I0214403

AMERICA *is* PLAGUED *with* CURSES

AMERICA *is* PLAGUED *with* CURSES

From the
"OUT HOUSE"
to the
"WHITE HOUSE"

DR. CURTIS G. HALL
& DR. CAROLYN HALL

Crutcher-Hall Management Trust

ISBN: 978-0-9701786-0-2

PRINTED IN THE UNITED STATES OF AMERICA

Contents

Introduction

The contents of this book are for the purposes of educating and enhancing the knowledge, wisdom, and understanding of all saints seeking closer relationships and closer daily walks with our Lord and Savior, Jesus Christ. In our secular society, knowledge is perceived as power and which also seem to turn the wheels of success in some of our daily lives.

As authors of this and other books, God tells us in Ecclesiastes that we may become weary in making books as there is no end There is no conclusion to this knowledge process, neither by providing it, nor by absorbing it and/or by seeking more of it.

Ecclesiastes 12:12 (KJV), "And further, by these, my son, be admonished: of making books there is no end; and much study is a weariness of the flesh."

Many Christians are constantly defeated in their prayers, their health, their finances, their marriages, their relationships, their jobs, and their lives as a whole. Sometimes we do all that we know to do, but when we take one step forward, we seemingly take several steps backwards in our Christian lives. Unfortunately, the key factor in our demise in most cases of our lives is merely ignorance, the lack of knowledge. Most of us are sincere in what we do for the Lord, but because of our ignorance, we are sometimes sincerely wrong. We sometimes question our own lives when we see the success of many unsaved persons as they accumulate wealth, live in huge and fabulous houses and/or estates.

We know that our Heavenly Father, God Almighty, has cattle on thousands of hills. He has many mansions and untold riches, but we as His children seemingly stand as poor and defeated ones in not only our secular lives, but our spiritual lives as well.

We have found in our experiences and in our extensive research for this book that even Christians can be defeated in their finances, their health, their marriages, their relationships, their spirituality in Christianity, their jobs and their everyday lives on this earth by turning from God, Almighty. We have found that Christians through their ignorance, through their lack of wisdom, through their lack of knowledge, and through their lack of understanding of God's holy word, they have separated and distance themselves from the grace, blessings, protection and the powerful anointing of God, Almighty.

Christians, your knowledge is power. Seek out, obtain and apply the power proclaimed in this book as in due time will enhance and empower the knowledge of the soul, the spiritual gifts of individuals and the secular well-being of their lives. As a result of their obtaining more of this type of knowledge, wisdom and understanding and apply them to their lives, they will have closer daily walks with our Lord and Savior, Jesus Christ.

Christians need to know that Satan and his demons comes, but to kill, steal and destroy. Jesus Christ comes that we may have everlasting life throughout eternity in heaven with Him.

We pray and trust that this book will not only excite the souls and spirits in the Christian family, but that it will shock some and prick the hearts of others into an enlightening sense of spiritual reality which will thereby excite them into action to destroy any and all of the curses of satanic and demonic influences and oppressions which are responsible for blocking their blessings.

CHAPTER 1

25 Percent of People in the World Are Christians

Jesus tells us in Matthew 13:3-9 (KJV) that only about twenty-five (25) percent of all people who hear the Word of God for salvation will accept it. Out of the twenty-five (25) percent of saved people, only about thirty (30) percent (the worse scenario) of them will actively seek the salvation of others. This is called sowing seeds in the field for bountiful harvests of new converts (born-again/saved ones). After speaking to the multitude of people in parables, Jesus explained to His disciples of what the SEEDS, the FIELD and the HARVESTS are.

Matthew 13:37-39 (KJV). 37) He answered and said unto them, He that soweth the good seed is the Son of man;

38. The FIELD IS THE WORLD; the GOOD SEED are the children of the kingdom; but the tares are the children of the wicked one;
39. The enemy that sowed them is the devil; the HARVEST is the end of the world; and the reapers are the angels.

You'll notice that the field (WORLD) human population is divided into four (4) quarters. Let's turn our attention to the first quarter beginning with Matthew 13:3 (KJV). 3) And he spake many things unto them in parables, saying, Behold, a sower went forth to sow;

First 25th Percent/1/4

4. And when he sowed, SOME SEEDS FELL BY THE WAY SIDE, and the fowls came and devoured them up:
19. When any one heareth the word of the kingdom, and understandeth it not, then cometh the WICKED ONE, and catcheth away that which was sown in his heart. This is HE WHICH RECEIVED SEED BY THE WAY SIDE.

Second 25th Percent/1/4

5. Some fell upon STONY PLACES, where they had not much earth: and forthwith they sprung up, because they had no deepnest of earth:
6. And when the sun was up, they were scorched; and because they had no root, they withered away.
20. But he that received the seed into stony places, THE SAME IS HE THAT HEARETH THE WORD, AND ANON WITH JOY RECEIVED IT;
21. Yet hath he not root in himself, but dureth for a while: for when TRIBULATION OR PERSECUTION ARISETH BECAUSE OF THE WORD, BY AND BY HE IS OFFENDED.

Third 25th Percent/1/4

7. And some fell among thorns; and the thorns sprung up, and choked them:
22. He also that received seed among the thorns is he that HEARETH THE WORD; and THE CARE OF THIS WORLD, and THE DECEITFULNESS OF RICHES, CHOKE THE WORD, HE BECOMETH UNFRUITFUL.

Fourth 25th Percent/1/4

8. But other fell into good ground, and brought forth fruit,

some an hundredfold, some sixtyfold, some thirtyfold.
23. But he that received seed into the good ground is he that
heareth the word, and understandeth it; which also beareth
fruit, and bringeth fort, some an hundredfold, some sixty,
some thirty.

CHAPTER 2

Terrorist Attack on America's Soil

The 911 Terrorist attacks on the soils of these United States of America is as a result of America's constant and continual practices of sins against Almighty God's commandments outlined in His words in the Christian Bibles. Not only do America's citizens take credit for these sins, but also the people whom they put in authority over them (i.e., presidents, governors, judges, legislators, congressmen, congresswomen, senators and many other elected people as well.

Below are some of the things that have open the doors of America to disasters which include, but not limited to the following sins and rebellious actions against Almighty God's Word:

1. Abortions - Murdering babies legally as well as illegally.
2. Stem Cell Research - Murdering babies for research.
3. Fornication - Sexual intercourse of unmarried couples.
4. Adultery/Infidelity - Sexual intercourse of married people outside of their marriage.
5. Incest - Sexual intercourse with close relatives.
6. Homosexuality (i.e., gay couples) - Sexual intercourse or sexual acts with same sex mates.
7. Rape - forced sex on an un-consenting person.
8. Pedophile actions - sexually molesting children.
9. Prejudices and racism against fellow humans.

10. Serving idol gods over Almighty God.
11. Outlawed the freedom to pray in our schools and in some public buildings.
12. Immigration Reform - Racism and discrimination (institutionalized).
13. Collegiate Voting System - Prejudicial, discrimination, and racism directed at the vast majority. Those types of votes are targeted at the lily white population for desired results.
14. Washington, D.C. denied statehood (racial overtones) as well as voter rights and representations. The District is under Jim Crow rule and slavery at the least. The majority black citizens still have to bow and shuffle to Mr. Charlie.
15. Wicca, witchcraft, and worshiping Satan.
16. Seeking the services and advisements of fortune tellers, psychics or soothsayers.
17. Children disobedient and disrespecting their parents, their grandparents, and other grownups.
18. Killers/murderers of human beings.
19. Robbers and thieves - forcefully seizing goods from others and taking things of others at will.
20. Worshiping in occult religions over Christianity.
21. Séances - attending meeting with a Medium officiating the attempts to call up dead people for their clients to talk to them. Actually, demons can manifest to look like the dead person and also mimic their voices. No one reach dead people through such methods.
22. Churches denying priest the opportunities to marry, especially in the Catholic churches under their Pope in Rome, Italy. There is no such commandment by Almighty God.
23. Alcoholism - habitual and excessive consumption of alcoholic beverages.
24. Drug addictions - habitual and excessive consumption of drugs.
25. Drug dealing - the selling or the directing of selling drugs illegally.

26. Gluttony - the excessive or habitual over eating of food and or drinks.
27. Shop Lifting - stealing goods, money, or things without paying for them.
28. Lotto or Lottery - official gambling by purchasing lottery tickets of chance.
29. Casinos - legalized gambling with various games of chance.
30. Gangs - organized violent groups with evil means of persuasion in mind.
31. Mobs - highly organized criminals

Deuteronomy 28 (KJV)

1. And it shall come to pass, if thou shalt hearken diligently unto the voice of the Lord thy God, to observe and to do all his commandments which I command thee this day, that the Lord thy God will set thee on high above all nations of the earth:
2. And all these blessings shall come on thee, and overtake thee, if thou shalt hearken unto the voice of the Lord thy God.
3. Blessed shalt thou be in the city, and blessed shalt thou be in the field.
4. Blessed shall be the fruit of thy body, and the fruit of thy ground, and the fruit of thy cattle, the increase of thy kine, and the flocks of thy sheep.
5. Blessed shall be thy basket and thy store.
6. Blessed shalt thou be when thou comest in, and blessed shalt thou be when thou goest out.
7. The Lord shall cause thine enemies that rise up against thee to be smitten before thy face: they shall come out against thee one way, and flee before thee seven ways.
8. The Lord shall command the blessing upon thee in thy storehouses, and in all that thou settest thine hand unto;

and he shall bless thee in the land which the Lord thy God giveth thee.

9. The Lord shall establish thee an holy people unto himself, as he hath sworn unto thee, if thou shalt keep the commandments of the Lord thy God, and walk in his ways.
10. And all people of the earth shall see that thou art called by the name of Lord; and they shall be afraid of thee.
11. And the Lord shall make thee plenteous in goods, in the fruit of thy body, and in the fruit of thy cattle, and in the fruit of thy ground, in the land which the Lord sware unto thy fathers to give thee.
12. The Lord shall open unto thee his good treasure, the heaven to give the rain unto thy land in his season, and to bless all the work of thine hand: and thou shalt lend unto many nations, and thou shalt not borrow.
13. And the Lord shall make thee the head, and not the tail; and thou shalt be above only, and thou shalt not be beneath; if that thou hearken unto the commandments of the Lord thy God, which I command thee this day, to observe and to do them:
14. And thou shalt not go aside from any of the words which I command thee this day, to the right hand, or to the left, to go after other gods to serve them.
15. But it shall come to pass, if thou wilt not hearken unto the voice of the Lord thy God, to observe to do all his commandments and his statutes which I command thee this day; that all these curses shall come upon thee, and overtake thee:
16. Cursed [shalt] thou [be] in the city, and cursed [shalt] thou [be] in the field.
17. Cursed shall be thy basket and thy store.
18. Cursed shall be the fruit of thy body, and the fruit of thy land, the increase of thy kine, and the flocks of thy sheep.
19. Cursed shalt thou be when thou comest in, and cursed shalt thou be when thou goest out.

20. The Lord shall send upon thee cursing, vexation, and rebuke, in all that thou settest thine hand unto for to do, until thou be destroyed, and until thou perish quickly; because of the wickedness of thy doings, whereby thou hast forsaken me.
21. The Lord shall make the pestilence cleave unto thee, until he have consumed thee from off the land, whither thou goest to possess it.
22. The Lord shall smite thee with a consumption, and with a fever, and with an inflammation, and with an extreme burning, and with the sword, and with blasting, and with mildew; and they shall pursue thee until thou perish.
23. And thy heaven that is over thy head shall be brass, and the earth that is under thee shall be iron.
24. The Lord shall make the rain of thy land powder and dust: from heaven shall it come down upon thee, until thou be destroyed.
25. The Lord shall cause thee to be smitten before thine enemies: thou shalt go out one way against them, and flee seven ways before them: and shalt be removed into all the kingdoms of the earth.
26. And thy carcase shall be meat unto all fowls of the air, and unto the beasts of the earth, and no man shall fray them away.
27. The Lord will smite thee with the botch of Egypt, and with the emerods, and with the scab, and with the itch, whereof thou canst not be healed.
28. The Lord shall smite thee with madness, and blindness, and astonishment of heart:
29. And thou shalt grope at noonday, as the blind gropeth in darkness, and thou shalt not prosper in thy ways: and thou shalt be only oppressed and spoiled evermore, and no man shall save thee.
30. Thou shalt betroth a wife, and another man shall lie with her: thou shalt build an house, and thou shalt not dwell

therein: thou shalt plant a vineyard, and shalt not gather the grapes thereof.

31. Thine ox shall be slain before thine eyes, and thou shalt not eat thereof: thine ass shall be violently taken away from before thy face, and shall not be restored to thee: thy sheep shall be given unto thine enemies, and thou shalt have none to rescue them.
32. Thy sons and thy daughters shall be given unto another people, and thine eyes shall look, and fail with longing for them all the day long; and there shall be no might in thine hand.
33. The fruit of thy land, and all thy labours, shall a nation which thou knowest not eat up; and thou shalt be only oppressed and crushed alway:
34. So that thou shalt be mad for the sight of thine eyes which thou shalt see.
35. The Lord shall smite thee in the knees, and in the legs, with a sore botch that cannot be healed, from the sole of thy foot unto the top of thy head.
36. The Lord shall bring thee, and thy king which thou shalt set over thee, unto a nation which neither thou nor thy fathers have known; and there shalt thou serve other gods, wood and stone.
37. And thou shalt become an astonishment, a proverb, and a byword, among all nations whither the Lord shall lead thee.
38. Thou shalt carry much seed out into the field, and shalt gather but little in; for the locust shall consume it.
39. Thou shalt plant vineyards, and dress them, but shalt neither drink of the wine, nor gather the grapes; for the worms shall eat them.
40. Thou shalt have olive trees throughout all thy coasts, but thou shalt not anoint thyself with the oil; for thine olive shall cast his fruit.
41. Thou shalt beget sons and daughters, but thou shalt not enjoy them; for they shall go into captivity.

42. All thy trees and fruit of thy land shall the locust consume.
43. The stranger that is within thee shall get up above thee very high; and thou shalt come down very low.
44. He shall lend to thee, and thou shalt not lend to him: he shall be the head, and thou shalt be the tail.
45. Moreover all these curses shall come upon thee, and shall pursue thee, and overtake thee, till thou be destroyed; because thou hearkenedst not unto the voice of the Lord thy God, to keep his commandments and his statutes which he commanded thee:
46. And they shall be upon thee for a sign and for a wonder, and upon thy seed for ever.
47. Because thou servedst not the Lord thy God with joyfulness, and with gladness of heart, for the abundance of all things;
48. Therefore shalt thou serve thine enemies which the Lord shall send against thee, in hunger, and in thirst, and in nakedness, and in want of all things: and he shall put a yoke of iron upon thy neck, until he have destroyed thee.
49. The Lord shall bring a nation against thee from far, from the end of the earth, as swift as the eagle flieth; a nation whose tongue thou shalt not understand;
50. A nation of fierce countenance, which shall not regard the person of the old, nor shew favour to the young:
51. And he shall eat the fruit of thy cattle, and the fruit of thy land, until thou be destroyed: which also shall not leave thee either corn, wine, or oil, or the increase of thy kine, or flocks of thy sheep, until he have destroyed thee.
52. And he shall besiege thee in all thy gates, until thy high and fenced walls come down, wherein thou trustedst, throughout all thy land: and he shall besiege thee in all thy gates throughout all thy land, which the Lord thy God hath given thee.
53. And thou shalt eat the fruit of thine own body, the flesh of thy sons and of thy daughters, which the Lord thy God hath

given thee, in the siege, and in the straitness, wherewith thine enemies shall distress thee:

54. So that the man that is tender among you, and very delicate, his eye shall be evil toward his brother, and toward the wife of his bosom, and toward the remnant of his children which he shall leave:
55. So that he will not give to any of them of the flesh of his children whom he shall eat: because he hath nothing left him in the siege, and in the straitness, wherewith thine enemies shall distress thee in all thy gates.
56. The tender and delicate woman among you, which would not adventure to set the sole of her foot upon the ground for delicateness and tenderness, her eye shall be evil toward the husband of her bosom, and toward her son, and toward her daughter,
57. And toward her young one that cometh out from between her feet, and toward her children which she shall bear: for she shall eat them for want of all things secretly in the siege and straitness, wherewith thine enemy shall distress thee in thy gates.
58. If thou wilt not observe to do all the words of this law that are written in this book, that thou mayest fear this glorious and fearful name, The Lord Thy God;
59. Then the Lord will make thy plagues wonderful, and the plagues of thy seed, even great plagues, and of long continuance, and sore sicknesses, and of long continuance.
60. Moreover he will bring upon thee all the diseases of Egypt, which thou wast afraid of; and they shall cleave unto thee.
61. Also every sickness, and every plague, which is not written in the book of this law, them will the Lord bring upon thee, until thou be destroyed.
62. And ye shall be left few in number, whereas ye were as the stars of heaven for multitude; because thou wouldest not obey the voice of the Lord thy God.
63. And it shall come to pass, that as the Lord rejoiced over

you to do you good, and to multiply you; so the Lord will rejoice over you to destroy you, and to bring you to nought; and ye shall be plucked from off the land whither thou goest to possess it.

64. And the Lord shall scatter thee among all people, from the one end of the earth even unto the other; and there thou shalt serve other gods, which neither thou nor thy fathers have known, even wood and stone.

65. And among these nations shalt thou find no ease, neither shall the sole of thy foot have rest: but the Lord shall give thee there a trembling heart, and failing of eyes, and sorrow of mind:

66. And thy life shall hang in doubt before thee; and thou shalt fear day and night, and shalt have none assurance of thy life:

67. In the morning thou shalt say, Would God it were even! and at even thou shalt say, Would God it were morning! for the fear of thine heart wherewith thou shalt fear, and for the sight of thine eyes which thou shalt see.

68. And the Lord shall bring thee into Egypt again with ships, by the way whereof I spake unto thee, thou shalt see it no more again: and there ye shall be sold unto your enemies for bondmen and bondwomen, and no man shall buy you.

CHAPTER 3

2008 Main Street/Wall Street Economic Crisis Predicted in 1999

America's root problem is basically that of sinful natures in all walks of life, in all nationalities, religions, skin colors, races and creeds. Sin is not prejudice, neither does it discriminate against certain people in the human race. The main sin is disobeying our Creator, Almighty God in heaven.

2 Chronicles 7 (KJV)

14. If my people, which are called by my name, shall humble themselves, and pray, and seek my face, and turn from their wicked ways; then will I hear from heaven, and will forgive their sin, and will heal their land.

This Prophetic Word was declared by Dr. Jane Lowder in Richmond, Virginia on the 3rd of January 1999.

I continue to see a vision of a building, and across that building is written these words "WESTING HOUSE". As I look upon these words "WESTINGHOUSE", I see that the letters begin to fall, starting with the "G" and "H" from the centre of it. They fall down as if in a drain. As these letters fall off of this building, I see this building crumble and fall. I hear the Lord say "The foundation is shaking of great companies that are in good standing and in good order. They shall fall and shall be no more." The Lord says "There shall be merging of small places with the larger places. Where the thinking is one of safety but it shall not be safety."

Suddenly, banks shall close without notice and the stock market shall hit an all time low, but the end is not yet, for it shall rise again and bring false hope to many says the Lord. These things shall be and thou shalt look upon them and know that I have warned thee. The oil and petroleum shall go sky high and there comes a time when the lines shall be long and the hearts shall fail and the anger shall erupt because of the things that are happening. These are days when I shall allow the extremes to come says the Lord. That which is precious to me shall be turned unto me. The soul of man is very precious.

Lift up thy hands and thy head, lift them up to thy Redeemer and know that even as the world shall rock, thou shall stand in a sure place with thy eyes upon Me. I would have you to hold steady in the midst of this trouble and these things that shall come upon the earth and upon all nations.

There comes also a wind, says the Lord, it is a wind that will be favorable, but I say unto thee it is not My wind and if thou shalt follow after this wind thou will find thyself shipwrecked, for in this wind it will seem that all things have been put together again and it would look as if things would bud, blossom and bloom and be fruitful. It shall be for a short season, but put not thy finances in it says the Lord. Invest not thy monies in it. That which thou think shall stand shall fall and that which others think would fall, shall stand.

Lift up thine eyes and behold thy King who sitteth upon the throne and who has thy name written in the palm of His hand and has His eye upon thee to lead thee and guide thee. Know ye this, that I shall steady thee and shall cause thee to stand and surely thou shalt be My light, My voice and My outreached hand.

Many of My people have as if it were their head in the sand for they hear and they see but they understand not with their hearts. Tell Me, can you feel the wind when it blows? Can you feel the cold air? Yea, I say unto thee when the electricity goes off does your house get cold? The Lord says unto you, take up thy head and look ye up unto Me for these elements shall touch all people and though thou art called a Christian thou shalt feel the coldness and the heat and thou shalt feel many things of that which is round about thee but I shall keep thee and uphold thee and make a way where there is no way. I do not want thee to be ignorant of all these things that shall come upon the earth and even upon thy neighborhood. I say unto thee lift up thine eyes unto thy Redeemer and let thy spirit see and understand, for I call thee to take a stand this day and follow after me with the wholeness of thy heart and know that I shall be thy shelter. I shall be thy up-lifter and thy helper. I shall keep thee, but know that these things shall come upon the earth and upon thine own country and in thine own city. Thou shalt know that I the Lord allow it. There be many that shall call upon My Name and they shall come to know Me.

Trust not in thy riches, nor in thy bank account. Trust not in the establishment of thy home. Let thy trust be in nothing that is made with hands, for the Lord says unto thee this world and the world system is built on sinking sand and surely thou shalt see many come crumbling down and sinking, but it is not so with thee, for thou art built upon a rock and established upon the going of the Eternal One.

I say unto thee this day, rejoice in Me. Rejoice, rejoice with exceeding gladness in thy heart. The Lord says thou hast said "signs and wonders" and signs and wonders it shall be. Rejoice for I the Lord stand in control and I have all things in control. Arise unto thy feet and lift up thy hands and declare unto the Lord that this day thou shalt hear and see with a seeing and thou shalt follow after Me. The time is short and the hour is at hand and thou shalt see the great movements of thy God and the rhythms of thy God that shall flow throughout the earth and into all nations.

I say unto thee, Australia also shall shake and the Asian countries. You would say they have already been shaken, but that was only a rattle says the Lord. I say unto thee there shall be a shaking that will cause the heart of man to fear and shall cry out unto Me. Therefore, sing ye unto thy God and sing ye often of My mercy and My goodness. Though all these elements come, My mercy, and My goodness shall never fail. They endure forever and you shall see as thou hast declared a great revival and a mighty incoming from those that are without. I am that I am and I change not and this is the beginning of a great shaking. It is not for my family that stands true and waits upon Me. Sing ye of My mercy and declare it in all places for you shall be the salt of the earth and you shall be the light and the hands that are stretched out to comfort and to build and to bring into order says the Lord.

CHAPTER 4

Abortions - Killing & Murdering of Babies - A Great Sin

Almighty God admonishes us in His 10 Commandments that we should not kill. When any abortions are performed, it is a form of killing and/or murdering of human souls. This is a great sin and abomination to Almighty God.

Exodus 20 (KJV)

13. Thou shalt not kill.

Abortions are performed through many arrangements; legally and illegally under certain environments including, but not limited to:

1. Abortion Clinics (legal) - Baby Murdering Clinics.
2. Small town hospitals (legal institution) - Not widely publicized - Baby Murdering Institutions.
3. Underground Abortion Clinics (illegal) - Baby slaughter Houses & Murdering Clinics.

God revealed to us that he knew us before the foundation of the world. So, why do ignorant an unlearned, and self-serving people proclaim that embryos aren't humans? As soon as a woman conceives, she has a human being in her womb.

Luke 2 (KJV)

21. And when eight days were accomplished for the circumcising of the child, his name was called Jesus, which was so named of the angel ***before he was conceived in the womb***.

Ephesians 1 (KJV)

4. According as he hath chosen us in him ***before the foundation of the world***, that we should be holy and without blame before him in love:

1 Peter 1 (KJV)

20. Who verily was ***foreordained before the foundation of the world***, but was manifest in these last times for you,

John 17 (KJV)

24. Father, I will that they also, whom thou hast given me, be with me where I am; that they may behold my glory, which thou hast given me: for thou lovedst me ***before the foundation of the world***.

Many people are in favor of abortions which is the murdering of babies.

Not only are the citizens of the United States of American in a serious state of moral deficiency, but the lawmakers, and the judicial system as well. We as U.S. citizens are in a very sad state of affairs. The United States of America is in danger of losing God, Almighty's protective hedge around her. The 911 terrorist and Hurricane Katrina that hit the gulf states including New Orleans, Louisiana, Biloxi, Mississippi and states were just a so-called mother nature fluke. These disasters were wake-up calls as warnings to set our spiritual lives in order because God is certainly watching us and taking note.

CHAPTER 5

About Generational Curses

Generational curses go back to the 3rd and 4th generations of a family's bloodline. It could have been something that their greatest grandparents did against the will and commandments of God, Almighty. It is very important that those curses be severed and broken. These curses could be the root of one's sickness, one's diseases, one's ailments, one's mental sickness or anything not good to one's body, soul or mind. Here are some verses that reference the depth of curses which could be lingering in such bloodline:

Exodus 20 (KJV)

1. And God spoke all these words, saying
2. I am the Lord thy God, which have brought thee out of the land of Egypt, out of the house of bondage.
3. Thou shalt have no other gods before me.
4. Thou shalt not make unto thee any graven image, or any likeness of any thing that is in heaven above, or that is in the earth beneath, or that is in the water under the earth.
5. Thou shalt not bow down thyself to them, nor serve them: for I the LORD thy God am a jealous God, visiting the iniquity of the fathers upon the children unto the **third and fourth generation** of them that hate me;

Exodus 34 (KJV)

1. And the Lord said unto Moses, Hew thee two tables of stone like unto the first: and I will write upon these tables the words that were in the first tables, which thou brakest.
2. And be ready in the morning, and come up in the morning unto mount Sinai, and present thyself there to me in the top of the mount.
3. And no man shall come up with thee, neither let any man be seen throughout all the mount; neither let the flocks nor herds feed before that mount.
4. And he hewed two tables of stone like unto the first; and Moses rose up early in the morning, and went up unto mount Sinai, as the Lord had commanded him, and took in his hand the two tables of stone.
5. And the Lord descended in the cloud, and stood with him there, and proclaimed the name of the Lord.
6. And the Lord passed by before him, and proclaimed, The Lord, The Lord God, merciful and gracious, longsuffering, and abundant in goodness and truth,
7. Keeping mercy for thousands, forgiving iniquity and transgression and sin, and that will by no means clear the guilty; visiting the iniquity of the fathers upon the children, and upon the children's children, unto the third and to the fourth generation.

Numbers 14 (KJV)

1. And all the congregation lifted up their voice, and cried; and the people wept that night.
2. And all the children of Israel murmured against Moses and against Aaron: and the whole congregation said unto them, Would God that we had died in the land of Egypt! or would God we had died in this wilderness!
3. And wherefore hath the Lord brought us unto this land, to

fall by the sword, that our wives and our children should be a prey? were it not better for us to return into Egypt?

4. And they said one to another, Let us make a captain, and let us return into Egypt.
5. Then Moses and Aaron fell on their faces before all the assembly of the congregation of the children of Israel.
6. And Joshua the son of Nun, and Caleb the son of Jephunneh, which were of them that searched the land, rent their clothes:
7. And they spake unto all the company of the children of Israel, saying, The land, which we passed through to search it, is an exceeding good land.
8. If the Lord delight in us, then he will bring us into this land, and give it us; a land which floweth with milk and honey.
9. Only rebel not ye against the Lord, neither fear ye the people of the land; for they are bread for us: their defence is departed from them, and the Lord is with us: fear them not.
10. But all the congregation bade stone them with stones. And the glory of the Lord appeared in the tabernacle of the congregation before all the children of Israel.
11. And the Lord said unto Moses, How long will this people provoke me? and how long will it be ere they believe me, for all the signs which I have shewed among them?
12. I will smite them with the pestilence, and disinherit them, and will make of thee a greater nation and mightier than they.
13. And Moses said unto the Lord, Then the Egyptians shall hear it, (for thou broughtest up this people in thy might from among them;)
14. And they will tell it to the inhabitants of this land: for they have heard that thou Lord art among this people, that thou Lord art seen face to face, and that thy cloud standeth over them, and that thou goest before them, by day time in a pillar of a cloud, and in a pillar of fire by night.

15. Now if thou shalt kill all this people as one man, then the nations which have heard the fame of thee will speak, saying,
1. Because the Lord was not able to bring this people into the land which he sware unto them, therefore he hath slain them in the wilderness.
2. And now, I beseech thee, let the power of my Lord be great, according as thou hast spoken, saying,
3. The LORD [is] longsuffering, and of great mercy, forgiving iniquity and transgression, and by no means clearing the guilty, visiting the iniquity of the fathers upon the children unto the ***third and fourth generation***.

Deuteronomy 5 (KJV)

1. And Moses called all Israel, and said unto them, Hear, O Israel, the statutes and judgments which I speak in your ears this day, that ye may learn them, and keep, and do them.
2. The Lord our God made a covenant with us in Horeb.
3. The Lord made not this covenant with our fathers, but with us, even us, who are all of us here alive this day.
4. The Lord talked with you face to face in the mount out of the midst of the fire,
5. (I stood between the Lord and you at that time, to shew you the word of the Lord: for ye were afraid by reason of the fire, and went not up into the mount;) saying,
6. I am the Lord thy God, which brought thee out of the land of Egypt, from the house of bondage.
7. Thou shalt have none other gods before me.
8. Thou shalt not make thee any graven image, or any likeness of any thing that is in heaven above, or that is in the earth beneath, or that is in the waters beneath the earth:
9. Thou shalt not bow down thyself unto them, nor serve them: for I the LORD thy God am a jealous God, visiting the

iniquity of the fathers upon the children unto the third and fourth generation of them that hate me,

Below are some of the curses you can expect to incur because of your sinful actions, your unbelief and your rebellious actions against God, Almighty:

Deuteronomy 28 (KJV)

15. But it shall come to pass, if thou wilt not hearken unto the voice of the Lord thy God, to observe to do all his commandments and his statutes which I command thee this day; that all these curses shall come upon thee, and overtake thee:
16. Cursed shalt thou be in the city, and cursed shalt thou be in the field.
17. Cursed shall be thy basket and thy store.
18. Cursed shall be the fruit of thy body, and the fruit of thy land, the increase of thy kine, and the flocks of thy sheep.
19. Cursed shalt thou be when thou comest in, and cursed shalt thou be when thou goest out.
20. The Lord shall send upon thee cursing, vexation, and rebuke, in all that thou settest thine hand unto for to do, until thou be destroyed, and until thou perish quickly; because of the wickedness of thy doings, whereby thou hast forsaken me.
21. The Lord shall make the pestilence cleave unto thee, until he have consumed thee from off the land, whither thou goest to possess it.
22. The Lord shall smite thee with a consumption, and with a fever, and with an inflammation, and with an extreme burning, and with the sword, and with blasting, and with mildew; and they shall pursue thee until thou perish.
23. And thy heaven that is over thy head shall be brass, and the earth that is under thee shall be iron.

24. The Lord shall make the rain of thy land powder and dust: from heaven shall it come down upon thee, until thou be destroyed.
25. The Lord shall cause thee to be smitten before thine enemies: thou shalt go out one way against them, and flee seven ways before them: and shalt be removed into all the kingdoms of the earth.
26. And thy carcase shall be meat unto all fowls of the air, and unto the beasts of the earth, and no man shall fray them away.
27. The Lord will smite thee with the botch of Egypt, and with the emerods, and with the scab, and with the itch, whereof thou canst not be healed.
28. The Lord shall smite thee with madness, and blindness, and astonishment of heart:
29. And thou shalt grope at noonday, as the blind gropeth in darkness, and thou shalt not prosper in thy ways: and thou shalt be only oppressed and spoiled evermore, and no man shall save thee.
30. Thou shalt betroth a wife, and another man shall lie with her: thou shalt build an house, and thou shalt not dwell therein: thou shalt plant a vineyard, and shalt not gather the grapes thereof.
31. Thine ox shall be slain before thine eyes, and thou shalt not eat thereof: thine ass shall be violently taken away from before thy face, and shall not be restored to thee: thy sheep shall be given unto thine enemies, and thou shalt have none to rescue them.
32. Thy sons and thy daughters shall be given unto another people, and thine eyes shall look, and fail with longing for them all the day long; and there shall be no might in thine hand.
33. The fruit of thy land, and all thy labours, shall a nation which thou knowest not eat up; and thou shalt be only oppressed and crushed alway:

34. So that thou shalt be mad for the sight of thine eyes which thou shalt see.
35. The Lord shall smite thee in the knees, and in the legs, with a sore botch that cannot be healed, from the sole of thy foot unto the top of thy head.
36. The Lord shall bring thee, and thy king which thou shalt set over thee, unto a nation which neither thou nor thy fathers have known; and there shalt thou serve other gods, wood and stone.
37. And thou shalt become an astonishment, a proverb, and a byword, among all nations whither the Lord shall lead thee.
38. Thou shalt carry much seed out into the field, and shalt gather but little in; for the locust shall consume it.
39. Thou shalt plant vineyards, and dress them, but shalt neither drink of the wine, nor gather the grapes; for the worms shall eat them.
40. Thou shalt have olive trees throughout all thy coasts, but thou shalt not anoint thyself with the oil; for thine olive shall cast his fruit.
41. Thou shalt beget sons and daughters, but thou shalt not enjoy them; for they shall go into captivity.
42. All thy trees and fruit of thy land shall the locust consume.
43. The stranger that is within thee shall get up above thee very high; and thou shalt come down very low.
44. He shall lend to thee, and thou shalt not lend to him: he shall be the head, and thou shalt be the tail.
45. Moreover all these curses shall come upon thee, and shall pursue thee, and overtake thee, till thou be destroyed;because thou hearkenedst not unto the voice of the Lord thy God, to keep his commandments and his statutes which he commanded thee:

Here is a sample prayer to break, sever, and loose yourself, your children, your grandchildren, your great grandchildren and their children to the third and fourth generations:

Heavenly Father,

in the name of ***Your Son, Jesus Christ, my personal Savior,***

I break myself, my wife, my children, my grandchildren, and my great grandchildren from all generational curses, all Agent Orange (Viet Nam) curses, all Buddhist Monk's (Viet Nam) curses, all Satanic curses, all unknown curses including, but not limited to diabetes, high blood pressure, heart diseases, heart attacks, kidney diseases, strokes, blindness in the eyes, eye diseases, cancers, and arthritis to the third and fourth generations, golng back to: my parents, my grandparents, and to my great grandparents, to the ***third and fourth generations.***

I loose myself, my wife, my children, my grandchildren, and my great grandchildren from all generational curses, all Agent Orange (Viet Nam) curses, all Buddhist Monk's (Viet Nam) curses, all Satanic curses, and all unknown curses including, but not limited to diabetes, high blood pressure, heart diseases, heart attacks, kidney diseases, strokes, blindness in the eyes, eye diseases, cancers, and arthritis to the third and fourth generations, going back to: my parents, my grandparents, and to my great grandparents, to the ***third and fourth generations.***

I cut and sever all bonds, all cords, all snares, all snares of death, all ties and all traps to myself, my wife, my children, my grandchildren and to my great grandchildren to the third and fourth generations from all links to all generational curses, all Agent Orange (Viet Nam) curses, all Buddhist Monk's (Viet Nam) curses, all Satanic curses, and all unknown curses including, but not limited to diabetes, high blood pressure, heart diseases, heart attacks, kidney diseases, strokes, blindness in the eyes, eye diseases, cancers, and arthritis to the third and fourth generations, going back to: my parents, my grandparents, and to my great grandparents, to the ***third and fourth generations.***

I rebuke all generational curses, all Agent Orange (Viet Nam) curses, all Buddhist Monk's (Viet Nam) curses, all Satanic curses, and all unknown curses including, but not limited to diabetes, high blood pressure, heart diseases, heart attacks, kidney diseases, strokes, blindness in the eyes, eye diseases, cancers, and arthritis for myself, my wife, my children, my grandchildren and my great grandchildren to the third and fourth generations, going back to: my parents,my grandparents, and to my great grandparents, to the ***third and fourth generations.***

I command that all generational curses, all Agent Orange (Viet Nam) curses, all Buddhist Monk's (Viet Nam) curses, all Satanic curses, and all unknown curses including, but not limited to diabetes, high blood pressure, heart diseases, heart attacks, kidney diseases, strokes, blindness in the eyes, eye diseases, cancers, and arthritis ***come out now*** and ***leave immediately and never return forever*** for myself, my wife, my children, my grandchildren and my great grandchildren to the third and fourth generations, going back to: my parents, my grandparents, and to my great grandparents, to the ***third and fourth generations.***

I bind my body, my wife's body, my children's bodies, my grandchildren's bodies, my great grandchildren's bodies to outstanding healthy bodies and vessels without diseases and sickness to the ***third and fourth generations***.

I bind myself, my wife, my children, my grandchildren, and my grandchildren to the Spirit of the Living ***God, God's Holy Spirit to the third and fourth generations***.

I bind myself, my wife, my children, my grandchildren, and my great grandchildren to God, Almighty's hedge of protection to the ***third and fourth generations***.
In the name of ***All Mighty God*** in Heaven and In the name of Almighty Jesus Christ in Heaven, and In the name of Almighty

Holy Spirit. Praise You, Almighty God, and Praise You, Almighty Jesus Christ, and Praise You, Almighty Holy Spirit! Amen.

- You can be more specific concerning a curse that you know is in your bloodline (i.e., murder, prostitution, homosexuality, mental illness, etc.). There can be many generational curses that you may have to deal with in your particular bloodline. Other curses can be early death because God, almighty promised us three score and ten years (70 years of age)) to 80 years of age and more. Many people are going to their deaths quite earlier than that with curses of cancer, heart attacks, drug and alcohol over dosages, high blood pressure, diabetes and the list goes on.

Psalms 90 (KJV)

10. The days of our years are threescore years and ten; and if by reason of strength they be fourscore years, yet is their strength labour and sorrow; for it is soon cut off, and we fly away.

CHAPTER 6

Adopting Children - Their Generational Curses

Many married couples desiring children of their own have been faced with dilemmas of not being able to conceive and/or birth them. Certain medical and/or physical conditions have contributed to their lack of not being endowed with the necessary blessings to conceive, birth and raise children of their own bloodline.

Various medical technologies have aided males in some instances where there were medical or physical deficiencies. On the other hand, females have been aided by various medical technologies as well. However when these aren't suitable or desired, then other means of acquiring children are desired outside of the couples relationship.

Adopting a child or children is a desired alternative to the natural birth of one's own child(ren). However, for Christians, this poses some problems which will have to be dealt with spiritually.

Galatians 4:3&8 (NKJV),

3. "Even so we, when we were children, were in bondage under the elements of the world.
8. But then, indeed, when you did not know God, you served those which by nature are not gods."

This reflects not only on our spiritual beings, but our physical beings as well.

These problems are embedded within what we'll call **"GENERATIONAL SINS"**. These are sins derived from one's own blood line. Within a blood line, various sins and curses are prevalent, but not limited to the following: there could be satanic worshiping, practicing of martial arts, prostitution, a prostitute's leader (pimp), masonic rituals, Jehovah Witnessing, horoscope reading, palm reading, fortune telling (psychic-foretelling), seeking the assistance of fortune tellers (psychics). The list can go on and on. There are many books written by Christians with reflections given on a Christian's perspective in print on these and other subjects at bible book stores or can be ordered from many book stores. These matters must be dealt with when adopting children outside of your own generation and within the realm of Christianity. Additionally, don't overlook your own generational sins and curses you may or may not know about. Make absolutely sure you take care of your own generational sins and curses first.

Generational sins and plagues of curses must be broken and severed between the blood line of the adopted child(ren) as soon as possible. Since the adoption is possibly not of a Christian generation, the child or children is/are outside of God's blessings. Even if the child(ren) did come from a Christian environment, there still could be generational sins and plagues of curses in their backgrounds.

Psalms 112:2 (KJV), "His seed shall be mighty upon earth: the generation of the upright shall be blessed."

If these curses and sins aren't broken and are allowed to linger throughout the life of the child(ren), Satan and/or his demons will reek havoc with not only the child(ren), but you and your natural family as well.

We know of one Christian family who did adopt two young boys who were blood brothers. This family constantly had problems with these boys after they became teenagers. It was learned that the boys were mentally unstable and they did reek havoc with the family. I don't believe anything was ever learned concerning the background of these boys family background. However, about five years ago, tragedy hit the family where one of the boys suffered a seizure and died immediately. Two weeks later the other son was vacationing over to the adopted mother's sister's home when he fell into the swimming pool and drowned.

These boys brought with them heavy baggages filled with plagues of curses from their ancestors' generational sins. This particular family didn't know what they were getting themselves into when they adopted these boys. They started out as a happy family with recorded videos of them and the boys when they were quite young. However, we later learned from the adopted parents older daughter that she was quite skeptical when her parents decided on adopting these boys. This young lady exemplifies that of a strong Christian young lady who had the gift of discernment, but her parents didn't. She was concerned that something was spiritually wrong with these boys who become her brothers. Her discernment was indeed manifested through the lives and death of those boys.

God Almighty can and will break and sever any and all generational curses and sins between your adopted child(ren), Satan and his demons. You must pray to Him and ask Him to do so in the name of Jesus with thanksgiving and praises. You may use this little simple prayer and/or modify it to your own needs and/or requirements.

"Our Father in heaven, in the name of Jesus, please forgive my infant child, (child's name) of all generational sins he/she has inherited from His/her ancestors. Father, please **BREAK AND SEVER ALL TIES** to all generational sins and curses between (child's name), his/her ancestors, and his/her generational blood line.

In the name of Almighty God, the Heavenly Father, and In the name of Almighty Jesus Christ in heaven, and In the name of Almighty Holy Spirit down here on earth with us!

Praise You Almighty God, the Heavenly Father, and Praise You Almighty Jesus Christ in heaven, and Praise You Almighty Holy Spirit down here on earth with us! Amen!

Now you must use your Christian authority to set Satan and his demons straight on whose property you and your infant son/daughter, are. Use your authority similar to the following:

"Satan, you heard it! We belong to God, Almighty, Jesus Christ, and the Holy Spirit. God, Almighty has forgiven my son/daughter, of all his/her generational sins and curses he/she has inherited from his/her ancestors.

I **COMMAND** that you, Satan, your head demons and all demons associated with his/her generational sins to **loose him/her** immediately in the name of Jesus.

I **COMMAND** that you, Satan, your head demons and all demons associated with his/her generational sins to **leave him/her** immediately in the name of Jesus.

I **BIND UP** each and every demon associated with his/her generational sins immediately in the precious name of Jesus Christ! Amen."

Back in the biblical days of Moses when he wrote the law or **"LAW OF MOSES"** under a period of time which we call the **"DISPENSATION OF LAW"**, God made provisions for the people and strangers of Moses to receive forgiveness for their sins. Through the sacrifice of animals blood (bullocks, rams, lambs or kids) these animals were cooked over open flames on an altar. These animals' were then offered as burnt offerings up to the Lord; for the sins of the people as well as for the sins of strangers who joined Moses' generation for the remission of their sins.

God explained to Moses on what he was to do for the atonement of his people's sins with all that were born in the country, specifically in his generation and any stranger who joined them also.

Numbers 15:13-16 (KJV), (13) "All that are born of the country shall do these things after this manner, in offering an offering made by fire, of a sweet savour unto the Lord.

14. And if a stranger sojourn with you, or whosoever be among you in your generations, and will offer an offering made by fire, of a sweet savour unto the Lord; as ye do, so he shall do.
15. One ordinance shall be both for you of the congregation, and also for the stranger that sojourneth with you, an ordinance for ever in your generation: as ye are, so shall the stranger be before the Lord.
16. One law and one manner shall be for you, and for the stranger that sojourneth with you.

Praise God! We don't have to sacrifice the blood of animals anymore for our sins.

Romans 10:4-5 (NKJV), (4) "For Christ is the end of the law for righteousness to everyone who believes.

5. For Moses writes about the righteousness which is of the law," "The man who does those things shall live by them.".

John 1:17 (NKJV), "For the law was given through Moses, but grace and truth came through Jesus Christ." We are now in the **"DISPENSATION OF GRACE"**.

Ephesians 3:2 (NKJV), "If indeed you have heard of the dispensation of the grace of God which was given to me for you."

Galatians 5:18 (NKJV), "But if you are led by the Spirit, you are not under the law."

However, the majority people of the Jewish nation who don't believe their Savior has come and are still waiting his appearance. They are still under the "Dispensation Of Law". Jesus spoke to the Jews in the following passage of scripture:

> 1 Corinthians 9:20 (NKJV), "And to the Jews I became as a Jew, that I might win Jews; to those are under the law, as under the law, that I might win those who are under the law;"

It is believed that the Jews will return to animal sacrifices when many of them return to their homeland, Israel and surrounding cities.

Jesus Christ was our only Lamb, the Lamb of God. When Jesus went to the cross, He ushered in the dispensation of grace and abolished the dispensation of Law. His blood was shedded for all of us whether we except it or not. Our sins are forgiven through Him and not through sacrifices of animals under the law. We have power through our words of authority and prayer by using the name of Jesus. We will essentially be using the magnificent authority of Jesus. When we are concluding our prayers, we must say, "In the Name of Jesus" or words to that effect. Any authority we use, we must say for example: "In the name of Jesus, I take authority over the curse of drug over my son/daughter, (child's name). Use what is suited to your situation. If you know some of the curses that your child has, then there is another approach to use as illustrated below.

Drugs was the ruler over a certain teenager's life whom we'll name Morris. We are not only admonished to pray for him, but we have been given the authority and opportunity to use the power of Jesus

Christ over Satan and his demons as well. Listed below are just a few examples with some powerful WORDS of authority in capital letters beginning with:

In the **NAME OF JESUS:**

I take **AUTHORITY** over the CURSE of drugs over my son, Morris.

I **BREAK** the curse of drugs over my son, Morris.

I **RENOUNCE** the curse of drug over my son, Morris.

I **REVERSE** the curse of drug over my son, Morris.

I **SEVER** all earthy ties between the curse of drug and my son, Morris.

I **COMMAND** you, Satan and any demons associated with the curse of drugs over my son, Morris to loose him, **NOW!**

I **COMMAND** you to leave him **NOW!**

I **BIND** up each and every demon associated with the drug curse over my son, Morris.

This is only a portion of the job with Morris. He must now have a sincere desire to accept Jesus as his personal saviour. Once he accepts Jesus as his personal saviour, he then must pray to God to forgive him for using drugs and being involved with drugs. He must thank God in the name of Jesus. He then must command the head drug demon to leave him **now** in the name of Jesus Christ.

Now, what if Morris doesn't desire to our Lord and Savior, Jesus Christ as his personal Savior? Well, you can't force a horse to eat and you certainly can't force Morris to accept Jesus Christ as his personal Savior. The demons will no doubt return to Morris with at least seven other demons more evil than they.

Mat 12:43 (KJV) "When the unclean spirit is gone out of a man, he walketh through dry places, seeking rest, and findeth none."

Mat 12:44 (KJV) "Then he saith, I will return into my house from whence I came out; and when he is come, he findeth it empty, swept, and garnished."

Mat 12:45 (KJV) "Then goeth he, and taketh with himself seven other spirits more wicked than himself, and they enter in and dwell there: and the last state of that man is worse than the first. Even so shall it be also unto this wicked generation."

When we know that there are generational sins of our adoptive child(ren) who are infants or not of an age to understand or comprehend, we must pray to God and ask Him to sever all ties to those specific generational sins as well as unknown generational sins. You can now do what Morris' parent(s) did with the authority that you also have through Jesus for the adopted child(ren).

CHAPTER 7

African (Black) Americans - America's Back-Bone and Foundation

African Americans and their ancestors were and are vital players in the foundation and vital back-bones of America. Free labor came from the backs of slave men, women and children in building the infrastructures, including roads, bridges, buildings, waterfronts, railroads, the White House, the nations Capitol and so on. Slaves free labor help to produce foods from many of the grain farms, hog farms, cattle farms, horse and mule farms, chicken farms, turkey farms, cotton mills, grain mills, cotton fields, corn fields, soy bean fields, sorghum and milo fields, strawberry, water melon, cantaloup, collar green, mustard green, turnip green, spinach, peanut, potatoe, and many other vegetable fields as well.

African (Black) Americans were not only labor intensive, but they also had high tech minds and intuitions that spawned many new inventions and innovations which are being used today, not only in America, but across many continents around the world. American's citizens lives are much better as they enjoy those vast innovations and inventions at their disposals.

Before the widespread establishment of chattel slavery, much labor was organized under a system of bonded labor known as indentured servitude. This typically lasted for several years for white and black alike, and it was a means of using labor to pay the costs of transporting people to the colonies. By the 18th century, court rulings established the racial basis of the American incarnation of slavery to apply chiefly to Black Africans and people of African descent, and occasionally to Native Americans. A 1705 Virginia law stated slavery would apply to those peoples from nations that were not Christian. In part because of the success of tobacco as a cash crop in the Southern colonies, its labor-intensive character caused planters to import more slaves for labor by the end of the 17th century than did the northern colonies. The South had a significantly higher number and proportion of slaves in the population. Religious differences contributed to this geographic disparity as well.

From 1654 until 1865, slavery for life was legal within the boundaries of much of the present United States. Most slaves were black and were held by whites, although some Native Americans and free blacks also held slaves; there were a small number of white slaves as well. The majority of slaveholding was in the southern United States where most slaves were engaged in an efficient machine-like gang system of agriculture. According to the 1860 U.S. census, nearly four million slaves were held in a total population of just over 12 million in the 15 states in which slavery was legal. Of all 8,289,782 free persons in the 15 slave states, 393,967 people (4.8%) held slaves, with the average number of slaves held by any single owner being 10. The majority of slaves were held by planters, defined by historians as those who held 20 or more slaves. Ninety-five percent of black people lived in the South, comprising one-third of the population there, as opposed to 2% of the population of the North. The wealth of the United States in the first half of the 19th century was greatly enhanced by the labor of African Americans.

But with the Union victory in the American Civil War, the slave-labor system was abolished in the South. This contributed to the decline of the postbellum Southern economy, but it was most affected by the continuing decline in the price of cotton through the end of the century. That made it difficult for the region to recover from the war, as did its comparative lack of infrastructure, which kept products from markets. The South faced significant new competition from foreign cotton producers such as India and Egypt. Northern industry, which had expanded rapidly before and during the war, surged even further ahead of the South's agricultural economy. Industrialists from northeastern states came to dominate many aspects of the nation's life, including social and some aspects of political affairs. The planter class of the South lost power temporarily. The rapid economic development following the Civil War accelerated the development of the modern U.S. industrial economy.

Twelve million Africans were shipped to the Americas from the 16th to the 19th centuries. Of these, an estimated 645,000 were brought to what is now the United States. The largest number were shipped to Brazil. The slave population in the United States had grown to four million by the 1860 Census.

Illegal slavery continues in the United States today. Modern slavery is often discussed in the framework of human trafficking.

CHAPTER 8

Alcoholic Beverages - Key Consumption - Do In Moderation

Christians must be very cautious and very careful if they decide to consume alcoholic beverages. The most important key to this is the term "Moderation". Alcoholic beverages must not be consumed excessively in a habitual manner which will enslave you into dependency upon it.

It is not a sin to consume wine or any other such alcoholic beverage with one's meals or at a given celebration where such beverages are served. Again, the key is moderation and not excessive drinking.
However, if you are in a setting where you think that it may be perceived as appearance on your behalf as a Christian, don't drink in that group's present of any alcoholic beverages. Be guided by the Almighty Holy Spirit for all of your actions.

Numbers 6:1-3, (1) "And the Lord spake unto Moses, saying,

2. Speak unto the children of Israel, and say unto them, When either man or woman shall separate themselves to vow a vow of a Nazarite, to separate unto the Lord:
3. He shall separate himself from wine and strong drink, neither shall he drink the liquor of grapes, nor eat moist grapes, or dried."

A Nazarite in the Old Testament scriptures is a religious sect or denomination of the Church. God put strict requirements on His servants in the biblical days, especially the servants working in His temple. They could lose their live for polluting their bodies, either by eating grapes, drinking grape juice, wine or hard liquor and then by entering certain places within the temple. This was also under the law of Moses which we call the "Dispensation of Law". We are under the "Dispensation of Grace/The Holy Ghost" where we aren't bound by the Law of Moses as such. We can still eat grapes, drink grape juice, drink wine in moderation and still be blessed by God, Almighty.

Wine Consumption In Moderation

The Apostle Paul in his letter to Timothy told him to drink a little wine for his stomach's sake.

1 Timothy 5:23 (KJV), "Drink no longer water, but use a little wine for thy stomach's and thine often infirmities."

Apparently, Timothy had a constant problem or weakness in his physical body and wine was sort of a medicine to that ailment. Paul didn't tell Timothy to be a habitual wine drinker, nor did he tell him to be a social drinker. In so many words, Paul is telling Timothy to use moderation in his wine drinking.

Wine And Strong Drinks Habitual Consumption Forbidden

Christians shouldn't become slaves to alcoholic beverages such as beer, whiskey, wine and/or many other types of alcoholic liquors or beverages. Alcoholic beverages are in the same class as drugs. With over indulgences of these liquors, a person can become addictive or become habit forming to them. Habitual consumption of alcohol can lead one to additional problems with the mind, the soul and the body. Some people are of the opinion that if you drink in moderation there shouldn't be a problem. However, many people can't seem to drink in moderation as one would think they could. They are lushes and drink like fish. These people are essentially not in control of their bodies, their souls, nor are they in control of their spirits.

Prov 20:1 (KJV) "Wine is a mocker, strong drink is raging: and whosoever is deceived thereby is not wise."

Prov 21:17 (KJV) "He that loveth pleasure shall be a poor man: he that loveth wine and oil shall not be rich."

Prov 23:30 (KJV) "They that tarry long at the wine; they that go to seek mixed wine."

Prov 31:4 (KJV) "It is not for kings, O Lemuel, it is not for kings to drink wine; nor for princes strong drink:"

Prov 31:5 (KJV) "Lest they drink, and forget the law, and pervert the judgment of any of the afflicted."

Prov 31:6 (KJV) "Give strong drink unto him that is ready to perish, and wine unto those that be of heavy hearts."

Eccl 9:7 (KJV) "Go thy way, eat thy bread with joy, and drink thy wine with a merry heart; for God now accepteth thy works."

Eccl 10:19 (KJV) "A feast is made for laughter, and wine maketh merry: but money answereth all things."

Isa 5:11 (KJV) "Woe unto them that rise up early in the morning, that they may follow strong drink; that continue until night, till wine inflame them!" Isa 5:12 (KJV) "And the harp, and the viol, the tabret, and pipe, and wine, are in their feasts: but they regard not the work of the LORD, neither consider the operation of his hands." Isa 5:22 (KJV) "Woe unto them that are mighty to drink wine, and men of strength to mingle strong drink:"

CHAPTER 9

All People Are Predominately Evil From Birth

Unfortunately, all people are predominately evil from birth. People have to be taught to be good and to do good. When they don't have the teachings to be good and to do good, they resort to their own evil nature which they were born with. Churches do poor jobs of getting this message across. Law officials and governmental officials have not a clue of this vast problem. If the U.S. Congress, the U.S. Senate, and the U.S. Supreme Court had any inkling of such a vast problem, then prayer would not have been an issue in our school systems. Prayer was no doubt a great thing in teaching our future generations the avenues of good behaviors through the good book, our Christian Bible. So, where good is not being allowed or not being taught, then evil prevails.

The bible tells us that all of us have sinned and come short of the glory of Almighty God. Therefore, we are all evil from birth and have to be taught to be good and to do good.

Romans 3 (KJV)

23. For all have sinned, and come short of the glory of God.

In order for us to learn to do good and to strive for goodness, we must obey the commandments of Almighty God or else face His consequences of curses upon us.

Exodus 20 (KJV)

12. Honour thy father and thy mother: that thy days may be long upon the land which the Lord thy God giveth thee.
13. Thou shalt not kill.
14. Thou shalt not commit adultery.
15. Thou shalt not steal.
16. Thou shalt not bear false witness against thy neighbour.
17. Thou shalt not covet thy neighbour's house, thou shalt not covet thy neighbour's wife, nor his manservant, nor his maidservant, nor his ox, nor his ass, nor any thing that is thy neighbour's.
18 And all the people saw the thunderings, and the lightnings, and the noise of the trumpet, and the mountain smoking: and when the people saw it, they removed, and stood afar off.
19. And they said unto Moses, Speak thou with us, and we will hear: but let not God speak with us, lest we die.
20. And Moses said unto the people, Fear not: for God is come to prove you, and that his fear may be before your faces, that ye sin not.
21. And the people stood afar off, and Moses drew near unto the thick darkness where God was.
22. And the Lord said unto Moses, Thus thou shalt say unto the children of Israel, Ye have seen that I have talked with you from heaven.
23. Ye shall not make with me gods of silver, neither shall ye make unto you gods of gold.

Leviticus 19 (KJV)

1. And the Lord spake unto Moses, saying,
2. Speak unto all the congregation of the children of Israel, and say unto them, Ye shall be holy: for I the Lord your God am holy.

3. Ye shall fear every man his mother, and his father, and keep my sabbaths: I am the Lord your God.
4. Turn ye not unto idols, nor make to yourselves molten gods: I am the Lord your God.
5. And if ye offer a sacrifice of peace offerings unto the Lord, ye shall offer it at your own will.
6 It shall be eaten the same day ye offer it, and on the morrow: and if ought remain until the third day, it shall be burnt in the fire.
7. And if it be eaten at all on the third day, it is abominable; it shall not be accepted.
8 Therefore every one that eateth it shall bear his iniquity, because he hath profaned the hallowed thing of the Lord: and that soul shall be cut off from among his people.
9. And when ye reap the harvest of your land, thou shalt not wholly reap the corners of thy field, neither shalt thou gather the gleanings of thy harvest.
10. And thou shalt not glean thy vineyard, neither shalt thou gather every grape of thy vineyard; thou shalt leave them for the poor and stranger: I am the Lord your God.
11. Ye shall not steal, neither deal falsely, neither lie one to another.
12. And ye shall not swear by my name falsely, neither shalt thou profane the name of thy God: I am the Lord.
13. Thou shalt not defraud thy neighbour, neither rob him: the wages of him that is hired shall not abide with thee all night until the morning.
14. Thou shalt not curse the deaf, nor put a stumblingblock before the blind, but shalt fear thy God: I am the Lord.
15. Ye shall do no unrighteousness in judgment: thou shalt not respect the person of the poor, nor honour the person of the mighty: but in righteousness shalt thou judge thy neighbour.
16. Thou shalt not go up and down as a talebearer among thy people: neither shalt thou stand against the blood of thy neighbour; I am the Lord.

17. Thou shalt not hate thy brother in thine heart: thou shalt in any wise rebuke thy neighbour, and not suffer sin upon him.
18. Thou shalt not avenge, nor bear any grudge against the children of thy people, but thou shalt love thy neighbour as thyself: I am the Lord.
19. Ye shall keep my statutes. Thou shalt not let thy cattle gender with a diverse kind: thou shalt not sow thy field with mingled seed: neither shall a garment mingled of linen and woollen come upon thee.

Deuteronomy 28 (KJV)

15. But it shall come to pass, if thou wilt not hearken unto the voice of the Lord thy God, to observe to do all his commandments and his statutes which I command thee this day; that all these curses shall come upon thee, and overtake thee:
16. Cursed shalt thou be in the city, and cursed shalt thou be in the field.
17. Cursed shall be thy basket and thy store.
18. Cursed shall be the fruit of thy body, and the fruit of thy land, the increase of thy kine, and the flocks of thy sheep.
19. Cursed shalt thou be when thou comest in, and cursed shalt thou be when thou goest out.
20. The Lord shall send upon thee cursing, vexation, and rebuke, in all that thou settest thine hand unto for to do, until thou be destroyed, and until thou perish quickly; because of the wickedness of thy doings, whereby thou hast forsaken me.
21. The Lord shall make the pestilence cleave unto thee, until he have consumed thee from off the land, whither thou goest to possess it.
22. The Lord shall smite thee with a consumption, and with a fever, and with an inflammation, and with an extreme

burning, and with the sword, and with blasting, and with mildew; and they shall pursue thee until thou perish.

23. And thy heaven that is over thy head shall be brass, and the earth that is under thee shall be iron.
24. The Lord shall make the rain of thy land powder and dust: from heaven shall it come down upon thee, until thou be destroyed.
25. The Lord shall cause thee to be smitten before thine enemies: thou shalt go out one way against them, and flee seven ways before them: and shalt be removed into all the kingdoms of the earth.
26. And thy carcase shall be meat unto all fowls of the air, and unto the beasts of the earth, and no man shall fray them away.
27. The Lord will smite thee with the botch of Egypt, and with the emerods, and with the scab, and with the itch, whereof thou canst not be healed.
28. The Lord shall smite thee with madness, and blindness, and astonishment of heart:
29. And thou shalt grope at noonday, as the blind gropeth in darkness, and thou shalt not prosper in thy ways: and thou shalt be only oppressed and spoiled evermore, and no man shall save thee.
30. Thou shalt betroth a wife, and another man shall lie with her: thou shalt build an house, and thou shalt not dwell therein: thou shalt plant a vineyard, and shalt not gather the grapes thereof.
31. Thine ox shall be slain before thine eyes, and thou shalt not eat thereof: thine ass shall be violently taken away from before thy face, and shall not be restored to thee: thy sheep shall be given unto thine enemies, and thou shalt have none to rescue them.
32. Thy sons and thy daughters shall be given unto another people, and thine eyes shall look, and fail with longing for them all the day long; and there shall be no might in thine hand.

33. The fruit of thy land, and all thy labours, shall a nation which thou knowest not eat up; and thou shalt be only oppressed and crushed alway:
34. So that thou shalt be mad for the sight of thine eyes which thou shalt see.
35. The Lord shall smite thee in the knees, and in the legs, with a sore botch that cannot be healed, from the sole of thy foot unto the top of thy head.
36. The Lord shall bring thee, and thy king which thou shalt set over thee, unto a nation which neither thou nor thy fathers have known; and there shalt thou serve other gods, wood and stone.
37. And thou shalt become an astonishment, a proverb, and a byword, among all nations whither the Lord shall lead thee.
38. Thou shalt carry much seed out into the field, and shalt gather but little in; for the locust shall consume it.
39. Thou shalt plant vineyards, and dress them, but shalt neither drink of the wine, nor gather the grapes; for the worms shall eat them.
40. Thou shalt have olive trees throughout all thy coasts, but thou shalt not anoint thyself with the oil; for thine olive shall cast his fruit.
41. Thou shalt beget sons and daughters, but thou shalt not enjoy them; for they shall go into captivity.
42 All thy trees and fruit of thy land shall the locust consume.
43. The stranger that is within thee shall get up above thee very high; and thou shalt come down very low.
44. He shall lend to thee, and thou shalt not lend to him: he shall be the head, and thou shalt be the tail.
45. Moreover all these curses shall come upon thee, and shall pursue thee, and overtake thee, till thou be destroyed; because thou hearkenedst not unto the voice of the Lord thy God, to keep his commandments and his statutes which he commanded thee:

46. And they shall be upon thee for a sign and for a wonder, and upon thy seed for ever.
47. Because thou servedst not the Lord thy God with joyfulness, and with gladness of heart, for the abundance of all things;
48. Therefore shalt thou serve thine enemies which the Lord shall send against thee, in hunger, and in thirst, and in nakedness, and in want of all things: and he shall put a yoke of iron upon thy neck, until he have destroyed thee.
49. The Lord shall bring a nation against thee from far, from the end of the earth, as swift as the eagle flieth; a nation whose tongue thou shalt not understand;
50. A nation of fierce countenance, which shall not regard the person of the old, nor shew favour to the young:
51. And he shall eat the fruit of thy cattle, and the fruit of thy land, until thou be destroyed: which also shall not leave thee either corn, wine, or oil, or the increase of thy kine, or flocks of thy sheep, until he have destroyed thee.
52. And he shall besiege thee in all thy gates, until thy high and fenced walls come down, wherein thou trustedst, throughout all thy land: and he shall besiege thee in all thy gates throughout all thy land, which the Lord thy God hath given thee.
53 And thou shalt eat the fruit of thine own body, the flesh of thy sons and of thy daughters, which the Lord thy God hath given thee, in the siege, and in the straitness, wherewith thine enemies shall distress thee:
54. So that the man that is tender among you, and very delicate, his eye shall be evil toward his brother, and toward the wife of his bosom, and toward the remnant of his children which he shall leave:
55. So that he will not give to any of them of the flesh of his children whom he shall eat: because he hath nothing left him in the siege, and in the straitness, wherewith thine enemies shall distress thee in all thy gates.

56. The tender and delicate woman among you, which would not adventure to set the sole of her foot upon the ground for delicateness and tenderness, her eye shall be evil toward the husband of her bosom, and toward her son, and toward her daughter,
57. And toward her young one that cometh out from between her feet, and toward her children which she shall bear: for she shall eat them for want of all things secretly in the siege and straitness, wherewith thine enemy shall distress thee in thy gates.
58. If thou wilt not observe to do all the words of this law that are written in this book, that thou mayest fear this glorious and fearful name, The Lord Thy God;
59. Then the Lord will make thy plagues wonderful, and the plagues of thy seed, even great plagues, and of long continuance, and sore sicknesses, and of long continuance.
60. Moreover he will bring upon thee all the diseases of Egypt, which thou wast afraid of; and they shall cleave unto thee.
61. Also every sickness, and every plague, which is not written in the book of this law, them will the Lord bring upon thee, until thou be destroyed.
62. And ye shall be left few in number, whereas ye were as the stars of heaven for multitude; because thou wouldest not obey the voice of the Lord thy God.
63. And it shall come to pass, that as the Lord rejoiced over you to do you good, and to multiply you; so the Lord will rejoice over you to destroy you, and to bring you to nought; and ye shall be plucked from off the land whither thou goest to possess it.

CHAPTER **10**

America's Manufacturers and Service Providers Produce Inferior Products and Services

The love for the almighty $dollar is the driving force behind America's entrepreneurship in producing goods and services. However, many goods and services are produced in such ways as to garner repeat purchases of inferior type quality goods and services for short term life spans for increased profits for the producers of the same.

1 Timothy 6 (KJV)

> 10. For the love of money is the root of all evil: which while some coveted after, they have erred from the faith, and pierced themselves through with many sorrows.

Here are some examples which include, but not limited to some of my experiences as well as others as follows:

Consumer Appliances

Waffle Maker - I purchased a waffle maker which was unsuited for making waffles. There was no indicator for to warn me when the waffle was finished baking. The waffle separated into two pieces and was not fit to be called a waffle.

I then went to Macy's and purchased a professional waffle maker which did exactly the way the restaurants make theirs.

Hand Mixer - We had previously purchased a hand mixer for mixing batter for breads, cakes and other dishes. This mixer soon wore out. We then purchased a Kitchen Aide Professional model which is still going and has been for the past 8 years.

Stove Counter Cook Top Upgrade

We purchased our present home was 12 years old. The cook Top Range was deteriorating and needed constant replacement parts. We finally replaced it with a Miele Counter Top Cook range.

Range: 1 Wok burner (propane), I large and 1 small burner (propane), 1 electric griddle, 1 large electric burner, and 1 small electric burner. This expensive unit came with a long term warranty.

Washer And Dryer Upgrade

Our washer and dryer was of inferior quality and didn't last long. We then purchased a Maytag Front-Loader washer and dryer which was more expensive than the top-loaders. Both of these machines have been going strong for the past 8 years without any repairs and is still going strong.

Television Sets And Stereo Equipment

We have purchased American made televisions and stereo equipment with frequent repairs and replacements and which were of inferior quality compared to Japanese made televisions and stereo equipment. We have found the best quality in Japanese made televisions and stereo equipment.

Automobiles

We have purchased many types of American made automobiles. We have purchased both new and used automobiles. We have purchased new auto with financing. By the time we made our last payment the auto was falling apart and needed major repairs. Many American made autos are made to only last a short while. On the other hand, Japanese made auto and European made autos usually last a number years before major repairs are needed.

Auto Mechanics And Service Centers

Some auto mechanics and auto service centers will sometimes provide inferior services at expensive or high costs to its customers. They will sometimes use cheap parts and charge more for profits to them. Normally, the customers are unaware of such practices.

Some years ago, my job had me traveling on the road quite frequently. My wife and daughter were at home alone, but my wife was also working and taking care of our home, the finances and our automobiles. One of the tires on my wife's auto had gone bad and had to be replaced. I called the service station and informed them that my wife was bringing her car in to have a tire replaced. I told the gentlemen to please give her a good tire for her auto. Well, he did provide a new tire for an expensive price. The tire was some off brand tire which he charged an expensive price for it. That tire lasted for 6 months. The life span of the tire proved to be very short. Normally before I purchase tires, I would seek out the brand of tires with long life spans comparable with the charges for those tires. I didn't have the opportunity to do my research on tires at that particular time, the reason why I was depending on that service station to give us a fair service. We did not get that fair service. Fortunately, that particular service station changed hands to new owners. Good riddance.

Another experience was with a local auto service center. We took my 1991 Chevrolet Silverado Pick-up truck in for numerous repairs and service, including an engine tune-up. The pick-up had not had a tune for over 8 years and none of the tune-up items had been replaced. We got the pick-up back with an expensive bill indicating that a tune-up had been done. As I sat in the pick-up with the engine idling, I noticed that the truck was not running smoothly. Being a "Shade Tree Type Mechanic" that I am, I surmised that a complete tune-up had not been done. One of the head mechanics told me that his technicians had checked the spark plug wires and found that they were alright when they weren't. My brother pulled some of the wires and checked them physically and found that they were either corroded or rusty at the most. Not only that, but the distributor cap and the rotor also needed to be replace. We did convince the mechanic to replace all of those with the best available parts and he did just that.

Also, we had the air conditioning compressor replaced and the system re-charge with freon. Later the system lost all of its freon and had to re-charged twice. We finally had the system checked by another mechanic from another auto service center. He found that the "O" ring at the hose connection was missing which allowed the freon to seep out. Not all auto service centers are willing to service your bet interests.

Grocery Store And Butcher Shop Services

My brother-in-law said that he was working at a grocery store, B-Lo's butcher shop at Chesapeake/Portsmouth, Virginia. The chief butcher had him to replenish the consumer refrigerators with ground beef. He noticed that there were two types of ground beef packages. One type of packaged beef was the lean type and the other type was beef filled with fat. He reached for the lean packages, but was immediately stopped by the head butcher who said that he could only stock the beef filled with the fat. Those packages were to be stocked for the Welfare mothers who came to shop on certain days. He then told my borother-in-law that the lean packages were for shoppers other than the welfare mothers.

There are also cases of butchers re-packaging old ground beef covered with fresh ground beef for re-stocking on the shelves for consumers as well.

Grocery Products Packaged Differently For Certain Grocery Stores

I normally buy souse (hog head cheese) which is a pork loaf made from the meat of a hog's head and is located for purchase in the cold-cut section of packaged meats. We normally purchased these meat packages from the Shopper's Food Warehouse where these souse packages are sliced from square loafs with a lot of vinegar in the ingredients. I did think that there was too much vinegar in it, but kept on buying it anyway. Well, just recently, we went to the Giant Food Store to make some grocery purchases because Giant carries some things that we like that Shopper's doesn't carry. So, while we were shopping, I told my wife that I was out of souse, so we proceeded to the cold-cut section to look for some souse. To our surprise Giant had some souse which was packaged by Gwalteney the packers who package souse for Shopper's. However, the packaging was round instead of the square design. When I opened the package and ate a sliced, it was mild to taste with a better flavor than the souse offered for sale at Shopper's. Now, you figure that one out.

Gasoline Quality Made Be The Same

Named brand gasolines at expensive prices may be purchased a t off brand gasoline service stations. In some cases the gas you purchased at off brand gasoline service stations may be the same at the more expensive stations. We have seen some tankers fill-up the tanks at named brand service stations, go right down the road fill-up off brand service stations as well. You will normally pay a lot less at the off brand service stations.

Attorney Services And Their Fees

Many attorneys provide little services for excessive fees and charges. We hired a young attorney for some problems that we had with the IRS. We filed a lawsuit against the IRS to no avail. The young attorney charged us excessive fees and charges. He even called our home while we were on vacation and left a message on our answering machine and charged us $75 for leaving us a message. We paid him over $25,000 for handling the lawsuit which was eventually withdrawn. He had previously told us that he had a certain strategy that he would us in our case. His so-called strategy didn't work for us.

We were back at square one in our situation with the IRS. Not only that, but we were out another $6,000 for CPA expenses for re-preparing previous returns which he didn't use as part of his so-called strategy. The attorney then increased our fees to another $20,000 for an alternate strategy. Of course we didn't agree to those fees. There should be a law against such.

Gas And Oil Drilling Sites In America

Exxon/Mobil Petroleum Operators are gouging America to the tune of $Billions on a quarterly basis and has just about brought us to our knees without any recourse. What we don't here in the media is that there are a lot of places to drill for gas and oil in America.

Arkansas and Louisiana are sitting on rivers of gas and oil under their farm lands. The state of Arkansas has two major oil shales: the Penters Shale and the Fayettville Shale. These shales encompasses a 100 mile long stretch to a 50 mile wide stretch across 10 counties. Many wells are have already been drilled with many more scheduled to be drilled in 2008. The transportation vehicle of pipe lines are presently being constructed as the transporting infrastructure.

CHAPTER 11

Ancestors' Acceptance of Un-Broken Curses

You are not only plagued with curses that your ancestors may have accepted, but also those that your immediate family has accepted as well. I, (Curtis) can remember coming home on leave from the Army and where I have taken my mother and my aunt to a fortune teller's house. They went there for readings, advice, and of course, fortune telling for things of the future. At the time that I took them there, I didn't know that I had opened a door for curses to come upon me. Additionally, I had visited a fortune teller myself with additional curses being placed on my life. One sad note is that I got winds that my step father had visited a fortune teller with promises that he would be healed from diabetes. Daddy really thought this woman was representing God. I was told later that my step father was quite angry with God for not healing him as he thought the promise came from God. It was bad enough that he had the curses of diabetes, but he went and accumulated more curses by seeking cures, advice, promises, and the Lord only knows what else from this spiritualist, Satan's representative.

The sad point of this matter is that these fortune tellers call themselves spiritualist which is a catchy word which Christians mistakenly associate them as being women or men of God, Almighty in heaven which we serve. Some have gone so far as to put the title of "Reverend" before their name which confuses Christians even more. In this town where we live, there is one such fortune teller calling herself a spiritualist and using the title of "Reverend". Years later after I found out that we are not supposed inquire of these fortune tellers, I revealed this information to my mother. She replied to me that the woman was a spiritualist and said in so many words that she didn't see anything wrong with it. I eventually convinced her that fortune tellers and other people who deals in this realm are representatives of Satan and not of God, Almighty in Whom we serve.

Years ago while I (Curtis) was still at home, I heard that my aunt through revelation from others had accepted certain rituals to do in her home to keep her husband from leaving her. This could include putting certain things in her husband's food, burning candles for so many days, burning incense for some many days, placing things under the steps outside of the house leading to the main doors. My aunt was heavily involve in the curse of adultery and was afraid the she would lose her husband through her own deeds of adultery. I was later informed while I was still in the army that her husband discovered her in bed having sex with her husband's male boss. After this particular episode, I took her and my mother to see the fortune teller. Nowadays, they call them psychics. Unbeknownst to me, all of us were cursed for visiting this fortune teller. There were three (3) generations of curses in my family.

1 Ki 9:6 (KJV) "But if ye shall at all turn from following me, ye or your children, and will not keep my commandments and my statutes which I have set before you, but go and serve other gods, and worship them:"

1 Ki 9:7 (KJV) "Then will I cut off Israel out of the land which I have given them; and this house, which I have hallowed for my name, will I cast out of my sight; and Israel shall be a proverb and a byword among all people:"

Exo 20:3-5 (KJV) Thou shalt have no other gods before me.

4. Thou shalt not make unto thee any graven image, or any likeness of any thing that is in heaven above, or that is in the earth beneath, or that is in the water under the earth:
5. Thou shalt not bow down thyself to them, nor serve them: for I the LORD thy God am a jealous God, visiting the iniquity of the fathers upon the children unto the third and fourth generation of them that hate me;

CHAPTER 12

Animals and Pets Don't Go to Heaven

Many people find comfort and fellowship with their pets sometimes over the friendship of human beings. There have been lawsuits initiated by families of deceased relatives in various courts over the huge inheritances they left to their pets resulting from their written wills. Many pet owners are concerned that when they leave for glory that their pets will follow them once they leave this life also. The bad news to them is that their pets will not follow them to heaven. Let's take for an example the dog as described below.

Deu 23:18 (KJV) "Thou shalt not bring the hire of a whore, or the price of a dog, into the house of the LORD thy God for any vow: for even **both these are abomination** unto the LORD thy God."

Dogs are placed in the same category as whoremongers, whom God despises. In other words, a dog is not acceptable to God as a sacrificial gift or offering. He doesn't actually hate the dog in itself because it is His creation. Both of these are abominations to Him. Since we don't sacrifice animals anymore for our sins, we can't even use animals for that purpose, either. Dogs certainly weren't God's choices for sacrificial offerings to Him. This applies to most of our common pets, (i.e., cats, parrots, fish, horses, cows, chickens, etc.).

Animals aren't accountable to God in any sense of the word from biblical point of view. While humans may have a body, soul and spirit. Animals have only a body of the animal kind and an animal soul (not accountable to God), but not a spirit which could essentially give them eternal life. Animals are only accountable to humanity while they live. Before God created humanity, He promised to give humanity rule and dominion over the earth.

Genesis 1:26 (KJV), "And God said, Let us make man in our image, after our likeness: and let them have dominion over the fish of the sea, and over the fowl of the air, and over the cattle, and over all the earth, and over every creeping thing that creepeth upon the earth."

Subsequently after God created humanity, He certainly did give them dominion over the whole earth.

Genesis 1:28 (KJV), "And God blessed them, and God said unto them, Be fruitful, and multiply, and replenish the earth, and subdue it: and have dominion over the fish of the sea, and over the fowl of the air, and over every living thing that moveth upon the earth."

First, these owners need to understand that only human beings have souls accountable to God. Souls and Spirits of humans are accountable to God whether their bodies are living or dead. The souls of humans never die contrary to the misconceptions, disbeliefs and erroneous teachings of various occult related organizations such as Jehovah Witnesses.

Finally, there are no biblical provisions for the salvation, sanctification, or justification for animals, fowls of the air, fish, crawling, creeping or anything else on the earth besides humanity. When your pets die, they are gone forever.

CHAPTER **13**

Battling Satan Without Almighty God's Permission

Whatever you do, don't play with Satan and don't just arbitrarily do out of pride, just attack him without just cause or without specifically receiving a commandment from God, Almighty to do so. Although we have power over Satan and his demons, we shouldn't take liberties or pleasures in going against them without just cause because we will be opening ourselves up for tremendous attacks on our lives. We can really get ourselves out there on a limb without a prayer or support in our battle and without help from God, Almighty. Sometimes God, Almighty will teach us some lessons by letting Satan and/or his demons attack us. If you are not a Christian or if you are not a strong Christian, then you don't have permission from God to attack Satan. You will simply not be equipped with the necessary armor or battle weapons to do so.

Acts 19:13-16 (KJV) Then certain of the vagabond Jews, exorcists, took upon them to call over them which had evil spirits the name of the Lord Jesus, saying, We adjure you by Jesus whom Paul preacheth.

14. And there were seven sons of one Sceva, a Jew, and chief of the priests, which did so.
15. And the evil spirit answered and said, Jesus I know, and Paul I know; but who are ye?

16. And the man in whom the evil spirit was leaped on them, and overcame them, and prevailed against them, so that they fled out of that house naked and wounded.

One interesting note is that the Chief of the priests should have been walking with God and serving Him. You see, demons know if you are in fact serving our living Savior, Jesus Christ and following the commandments of our Father, God, Almighty.

Ridiculing Satan

You can get yourself in a lot trouble when you call yourself kidding with Satan and/or his demons. For example, you could without being prompted by anything and tell Satan and his demons that they are going to burn in hell forever. What you have just done was to invite Satan and his demons to attack you at will. Don't just do this just out of spite. Make sure that Satan and/or his demons are attacking you, before you attack them. You must exercise selfrestraint in this matter.

1 Cor 7:5 (KJV) "Defraud ye not one the other, except it be with consent for a time, that ye may give yourselves to fasting and prayer; and come together again, that Satan tempt you not for your **incontinency**."

192. akrasia, ak-ras-ee'-a; from G193; want of **self-restraint**:--excess, **incontinency**.

Eph 4:27 (KJV) "Neither give place to the devil."

James 4:7 (KJV) "Submit yourselves therefore to God. Resist the devil, and he will flee from you."

CHAPTER **14**

Bigamy and Polygamy Are Biblically Prohibited

Bigamy: Definition

The criminal offense of marrying one person while still legally married to another.

Polygamy: Definition

The condition or practice of having more than one spouse at one time. Also called plural marriage.

There are many polygamist groups residing in these United States of America, including, but limited to the states of Texas, Arizona, and Virginia, just to name a few. The leaders of those groups believe that old testament scriptures gives them the rights to do so. They think that they are sincerely right. However, they are sincerely wrong.

During the initial stages of creation, beginning with Adam and Eve, Almighty God permitted them to marry within the family to multiply the earth. Even up to the leadership of the Jews by the Prophet Moses, some men had many wives and concubines. Even King Solomon had about 300 wives and 700 concubines. Jesus Christ came along and that particular history was changed to only one wife per man. Anything different from that was adultery.

Almighty God gave Moses two (2) tablets with the 10 commandments prohibiting both bigamy and polygamy, that is prohibiting them from having more than one (1) wife.

Exodus 20 (KJV)

14. Thou shalt not commit adultery.

Matthew 5 (KJV)

27. Ye have heard that it was said by them of old time, Thou shalt not commit adultery:
28. But I say unto you, That whosoever looketh on a woman to lust after her hath committed adultery with her already in his heart.

Almighty God emphasizes in the book of Matthew that marriage is for one husband (male), and one woman (female). In marriage, they are joined as one soul, not multiple souls.

Matthew 19 (KJV)

5. And said, For this cause shall a man leave father and mother, and shall cleave to his wife: and they twain shall be one flesh?
6. Wherefore they are no more twain, but one flesh. What therefore God hath joined together, let not man put asunder.

Even men of Almighty God prohibited from marrying more than one wife and she must be a virgin. He must not marry a prostitute (harlot) or a whore. Neither should he marry a widow, a profane woman, or a woman who has been divorced. See verse 14 below.

Leviticus 21 (KJV)

1. And the Lord said unto Moses, Speak unto the priests the sons of Aaron, and say unto them, There shall none be defiled for the dead among his people:
2. But for his kin, that is near unto him, that is, for his mother, and for his father, and for his son, and for his daughter, and for his brother.
3. And for his sister a virgin, that is nigh unto him, which hath had no husband; for her may he be defiled.
4. But he shall not defile himself, being a chief man among his people, to profane himself.
5. They shall not make baldness upon their head, neither shall they shave off the corner of their beard, nor make any cuttings in their flesh.
6. They shall be holy unto their God, and not profane the name of their God: for the offerings of the Lord made by fire, and the bread of their God, they do offer: therefore they shall be holy.
7. They shall not take a wife that is a whore, or profane; neither shall they take a woman put away from her husband: for he is holy unto his God.
8. Thou shalt sanctify him therefore; for he offereth the bread of thy God: he shall be holy unto thee: for I the Lord, which sanctify you, am holy.
9. And the daughter of any priest, if she profane herself by playing the whore, she profaneth her father: she shall be burnt with fire.
10. And he that is the high priest among his brethren, upon whose head the anointing oil was poured, and that is consecrated to put on the garments, shall not uncover his head, nor rend his clothes;
11. Neither shall he go in to any dead body, nor defile himself for his father, or for his mother;
12. Neither shall he go out of the sanctuary, nor profane the

sanctuary of his God; for the crown of the anointing oil of his God is upon him: I am the Lord.

13. And he shall take a wife in her virginity.
14. A widow, or a divorced woman, or profane, or an harlot, these shall he not take: but he shall take a virgin of his own people to wife.

Almighty God re-emphasizes the point that He is the Higher Power that everyone on earth should recognize and honor Him by obeying His commandments. He re-emphasizes the commandment, "Thou Shalt not commit adultery!"

Romans 13 (KJV)

1. Let every soul be subject unto the higher powers. For there is no power but of God: the powers that be are ordained of God.
2. Whosoever therefore resisteth the power, resisteth the ordinance of God: and they that resist shall receive to themselves damnation.
3. For rulers are not a terror to good works, but to the evil. Wilt thou then not be afraid of the power? do that which is good, and thou shalt have praise of the same:
4. For he is the minister of God to thee for good. But if thou do that which is evil, be afraid; for he beareth not the sword in vain: for he is the minister of God, a revenger to execute wrath upon him that doeth evil.
5. Wherefore ye must needs be subject, not only for wrath, but also for conscience sake.
6. For this cause pay ye tribute also: for they are God's ministers, attending continually upon this very thing.
7. Render therefore to all their dues: tribute to whom tribute is due; custom to whom custom; fear to whom fear; honour to whom honour.
8. Owe no man any thing, but to love one another: for he that loveth another hath fulfilled the law.

9. For this, Thou shalt not commit adultery, Thou shalt not kill, Thou shalt not steal, Thou shalt not bear false witness, Thou shalt not covet; and if there be any other commandment, it is briefly

Almighty God specifically said to His servants on earth that they must be a husband or wife of one (1) spouse. You won't find the words "Bigamy" or "Polygamy" in the Holy Scriptures of the Bible, but you find that the contents or context of this fit right in the meaning of adultery.

Bishops Specifically Prohibited From Bigamy and Polygamy

1 Timothy 3 (KJV)

1. This is a true saying, If a man desire the office of a bishop, he desireth a good work.
2. A bishop then must be blameless, the husband of one wife, vigilant, sober, of good behaviour, given to hospitality, apt to teach;

Deacons Specifically Prohibited From Bigamy or Polygamy

12. Let the deacons be the husbands of one wife, ruling their children and their own houses well.

Adultery Destroys Your Soul

Proverbs 6 (KJV)

32. But whoso committeth adultery with a woman lacketh understanding: he that doeth it destroyeth his own soul.

Lust For A Woman/Man In The Heart Is Adultery

Matthew 5 (KJV)

28. But I say unto you, That whosoever looketh on a woman to lust after her hath committed adultery with her already in his heart.

CHAPTER 15

Blaspheming the Holy Spirit Is Un-Forgivable

Many Christians have wondered if they had by chance blasphemed or had hatred against the Holy Spirit. They can rest easy if they in fact are born again or saved Christians. Nobody who loves the Lord could not have that type of evil in their spirits. Blaspheming the Holy Spirit will never be forgiven in this world, nor in the world to come. Jesus had this to say about people who blaspheme against the Holy Ghost:

Matthew 12 (KJV)

31. Wherefore I say unto you, All manner of sin and blasphemy shall be forgiven men: but the blasphemy against the Holy Ghost shall not be forgiven unto men.

The word man implies a certain man in which you will learn later is an evil man who is one of Satan's family of evil. That word man was derived from the Greek translation G444 anthropos, anth'-ro-pos; man-faced, i.e. a human being:--certain, man. If you were totally sold out (never to become a Christian) to Satan, then you would have blasphemed the Holy Ghost. Satan is the father of blasphemy.

Revelation 13 (KJV)

6. And he opened his mouth in blasphemy against God, to blaspheme His name, and his tabernacle, and them that dwell in heaven." That includes the Holy Ghost.

Many Christians are concerned that maybe in their sinful state before they were saved, they could have possibly blasphed the Holy Ghost and not be forgiven for it. By the mere fact you sincerely became a Christian, you have never blasphemed the Holy Spirit.

If you have talked evil about God or Jesus Christ, you can and will be forgiven. Of course if you are a Christian you've already been forgiven by the mere fact you are in Christianity. Jesus went on to explain that blaspheming the Holy Ghost will never be forgiven.

Matthew 12 (KJV),

32. And whsoever speaketh a word against the Son of Man, it shall be forgiven: but whosoever speaketh against the Holy Ghost, it shall not be forgiven him, neither in this world, neither in the world to come."

CHAPTER **16**

Bless Almighty God First, Then Ask Him to Bless America

Often-times we hear America's patriotic citizens use the phrase, "God, Bless America!". What they fail to understand is that blessing are two-fold. One has to give in order to receive. If you never give to others, including our Creator, our Deity, our Lord, our Almighty God, then your request for blessings will go un-answered. Almighty God lives in praises.

Psalms 22 (KJV)

3. But thou art holy, O thou that inhabitest the praises of Israel.

We must praise Almighty God with every fiber of our being for His mighty blessings. The book of Psalms 150 gives us an eye opening glimpse of how we should direct our praises to Almighty God as listed below and found in your Christian Bibles.

Psalms 150 (KJV)

1. Praise ye the Lord. Praise God in his sanctuary: praise him in the firmament of his power.
2. Praise him for his mighty acts: praise him according to his excellent greatness.
3. Praise him with the sound of the trumpet: praise him with the psaltery and harp.

4. Praise him with the timbrel and dance: praise him with
stringed instruments and organs. 5. Praise him upon the
loud cymbals: praise him upon the high sounding cymbals.
6. Let every thing that hath breath praise the Lord. Praise ye
the Lord.

CHAPTER 17

Bless Your Food by Giving Thanks to Almighty God

We are admonished to bless, that is to thank Almighty God for all of our blessings and gifts which He provides to us without ceasing. Many people are ashamed to publically give thanks to Almighty God before they consume their meals or snacks at eating places and restaurants. If one deny Him, then He will deny them as well. So, don't be ashamed to bow your heads and give Almighty God the blessings of your food before you consume it.

Matthew 10:33 (KJV), "But whosoever shall deny me before men, him will I also deny before my Father which is in heaven." Often time we as Christians are reluctant to bless or give thanks to God for the food we are about to eat in public places, among crouds and/or our acquantances. He goes on to tell us that in everything give thanks to God, our Father in heaven.

I Thessalonians 5:18 (KJV), "In every thing give thanks: for this is the will of God in Christ Jesus concerning you."

In these days some people forbid themselves from eating meats or certain kinds of meats in that some become vegetarians. Some feel that they will acquire better health by doing so. God said that any thing he created for us to eat should be received with thanksgiving because it is sanctified by the word of God and prayer.

1 Timothy 4:1-5 (KJV),

1. Now the Spirit speaketh expressly, that in the latter times some shall depart from the faith, giving heed to seducing spirits, and doctrines of devils;
2. Speaking lies in hypocrisy; having their conscience seared with a hot iron.
3. Forbidding to marry, and commanding to abstain from meats, which God hath created to be received with thanksgiving of them which believe and know the truth.
4. For every creature of God is good, and nothing to be refused, if it be received with thanksgiving:
5. For it is sanctified by the word of God and prayer."

However, we do have to watch our animal fat intake which is detrimental to our health.

Leviticus 3:17 (KJV), It shall be a perpetual statute for your generations throughout all your dwellings, that ye eat neither fat nor blood.

17. It shall be a perpetual statute for your generations throughout all your dwellings, that ye eat neither fat nor blood.

Leviticus 3:23 (KJV), Speak unto the children of Israel, saying, Ye shall eat no manner of fat, of ox, of sheep, or of goat.

Even in the secular world of medical science would agree that we should limit or abstain from absorbing too much fat which could aid in clogging our blood vessels and/or our arteries.

CHAPTER **18**

Bodily Exercise Profits You Little

There are many types of exercise programs on the market to so called help keep a person fit so their lives could possibly be prolonged with better health.

1 Timothy 4 (KJV)

8. For bodily exercise profiteth little: but godliness is profitable unto all things, having promise of the life that now is, and of that which is to come.
9. This is a faithful saying and worthy of all acceptation.

There was a gentleman who exercised daily, ate a vegetarian diet, abstained from drinking alcoholic beverages, he didn't smoke, but still died early in his life. The Bible tells us that bodily exercise will profit us little. The longevity and health of our lives aren't dependent upon how much we exercise our bodies. As long as we keep our eyes on the Maker of our bodies, then our health can be preserved and maintained in a suitable way.

CHAPTER 19

Body Is a Living Sacrifice to Almighty God

Our Christian bodies are living sacrifices unto God Almighty, our heavenly Father. We can't be drug abusers, alcoholics, winos, sex offenders, habitual over eaters (gluttons) or whatever causes harm to our bodies.

Romans 12:1 (KJV), "I beseech you therefore, brethren, by the mercies of God, that ye present your bodies a living sacrifice, holy, acceptable unto God, which is your reasonable service.

1 Corinthians 6:15-20 (KJV), "15) Know ye not that your bodies are the members of Christ? Shall I then take the members of Christ, and make them members of an harlot? God forbid.

16. What? Know ye not that he which is joined to an harlot is one body? For two, saith He, shall be one flesh.
17. But he that is joined unto the Lord is one spirit.
18. Flee fornication. Every sin that a man doeth is without the body; but he that committeth fornication sinneth against his own body.
19. What? Know ye not that your body is the temple of the Holy Ghost which is in you, which ye have of God, and ye are not your own?
20. For ye are bought with a price: therefore glorify God in your body, and in your spirit, which are God's.

Celibacy - Abstaining From Having Sex Is A Choice

Some people desire to remain celibate, that is they don't want to marry and thereby totally abstain from having sex intercourse with the opposite sex. There is nothing wrong with a person's desire to abstain from marriage and thereby abstaining from having sex intercourse with the opposite sex. Some church denominations require that their ministers or their clergy staff and their support staff of people make vows of celibacy while they serve that particular denomination. It means that they have been forbidden to marry which requires that they totally abstain from having sex with the opposite sex regardless of their desires to do so. Prohibiting one from marriage when they have the desire to so is not biblically correct. Although God is not forbidding us to marry, but man is forbidding us to marry. This is a form of bondage. This type of prohibition is not of God, but of Satan.

1 Corinthians 7:8-9 (KJV), "8) I say therefore to the unmarried and widows, It is good for them if they abide even as I.

9. But if they cannot contain, let them marry: for it is better to marry than to burn."

Contain. Greek translation G1467 Egkrateuomai, eng-krat-yoo'-om-ahee; to exercise self-restraint.

If you feel that you need to fulfil your desires of having sex with the opposite sex, then you need to get married. Otherwise, you are in danger of being inflamed with anger, grief, and lust in your heart which is basically the same as actually committing a sex act with the person you desire to be with. This is what the word "burn" means as the last word in the above scripture.

Burn is Greek translation G4440 Puro, Poo-ro-o; to be inflamed (with anger, grief, lust):--burn.

It is definitely not a sin to marry if you so desire. Listen what the scriptures has to say about the matter of getting married.

1 Corinthian 7:28 (KJV), "But and if thou marry, thou hast not sinned; and if a virgin marry, she hath not sinned. Nevertheless such shall have trouble in the flesh: but I spare you."

This is a warning about the flesh in trials and tribulations and of course burdens. The next three verses are warning you about doctrines of devils spreading lies that you shouldn't marry.

1 Timothy 4:1-3 (KJV), "1) Now the Spirit speaketh expressly, that in the latter times some shall depart from the faith, giving heed to seducing spirits, and doctrines of devils;

2. Speaking lies in hypocrisy; having their conscience seared with a hot iron;
3. Forbidding to marry, and commanding to abstain from meats, which God hath created to be received with thanksgiving of them which believe and know the truth."

These lies are alive and well now. Many couples think it is right that they are living together, having children, but they desire to maintain their lives outside of marriage. Some Christians are no less doing some of these things by living together outside of marriage. Some religions require their members to abstain from eating certain meats which our God has provided for us to receive. You must gain the necessary wisdom, knowledge and understanding to know what God's will is and carry it out to the best of your abilities. That is why you are reading this book to aid you in gaining the necessary wisdom, knowledge and understanding of God's unadulterated word.

Sex outside of marriage is lust and not love. Many people, young and old confuse their lustful desires with Christian love. Although, we humans are weak, but as Christians, we must exercise restraint during the stages of our single lives. When you get to a point in your lives where you feel that you just can not contain your lustful desires to have sexual intercourse with the opposite sex, then you should earnestly and sincerely ask God to send you a Spirit-filled mate to marry and He will. Remember, this marriage is for life.

Prov 6:25 (KJV) "Lust not after her beauty in thine heart; neither let her take thee with her eyelids."

Mat 5:28 (KJV) "But I say unto you, That whosoever looketh on a woman to lust after her hath committed adultery with her already in his heart."

Gal 5:16 (KJV) "This I say then, Walk in the Spirit, and ye shall not fulfil the lust of the flesh."

James 1:14 (KJV) "But every man is tempted, when he is drawn away of his own lust, and enticed."

James 1:15 (KJV) "Then when lust hath conceived, it bringeth forth sin: and sin, when it is finished, bringeth forth death."

James 4:2 (KJV) "Ye lust, and have not: ye kill, and desire to have, and cannot obtain: ye fight and war, yet ye have not, because ye ask not."

2 Pet 1:4 (KJV) "Whereby are given unto us exceeding great and precious promises: that by these ye might be partakers of the divine nature, having escaped the corruption that is in the world through lust."

2 Pet 2:10 (KJV) "But chiefly them that walk after the flesh in the lust of uncleanness, and despise government. Presumptuous are they, selfwilled, they are not afraid to speak evil of dignities."

1 John 2:16 (KJV) "For all that is in the world, the lust of the flesh, and the lust of the eyes, and the pride of life, is not of the Father, but is of the world."

1 John 2:17 (KJV) "And the world passeth away, and the lust thereof: but he that doeth the will of God abideth for ever."

CHAPTER **20**

Bosses Are Not to Be Despised

The Bible really tells us to honor and obey ones who are appointed over us, especially in the work force. Many young people tend to rebel against those who are placed in authority over them. God put governments and other instruments of authority in place for his reason. Although, many people who are fortunate to be in somewhat of authority position are not always honest, un-bias, or righteous in nature towards their subordinates, but as Christians under them, we should be honest, righteous, dedicated and trustworthy to our bosses or supervisors.

Those who are practicing Christians and who have authority over us deserve special honor and dedication as God, Almighty may have a hand in directing their path to their authoritative position. God does not have a hand in directing the paths of un-saved bosses.

1 Timothy 6 (KJV)

1. Let as many servants as are under the yoke count their own masters worthy of all honour, that the name of God and his doctrine be not blasphemed.
2. And they that have believing masters, let them not despise them, because they are brethren; but rather do them service, because they are faithful and beloved, partakers of the benefit. These things teach and exhort.

Now, if your boss is wicked and is certainly not a Christian and despises you because you are a Christian, then pray this prayer:

Psalms 140 (KJV)

1. Deliver me, O Lord, from the evil man: preserve me from the violent man;
2. Which imagine mischiefs in their heart; continually are they gathered together for war.
3. They have sharpened their tongues like a serpent; adders' poison is under their lips. Selah.
4. Keep me, O Lord, from the hands of the wicked; preserve me from the violent man; who have purposed to overthrow my goings.
5. The proud have hid a snare for me, and cords; they have spread a net by the wayside; they have set gins for me. Selah.
6. I said unto the Lord, Thou art my God: hear the voice of my supplications, O Lord.
7. O God the Lord, the strength of my salvation, thou hast covered my head in the day of battle.
8. Grant not, O Lord, the desires of the wicked: further not his wicked device; lest they exalt themselves. Selah.
9. As for the head of those that compass me about, let the mischief of their own lips cover them.
10. Let burning coals fall upon them: let them be cast into the fire; into deep pits, that they rise not up again.
11. Let not an evil speaker be established in the earth: evil shall hunt the violent man to overthrow him.
12. I know that the Lord will maintain the cause of the afflicted, and the right of the poor.
13. Surely the righteous shall give thanks unto thy name: the upright shall dwell in thy presence.

CHAPTER 21

Broken Dedications to Satan Reap You More Curses

Now, if you have been associating with Satan in some form or fashion as a Satanist or if you have been or you are now dabbling in satanic rituals, playing with Ouija boards, Dungeon and Dragon games, power games, and/or items or sources of satanic influence, listening to acid rock music, hard rock music, rap music with demonic lyrics, you have certainly opened up doors for those curses to come into your lives. One big problem comes when you try to separate yourself from these demonically influence things. These curses have flooded your life such that Satan doesn't want you to leave and he will reek havoc with your life because you have broken your vow of dedication to him by attempting to break your relationship with him and your attempt to sever your ties to him. You have actually made an UNSPOKEN VOW or PLEDGE to him. Now you want to break that vow or pledge, but Satan will charge you a dear penny of penalties for withdrawing your support from him. In our church, babies are regularly dedicated to God, Almighty. The parents, their families and their friends take vows or promises to assist in the Christian upbringing of those babies. The church members are also ask to take vows or promises to assist in the Christian upbringing of those babies as well. Now, if babies are dedicated in non Christian churches, then those babies are in fact dedicated to Satan and their little lives are plagued with curses. THE STAKES ARE HIGH HERE!

1 Ki 9:6 (KJV) "But if ye shall at all turn from following me, ye or your children, and will not keep my commandments and my statutes which I have set before you, but go and serve other gods, and worship them:"

1 Ki 9:7 (KJV) "Then will I cut off Israel out of the land which I have given them; and this house, which I have hallowed for my name, will I cast out of my sight; and Israel shall be a proverb and a byword among all people:"

Exo 20:3-5 (KJV) Thou shalt have no other gods before me.

4. Thou shalt not make unto thee any graven image, or any likeness of any thing that is in heaven above, or that is in the earth beneath, or that is in the water under the earth:
5. Thou shalt not bow down thyself to them, nor serve them: for I the LORD thy God am a jealous God, visiting the iniquity of the fathers upon the children unto the third and fourth generation of them that hate me;

CHAPTER 22

Broken Vows to Almighty God Reap You More Curses

Christians who pledge vows to Almighty God, then break them, could result in more curses to themselves their family and their future generations. If you break a vow to Almighty God, then you must ask Him for forgiveness. He will without a doubt, forgive you.

Eccl 5:4-5 (KJV) When thou **vowest a vow** unto God, defer not to pay it; for he hath no pleasure in fools: pay that which thou hast vowed.

5. Better is it that thou shouldest not vow, than that thou shouldest vow and not pay.

Vow. Hebrew definition: 5087. nadar, naw-dar'; a prim. root; **to promise** (pos., to do or give something to God):--(make a) vow

Sometimes in our lives we make certain vows to God, Almighty and find later that evil things start happening. Then, we need to check out any promises that we made to God and see if we are meeting our commitments to Him. If you were several years ago, a few months ago or just a few years ago and now decided to go back into the world, then you have broken your vow to follow in the footsteps of Jesus Christ. This is certainly a broken vow. Maybe, while you were on your death bed, you were able to speak or pray a few words for

Jesus to come into your heart and that you promised Him that you would serve Him for the rest of your life. However, you are up and running around in fair health or maybe in great health, but you feel that you haven't seen or done what you wanted to see or do in the WORLD, so you left the church. You also thought that you had more fun out there in the world and you felt that you missed those happenings out there. Well, my brother or my sister, you are plagued with curses of a broken vow or vows to God. God, Almighty will allow you to be cursed if break you vow with Him. He is a Just and Righteous God. He will bless you as well as punish you.

1 Cor 10:5-11 (KJV) But with many of them God was not well pleased: for they were overthrown in the wilderness.

6. Now these things were our examples, to the intent we should not lust after evil things, as they also lusted.
7. Neither be ye idolaters, as were some of them; as it is written, The people sat down to eat and drink, and rose up to play.
8. Neither let us commit fornication, as some of them committed, and fell in one day three and twenty thousand.
9. Neither let us tempt Christ, as some of them also tempted, and were destroyed of serpents.
10. Neither murmur ye, as some of them also murmured, and were destroyed of the destroyer.
11. Now all these things happened unto them for ensamples: and they are written for our admonition, upon whom the ends of the world are come.

Lev 26:21-25 (KJV) And if ye walk contrary unto me, and will not hearken unto me; I will bring **seven times more plagues** upon you according to your sins.

22. I will also send wild beasts among you, which shall rob you

of your children, and destroy your cattle, and make you few in number; and your high ways shall be desolate.

23. And if ye will not be reformed by me by these things, but will walk contrary unto me;
24. Then will I also walk contrary unto you, **and will punish you yet seven times for your sins.**
25. And I will bring a sword upon you, that shall avenge the quarrel of my covenant: and when ye are gathered together within your cities, I will send the pestilence among you; and ye shall be delivered into the hand of the enemy.

An example of broken vows are the sins of the children of Israel toward God Who was sustaining their livelihood, feeding them daily and protecting them during their 40 years of wondering in the wilderness.

Num 21:5-9 (KJV) And the people spake against God, and against Moses, Wherefore have ye brought us up out of Egypt to die in the wilderness? for there is no bread, neither is there any water; and our soul loatheth this light bread.

6. And the LORD sent fiery serpents among the people, and they bit the people; and much people of Israel died.
7. Therefore the people came to Moses, and said, We have sinned, for we have spoken against the LORD, and against thee; pray unto the LORD, that he take away the serpents from us. And Moses prayed for the people.
8. And the LORD said unto Moses, Make thee a fiery serpent, and set it upon a pole: and it shall come to pass, that every one that is bitten, when he looketh upon it, shall live.
9. And Moses made a serpent of brass, and put it upon a pole, and it came to pass, that if a serpent had bitten any man, when he beheld the serpent of brass, he lived.

CHAPTER 23

Capital Punishment - Killing & Murdering Authorities

Government officials in authority who direct that people in prisons on death row be put to death are in fact disobeying the Commandments of Almighty God, our Creator and Heavenly Father. He admonishes us not to have blood on our hands for taking another human beings life. Since we can't give life, then we don't have the right to take anyone's life. Government officials don't merely have the right to take anybody's life, no matter what the alleged crime was purported to have been committed.

Exodus 20 (KJV)

13. Thou shalt not kill.

Officials who authorize capital punishment processes have ignored and disobeyed God, Almighty's command when He tells us to leave way for His wrath because vengeance is His responsibility and that He will repay:

Romans 12 (KJV)

19. Dearly beloved, avenge not yourselves, but rather give place unto wrath: for it is written, Vengeance is mine; I will repay, saith the Lord.

20. Therefore if thine enemy hunger, feed him; if he thirst, give him drink: for in so doing thou shalt heap coals of fire on his head.
21. Be not overcome of evil, but overcome evil with good.

Capital punishment is plain and simple: Murder sanctioned by people seeking vengeance with no thoughts of the ramifications in their desires for murdering someone else. They are ignorant to the fact that they are as guilty of murder as is the authorities who giving the orders to carry out such murders. The bible tells that what we think is what we are. So, if you think that capital punishment is the way to go to get closure in your life. Wrong! There is no such closure to be had with murder on your mind. You are just as guilty as the murderer on death row. Some of the processes used include, but are not limited to:

Lethal Injections. The persons preparing the criminal for the injection, the person, the person who starts the injection process and the person or persons who prepared the lethal drugs for the execution.

Electrocution: All are guilty of murder whomever assisted in the preparation of the person who was executed. The person who pulled the switch to cause the electrocution of the is just as guilty of murder as well. The authorizing officials now have blood on their hands and now are guilty of murder as well. They will also be judged by God, Almighty.

Gas Chamber: This one reminds one of the Jewish Holocaust where many jews were murdered in those awful gas chambers. The people who carry out the process of murdering humans in these gas chambers are guilty of murder along with the authorizing officials as well. All will be judged for their actions by God, Almighty.

Hanging: Although the former dictator of Iraq and his close associates were hunged after they were tried in court, these were also murders which inluded the judges, the preparers, the hangman, and the authorizing officials who directed the execution. All are guilty of murder and will be judged by God, Almighty.

Firing Squad: In 1978 as I, Curtis, was attending the Advanced Non-Commissioned Officer Course at the Administration School at Fort Benjamin Harrison, Indiana, a news broadcast aired that a gentleman was either in prison for life or on death row. Anyway, he requested that he be executed by a firing squad. Well, during a break from our class, we were standing around talking about that particular sitation of a firing squad. There about 5 black students and about 10 white students in the class. All of the white students voiced their desires for the opportunity to be part of that firing squad. None of the black students wanted to take part in the firing squad. This was a shock to me. Although those white students don't know that they are just as guilty as the ones who participated on the firing squad along with the authorizing officials.

One of the key issues is a spiritual one. So whatever a person's thoughts are in their hearts, so are they whether commits the act or not:

Proverbs 23 (KJV)

7. For as he thinketh in his heart, so is he: Eat and drink, saith he to thee; but his heart is not with thee.

The president of the United States of America along with governors who have the authority to stop capital punishments including the execution of humans are just as guilty of murder as those mentioned above as well. They will also be judged by God, Almighty.

Matthew 5 (KJV)

21. Ye have heard that it was said by them of old time, Thou shalt not kill; and whosoever shall kill shall be in danger of the judgment:

Psalms 10 (KJV)

1. Why standest thou afar off, O Lord? why hidest thou thyself in times of trouble?
2. The wicked in his pride doth persecute the poor: let them be taken in the devices that they have imagined.
3. For the wicked boasteth of his heart's desire, and blesseth the covetous, whom the Lord abhorreth.
4. The wicked, through the pride of his countenance, will not seek after God: God is not in all his thoughts.
5. His ways are always grievous; thy judgments are far above out of his sight: as for all his enemies, he puffeth at them.
6. He hath said in his heart, I shall not be moved: for I shall never be in adversity.
7. His mouth is full of cursing and deceit and Fraud: under his tongue is mischief and vanity.
8. He sitteth in the lurking places of the villages: in the secret places doth he murder the innocent: his eyes are privily set against the poor.

Not only is the accused party guilty of murder in he/she did in fact commit the crime, but following who assists in carrying out the capital punishment, along with the authorizing officials:

Psalms 94 (KJV)

1. O Lord God, to whom vengeance belongeth; O God, to whom vengeance belongeth, shew thyself.
2. Lift up thyself, thou judge of the earth: render a reward to the proud.
3. Lord, how long shall the wicked, how long shall the wicked triumph?
4. How long shall they utter and speak hard things? and all the workers of iniquity boast themselves?

5. They break in pieces thy people, O Lord, and afflict thine heritage.
6. They slay the widow and the stranger, and murder the fatherless.

Hosea 6 (KJV)

9. And as troops of robbers wait for a man, so the company of priests murder in the way by consent: for they commit lewdness.

Matthew 19 (KJV)

17. And he said unto him, Why callest thou me good? there is none good but one, that is, God: but if thou wilt enter into life, keep the commandments.
18. He saith unto him, Which? Jesus said, Thou shalt do no murder, Thou shalt not commit adultery, Thou shalt not steal, Thou shalt not bear false witness,
19. Honour thy father and thy mother: and, Thou shalt love thy neighbour as thyself.

Romans 1 (KJV)

29. Being filled with all unrighteousness, fornication, wickedness, covetousness, maliciousness; full of envy, murder, debate, deceit, malignity; whisperers,
30. Backbiters, haters of God, despiteful, proud, boasters, inventors of evil things, disobedient to parents,
31. Without understanding, covenant breakers, without natural affection, implacable, unmerciful:
32. Who knowing the judgment of God, that they which commit such things are worthy of death, not only do the same, but have pleasure in them that do them.

CHAPTER 24

Celebrating Holidays vs. Worshiping Almighty God

Secular celebrations are commonly misconstrued with the Christian traditions of worshiping God, Almighty, His Son, Jesus and His Holy Spirit. Not only are secular type of parties and fellowships popular and prevalent in our society, but the commercialization of products and services by retailers depends on this niche for their marketing and reaping massive profits.

Marketing strategies are developed around certain holidays or holy days such as the 4th of July, Easter, Thanksgiving, Christmas and New Years. We as Americans celebrate the 4th of July to commemorate the freedom which we so richly enjoy. Easter is a day set aside for family reunions, picnics, bar-b-ques, and/or family gatherings. Retailers such as store owners enjoys selling Easter candy, bunny rabbits whether they are alive or just stuffed animals, chicken eggs for boiling and coloring, clothing (Easter frocks) and Easter baskets. Thanksgiving provides the retailers a market for selling turkeys, hams and many other food products for this special day. Thanksgiving day is a great day of festivity where families get together for dinner to celebrate in their own way the birth of America. Christmas is probably the greatest holiday for targeting consumers for marketing and selling. The Christmas season can either break or make retailers in the quest to sell an abundance of goods and services. The Christmas season is the biggest profit period of the year. The next largest season for celebrations is New Years day. Parties are prevalent everywhere. Party foods, liquors: soft drinks and alcoholic drinks, goods and services are very marketable for New Years celebrations.

We as Christians should be really aware or cognizant of whether we are to celebrate as the secular world does or whether we should worship God instead. The bible admonishes us not to celebrate as the secular world does. Many times we are found doing what the world does just because they represent the majority and it seems like the thing to do. Just because the majority says it is right, it is not necessarily the truth. Let's see what God tells us to do in the verse referenced by two different translations of the Bible. Although they reflect different definitions, they are actually saying the same thing with the abilities to enhance our understanding.

Colossians 2:16 (Revised Standard) "Therefore let no one pass judgement on you in questions of food and drink or with regard to a festival of a new moon or a sabbath."

Colossians 2:16 (Simple English) "So, don't let anyone condemn you for what you eat or drink, or a religious festival, or the new moon holiday, or Sabbaths."

JULY 4TH is a family oriented holiday combined with family vacations. Families usually come together for family reunions, class reunions and/or various other reunions. This is a grand opportunity for Christians to attend such functions to witness for Jesus Christ. This is in fact a form of worshiping for all Christians who participates in such events or functions. Let your light so shine that men, women, boys and girls will see Jesus in you. This is a pagan holiday and certainly not a Christian one.

EASTER is a day set aside to recognize the death and resurrection of our Lord and Savior Jesus Christ. We don't recognize Easter as a day of celebration, but a special day to praise, worship and recognition our Lord, Jesus. The world anticipates and celebrates the days immediately preceding Easter as high volume sales days before this day arrives for profits. Easter is really a pagan holiday. Easter is not a holy day in itself. Christians have taken or set aside this day as a day for special worship of God, Almighty for His Son's death on the cross for our sins.

John 9:31 (KJV) "Now we know that God heareth not sinners: but if any man be a worshipper of God, and doeth his will, him he heareth."

HALLOWEEN (October 31st) is a special satanic day of worship with various costume parties and gatherings. Children are allowed to participate by dressing up in their costumes as they travel door-to-door for tricks or treats. This seems harmless for children to do, but they are really honoring Satan and his demons by participating in such. Many parents are ignorant of this fact and allow their children to do such. Christians no doubt have their own versions in participating in various functions held at churches. Even having functions at church with costumes aren't good ideas. It is still a form of worshiping Satan and his demons. Christians shouldn't wear costumes even at a church sponsored function on Halloween day or night. Christians shouldn't do anything which gives credence to the celebration of Halloween.

THANKSGIVING is a day set aside as a holiday of giving thanks to God, Almighty with feasting of food and family gatherings by the American people to commemorate the Pilgrim's celebration of the good harvest of 1621. Christians should be celebrating Christ's death and resurrection and giving thanks on a daily basis including Thanksgiving day.

CHRISTMAS DAY is a pagan holiday which the merchants and retailers love. During mid August, some merchants and retailers start their marketing strategies for selling their wares targeted at Christmas shoppers for so called Christmas gifts, dinners, parties and such. Christians often use and should use this pagan holiday for family gatherings and a special day for worshiping God for the birth of His Son, Jesus while they commemorate His birth. Santa Claus has no place in the Christian life. He is a satanic diversion from Jesus Christ, our hero. Christmas trees have no place in the Christian home. It is a representation of the pagan holiday, Christmas. Participating in the gift buying craze is representive of the pagan holiday as well. Many people go in debt just to buy someone a gift because it was in their tradition to do so. This is satanic bondage and shouldn't be. Christians should sever all ties between the pagan holiday rituals of the pagan holiday called Christmas. Although Christmas sounds like a religious holy day, it really isn't. Some will say that Christmas is a combination of "Christ" and "Mas(s)" is a deception. Christianity has nothing to do with the formation of Christmas day.

NEW YEARS DAY is another pagan holiday which brings many celebrations of parties, family and friends gatherings, and/or vain promises for doing better during the coming year. Traditional ethnic dishes are normally cooked and served for superstitious reasons.

Acts 17:22 (KJV) "Then Paul stood in the midst of Mars' hill, and said, Ye men of Athens, I perceive that in all things ye are too superstitious."

Acts 17:23 (KJV) "For as I passed by, and beheld your devotions, I found an altar with this inscription, TO THE UNKNOWN GOD. Whom therefore ye ignorantly worship, him declare I unto you."

Here again, Christians should be aware of the reasons for these pagan holidays and the superstitions that go along with them. When you are superstitious, you are in fact relying on an unnamed god, represented by Satan and his demons. Abstain from participating in such parties and/or celebrations. When you cook food during these seasons of secular celebrations, cook for your blessings from God, Almighty and not for some superstition.

CHAPTER 25

Celibacy vs. Having Sex

Some people desire to remain celibate, that is they don't want to marry and thereby totally abstain from having sex with the opposite sex. There is nothing wrong with a person's desire to abstain from marriage and sex. Some church denominations require that their ministers or their clergy staff and their support staff of people make vows of celebacy while they serve that particular denomination. It means that they have been forbidded to marry which requires that they totally abstain from having sex with the oposite sex regardless of their desires to do so. Prohibiting one from marriage when they have the desire to do so is not biblically correct.

Now, in the book of Matthew, Jesus tells us males and his disciples that if we so desire and can stand it, we can become Eunuchs. Eunuchs are men who choose to be castrated, that is having their testicles removed. This will prevent them from having sexual desires towards the feminine sex.

Matthew 19 (KJV)

12. For there are some eunuchs, which were so born from their mother's womb: and there are some eunuchs, which were made eunuchs of men: and there be eunuchs, which have

> made themselves eunuchs for the kingdom of heaven's sake. He that is able to receive it, let him receive it.

Although God is not forbidding us to marry, but man is forbidding us to marry. This is a form of bondage. This type of prohibition is not of God, but of Satan.

1 Corinthians 7:8-9 (KJV), "8) I say therefore to the unmarried and widows, It is good for them if they abide even as I. 9) But if they cannot contain, let them marry: for it is better to marry than to burn."

Here the word "contain" is derived from the Greek translation G1467 Egkrateuomai, eng-krat-yoo'-om-ahee; to exercise self-restraint.

If you feel that you need to fulfill your desires of having sex with the opposite sex, then you need to get married. Otherwise, you are in danger of being inflamed with anger, grief, and lust in your heart which is basically the same as actually committing a sex act with the person you desire to be with. This is what the word "burn" means as the last word in the above scripture. Burn is derived from the Greek translation G4440 Puro, Poo-ro-o; to be inflamed (with anger, grief, lust):--burn. It is definitely not a sin to marry if you so desire. Listen what the scriptures hace to say about the matter of getting married.

1 Corinthian 7:28 (KJV), "But and if thou marry, thou hast not sinned; and if a virgin marry, she hath not sinned. Nevertheless such shall have trouble in the flesh: but I spare you."

This is a warning about the flesh in trials and tribulations and of course burdens. The next three verses are warning you about doctrines of devils spreading lies that you shouldn't marry.

1 Timothy 4 (KJV)

13. Now the Spirit speaketh expressly, that in the latter times

some shall depart from the faith, giving heed to seducing spirits, and doctrines of devils;

14. Speaking lies in hypocrisy; having their conscience seared with a hot iron;
15. Forbidding to marry, and commanding to abstain from meats, which God hath created to be received with thanksgiving of them which believe and know the truth."

These lies are alive and well now. Many couples think it is right that they are living together, having children, but they desire to maintain their lives outside of marriage. Some Christians are no less doing some of these things by living together outside of marriage. Some religions require their members to abstain from eating certain meats which our God has provided for us to receive. You must gain the necessary wisdom, knowledge and understanding to know what God's will is and carry it out to the best of your abilities. That is why you are reading this book to aid you in gaining the necessary wisdom, knowledge and understanding of God's unadulterated word.

CHAPTER 26

Charisma and Charismatic Christians

Most churches, especially the Baptist denominations don't have the foggiest idea of what charisma or charismatic is because most of their leaders are still babes in Christ. They lack the wisdom, knowledge and understanding of the gifts of the Holy Spirit. Most of the Baptist churches believe that once a person is saved or born-again, they are endowed with the gifts of the Holy Spirit. However, there is one startling fact about their summations of those gifts and that is that none of the Spiritual gifts are being manifested through their pastors.

We recently attended a Sunday Morning Worship Service at this particular Baptist Church where the Sanctuary was at full capacity. The speaker for the morning was speaking on the Subject: "Am I Charismatic". He took his text from I Corinthians 12:1-7. Baptist preachers have always stopped short of God's explanation of the Gifts of the Holy Spirit. This is just what he did. He did go on to explain his definition of the gifts. He then went on to explain that each and every Christian is in a sense endowed with those gifts, but they are hidden and they need to pull them out and use them. Let's look at the world's definition of Charisma and Charismatic as defined in Webster's dictionary:

Charisma. Webster's definition. "Gift of God's grace............ 1.

Christian Theology. A divinely inspired gift, grace, or talent, as for **prophesying, healing,** etc.: ...."

Charismatic. Webster's definition. Adj. "1. Of, having, or resulting from charisma. 2. Designating or of any of various religious groups or movements that stress direct divine inspiration, manifested as in **glossolalia, healing powers,** etc. -N. 1. A member of a charisma group or movements. 2. A person who supposedly has some **divinely inspired power**, as the ability to **prophesy.**"

Glossolalia is Webster's definition for the gift of Spirit, "Gifts of Tongues". This is where one speaks in another language or a heavenly language. Most Baptists don't even believe in the gifts of speaking in tongues. Webster's definitions are clearly talking about the gifts of the Holy Spirit.

There are nine (9) gifts of the spirit and all of them are quite active today.

1 Cor 12:8-10 (KJV) For to one is given by the Spirit the **word of wisdom**; to another the **word of knowledge** by the same Spirit;

9. To another **faith** by the same Spirit; to another the **gifts of healing** by the same Spirit;
10. To another the **working of miracles**; to another **prophecy**; to another **discerning of spirits**; to another **divers kinds of tongues**; to another the **interpretation of tongues**:

These gifts of the Holy Spirit are not automatically given to believers. They must petition God for them, but in addition to that, some require much fasting to be endowed with them. Most Christians are not at a point in their Christian lives to receive any of the Spiritual gifts. Many are in fact babes in Christ. They refuse to believe these things are most prevalent today. God has not only told us to study to show ourselves approved unto Him, but with the knowledge, wisdom and understanding that we receive, we need not be ashamed when we rightly divide the word of truth.

2 Tim 2:15 (KJV) "Study to show thyself approved unto God, a workman that needeth not to be ashamed, rightly dividing the word of truth."

Eccl 12:11-13 (KJV) The words of the wise are as goads, and as nails fastened by the masters of assemblies, which are given from one shepherd.

12. And further, by these, my son, be admonished: of making many books there is no end; and much study is a weariness of the flesh.
13. Let us hear the conclusion of the whole matter: Fear God, and keep his commandments: for this is the whole duty of man.

God specifically tells us to teach His people the differences between the holy things, the unholy things, the clean things and the unclean things.

Ezek 44:23 (KJV) "And they shall teach my people the difference between the holy and profane, and cause them to discern between the unclean and the clean."

CHAPTER **27**

Child Abusers Warning from Jesus Christ

Our Savior, Jesus Christ warns us concerning the affairs and cares of little children. There are dire consequences for those who do abuse, mistreat and harm little children. Man can never punish abusers of children as much as Almighty God's wrath can. He is the ultimate Punisher and Avenger.

Matthew 18 (KJV)

1. At the same time came the disciples unto Jesus, saying, Who is the greatest in the kingdom of heaven?
2. And Jesus called a little child unto him, and set him in the midst of them,
3. And said, Verily I say unto you, Except ye be converted, and become as little children, ye shall not enter into the kingdom of heaven.
4. Whosoever therefore shall humble himself as this little child, the same is greatest in the kingdom of heaven.
5. And whoso shall receive one such little child in my name receiveth me.
6. But whoso shall offend one of these little ones which believe in me, it were better for him that a millstone were hanged about his neck, and that he were drowned in the depth of the sea.

7. Woe unto the world because of offences! for it must needs be that offences come; but woe to that man by whom the offence cometh!
8. Wherefore if thy hand or thy foot offend thee, cut them off, and cast them from thee: it is better for thee to enter into life halt or maimed, rather than having two hands or two feet to be cast
9. And if thine eye offend thee, pluck it out, and cast it from thee: it is better for thee to enter into life with one eye, rather than having two eyes to be cast into hell fire.
10. Take heed that ye despise not one of these little ones; for I say unto you, That in heaven their angels do always behold the face of my Father which is in heaven.
11. For the Son of man is come to save that which was lost. into everlasting fire.

CHAPTER 28

Child Spankings or Whippings Are Not Biblically Forbidden

Nowadays, parents hands are tied because of local governmental laws, ordinances and regulations which forbid them their rights to properly chastise their children with spankings and/or whippings without reaching the point of abusing them in the process.

The baby boomer generation of children experienced spankings with paddles, rulers and the palms of adult hands. Whippings were harsher than spankings. We were whipped with switches which were slender limbs from trees, ironing cords, razor straps, belts from trousers and such. Nowadays, parents are subject to being arrested, handcuffed, and hauled off to jailed by law enforcement officials for trying to raise their children right. Granted, there are many instances of child abuse out there in the world where raising children aren't the abusers primary purpose or issue.

Churches should be ashamed of themselves for allowing outsiders such as the law and governments to dictate them on how to raise their children. Older generations including our parents and grandparents punished us with switches that they cut from trees, razor straps, belts, paddles, rulers, ironing cords or whatever was available to produce the process of whipping.

Spankings were the softer side of whippings which was usually done with the hands on one's buttocks or more bluntly, one's butt. These types of punishments really got our attention to say the least. We learned a great deal of respect for not only our parents, but any grownups, elderly persons, and senior people around the ages of our grandparents.

Nowadays, if you whip your children and your neighbor learn of it and calls the police, you could be arrested and hauled off to jail for child abuse. Now, there are some people out there who really do abuse children and they should be arrested and locked up and charged for abusing children. There is a difference between correcting your child and abusing your child. Christians should have the knowledge, wisdom and understanding to know the difference. We are admonished by God, Almighty to chastise our children by using the tools of corrections such as belts, paddles or our hands. These seem to get the children's attention when just talking to them doesn't work at times. Our own bible tells gives us guidelines on how to effectively and efficiently raise our children.

Prov 10:13 (KJV) "In the lips of him that hath understanding wisdom is found: but a rod is for the back of him that is void of understanding."

Prov 13:24 (KJV) "He that spareth his rod hateth his son: but he that loveth him chasteneth him betimes."

Prov 14:3 (KJV) "In the mouth of the foolish is a rod of pride: but the lips of the wise shall preserve them."

Prov 22:15 (KJV) "Foolishness is bound in the heart of a child;but the rod of correction shall drive it far from him."

Prov 23:13 (KJV) "Withhold not correction from the child: for if thou beatest him with the rod, he shall not die."

Prov 23:14 (KJV) "Thou shalt beat him with the rod, and shalt deliver his soul from hell."

Prov 26:3 (KJV) "A whip for the horse, a bridle for the ass, and a rod for the fool's back."

Prov 29:15 (KJV) "The rod and reproof give wisdom: but a child left to himself bringeth his mother to shame."

CHAPTER 29

Child Training Should Start at Home

The bible specifically tells us to train up our children the way they should go and when they are old, they will not depart from those teachings. Many children are out of control even before they become teenagers. The simple fact is that they were not properly trained in the first place or they weren't trained at all. They took on the attitudes and the non trained state of minds from their peers.

Prov 22:6 (KJV) "Train up a child in the way he should go: and when he is old, he will not depart from it."

Eph 6:4 (KJV) "And, ye fathers, provoke not your children to wrath: but bring them up in the nurture and admonition of the Lord."

Prov 20:11 (KJV) "Even a child is known by his doings, whether his work be pure, and whether it be right."

Prov 22:15 (KJV) "Foolishness is bound in the heart of a child; but the rod of correction shall drive it far from him."

Prov 23:13 (KJV) "Withhold not correction from the child: for if thou beatest him with the rod, he shall not die."

Prov 23:24 (KJV) "The father of the righteous shall greatly rejoice:

and he that begetteth a wise child shall have joy of him."
Prov 29:15 (KJV) "The rod and reproof give wisdom: but a child left to himself bringeth his mother to shame."

Prov 29:21 (KJV) "He that delicately bringeth up his servant from a child shall have him become his son at the length."

Eccl 4:13 (KJV) "Better is a poor and a wise child than an old and foolish king, who will no more be admonished."

My, (Curtis) brother-in-law told me that he witness unfortunate incidents of children disrespecting their parents in his neighborhood quite frequently. He said that one young man curses at his mother and calls her all kinds of evil names. But, she humbles herself and calls him to dinner. He still curses and disrespects her. Well, he will have a very short life because my bible said that he would.

Exo 20:12 (KJV) "Honour thy father and thy mother: that thy days may be long upon the land which the LORD thy God giveth thee."

Deu 5:16 (KJV) "Honour thy father and thy mother, as the LORD thy God hath commanded thee; that thy days may be prolonged, and that it may go well with thee, in the land which the LORD thy God giveth thee."

Mat 15:4 (KJV) "For God commanded, saying, Honour thy father and mother: and, He that curseth father or mother, let him die the death."

Eph 6:2 (KJV) "Honour thy father and mother; which is the first commandment with promise;"

Eph 6:3 (KJV) "That it may be well with thee, and thou mayest live long on the earth."

CHAPTER 30

Childhood Gangs and Violence

One of the mainstream problems with our children are childhood gangs and violence which is associated with many gangs. These problems are results from our lack in not training our children at their earliest age of understanding properly or not at all. Additionally, we aren't properly instructing them on biblical principles at their earliest age of understanding which will instill within their souls good moral characters with solid foundations with salvation in our Lord and Savior, Jesus Christ. Otherwise, without such teachings and instructions, our children are getting their training and their instructions from gangs and their institutions of violence, immorality, murder, stealing, car jacking and many other imaginable crimes. We are admonished and commanded by God to train and teach our children in the way that we should. Many children have never studied with a Sunday School Class at any church.

Prov 22:6 (KJV) "Train up a child in the way he should go: and when he is old, he will not depart from it."

Prov 1:8-33 (KJV) My son, hear the instruction of thy father, and forsake not the law of thy mother:

9. For they shall be an ornament of grace unto thy head, and chains about thy neck.

10. My son, if sinners entice thee, consent thou not.
11. If they say, Come with us, let us lay wait for blood, let us lurk privily for the innocent without cause:
12. Let us swallow them up alive as the grave; and whole, as those that go down into the pit:
13. We shall find all precious substance, we shall fill our houses with spoil:
14. Cast in thy lot among us; let us all have one purse:
15. My son, walk not thou in the way with them; refrain thy foot from their path:
16. For their feet run to evil, and make haste to shed blood.
17. Surely in vain the net is spread in the sight of any bird.
18. And they lay wait for their own blood; they lurk privily for their own lives.
19. So [are] the ways of every one that is greedy of gain; [which] taketh away the life of the owners thereof.
20. Wisdom crieth without; she uttereth her voice in the streets:
21. She crieth in the chief place of concourse, in the openings of the gates: in the city she uttereth her words, [saying],
22. How long, ye simple ones, will ye love simplicity? and the scorners delight in their scorning, and fools hate knowledge?
23. Turn you at my reproof: behold, I will pour out my spirit unto you, I will make known my words unto you.
24. Because I have called, and ye refused; I have stretched out my hand, and no man regarded;
25. But ye have set at nought all my counsel, and would none of my reproof:
26. I also will laugh at your calamity; I will mock when your fear cometh;
27. When your fear cometh as desolation, and your destruction cometh as a whirlwind; when distress and anguish cometh upon you.
28. Then shall they call upon me, but I will not answer; they shall seek me early, but they shall not find me:

29. For that they hated knowledge, and did not choose the fear of the LORD:
30. They would none of my counsel: they despised all my reproof.
31. Therefore shall they eat of the fruit of their own way, and be filled with their own devices.
32. For the turning away of the simple shall slay them, and the prosperity of fools shall destroy them.
33. But whoso hearkeneth unto me shall dwell safely, and shall be quiet from fear of evil.

Curses From God, Almighty

Interesting enough, God Almighty will send or allow curses to be upon you if you aren't sincere in your heart about Him. If you proclaim your love for God and His Son, Jesus Christ with your mouth, but you believe or do something else in your heart, then you will be cursed by God, Almighty. Even the blessings which you think you have will be cursed. Let's say that you exclaim with your mouth to a man or woman, "I love you my brother or my sister", but in your heart you can't stand the ground which that person walks on. That's hatred and you are definitely cursed by God. You are therefore not giving glory to God's name.

Mal 2:2 (KJV) "If ye will not hear, and if ye will not lay it to heart, to give glory unto my name, saith the LORD of hosts, I will even send a curse upon you, and I will curse your blessings: yea, I have cursed them already, because ye do not lay it to heart."

Gal 3:10 (KJV) "For as many as are of the works of the law are under the curse: for it is written, Cursed is every one that continueth not in all things which are written in the book of the law to do them."

CHAPTER **31**

Children Cursing and Dishonoring Their Parents

In today's society, many children have no respect for not only their parents, but they have no respect for their elders or our senior citizens. It is common thing to hear youngsters spewing out curse words among each other. It is not uncommon to hear them curse at their elders or senior citizens. God promised that death is the curse and a very short life is the penalty for those who use this type of language at not only their parents, but anybody who is an elder to them.

Exo 21:17 (KJV) "And he that curseth his father, or his mother, shall surely be put to death."

Exo 20:12 (KJV) "Honour thy father and thy mother: that thy days may be long upon the land which the LORD thy God giveth thee."

Deu 5:16 (KJV) "Honour thy father and thy mother, as the LORD thy God hath commanded thee; that thy days may be prolonged, and that it may go well with thee, in the land which the LORD thy God giveth thee."

Mat 15:4 (KJV) "For God commanded, saying, Honour thy father and mother: and, He that curseth father or mother, let him die the death."

Many news events have been publicize concerning children taking their parents to court in order to divorce them. This is a great dishonor to parents and will not go unpunished by God, Almighty. He said that if you honor your mother and your father, your days will be prolonged or extended upon this earth. However, you dishonor them, your life will be shorten and death will visit you early.

Eph 6:1-3 (KJV) Children, obey your parents in the Lord: for this is right.

2. Honour thy father and mother; which is the first commandment with promise;
3. That it may be well with thee, and thou mayest live long on the earth.

Example Of Biblical Day Punishments

Here is a typical example of shorten lives and quick deaths to children dishonoring one particular elderly and senior person to them. The prophet Elijah was an old bald headed man of God. These children had heard that Elijah had previously gone up to heaven in a fiery chariot. So, they tried to provoke him to go up again. They made Elijah angry and he cursed them in the name of God, Almighty. God allowed two (2) female bears to come out of the woods and they killed 42 children. Food for thought! Old people didn't get old by being disobedient, disrespectful or by dishonoring their parents, elders or senior citizens.

2 Ki 2:23-24 (KJV) And he went up from thence unto Bethel: and as he was going up by the way, there came forth little children out of the city, and mocked him, and said unto him, Go up, thou bald head; go up, thou bald head.

24. And he turned back, and looked on them, and cursed them in the name of the LORD. And there came forth two she bears out of the wood, and tare forty and two children of them.

CHAPTER **32**

Children Watching Their Mothers Giving Birth

The is a phenomenon going on where some parents allow their older children to witness the birth of their new born brother(s) and/or their newborn sisters. Biblically speaking, children aren't supposed to see the nakedness of their parents. It is morally and spiritually respectable that once they inadvertently see their parents in a position of nakedness that they turn their eyes away immediately. If that parent is sleep, then that child or children shall as soon as possible cover up that parent's nakedness without directly viewing their parent's naked body.

Noah was found drunk and naked by one of his sons who then told two of his brothers. These two brothers took a garment as they walked backwards and laid the garment on their father. Noah learned later what had happened and he then blessed the two sons who covered his nakedness and punished the one son who saw him first lying naked, but who did nothing to cover him. You'll notice that not only was that particular son punished, but his next generation of children were punished as well. There is a sense of high respect in not seeing the nakedness of our parents.

Gen 9:21-27 (KJV) And he drank of the wine, and was drunken; and he was uncovered within his tent.

22. And Ham, the father of Canaan, saw the nakedness of his father, and told his two brethren without.
23. And Shem and Japheth took a garment, and laid it upon both their shoulders, and went backward, and covered the nakedness of their father; and their faces were backward, and they saw not their father's nakedness.
24. And Noah awoke from his wine, and knew what his younger son had done unto him.
25. And he said, Cursed be Canaan; a servant of servants shall he be unto his brethren.
26. And he said, Blessed be the LORD God of Shem; and Canaan shall be his servant.
27. God shall enlarge Japheth, and he shall dwell in the tents of Shem; and Canaan shall be his servant.

CHAPTER **33**

Christian Husbands' Responsibilities

Some Christian husbands have failed in their leadership of their families in not only the secular society, but their Christian environment as well. This is a curse that has followed many of them throughout many generations including their own. With this in mind, their children are effected with a total of several generations to come if this trend is not broken.

Christian husbands are charged by God to be responsible for their families in not only their secular environments, but specifically their Christian environments. Man is the head of his family, Jesus is the head of the Church, and God Almighty is the head of Jesus. So, God had to hold someone responsible for the family, He chose man as the responsible party.

1 Cor 11:3 (KJV) "But I would have you know, that the head of every man is Christ; and the head of the woman is the man; and the head of Christ is God."

Eph 5:23 (KJV) "For the husband is the head of the wife, even as Christ is the head of the church: and he is the saviour of the body."

Eph 5:24 (KJV) "Therefore as the church is subject unto Christ, so let the wives be to their own husbands in every thing."

Eph 5:25 (KJV) "Husbands, love your wives, even as Christ also loved the church, and gave himself for it;"

Eph 5:33 (KJV) "Nevertheless let every one of you in particular so love his wife even as himself; and the wife see that she reverence her husband."

Col 3:18 (KJV) "Wives, submit yourselves unto your own husbands, as it is fit in the Lord."

Col 3:19 (KJV) "Husbands, love your wives, and be not bitter against them."

1 Pet 3:5 (KJV) "For after this manner in the old time the holy women also, who trusted in God, adorned themselves, being in subjection unto their own husbands:"

1 Pet 3:6 (KJV) "Even as Sara obeyed Abraham, calling him lord: whose daughters ye are, as long as ye do well, and are not afraid with any amazement."

1 Pet 3:7 (KJV) "Likewise, ye husbands, dwell with them according to knowledge, giving honour unto the wife, as unto the weaker vessel, and as being heirs together of the grace of life; that your prayers be not hindered."

CHAPTER **34**

Christians Don't Stand in the Gap for Others

Most Christians are unaware that they can provide protection (a hedge) around someone and stand in the gap (stand in place of someone) for not only their own children, but sinners or other people as well. When your child or children rebel and stop going to church, you can be a hedge for them and stand in the gap for them. Let's say for an example that your child is not saved, but some how won't give his or her life to Jesus Christ for salvation. There are really evil spiritual forces preventing your child from accepting Jesus Christ as his or her personal Savior. Instead of them being bombarded with evil spirits, you need to protect them from these evil spirits by putting them in a hedge of protection and standing in the gap, that is taking their place. You will be helping to fight their battle with the principalities and evil demons in this world.

When you stand in the gap, you are standing in the place of your child(ren) and you are a fence of protection (hedge) where that evil spirit can't get to your child(ren). Every time any evil spirits try to attack or influence your child(ren), it or they sees only you, the fence of protection. You are the strong one and you know just what to do to put on your shield of armor for protection for you and your child(ren). Allow me to warn you that Satan and his demons will attempt to attack you instead of your children or whomever you are standing in the gap for. All hell will break loose on you, my sweethearts!

There is biblical account that God had put a hedge of protection around an upright and perfect man of God named Job. Not only was this hedge of protection around Job, but everything that Job owned was protected. Additionally, Job's possessions increased tremendously where he was the richest man on the Eastern part of the world where most humans lived. In order for Satan to attempt to destroy Job, God had to remove the hedge around him and his possessions.

Job 1:10 (KJV) "Hast not thou made an hedge about him, and about his house, and about all that he hath on every side? thou hast blessed the work of his hands, and his substance is increased in the land."

I, (Curtis) usually stand in the gap for all sinners during the call to discipleship (invitation to salvation). I pray a very short prayer to God, Almighty by saying, "Father in heaven, please allow me to stand in the gap for all of these sinners to come to salvation. I thank you in the name of Jesus Christ. Amen."

Ezek 22:30 (KJV) "And I sought for a man among them, that should ***make up the hedge, and stand in the gap*** before me for the land, that I should not destroy it: but I found none."

Hedge. Hebrew definition. 1447. gader, gaw-dare'; from H1443; a circumvallation; by impl. an inclosure:--fence, hedge, wall.

Stand. Hebrew definition. 5975. 'amad, aw-mad'; a prim. root; to stand, in various relations (lit. and fig., intrans. and trans.):--abide (behind), appoint, arise, cease, confirm, continue, dwell, be employed, **endure**, establish, leave, make, ordain, be [over], place, (be) **present (self)**, raise up, remain, repair, + serve, set (forth, over, -tle, up), (make to, make to be at a, with-) stand (by, fast, firm, still, up), (be at a) stay (up), tarry.

Gap. Hebrew definition. 6556. perets, peh'-rets; from H6555; a break (lit. or fig.):--breach, breaking forth (in), X forth, gap.

Here is one scenario where some rich people were cheating and misusing poor people. God, Almighty didn't like what was happening and so He looked for someone to stand in the gap, but He found not one soul among those rich people because He didn't want to destroy them with His wrath. God is just, but He is also merciful. Because He is merciful He sought someone to stand in the gap and since He is just, somebody had to pay for those evil deeds. Had someone stood in the gap for those rich people, they could have possibly been converted and saved from God's wrath. Since nobody was found to stand in the gap, those rich people suffered God's wrath by being consumed or burned up by fire.

Ezek 22:31 (KJV) "Therefore have I poured out mine indignation upon them; I have consumed them with the fire of my wrath: their own way have I recompensed upon their heads, saith the Lord GOD."

CHAPTER 35

Church and State - Biblically Bound Together

Many politicians, including judges often push for separation of church and state. Almighty God never separated the two when he had kings anointed to lead his people. Almighty God recognized such leaders by anointing them and empowering them with his Holy Spirit. They had favoritism with Him when anointed and empowered them to lead his people.

There are four (4) such kings among many who Almighty God had favoritism with: King Saul, King David, King Solomon, King and Priest Melchilsedec.

King Saul

1 Samuel 9 (KJV)

1. Now there was a man of Benjamin, whose name was Kish, the son of Abiel, the son of Zeror, the son of Bechorath, the son of Aphiah, a Benjamite, a mighty man of power.
2. And he had a son, whose name was Saul, a choice young man, and a goodly: and there was not among the children of Israel a goodlier person than he: from his shoulders and upward he was higher than any of the people.

15. Now the Lord had told Samuel in his ear a day before Saul came, saying,
16. To morrow about this time I will send thee a man out of the land of Benjamin, and thou shalt anoint him to be captain over my people Israel, that he may save my people out of the hand of the Philistines: for I have looked upon my people, because their cry is come unto me.
17. And when Samuel saw Saul, the Lord said unto him, Behold the man whom I spake to thee of! this same shall reign over my people.

1 Samuel 15 (KJV)

Samuel also said unto Saul, The Lord sent me to anoint thee to be king over his people, over Israel: now therefore hearken thou unto the voice of the words of the Lord.

King Saul's Demise For Disobeying Almighty God

1 Samuel 16 (KJV)

14. But the Spirit of the Lord departed from Saul, and an evil spirit from the Lord troubled him.
15. And Saul's servants said unto him, Behold now, an evil spirit from God troubleth thee.
16. Let our lord now command thy servants, which are before thee, to seek out a man, who is a cunning player on an harp: and it shall come to pass, when the evil spirit from God is upon thee, that he shall play with his hand, and thou shalt be well.
17. And Saul said unto his servants, Provide me now a man that can play well, and bring him to me.
18. Then answered one of the servants, and said, Behold, I have seen a son of Jesse the Bethlehemite, that is cunning in playing, and a mighty valiant man, and a man of war,

and prudent in matters, and a comely person, and the Lord is with him.

19. Wherefore Saul sent messengers unto Jesse, and said, Send me David thy son, which is with the sheep.
20. And Jesse took an ass laden with bread, and a bottle of wine, and a kid, and sent them by David his son unto Saul.
21. And David came to Saul, and stood before him: and he loved him greatly; and he became his armourbearer.
22. And Saul sent to Jesse, saying, Let David, I pray thee, stand before me; for he hath found favour in my sight.
23. And it came to pass, when the evil spirit from God was upon Saul, that David took an harp, and played with his hand: so Saul was refreshed, and was well, and the evil spirit departed from him.

1 Samuel 16 (KJV)

1. And the Lord said unto Samuel, How long wilt thou mourn for Saul, seeing I have rejected him from reigning over Israel? fill thine horn with oil, and go, I will send thee to Jesse the Bethlehemite: for I have provided me a king among his sons.
2. And Samuel said, How can I go? if Saul hear it, he will kill me. And the Lord said, Take an heifer with thee, and say, I am come to sacrifice to the Lord.

King David

1 Samuel 16 (KJV)

1. And the LORD said unto Samuel, How long wilt thou mourn for Saul, seeing I have rejected him from reigning over Israel? fill thine horn with oil, and go, I will send thee to Jesse the Bethlehemite: for I have provided me a king among his sons.

11. And Samuel said unto Jesse, Are here all thy children? And he said, There remaineth yet the youngest, and, behold, he keepeth the sheep. And Samuel said unto Jesse, Send and fetch him: for we will not sit down till he come hither.
12. And he sent, and brought him in. Now he was ruddy, and withal of a beautiful countenance, and goodly to look to. And the Lord said, Arise, anoint him: for this is he.
13. Then Samuel took the horn of oil, and anointed him in the midst of his brethren: and the Spirit of the Lord came upon David from that day forward. So Samuel rose up, and went to Ramah.

King Solomon

1 Kings 1 (KJV)

32. And king David said, Call me Zadok the priest, and Nathan the prophet, and Benaiah the son of Jehoiada. And they came before the king.
33. The king also said unto them, Take with you the servants of your lord, and cause Solomon my son to ride upon mine own mule, and bring him down to Gihon:
34. And let Zadok the priest and Nathan the prophet anoint him there king over Israel: and blow ye with the trumpet, and say, God save king Solomon.
35. Then ye shall come up after him, that he may come and sit upon my throne; for he shall be king in my stead: and I have appointed him to be ruler over Israel and over Judah.
36. And Benaiah the son of Jehoiada answered the king, and said, Amen: the Lord God of my lord the king say so too.
37. As the Lord hath been with my lord the king, even so be he with Solomon, and make his throne greater than the throne of my lord king David.
38. So Zadok the priest, and Nathan the prophet, and Benaiah the son of Jehoiada, and the Cherethites, and the Pelethites,

went down, and caused Solomon to ride upon king David's mule, and brought him to Gihon.

39. And Zadok the priest took an horn of oil out of the tabernacle, and anointed Solomon. And they blew the trumpet; and all the people said, God save king Solomon.

King And Priest Melchizedek (Hebrew)/Melchisedec(Greek)

Genesis 14 (KJV)

18. And Melchizedek king of Salem brought forth bread and wine: and he was the priest of the most high God.

CHAPTER **36**

Church and State Are Biblically Bound Together - Government Attempts to Separate Them

During certain periods of time within the bible, Almighty God attempted to bring humanity closer to Him by establishing certain laws and guidelines for man to follow. However, man failed on grounds. These periods of time are called Dispensations. There are seven dispensations from the Book of Genesis to the Book of Revelation as listed below.

The third dispensation which is the Dispensation of Human Government which Almighty God instituted with Noah when he and his family left the Ark to establish their presence on the earth. Almighty God is the ultimate driving force behind establishing world governments whether man wants to include Him or not.

Third Dispensation of Human Government

From Noah's exit from the ark to Abraham.

Man failed God in the dispensation of Conscience and received the judgment of the flood. Now the dispensation of Human Government begins. This means that man is now responsible for governing the earth for God.

God's Covenant with Noah

God would not curse the ground any more nor destroy all living things again by flood.

1. Genesis 9:1 Noah and his descendants were to be fruitful and multiply and replenish the earth.
2. Genesis 9:2-4 Man could now eat the flesh of every living thing.
3. Genesis 9:5-6 The law of capital punishment was established.
4. Genesis 9:8-11 The earth was never again to be destroyed by flood.
5. II Peter 3:6-7 The next time the earth is destroyed will be by fire.
6. Genesis 9:12-17 God used the rainbow as the token of the covenant that He made with man.

Here is what happened to one governing king of Judaea, King Herod who would not give Almighty God the credit or even honor Almighty God. King Herod was a cocky, stubborn, ignorant and deceitful man, just to describe a few things about him. Well, to his demise, he was struck down by Almighty God's Angel and the worms ate him alive which resulted in his immediate death. Now, do you still think that you should separate Church from State or Governments? Personally, I should think not!.

Acts 12 (KJV)

21. And upon a set day Herod, arrayed in royal apparel, sat upon his throne, and made an oration unto them.
22. And the people gave a shout, saying, it is the voice of a god, and not of a man.
23. And immediately the angel of the Lord smote him, because he gave not God the glory: and he was eaten of worms, and gave up the ghost.

Below are outlines of all seven dispensations of the Holy Bible:

Outlines Of Seven Dispensations Of The Bible

First Dispensation - Innocence

Creation of man until his fall to sin.
Adam and Eve created in Innocence

The first chapter of Genesis tells us about the six days of creation and what was created on each day. In chapter two we are given the details of the events that took place on the sixth day of creation.

1. Genesis 2:7 God formed man and he became a living soul.
2. Genesis 2:8 God planted a garden eastward in Eden.
3. Genesis 2:8-15 God placed the man whom he had formed in the garden to dress it and keep it.
4. Genesis 2:17 God commanded the man not to eat of the tree of the knowledge of good and evil. God gave the man free will to choose his destiny. He could obey God and live forever or disobey God and die.
5. Genesis 2:18-25 God made a woman using a rib which he had taken from Adam.

Second Dispensation - Conscience

From the fall of man until the flood
Adam and Eve outside the garden of Eden

Along with the knowledge of good and evil Adam and Eve received a conscience. Existence for them was quite different from before. Before, the first man and woman were to dress and keep paradise. Now Adam had to toil by the sweat of his brow in an unending battle against weeds and briars. Eve also discovered what God meant when He said "I will greatly multiply thy sorrow and thy conception; in sorrow shalt thou bring forth children"(Genesis 3:16).

Third Dispensation - Human Government

From Noah's exit from the ark to Abraham.

Man failed God in the dispensation of Conscience and received the judgment of the flood. Now the dispensation of Human Government begins. This means that man is now responsible for governing the earth for God.

God's Covenant with Noah

God would not curse the ground any more nor destroy all living things again by flood.

1. Genesis 9:1 Noah and his descendants were to be fruitful and multiply and replenish the earth.
2. Genesis 9:2-4 Man could now eat the flesh of every living thing.
3. Genesis 9:5-6 The law of capital punishment was established.
4. Genesis 9:8-11 The earth was never again to be destroyed by flood.
5. II Peter 3:6-7 The next time the earth is destroyed will be by fire.
6. Genesis 9:12-17 God used the rainbow as the token of the covenant that He made with man.

Fourth Dispensation - Promise

The Dispensation of Promise consists of the promises made to Abraham, Isaac, and Jacob.

Almost the entire human race turns away from God to idolatry. Men began to worship the sun, the moon, the stars, and everything else they could think of except the one true God. Man had become just as bad as the people that were destroyed by the flood but God has promised not to ever destroy everyone in a flood again.

The dispersion of the world's population is the last time God deals with the entire human race as a whole.

With the call of Abram, God's attention is focused upon a chosen people.

God now selects a man out of which to make a special and holy nation. This nation was to preserve God's truth and be a channel through which the whole world would ultimately be blessed.

God's chosen people were to be the channel through which Messiah was to come.

Genesis 3:15 The seed of the woman (the human race).

1. Genesis 22:18 The seed of Abraham (the nation of Israel).
2. Genesis 49:10 The seed of Judah (the tribe of Judah).
3. II Samuel 7:12 The seed of David (the family of David).
4. Isaiah 7:14 Prophesied that He should come through a virgin.
5. Luke 1:26-33 The name of the virgin was Mary.

Fifth Dispensation - The Law and the Prophets

The Law and the Prophets Part 1
The birth of Moses to entering the Promised Land

Exodus 1:5-7 The children of Israel came to Egypt in a family group of seventy persons, and at the beginning of this lesson they have multiplied exceedingly and the land was filled with them.

Exodus 1:8-14 Because of Pharaoh's fear that these people would rise up against him, He oppressed them and they became slaves instead of remaining the free group that had come down to Egypt to live.

Exodus 1:15-22 The king of Egypt made a decree that the midwives to the Hebrew women were to kill a baby if it was a son and let it live if it was a daughter. But the midwives did not do as the king of Egypt commanded because they feared God and the people continued to multiply.

Moses - There are three distinct 40 year periods in the life of Moses.

The first forty years were learning in the courts of Egypt.

The second forty years were spent on the back side of the desert on the plains of Sinai herding sheep

The third forty years were spent leading the children of Israel to the Promised Land.

The first forty years of Moses

1. Exodus 2:1-4 birth of Moses. Because of the decree of Pharaoh the mother of Moses was trying to keep him hidden.
2. Exodus 2:5-6 Pharaoh's daughter finds Moses and has compassion on him and wants him for her own.
3. Exodus 2:7-9 The mother of Moses was paid by Pharaoh's daughter to nurse him.
4. Exodus 2:10 Moses becomes the son of Pharoah's daughter.
5. Exodus 2:11-12 Moses slays an Egyptian that was smiting an Hebrew.

The second forty years of Moses

1. Exodus 2:13-13-15 Moses flees from the wrath of Pharaoh.
2. Exodus 2:16-25 Moses becomes a shepherd.

3. Exodus 3:1-10 The burning bush. God tells Moses that he is to bring the children of Israel out of Egypt.
4. Exodus 4:10-17 Moses argued with God and the anger of the Lord was kindled against Moses. God sends Aaron with Moses to Pharaoh.

The third forty years of Moses

Moses the deliverer.

1. Exodus 5:1-9 Moses and Aaron meet with Pharaoh. Pharaoh is angered and increases the peoples workload by making them gather their own straw to make bricks.
2. Exodus 7:7 Moses was eighty years old when he spoke to Pharaoh.
3. Exodus 7:8-13 Pharaoh refuses to hear what Moses and Aaron have to say.

The Law and the Prophets Part 2

Deuteronomy 34:1-8.

Realizing that his work was coming to and end, Moses gives his farewell address to the children of Israel. This farewell address takes up the entire book of Deuteronomy.

After he has finished speaking to the people, Moses goes to the top of Mount Pisgah where God let him see all the Promised Land before he died.

God buried Moses in a valley in the land of Moab and no one knows the location of his grave.

Deuteronomy 34:9 Joshua takes over as leader of Israel.

Joshua 1:1-9 God tells Joshua to be strong and very courageous and promises to stand by Joshua just as he did Moses.

Joshua 1:10-11 Joshua tells the people to get ready to cross the Jordan river.

Joshua chapter 2 is the story of the two spies Joshua sent to check out Jericho.

Joshua 3:14-17 The priests enter the Jordan river and the waters part and they stand on dry ground as the people pass over Jordan.

Joshua 4:1-10 God commanded Joshua to have twelve men each take a stone from the Jordan to set up at the place where they would lodge that night. Joshua did as the Lord had commanded and also placed twelve stones as a memorial in the Jordan where the feet of the priests stood.

Joshua 4:15-18 God orders the priests out of the Jordan so the waters could flow as before.

Joshua 4:19-24 Joshua had the twelve stones set up in Gilgal where the children of Israel camped that night.

Joshua chapter 5 When the children of Israel camped at Gilgal, all the males had to be circumcised, it was the time of the passover, and after the passover the manna ceased and they ate the fruit of the land of Canaan that year.

Joshua chapter 6 The story about the fall of Jericho.

Joshua chapter 7 Achan's sin. There is no victory where there is sin.

Joshua chapter 8 Victory over Ai and an altar built on mount Ebal.

Joshua leads the people through victory after victory until all of the Promised Land is theirs as God had promised them.

Joshua 24:29-30 Joshua dies.

The Judges

Judges 2:10-23 The period of time from the death of Joshua until the crowning of Saul as king of Israel is known as the time of the judges.

God told his people to have nothing to do with the remaining inhabitants of the land, but to utterly destroy them. Instead, the children of Israel would make alliances with them and even took their daughters to wife and worshipped idol gods.

This brought the judgments of God upon Israel in the form of bondage and slavery to other nations.

In their distress, Israel would turn back to God and call upon Him for help. At this time God would raise up a deliverer. During the lifetime of this leader the children of Israel would remain faithful and true to God. After this judge would die, Israel would relax and turn back to sin again. This is a cycle that is repeated a number of times.

In The Bible we find the names of 16 Judges.

1. Othniel (Judges 3:9-11)
2. Ehud (Judges 3:12-30)
3. Shamgar (Judges 3:31)
4. Deborah (Judges 4:5)
5. Barak (Judges 4:6-10)
6. Gideon (Judges 6:7-23) (Judges 8:33)
7. Abimelech (Judges chapter 9)

8. Tola (Judges 10:1-2)
9. Lair (Judges 10:3-5)
10. Jephthah (Judges chapter 12:7)
11. Ibson (Judges 12:8-10)
12. Elon (Judges 12:11-12)
13. Abdon (Judges 12:13-15)
14. Sampson (Judges chapter 13,14,15,16)
15. Eli (I Samuel chapters 1 and 2)
16. Samuel (I Samuel chapter 3)

The Law and the Prophets Part 3
General view of the New Testament

Division of New Testament Books.

1. The first four books of the New Testament are known as the gospels. In the gospels is recorded the history of the events which took place in the life of Jesus. The gospels are listed as part of the New Testament, but the period which they cover is still under the law of Moses. Luke 16:16 The law and the prophets were until John.
2. The book of Acts tells us how to become Christians. The book of Acts contains the history of the early church.
3. The epistles instruct us on how to live the Christian life. These books were written to people who had already become Christians There was no need to give them instructions on how to be saved because they already were born again of the water and the Spirit. John 3:5
4. Revelation is the only book of prophesy in the New Testament.

Theme of New Testament (We have found him)

5. Philip said,"We have found him,of whom Moses in the law, and the prophets, did write".
6. The prophets of old inquired and searched diligently to find

the salvation that we enjoy today. Even the angels desire to look into it. I Peter 1:10-12

Four hundred silent years

The Jews

1. During the 400 years of silence there were no prophets heard and no inspired literature written.
2. Many changes occurred in Jewish habits, customs, and religious views during this time.
3. Their sufferings under foreign domination greatly intensified their hope for the promised Messiah.
4. God's purpose for the Jews of being a model nation and an example to the heathen nations was altered to use them to prepare the way for his son, Jesus Christ.

World power shifted

1. When Judah was taken captive, the world was ruled by the Babylonians.
2. During the seventy years of captivity the Medes and Persians began to rule. They ruled until 331 B.C.
3. Greece then became world ruler.
4. For around one hundred years after the fall of Greece the Jews had an independent state under the reign of the Maccabees which were a priestly family of rulers.
5. Around 63 B.C. the Romans came into power and Julius Caesar became the emperor of Rome. After his death, Herod the Great was made king of the Jews. To win the favor of the Jews he built many great public buildings including a new temple for the Jews. This is the same Herod that was in power when Jesus was born.

Sixth Dispensation - The Holy Ghost Part 1

1. The Holy Ghost is poured out and Church established. The disciples go to Jerusalem to wait for the Holy Ghost. Acts 1:4-14
2. Descent of the Holy Ghost. Prophesy Joel 2:28-29 Fulfilled Acts 2:1-18
3. The Church is established.

With this outpouring of the Holy Ghost on this group of believers, the Church was born.

The word "Church" means an assembly of called out ones. During this church age God is calling out, through the Holy Ghost, individuals from both Jews and Gentiles to form a new body (the Church).

Paul refers to the forming of the Church as a mystery. The mystery was the purpose of God to unite the Jews and Gentiles into a new thing, the Church, which is His body. Galations 3:28-29, Ephesians 1:22-23, Colossians 3:11

Dispensation of the Holy Ghost Part 2
The Gifts of the Spirit to the Dark Ages.

A - The Gifts of the Spirit

1. Word of Wisdom
   This is a wise utterance spoken through the operation of the Holy Spirit. It applies the revelation of God's Word or the Holy Spirit's wisdom to a specific situation or problem (Acts 6:10; 15:13-22). It is not, however, the same as having the wisdom of God for daily living. The latter is obtained by diligent study and meditation on God's ways and Word, and by prayer (James 1:5-6)

2. Word of knowledge
   This is an utterance inspired by the Holy Spirit that reveals knowledge about people, circumstances, or Biblical truth. It is often connected closely with prophecy (Acts 5:1-10; I Corinthians 14:24-25)

3. Gift of faith
   This is not saving faith, but rather a special supernatural faith imparted by the Holy Spirit that enables the Christian to believe God for the extraordinary and miraculous. It is a faith that removes mountains (I Corinthians 13:2) and is often found in combination with other manifestations such as healings and miracles (Matthew 17:20; Mark 11:22-24; Luke 17:6).

4. Gifts of healing
   These gifts are given to the church to restore physical health by divinely supernatural means (Matthew 4:23-25; Matthew 10:1; Acts 3:6-8; Acts 4:30). The plural (gifts) indicates healing of various illnesses and suggests that every act of healing is a special gift of God. Although gifts of healing are not given to every member of the body in a special way (I Corinthians 12:11,30), all members may pray for the sick. When faith is present, the sick will be healed. Healing may also occur as a result of obedience to the instructions of James 5:14-16.

5. Miracles
   These are deeds of supernatural power which alter the normal course of nature. They include divine acts in which God's kingdom is manifested against Satan and evil spirits.

6. Prophecy
   We must distinguish between prophecy listed in I Corinthians 12:10 as a temporary manifestation of the Spirit from prophecy cited as a ministry gift of the church in Ephesians

4:11. As a ministry gift, prophecy is given only to some believers, who must then function as prophets within the church. As a spiritual manifestation, prophecy is potentially available to every Spirit-filled Christian (Acts 2:17-18). Concerning the second of these two forms of prophecy, observe the following:

Prophecy is a special gift that enables a believer to bring a word or revelation directly from God under the impulse of the Holy Spirit (I Corinthians 14:24-25,29-31). It is not the delivery of a previously prepared sermon.

In both the Old Testament and the New Testament, prophecy is not primarily foretelling the future, but proclaiming the will of God and exhorting God's people to righteousness, faithfulness, endurance, and encouragement (I Corinthians 14:3).

The message may expose the condition of a person's heart (14:25) or offer edification, exhortation, comfort, warning, and judgment (I Corinthians 14:3, 25-26, 31).

The church must not receive such prophecy as an infallible message, for many false prophets will enter the church (I John 4:1). Therefore, all prophecies must be tested as to their genuineness and truth (I Corinthians 14:29,32; I Thessalonians 5:20-21) by whether they conform to the Word of God (I John 4: 1), by whether they promote godly living (1 Timothy 6:3), and by whether they are uttered by one who is sincerely living under the Lordship of Christ (I Corinthians 12:3).

Prophecy operates under the will of God and not man. The N.T. never indicates that the church actively sought revelation or direction from those who claimed they were prophets. Prophecy was given to the church only when

God initiated the message (1 Corinthians 12:11; II Peter 1:21).

7. Discerning of spirits
   This gift is a special ability given by the Spirit to properly discern and judge prophecies and to distinguish whether an utterance is from the Holy Spirit or not (I Corinthians 14:29; I John 4:1). Towards the end of the age when false teachers (Matthew 24:5) and distortion of Biblical Christianity will greatly increase (I Timothy 4:1), this gift will be extremely important for the church.

8. Divers kinds of tongues
   Concerning "tongues" (Gk. glossa, meaning language) as a supernatural manifestation of the Spirit, the following must be pointed out.

   Tongues may be an existing spoken langnage (Acts 2:4-6) or a language unknown on earth, e.g., "tongues ... of angels" (I Corinthians 13:1). Such speech has not been learned and is often unintelligible both to the speaker (I Corinthians 14:14) and to the hearers (I Corinthians 14:16).

   Speaking in tongues involves the spirit of man and the Spirit of God intermingling so that the believer communicates directly to God (i.e., in prayer, praise, blessing, or thanksgiving), giving expression or utterance at the level of one's spirit rather than the mind (I Corinthians 14:2,14) and praying for oneself or others under the direct influence of the Holy Spirit apart from the activity of the mind (I Corinthians 14:2,4,15,28; Jude 20). Speaking in tongues with interpretation may at times contain a revelation, knowledge, prophecy, or teaching for the assembly of believers (I Corinthians 14:6).

Tongues in the congregation must be accompanied by a Spirit-given interpretation that communicates the content and meaning of the utterance to the community of believers (I Corinthians 14:3,27-28). When interpreted to the congregation, they function either as a form and directive to worship and prayer or as prophecy. The entire body of believers can then participate in this Spirit-inspired revelation. Interpreted tongues can thus be a means of edification as the whole congregation responds to the utterance (I Corinthians 14:6,13).

Speaking in tongues within the congregation must be regulated. The speaker may never be in "ecstasy" or "out of control" (I Corinthians 14:27-28

9. Interpretation of tongues
   This is the ability given by the Holy Spirit to understand and make known the meaning of an utterance given in tongues. The gift may be given to the one who speaks in tongues or to someone else. Those who speak in tongues should pray also for the gift of interpretation (I Corinthians 14:13).

Dispensation of the Holy Ghost Part 3
Reformation to Vials of Wrath.

A - Reformation

The Reformation began the journey back to Pentecost.

1. Lutheran.
   In 1517 Martin Luther, a Catholic monk, gave the first ray of light to the darkened church. He broke away from the Catholic church and formed the first protestant church (Lutheran). He taught justification by

faith but retained the trinity doctrine, sprinkling, and infant baptism.

2. Presbyterian.
   In 1536 John Calvin went a little further by organizing his churches with local presbyters and observing communion (The Lord's Supper) as a memorial of Jesus' sufferings and death.

3. Congregational.
   In 1580 Robert Browne led the Congregational church in separating church and state.

4. Baptist.
   In 1609 John Smythe brought back baptism by immersion. This was the beginning of the Baptist church.

5. Methodist.
   In 1739 John Wesley brought a great revival to England and taught holiness and a genuine conversion. John Wesley was one of the founders of the Methodist church.

6. Christian Churches.
   In 1820 the Christian church was formed bringing back baptism for the remission of sins.

7. Trinity Pentecostal Churches.
   In 1900 baptism of the Holy Ghost was brought back (Evidence: speaking in tongues).

8. Oneness Pentecostal Churches.
   In 1914 the revelation of God in Christ was restored to the Church. The original Church is finally restored.

B - Signs of the End Times

The disciples asked Jesus three questions about the end times. (Matthew 24:3) When will these things be? What will be the sign of thy coming, and the end of the world?

Jesus answered.No man knoweth when your Lord doth come. (Matthew 24:36-42) When these signs begin to come to pass, look up. (Luke 21:25-28) As it was in the days of Noah. Compare Genesis 6:5-11 with Matthew 24:37-44, Philippians 3:17-19, Luke 17:26-30, Luke 21:34-35, II Timothy 3:1-4, II Peter 3:3-7. Eating and drinking. Philippians 3:17-19

There is nothing wrong with eating and drinking. These are a normal part of life, even though some people go to the extreme and make a god of their belly.

But the carnal person is only concerned with feeding his natural body. There is little indication that the people before the flood had any interest in talking to God (Praying) as did Adam, or sacrifice to God as did Abel, or walk with God as did Enoch.

1. Marrying and giving in marriage. II Peter 3:3-7

Marriage is not sinful, nor is it wrong for a man to give his daughter in marriage.

In Genesis 6:1-2 it appears that the godly line of Seth began to intermarry with the carnal line of Cain. Their behavior had degenerated to the point that they had become scoffers and doubters. They had forgotten God's judgment on Adam, Eve, and Cain because Lamech boasted of slaying a man with no regard for judgment.(Genesis 4:19-23)

2. Buying, selling, planting, and building. Luke 17:26-30

There is nothing inherently wrong with buying, selling, planting, and building. Humans were developing skills and talents in many areas. Lamech's three sons excelled in making tents, raising cattle, music and industry. They now had music for entertainment. Their simple nomadic lives were becoming sophisticated, materialistic, and corrupt.(Genesis 6:5-13) God said, "I will destroy them with the earth.

3. They knew not

Matthew 24:38-39 Life was going on as usual, everyone was engaged in their normal activities, the day before the judgment looked like any other day to them. There was no advance warning on exactly when judgment would come. So shall also the coming of the Son of man be.

4. The same extreme wickedness

II Timothy 3:1-7 clearly describes our generation and declares these characteristics to be signs of the last days. Just as the flood came upon the unsuspecting people in the days of Noah and destroyed all those who did not make themselves right with God, so is the judgment of God coming on the generation of the last days. There will be no warning of the exact time of his coming. (Matthew 24:36-37)

5. Noah prepared.

Noah was probably a strange looking character, working for many years on a strange looking vessel and talking about an impending flood. Most likely he was the subject of many jokes and laughter. But when the flood came, Noah, who had obeyed God, was inside the ark floating away while the scoffers and unbelievers were suffering the penalty of their sins.

Are we ready to meet Him if he should come right now? Is there a longing and an anticipation in our hearts to see our saviour, Jesus Christ? If there isn't, then let us check up on our lives to see if we are fully prepared for that great day.

C - The Rapture

1. I Thessalonians 4:13-18 The Rapture is the catching away of that chosen group from all nations of the earth who have been born again. The dead in Christ shall rise first: then we which are alive and remain sahll be caught up together with them in the clouds.
2. I Thessalonians 5:9 The Rapture of the Church will happen before the great tribulation.
3. Revelation 19:7-10 Those of the Rapture go to the Marriage Supper of the Lamb.

D - Manifestation and Reign of Anti-Christ

1. II Thessalonians 2:3-12 His coming is after the work of Satan.
2. Revelation 13:16-18 Rich and poor forced to take the mark of the beast to buy and sell.
3. Revelation 14:9-11 Anyone who worships the beast or accepts his mark will be tormented forever with fire and brimstone.

E - Vials of Wrath

1. Revelation 16:1 During the last three years of the great tribulation the vials of the wrath of God will be poured out on the earth.
2. Revelation 16:2 Sores on men.
3. Revelation 16:3 Everything in the sea dies.
4. Revelation 16:4-7 Rivers and fountains of waters become blood.

5. Revelation 16:8-9 Sun scorches men with fire.
6. Revelation 16:10-11 Darkness.
7. Revelation 16:12-16 Demonic spirits.
8. Revelation 16:17-21 Earthquake and hail.

Seventh Dispensation - Millenium

A - Marriage Supper of the Lamb.

Revelation 19:7-10 While the rest of the world is going through the great tribulation period the dead in Christ that were resurrected and those in Christ who were yet alive and caught away will be enjoying the Marriage Supper of the Lamb.

B - The Return of Christ.

Revelation 17:14; Revelation 19:11-16 After the Marriage Supper of the Lamb, Christ will return to earth to destroy anti-christ and set up His 1000 year reign and all the people who were caught away in the rapture will be with Him.

C - Battle of Armageddon

Revelation 19:17-21; Revelation 16:13-16; Revelation 17:12-14 The beast and the false prophet are cast alive into the lake of fire and the remnant were slain with the sword. The fowls were filled with their flesh.

D - Satan Bound for 1000 years.

Revelation 20:1-3 Satan is bound in chains and put in the bottomless pit for 1000 years.

E - Christ reigns for 1000 years.

Revelation 17:14 Christ's raptured saints will be with him when he returns to earth. They that are with him are called, chosen, and faithful.

Revelation 20:4-6 Those who were beheaded for Christ will be resurrected and reign with him for 1000 years. The rest of the dead will not be raised until the 1000 years are finished.

This is the First Resurrection (Revelation 20:5)

The third day of Hosea 6:2

All the Jews will live in his sight for 1000 years.

F - Satan is released from the pit

Revelation 20:7-9 When Satan is released, he tries one last time to fight God and His people. Satan's armies are devoured by fire.

Revelation 20:10 Satan is cast into the lake of fire where the beast and the false prophet are.

G - The Second Resurrection and Final Judgment

Revelation 20:11; II Peter 3:7-10 The earth and the heaven fled away.

The second resurrection (Revelation 20:12-13) The dead, small and great, are resurrected and stand before God to be judged.

H - Where will you spend Eternity?

1. With Christ
   Revelation 21:1-7 In the New Heaven and New Earth.
   Revelation 21:9-27 In the New Jerusalem.

2. With Satan
   Revelation 20:14-15; Revelation 21:8In the Lake of Fire.

I - One final warning

Revelation 22:18-19

18. For I testify unto every man that heareth the words of the prophecy of this book, If any man shall add unto these things, God shall add unto him the plagues that are written in this book:
19. And if any man shall take away from the words of the book of this prophecy, God shall take away his part out of the book of life, and out of the holy city, and from the things which are written in this book.

CHAPTER 37

Churches - Amen - Agreeing with the Spoken Word

Amen is not only a word of agreement, affirmation or concurrence in the bible (KJV), but is the shortest scripture in the bible. When a Christian uses this word, it is a statement of affirmation of what has been said is the truth. Many Christians who use this word have not the foggiest idea of the ramifications of what they are saying. You are essentially concurring with what was said as being the truth. You're also saying that you are sure that it is the truth. Amen is a powerful word to use when making an affirmation or concurrence.

Old Testament

Amen. Hebrew definition. 543. 'amen, aw-mane'; from H539; sure; abstr. faithfulness; adv. truly:--Amen, so be it, truth.

New Testament

Amen. Hebrew definition. 281. amen, am-ane'; of Heb. or. [H543]; prop. firm, i.e. (fig.) trustworthy; adv. surely (often as interj. so be it):--amen, verily.

CHAPTER **38**

Churches - Angel Worshiping Is Strictly Forbidden

There are good angels who are dedicated to God, Almighty. They serve Him and obey His every command. Then there are evil angels who are dedicated to Satan, the prince of darkness. These are the fallen angels which were the third of angels who fell from grace in heaven with Satan. In other words, they changed their allegiances to God to that of Satan. They decided not to serve God, but to serve Satan instead. These angels perpetuate each and every evil deed possible on Christians as well as non-christians. God's angels don't perpetuate evil on anyone. They only act as God, Almighty commands them. God doesn't perpetuate evil on anybody. He allows Satan to do evil on humanity.

Angel worshiping or so called recognition of personal angels is an increasing trend or phenomenon among not only children, but adults as well. Some people allegedly have what is called their guardian angel(s) who purportedly looks over them on a daily basis. Unfortunately, some Christians are caught up in this craze or growing angelic phenomenon. Christians must know that angel worship is forbidden.

Colossians 2:18 (KJV), "Let no man beguile you of your reward in a voluntary humility and **WORSHIPPING** of angels, intruding into those things which he hath not seen, vainly puffed up by his fleshly mind,".

Now, Jesus did give us a hint that little children have angels watching over them. In His parables, He was explaining to us that we must humble ourselves and become as little children to Him. He also warns those who offend His little children of dire consequences.

Mat 18:4 (KJV) "Whosoever therefore shall humble himself as this little child, the same is greatest in the kingdom of heaven."

Mat 18:5 (KJV) "And whoso shall receive one such little child in my name receiveth me."

Angels Report Child Abuse To God

Mat 18:6 (KJV) "But whoso shall offend one of these little ones which believe in me, it were better for him that a millstone were hanged about his neck, and that he were drowned in the depth of the sea."

Angels of Children

Mat 18:10 (KJV) "Take heed that ye despise not one of these little ones; for I say unto you, That in heaven their angels do always behold the face of my Father which is in heaven."

Evil Angels And Satan Attacks Christians

When Christians foster intimate relationships with God Almighty, He will place a shield of protection around them, their properties and their possessions as he did with Job.

Job was a man of God who walked with Him. He lived uprighteously and did what God commanded him. However, Satan petitioned God to remove the **HEDGE** (protection) around him so he could tempt Job and make him turn from God.

Job 1:10-11 (KJV), (10) "Hast not thou made an **HEDGE** about him, and about his house, and about all that he hath on every side? thou hast blessed the work of his hands, and his substance is increased in the land.

But put forth thine hand now, and touch all that he hath, and he will curse thee to thy face."

These verses clearly reveals to us the protection we can have by walking with God and doing his perfect will. Neither Satan nor his demons can break God's protective barrier (**HEDGE**) that He has placed around and about us.

Read the entire story of the book of Job. You will find that Job was richly blessed in every aspect of his life before Satan attacked him. He was even more blessed after Satan's attack because of his patience and fear of God. In God's infinite wisdom and knowledge He knows that not all Christians are walking with Him or doing His perfect will as He desires of them. These Christians don't have that hedge or protection around them. So, occasionally He has to send an angel or angels to protect or safeguard His own. He has done this back in the bible days as well as today.

There are a number of instances where plans were attempted to murder some evangelist unbeknownst to them while they were at their homes. The people who were attempting the murders reached the targeted victims homes only to find them surrounded by men dressed in white robes protecting the houses. These were God's angels sent to protect the men and women of God. However, please note that these were not those targeted victims personal or guardian angels. They were God's personal angels, His servants.

Traditionally, angels are depicted and described as with human like features clothed in white robes and with two (2) wings extended from the rear of their bodies. Although, there is mentioned about

God's messaging, ministering and warring angels ascending and descending throughout the bible, but there is nothing mentioned about these angels having wings. Biblical references of these angels are in human form. These angels have the power to transform themselves from their spiritual form and materialize to that of similar human forms as humanity is today. They can penetrate walls and solid objects as well.

Some of our prominent Evangelicals, Ministers, Pastors, Theologians and other men and women of God can attest to the fact they have seen and witnessed the presence of God's angels. Carlton Pierson, a Pastor and Evangelist said that he was lying in his bed at his hotel room prior to his preaching engagement when several or more demons had bound him in the bed and held his speech where he couldn't speak for about an hour. When he finally could speak, he yell out, "JESUS!!!". Immediately, two tall men (angels) came through the door (as spirits can do) and pointed their fingers at the demons. The demons immediately vanished and momentarily as did the angels as well.

Dr. Rebecca Brown who authored three books, "He Came To Set The Captives Free", "Prepare For War", and "Becoming A Vessel Of Honor" has had a remarkable experience with God's angels. Through her trials and tribulations with her ministry with God, He sent an angel to her while she sat at a table near a tree out in the yard. After Dr. Brown had made a determination of whom the angel was serving, she had a conversation in the form of questions with him. Even before the angel would answer any of Dr. Brown's questions, he said to her that she was full of questions. He then seemed to be getting permission from God to answer her questions. The angel then crossed his legs and said to her, Father said you can ask me any question you so desire or words to that effect. Dr. Brown's description of the angel was a man of a human form with a bronze colored face, white baggy pants and white shirt, a gold belt, sandals, a gold sheath and sword at his side and various other items, but not wings. The angel didn't give his name to Dr. Brown, either.

Except for Archangel Michael, Gabriel and Raphael and probably the other angels around God's throne, God's angels' names are secret. Angels are not to be honored in no way, shape or form. God gets all the glory and honour, but not his angels.

Note: The angel Raphael is found in the apocrypha book of Tobit. The book of Tobit is found in "The Modern Reader's Bible" printed in 1910 and the Catholic's denominational bible, "The New American Bible". This book of Tobit was once allegedly a lost book and is not found in Christian or Jewish bibles as a recognized book of the bible. In 1955 there were fragments of Tobit recovered with other books. These books were translated from fragments of the Aramaic and Hebrew languages from lost dead sea scrolls (centuries old) found in cave IV at Qumran. The location of this cave is a mile or so West of the Northwestern corner of the dead sea. Some theologians differ on the authenticity or their lack in recognizing that these books were prophetically inspired by God, Almighty.

Before Samson was born, an angel came unto his mother and told her that she would conceive and bare him. All she could tell was that the man's face was that of a man of God. Neither she nor her husband, Manoah knew that this man of God was actually an angel of God.

Judges 13:16 (KJV), "......For Manoah knew not that he was an angel of the Lord. Monoah ask the angel of his name so that she could honour him.

Judges 13:17 (KJV), "And Manoah said unto the angel of the Lord, What is thy name, that when thy sayings come to pass we may do thee honour?"

Judges 13:18 (KJV), "And the angel of the Lord said unto him, Why askest thou thus my name, seeing it is secret?"

As we can see, this angel wouldn't reveal his name to Manoah. Also, we see that Manoah could only distinguish this man as an angel by his face (possibly bronze in color) and not by any wings, because he had none. After Manoah had taken a kid and offered it to the Lord for a meat offering, the angel went up in the flame from the altar and was never seen again by them.

Judges 13:19-20 (KJV), (19) "So Manoah took a kid with a meat offering, and offered it upon a rock unto the Lord: and the angel did wonderously; and Manoah and his wife looked on.

(20) "For it came to pass, when the flame went up toward heaven from off the altar, that the angel of the Lord ascended in the flame of the altar. And Manoah and his wife looked on it, and fell on their faces to the ground.

Biblically speaking, God Almighty's angels are only at His disposal and only at His command or His Son Jesus' command and disposal. We can't pray to or ask God's angels to do anything for us. No unsaved human being, whether they be man, woman, boy or girl on the other hand have no authority or communion with heavenly angels. Heavenly angels will only act upon the command of God the Father, God the Son, or God the Holy Spirit which are three heads in one, the Holy Trinity.

We can reference at least the names of three (3) of God's angels and they are Michael, the archangel (chief/head and a warrior), Gabriel (messenger), and Raphael (guardian, intercessor, and warrior), apocrypha book of Tobit in the Old Testament.

Jude 1:9 (KJV), "Yet Michael the archangel, when contending with the devil he disputed about the body of Moses, durst not bring against him a railing accusation, but said, The Lord rebuke thee."

Michael is not only the archangel, but a warrior as well.

Revelation 12:7 (KJV), "And there was war in heaven: Michael and his angels fought against the dragon; and the dragon fought and his angels,".

On the other hand, Gabriel is one of God's personal messengers. Gabriel was the angel who brought the message to Mary, Jesus's earthy mother that she would become pregnant and give birth to Jesus. Prior to that Gabriel took the message to Mary's Aunt Elisabeth's husband, Zecharias that his prayer was heard and answered by God that his wife would become pregnant with a son to be named John.

Luke 1:13 (KJV), "But the angel said unto him, Fear not, Zacharias: for thy prayer is heard; and thy wife Elisabeth shall bear the a son, and thou shall call his name John.

Luke 1:18-19 (KJV), (18) "And Zacharias said unto the angel, Whereby shall I know this? for I am an old man, and my wife well stricken in years.

19. And the angel answering said unto him, I am Gabriel, that stand in the presence of God; and am sent to speak unto thee, and to show thee these glad tidings."

In the Old Testament Apocrypha book of Tobit (Catholic - NAB), Raphael (also stands at the throne of God) appeared unto Tobit's son, Tobiah as a man of their tribe. Raphael guarded Tobiah, healed Tobiah's father Tobit from blindness, healed Tobiah's wife Sarah from demonic afflictions of the demon named Asmodeus.

Tobit 3:8 (Catholic - NAB), demon Asmodeus had previously killed seven (7) of Sarah's husbands before her marriages to them were consummated (marital sexual intercourse).

Tobit 8:3 (Catholic - NAB) Raphael pursued, caught and bound both hands and feet of the demon named Asmodeus.

Some of God's angels are guardian angels, ministering angels, some are messengers and some are warriors. All act only at the commands of God the Father, God the Son or God the Holy Spirit for the sake of Christians and not for the sake of the secular world. God's Archangel Michael and many of His angels are constantly at war with Satan and his demonic angels. This war is called spiritual warfare. We fight not against flesh and blood, but it is a war against principalities and evil spirits in high places. As Christians, we are partakers in this war also.

Ephesians 6:12 (KJV), "For we wrestle not against flesh and blood, but against principalities, against powers, against the rulers of the darkness of this world, against spiritual wickedness in high places."

CHERUB AND CHERIBIMS

Cheribims are God's personal servants and they are another order of spiritual beings which is in fact quite interesting and fascinating in that they have more than two (2) wings as well. Cheribims have four (4) wings and under their wings, they have hands in the likeness of a man. Each cherub has four (4) individual heads.

Ezekiel 10:14 (KJV), "And every one had four faces: the first face was the face of a cherub, and the second face was the face of a man, and the third face of a lion, and the fourth the face of an eagle."
Ezekiel 10:21 (KJV), "Every one had four faces apiece, and every one four wings; and the likeness of the hands of a man was under their wings."

Another interesting fact that might give credence to the misconception and the phenomenon of the two (2) winged angels is when the images or the statues of cherubims were made. Let's not forget that a cherub has four (4) wings and four (4) faces. In the description of making images or statues of the cherubims, only two (2) wings were mentioned to be spread out over the ark of the Lord's covenant reaching the wall of the most holy house. Also, there was nothing mentioned about taking away the other two (2) wings. They weren't extended as the other two wings.

2 Chronicles 3:10-12 (KJV) (10) "And in the most holy house he made two cherubims of image work, and overlaid them with gold.

11. And the wings of the cherubims were twenty cubits long: one wing of the one cherub was five cubits, reaching to the wall of the house: and the other wing was likewise five cubits, reaching to the wing of the other cherub.
12. And one wing of the other cherub was five cubits, reaching to the wall of the house: and the other wing was five cubits also, joining to the wing of the other cherub."

SERAPHIMS

Now you are probably wondering where did the concept of angels with two (2) wings come from. One interesting fact in God's description of His seraphims might give us a clue as to where the angels with the two (2) wings phenomenon comes from. The book of Isaiah describes God's seraphims with six wings; two wings covered his face, two wings covered his legs, and he used two wings to fly. Isaiah saw these seraphims standing above God's Holy Throne.

Isaiah 6:2 (KJV), "Above it stood the seraphims: each one had six wings; with twain he covered his face, and with twain he covered his feet, and with twain he did fly."

As you can see, these seraphims had a total of six wings. Seraphims are God's personal servants, also. Isaiah then saw one of the seraphims did fly as he describes in scripture

Isaiah 6:6 (KJV), "Then flew one of the seraphims unto me, having a live coal in his hand, which he had taken with the tongs from the altar:"

As you can see, these seraphims also have hands and they can talk and communicate with humanity as well.

Isaiah 6:3 (KJV), "And one cried to another, and said, Holy, holy, holy, is the Lord of host: the whole earth is full of His glory."

It is not mentioned that these seraphims ever did any ministering to man, except to make acknowledgments and to make confirmations to man of God's glory.

Isaiah 6:7 (KJV), "And he laid it upon my mouth, and said, Lo, this has touched thy lips; and thine iniquity is taken away, and thy sin purged."

It is not mentioned that they did any battles on man's behalf. These are tasks that God has reserved for his angels without wings to do, but not cherubims or seraphims. The cherubims description of four (4) wings and the seraphims description of six (6) wings contradicts the traditions that angels only have two (2) wings with which to fly. Not only that, but tradition has it that they are mostly adorned in white apparel or white robes. All of us could possibly identify them in this type of garb. However, this is not the case. One word of caution is that if a so called angel appears to you in this type of garb, question him immediately by asking him "who is your master?". If he doesn't answer that his master is Jesus, then he is not God's angel. Immediately call out Jesus' name. You'll probably see one or more of God's angels to command this demon or demons to depart from your presence or to escort the demon(s) from your presence.

Remember, God's guardian angels, ministering angels, and/or warring angels can manifest themselves as common human beings without the slightest intuition or hint that they are angels. Most likely they will be wearing clothes similar to that which humanity is presently wearing in a particular region or sector of the world. However, some Theologians, men and woman of God have seen real angels dressed in white baggy looking shirts and trousers with sandals on their feet. Paul tells us that angels can commonly look like us humans.

Hebrews 13:2 (KJV), "Be not forgetful to entertain strangers: for thereby some have entertained angels unawares."

CHAPTER 39

Churches - Appearance of Sinning Is Forbidden

Christians are reminded that they should abstain from the appearance of sinning. An example is when one is in the company of someone or a group of people who are in fact taking part in something which seems to be wrong, whether it is or not. You can be at the wrong place at the wrong time and be charged for a crime that you didn't commit.

There is a misconception that people are predominately good, but the Bible tells differently. All of us are sinners from birth and have fallen short of the glory of God. Although we are Christians saved by grace, we are surrounded by a world of evil and wickedness.
John 5:19 (KJV), "And we know that we are of God, and the world lieth in wickedness."

We are admonished to separate ourselves from any appearance of wickedness. We shouldn't be seen frequenting bars, clubs, gambling casinos or supporting lotteries, raffles or any form of gambling.

1 Thessalonians 5:22 (KJV), "Abstain from all appearance of evil.".

1 Thessalonians 5:22 (Simple English), "Stay away from every kind of evil--even from what looks like evil."

Many people have become victims of somebody else's evil and sin. By law, you can be charged as an accessory to a crime if you are present during the conduct of such a crime, which is an evil and a sin. Your mere association with a person perpetuating a sin can cause you many sleepless nights, headaches, heartaches and worries, just to name a few problems. Very carefully, choose your friends and/or your associates. All of your friends don't have to be Christians.

You can be a lights to those of the world to lead them to Christ. The world is constantly watching Christians even when we don't realize they doing so. They expect us to set examples for them whether they follow suit or not. Constantly watch your actions as if you know of certainly that someone is watching you. Let your Christian light so shine that men, women, boys and girls will see Jesus in you. Christ explains to us why we are the lights of the world in the following scriptures:

Matthew 5:14 (KJV), "Ye are the light of the world. A city that is set on an hill cannot be hid.

Matthew 5:15 (KJV), "Neither do men light a candle, and put it under a bushel, but on a candlestick; and giveth light unto all that are in the house.

Matthew 5:16 (Living), "Don't hide your light! Let it shine for all; let your good deeds glow for all to see, so that they will praise your heavenly Father."

CHAPTER **40**

Churches - Armor of Protection Lacking in Christians

Christians as a whole are unaware that they should put on God's complete armor of protection on a daily basis. We aren't fighting against flesh and blood, but evil spirits.

Ephesians 6:11 (Living), "Put on all of God's Armor so that you will be able to stand safe against all strategies and tricks of Satan."

Ephesians 6:12 (Living), "For we are not fighting against people made of flesh and blood, but against persons without bodies--the evil rulers of the unseen world, those mighty satanic beings and great evil princes of darkness who rule this world; and against huge number of wicked spirits in the spirit world."

Ephesians 6:13 (Simple English) "This is why you must take up all of God's armor. Then when the time for battle comes, you will be able to resist. And after you have fought your best, you will stand.".

Ephesians 6:14 (NIV) "Stand firm then, with the belt of truth buckled around your waist, with the breastplate of righteousness in place,"

Ephesians 6:15 (Living) "Wear shoes that are able to speed you on as you preach the Good News of peace with God."

Ephesians 6:16 (Living) "In every battle you will need faith as your shield to stop the fiery arrows aimed at you by Satan.

Ephesians 6:17-18 (KJV) (17) "And take the helmet of salvation, and the sword of the Spirit, which is the word of God:

18. Praying always with all prayer and supplication in the Spirit, and watching thereunto with all perseverance and supplication for all saints."

In order for us to fully understand what God's full armor is, we need to expound on each element which God provides for our protection against Satan. When fighting soldiers are preparing for war, they are provided with helmets to protect their heads, flack jackets to protect their chest and vital organs, certain protective wear for the groin area, and suitable shoes or boots conducive to the terrain and/or the environment where the battle is to take place. Additionally, soldiers are given the proper weapons for which to use in their battles. So, Christians must be properly prepared and equipped with the necessary protective armor and fighting weapons as well. This includes the physical aspect as well as the spiritual aspect of a Christian's being. Let's explore this fighting armor of a Christian.

BELT OF TRUTH

Ephesians 6:14 (NIV) "Stand firm then, with the **belt of truth** buckled around your waist,..."

First, we must buckle around our waists the belt of truth. We must be truthful in everything we do in our daily walk with God. This belt of truth keeps our backs straight and in an upright position. Lies will only make our backs be in bent over positions. The enemy can only defeat us if our backs are bent from lying. It is easy to whip somebody while they are bent over or down on the ground. Many

Christians are worshiping God in a lie. When they aren't worshiping God in Spirit and Truth, then it is a lie.

John 4:23 (Living) "Jesus replied, "The time is coming, ma'am, when we will no longer be concerned about whether to worship the Father here or in Jerusalem. For it's not where we worship that counts, but how we worship-is our worship spiritual and real? Do we have the Holy Spirit's help? For God is Spirit, and we must have His help to worship as we should. The Father wants this kind of worship from us. But you Samaritans know so little about Him, **WORSHIPING BLINDLY**, while we Jews know all about him, for salvation comes to the world through the Jews."

Many Christians believe that true worship is highlighted only through much emotions and/or shoutings, but this is only part of worshiping which is the **FIRST PHASE** of worshiping God. This second phase of worshiping God includes being silent momentarily while patiently waiting for the Holy Spirit's entrance to our presence. Normally after all the dramatics of worshiping God are over, then the Holy Spirit makes His Grand Entrance and performs His work which is the **SECOND PHASE** of worshiping God. We have to know that we are in God's perfect will.

The Holy Spirit will use God's **SPECIAL** chosen vessels; highly anointed men and women of God endowed with **POWER.**

Acts 1:8 (KJV), "But ye shall receive power, after that the Holy Ghost is come upon you: and ye shall be witnesses unto me both in Jerusalem, and in all Judea, and in Samaria, and unto the uttermost part of the earth."

Acts 4:33 (KJV), "And with great power gave the apostles witness of the resurrection of the Lord Jesus: and great grace was upon them all." This power was included with certain gifts of the Spirit. (I Cor. 12:8-10 explained in next paragraph). Most Christians are not endowed with power, neither do many of them have either one or more of the gifts of the Spirit. Secular gifts (talents) are often confused with spiritual gifts.

Upon being saved, we are only filled with the Holy Spirit. This is our first gift from God, Almighty. As we grow in Christ, we can earnestly and sincerely pray to God through Jesus Christ and ask Him for certain gifts of the Spirit. These gifts don't come automatically just because we are Christians, we have to ask God for them. There are 9 gifts of the Spirit which we can receive.

I Corinthians 12:8-10 (KJV), "For to one is given by the Spirit the **word of wisdom**; to another the **word of knowledge** by the same Spirit; To another **faith** by the same Spirit; to another **gifts of healing** by the same Spirit; To another the **working of miracles**; to another **prophecy**; to another **discerning of spirits**; to another **divers kinds of tongues**; to another **interpretation of Tongues**:

However, before we receive any of these gifts, we must be baptized in the Holy Spirit. This is our second level of anointing. Once we are baptized in the Holy Spirit, we will receive and speak a Holy language which allows us the opportunity to speak and pray to God in the Spirit. This not only opens up our line of communication to God, Almighty, but allows us to speak the language(s) of man as well (i.e., prophecy, and/or Word of Knowledge). We must understand this in order for us to worship God in Spirit and in Truth, we must have a very close relationship with His Holy Spirit. Just attending Church Services on Sundays to listen to the choir sing praises and to the pastor's sermon may not be true complete worshiping of God. We must involve the Spirit of the Living God, the Holy Spirit always.

BREASTPLATE OF RIGHTEOUSNESS

Ephesians 6-14 (NIV) "Stand firm then, ... with the **breastplate of righteousness** in place,"

Secondly, one must be righteous to be afforded the breastplate of protection. You can't just do what you think is right in return for right from somebody else. You must be in fact a righteous person. Doing right or merely doing good outside of salvation doesn't mean a hill of beans to God.

Romans 3:22 (Living) "But now God has shown us a different way to heaven --NOT "BEING GOOD ENOUGH" and trying to keep the law, but by a new way (though not new, really, for the Scriptures told about it long ago). Now God says He will accept and acquit us--declare us "not guilty"--if we trust Jesus Christ to take away our sins. And we all can be saved in this same way, by coming to Christ, no matter who we are or what we have been like."

Romans 3:22 (Simple English) "Committing oneself to Jesus Christ is what makes a person right with God. Is for anyone who believes! It makes no difference."

As you can see, you can only be a righteous person by accepting Jesus Christ as your person savior. There is no other way under God's word.

WEAR SHOES TO SPEED YOU ON

Ephesians 6:15 (Living) "Wear shoes that are able to speed you on as you preach the Good News of peace with God."

Thirdly, we must be prepared and grounded in God's unadulterated (not watered down) word with firm and steadfast foundations from with which to preach, proclaim and teach. In other words we need to know what we are talking about when we attempt to use God's word. One way is to study and read the holy bible on a regular basis, possibly on a daily basis.

2 Timothy 2:15 (Simple) "Do your best to present yourself to God

as one who has passed the test. Be a worker who has nothing to be ashamed of. "Interpret the message of truth in the proper way." This work includes studying our bibles. We can study God's word on our own, but we need to attend weekly bible studies Sunday School classes and Sunday morning worship services as well. When possible, we need to also attend various seminars and conferences for our spiritual growth and spiritual enlightenments.

FAITH AS YOUR SHIELD

Ephesians 6:16 (Living) "In every battle you will need **faith as your shield** to stop the fiery arrows aimed at you by Satan."

Fourthly, we must have faith over everything else that we have. Faith is one of our most powerful weapons that we can use to protect ourselves from the battle of the enemy, Satan. What is this faith thing? Well, one can understand that faith is the belief that what God says in His word is true without physical proof of it at that moment. Furthermore, we must have the belief that God's word will not return void. We must believe His word will come to past and this is our hope while we patiently wait upon Him.

Hebrews 11:1 (Living) "What is faith? It is the confident assurance that something we want is going to happen. It is the certainly that what hope for is waiting for us, even though we cannot see it."

Wait a moment! The scripture mentioned a **shield of faith**, didn't it? This faith is part of our armor. The Greek translation says that the shield is a large shield (as door-shaped). It protects our entire bodies from attacks by Satan and his demons.

HELMET OF SALVATION

Ephesians 6-17 (KJV) "And take the helmet of salvation, ..."

Fifthly, you must have already changed your heart from sin, immersed in water and saved through the atoning blood of Jesus Christ to have the helmet of salvation.

Acts 2:38 (Simple) "Then Peter answered, "Change your hearts and each one of you must be immersed by the authority of Jesus the Messiah so that your sins may be forgiven. Then you will receive the gift of the Holy Spirit."

Romans 6:4 (Simple English) "So, through immersion, we were buried with Him into death. Christ was raised from death through the glory of the Father. In the same way, we will live a new life."
However, if you aren't saved, then God's complete armor is not provided for your protection. So, the "Helmet Of Salvation" helps to protect your body, your soul and your spirit. Obviously, people who are mentally unstable and/or who have experienced nervous breakdowns aren't protected with God's armor. People who are mentally unstable are essentially possessed with demonic spirit(s), defeated and controlled by Satan and his evil spirits. These mentally unstable people can of course change their hearts by seeking salvation through repenting, asking Christ to come into their hearts and by becoming totally immersed in water (water baptism). They will then receive the gift of the Holy Spirit (filled with the Holy Spirit) which will replace Satan and his evil spirits.

SWORD OF THE SPIRIT

Ephesians 6:17 "And take the ...., and the **sword of the Spirit**, which is the word of the Lord."

Sixthly, we must use as our weapon of spiritual battle the Bible, God's holy word. We must however be proficient in handling the word of God. He tells us in 1 Timothy 2:15 (KJV) "Study to shew thyself approved unto God, a workman that needeth not to be ashamed, rightly dividing the word of truth."

So, we must regularly and continually study our bibles to acquire wisdom, knowledge and understanding of God's perfect will of our lives. We should not be Christians who are ignorant in His word, because Satan will use this ignorance against us in every way possible.

PRAYING ALWAYS

Ephesians 6:18 (KJV) "Praying always with all prayer and supplication in the Spirit, and watching thereunto with all perseverance and supplication for all saints;"

CHAPTER 41

Churches - Babes in Christ Are Un-Skilled Christians

New or born-again Christians are often referred to as babes in Christ. They are inexperienced in Christianity and who lack solid foundations in the wisdom, knowledge, and understanding in God's word, the bible.

Hebrews 5:13-14 (KJV), "13) For every one that useth milk is unskilful in the word of righteousness: for he is a babe.

14. But strong meat belongeth to them that are of full age, even those who by reason of use have their senses exercised to discern both good and evil."

When new babies are born, they will most likely be fed and nourished with milk or formula like substances specially prepared and packaged for them. They don't have the necessary eating equipment such as teeth to chew nor do they have strong digestive systems to absorb meat and other solid foods properly. Their bodies and their digestive systems aren't capable of consuming foods which older humans consume. Many types of foods are processed and sold through grocery stores just for babies and toddlers. Babes in Christ are similar to new born babies and toddlers, they need to eat food that they can comfortably consume and digest. They must be nourished and nurtured with the basics of biblical teachings whereby they can gain the wisdom, knowledge and understanding to shine as Christians should.

The Apostle Paul tells us in

2 Timothy 2:15 (KJV), "Study to shew thyself approved unto God, a workman that needeth not to be ashamed, rightly dividing the word of truth." .

A babe in Christ doesn't have the necessary biblical knowledge whereby he/she can stand on his/her own. Although we are warned in the book of Ecclesiastes that there is no end to making books which the study of them makes us weary.

Ecclesiastes 12:12 (KJV), "And further, by these, my son, be admonished: of making books there is no end; and much study is a weariness of the flesh."

He/she must eat, that is consume God's word until he/she is at the point of weaning just like a baby in our physical lives. Even when we are weaned from milk, we still must continue to learn God's word in order to keep growing in biblical wisdom, knowledge and understanding.

In order to attain a well rounded life, we also must educate ourselves to the way of the world as well. If we only learn God's word and not the way of our secular societies, we are in for some great surprises. We can't be so holy that we aren't any worldly good. Many Christians have made the mistake of already knowing where their spiritual lives are headed right after baptism. They believe they are called to preach, teach or whatever before their spiritual lives are even shaped. If they are really sincere in walking with Jesus and doing God's will, they will go through many trials and tribulations.

New Christians who are babes in Christ often misconstrue their calling in thinking that they should be in full-time ministries as they enter into their Christian walk with Christ. Some of them have quit their full-time secular jobs because they believe God has called them into full-time Christian ministries. Often time, this is a misreading or a misconception on their part. Maybe God is calling them into full-time ministries, but not at that particular time. Often time God will take you through something again, again, and again.......... in order to prepare you for that ministry.

1 Peter 1:6-7 (KJV), "6) Wherein ye greatly rejoice, though now for a season, if need be, ye are in heaviness through manifold temptations:

7. That the trial of your faith with fire, might be found unto praise and honour and glory at the appearing of Jesus Christ."

This is called taking you through the fire.

Isaiah 13:12 (KJV), "I will make a man more precious than fine gold; even a man than the golden wedge of Ophir."

John the Baptist tells us about fire in

Matthew 3:11 (KJV), "I indeed baptize you with water unto repentance: but He that cometh after me is mightier than I, Whose shoes I am not worthy to bear: He shall baptize you with the Holy Ghost, and with Fire."

Consider this, when gold is refined, it becomes a high quality precious metal, after it is heated by fire at hundreds of degrees in a smelting pot by a smelting professional.

Mark 9:49-50 (KJV), "49) For every one shall be salted with fire, and every sacrifice shall be salted with salt.

50. Salt is good: but if the salt have lost his saltness, wherewith will ye season it? Have salt in yourselves, and have peace one with another."

Normally at a given meal at the dinner table we have condiments of seasonings for our foods such as salt and pepper to name a few. One of the condiments which is salt is regularly used to bring out the taste of an otherwise great meal. This spiritual fire is God's condiment, the salt to bring out the good in us. Without salt which is our proper seasonings and spiritual fire, we won't be properly refined or seasoned. To simply explain this spiritual fire, let us consider what the Apostle Paul said about the fire.

Hebrews 12:29 (KJV), "For our God is a consuming fire."

So, Almighty God allows us to be tried, and tried and tried again by Satan and his demons until we are refined as precious metals. So God is the Fire by which we are refined.

Although Almighty God, the Son, Jesus Christ came down here in human form, he waited on His full-time ministry for thirty (30) years after He was baptized by John the Baptist.

Luke 3:21-23 (KJV), "21) Now when all the people were baptized, it came to pass, that Jesus also being baptized, and praying, the heaven was opened,

22. And the Holy Ghost descended in a bodily shape like a dove upon Him, and a voice came from heaven, which said, Thou art my beloved Son; in Thee I am well pleased.
23. And Jesus Himself began to be about thirty years of age, being (as was supposed) the son of Joseph, which was the son of Heli,".

He was a carpenter and a minister before he took on His full-time ministry with His disciples. If God thrusts you into a full-time ministry, He will also provide you with the means for food, clothing and the necessities of life as well. You won't have to go out raking and scrapping for everything you need because you thought you were called to a full-time ministry at that particular time. The key is to wait on your calling. Don't try to rush things. God will only work as He will and not necessarily because of your will.

One note of encouragement is that if you have not experienced many trials and/or tribulations while you walk with Christ on a daily basis, then you are probably still a babe in Christ. The closer your walk with Christ, the more Satan and his demons will oppress you increasingly on a daily basis.

One other thing to think about is that God, Almighty will never tempt you. Good can't tempt evil as we are in the natural sense, evil human beings.

James 1:13-14 (KJV), "13) Let no man say when he is tempted, I am tempted of God: for God cannot be tempted with evil, neither tempteth He any man:

14. But every man is tempted, when he is drawn away of his own lust, and enticed."

God allows Satan and his demons to do such. Jesus was first tempted by Satan in Matthew 4:1 (KJV), "Then was Jesus led up of the Spirit into the wilderness to be tempted of the devil."

So please, don't ever say that you did something because you were tempted by God. Satan and his head demons are responsible for your trials, tribulations and your temptations. Remember that Christ is always with you throughout all of your temptations.

1 Corinthians 10:13 (KJV), "There hath no temptation taken you but such as is common to man: but God is faithful, who will not suffer you to be tempted above that ye are able; but will with the temptation also make a way to escape, that ye may be able to bear it."

Finally, may God, Almighty continue to bless and protect you as you grow in your walk with our Savior Jesus Christ. Pray to God, Almighty through His Son, Jesus Christ daily for wisdom, knowledge and understanding. WISDOM is the key to understanding God's word and His will, the source of treasure, the source of prosperity and the foundation for all of God's blessings. Wisdom also includes the bestowing of great honor upon you. Precious ones, seek WISDOM at all costs.

I, (Curtis) in the name of Jesus Christ, I request that You, Father in heaven allow me to sincerely stand in the GAP for ALL who seek after Your Wisdom.

CHAPTER 42

Churches - Bar Hopping by Christians Is Forbidden

The frequent attending and/or fellow shipping in bars and beer joints is a fad for people, young and old of the world. Local bars seem to be magnets for not only fellowship, but the consumption of alcohol, smoking, playing pool for some monetary value such as money, and other forms of gambling. These worldly social gathering places also provide for ideal meeting places to meet potential partners for sex, drugs and the like.

Ephesians 5:11 (KJV), "And have no fellowship with the unfruitful works of darkness, but rather reprove them."

Christians are admonished not to take part or fellowship with such. Even though you may not take part in the aforementioned evils, you can compromise your walk with Christ by the mere fact of your presence there.

2 Corinthians 6:14 (KJV), "Be ye not unequally yoked together with unbelievers: for what fellowship hath righteousness with unrighteousness? and what communion hath light with darkness?" When a Christian goes into one of the world's bars to fellowship with the fellows or ladies, they are actually not alone. Christians are in fellowship with their Lord and Savior, Jesus Christ.

1 Corinthians 1:9 (KJV), "God is faithful, by whom ye were called unto the fellowship of His Son Jesus Christ our Lord."

Remember, Christians have Jesus Christ, the Holy Spirit in their heart. So, when you walk in those clubs or bars to fellowship, you are taking Jesus in with you. You really need to ask yourself, "Do I Really Want To Do This?". Your answer should be "NO, AND I REALLY SHOULDN'T". Ask God to forgive you in the name of Jesus Christ for the thought, then thank Him and go on about your life.

We were sadden by an experience of an older minister who was also a pastor of a large church. He told us he visited his brothers and relatives in New York. During his stay with them, they decided to go bar hopping and they did stop to visit one of the local bars. This minister was encourage to join them. He said that everybody who accompanied them to the bar ordered alcohol beverages, but he ordered a glass of milk (as if this was saying lot) for him because he was a minister. First, the minister had no business following the crowd to the bar whether they are relatives or otherwise. Secondly, the minister should have been an example of the light of Jesus in him. Finally, he should have been aware of the scriptures admonishing us of this type of fellowship with the world. This type of lack in Christian wisdom, knowledge and understanding has some far reaching consequences which will heighten our concerns as to his Christian spirituality, his walk with Jesus Christ and his loyalty to the commandments of our Lord and Savior.

CHAPTER **43**

Churches - Holy Spirit - Praise and Worship Him Tremendously

Christians are taught to worship Almighty God, the Father, and Almighty God, The Son, Jesus Christ, but rarely, the worshiping of Almighty God, the Holy Spirit, Who is also called the Holy Ghost or Spirit of the Living God. The worshiping of the Holy Spirit is tremendously lacking in not only our personal lives, but in churches around the world as well. Let's explore Who the Holy Spirit really is.

1. First, the Holy Spirit is not an "IT" as many people believe He is.
2. Secondly, He is not any less than the God Head even though He is the 3rd Person of the God-Head.
3. Thirdly, He is the 3rd Person of the God-Head.
4. Fourthly, He is the most powerful person in the universe.
5. Fifthly, He is Almighty God down here on earth.
6. Sixthly, He deserves as much praise and worshiping as Almighty God, the Father, and Almighty God, the Son, Jesus Christ.
7. Seventhly, He is Almighty God, the Holy Spirit.

Almighty God, the Father, Almighty God, The Son, Jesus Christ, and Almighty God, the Holy Spirit are three (3) heads in one, three (3) partitions, or triune heads. They are all our creators as depicted in the following scripture. Almighty God said, "Let us ......", meaning let Myself, Jesus Christ, and the Holy Spirit create man in our own image and in our own likeness. All three of these Heads created man, not just Almighty God. Each one had a task to do in creating man in their own images and likenesses.

Creators, Including The Holy Spirit

The Holy Spirit moved upon the face of the waters, formed the earth and haevens and brought light to it, then Almighty God divided the light from the darkness. The light He called day and the darkness, He called night. Mainly speaking, when Almighty God spoke something into being, Jesus Christ, who is the administrator, hands it off to the Holy Spirit, then Holy Spirit will manifest or brings those things in to being or He actually make things happen.

Genesis 1 (KJV)

1. In the beginning God created the heaven and the earth.
2. And the earth was without form, and void; and darkness was upon the face of the deep. And the Spirit of God moved upon the face of the waters.
3. And God said, Let there be light: and there was light.

Genesis 1 (KJV)

26. And God said, Let us make man in our image, after our likeness: and let them have dominion over the fish of the sea, and over the fowl of the air, and over the cattle, and over all the earth, and over every creeping thing that creepeth upon the earth.

1 John 5 (KJV)

7. For there are three that bear record in heaven, the Father, the Word, and the Holy Ghost: and these three are one.

8. And there are three that bear witness in earth, the spirit, and the water, and the blood: and these three agree in one.

Jesus Christ's Human Birth Manifested By The Holy Spirit

The Holy Ghost (Holy Spirit) manifested the birth of Almighty God's Son, Jesus Christ as a human being, a Jew/Hebrew.

Matthew 1 (KJV)

18. Now the birth of Jesus Christ was on this wise: When as his mother Mary was espoused to Joseph, before they came together, she was found with child of the Holy Ghost.
20. But while he thought on these things, behold, the angel of the Lord appeared unto him in a dream, saying, Joseph, thou son of David, fear not to take unto thee Mary thy wife: for that which is conceived in her is of the Holy Ghost.

Salvation, Gift Of The Holy Ghost - First (1st) Level Of Christianity

Acts 2 (KJV)

38. Then Peter said unto them, Repent, and be baptized every one of you in the name of Jesus Christ for the remission of sins, and ye shall receive the gift of the Holy Ghost.
39. For the promise is unto you, and to your children, and to all that are afar off, even as many as the Lord our God shall call.

Salvation Is Only Part Of Christianity

Acts 8 (KJV)

14. Now when the apostles which were at Jerusalem heard that

Samaria had received the word of God, they sent unto them Peter and John:

Who, when they were come down, prayed for them, that they might receive the Holy Ghost:

16. (For as yet he was fallen upon none of them: only they were baptized in the name of the Lord Jesus.)
17. Then laid they their hands on them, and they received the Holy Ghost.

Baptism In The Holy Ghost - Second Level Of Christianity After Salvation

Matthew 3 (KJV)

11. I indeed baptize you with water unto repentance: but he that cometh after me is mightier than I, whose shoes I am not worthy to bear: he shall baptize you with the Holy Ghost, and with fire:

Acts 11 (KJV)

16. Then remembered I the word of the Lord, how that he said, John indeed baptized with water; but ye shall be baptized with the Holy Ghost.

Baptism In The Holy Ghost Brings On A New Language

Acts 2 (KJV)

1. And when the day of Pentecost was fully come, they were all with one accord in one place.
2. And suddenly there came a sound from heaven as of a rushing mighty wind, and it filled all the house where they

were sitting.

3. And there appeared unto them cloven tongues like as of fire, and it sat upon each of them.
4. And they were all filled with the Holy Ghost, and began to speak with other tongues, as the Spirit gave them utterance.

Acts 19 (KJV)

1. And it came to pass, that, while Apollos was at Corinth, Paul having passed through the upper coasts came to Ephesus: and finding certain disciples,
2. He said unto them, Have ye received the Holy Ghost since ye believed? And they said unto him, We have not so much as heard whether there be any Holy Ghost.
3. And he said unto them, Unto what then were ye baptized? And they said, Unto John's baptism.
4. Then said Paul, John verily baptized with the baptism of repentance, saying unto the people, that they should believe on him which should come after him, that is, on Christ Jesus.
5. When they heard this, they were baptized in the name of the Lord Jesus.
6. And when Paul had laid his hands upon them, the Holy Ghost came on them; and they spake with tongues, and prophesied.
7. And all the men were about twelve.

Blashemy Against The Holy Ghost Cannot Be Forgiven

Matthew 12 (KJV)

31. Wherefore I say unto you, All manner of sin and blasphemy shall be forgiven unto men: but the blasphemy against the Holy Ghost shall not be forgiven unto men.
32. And whosoever speaketh a word against the Son of man,

it shall be forgiven him: but whosoever speaketh against the Holy Ghost, it shall not be forgiven him, neither in this world, neither in the world to come.

There is a misconception in the Christian churches, especially, in the Apostolic and some Pentecostal churches that when they do water baptisms of their members, that they must use the phrase, "in Jesus name", thereby omitting the names of Almighty God, the Father, and Almighty God, the Holy Spirit, the Great manifester, Himself.

Matthew 28 (KJV)

19. Go ye therefore, and teach all nations, baptizing them in the name of the Father, and of the Son, and of the Holy Ghost:

Holy Ghost - Devine Teacher To Christians

John 14 (KJV)

26. But the Comforter, which is the Holy Ghost, whom the Father will send in my name, he shall teach you all things, and bring all things to your remembrance, whatsoever I have said unto you.

1 Corinthians 2 (KJV)

13. Which things also we speak, not in the words which man's wisdom teacheth, but which the Holy Ghost teacheth; comparing spiritual things with spiritual.
14. But the natural man receiveth not the things of the Spirit of God: for they are foolishness unto him: neither can he know them, because they are spiritually discerned.
15. But he that is spiritual judgeth all things, yet he himself is judged of no man.

16. For who hath known the mind of the Lord, that he may instruct him? But we have the mind of Christ.

Spiritual Gifts Given By The Holy Ghost

1 Corinthians 12 (KJV)

1. Now concerning spiritual gifts, brethren, I would not have you ignorant.
2. Ye know that ye were Gentiles, carried away unto these dumb idols, even as ye were led.
3. Wherefore I give you to understand, that no man speaking by the Spirit of God calleth Jesus accursed: and that no man can say that Jesus is the Lord, but by the Holy Ghost.
4. Now there are diversities of gifts, but the same Spirit.
5. And there are differences of administrations, but the same Lord.
6. And there are diversities of operations, but it is the same God which worketh all in all.
7. But the manifestation of the Spirit is given to every man to profit withal.
8. For to one is given by the Spirit the word of wisdom; to another the word of knowledge by the same Spirit;
9. To another faith by the same Spirit; to another the gifts of healing by the same Spirit;
10. To another the working of miracles; to another prophecy; to another discerning of spirits; to another divers kinds of tongues; to another the interpretation of tongues:
11. But all these worketh that one and the selfsame Spirit, dividing to every man severally as he will.
12. For as the body is one, and hath many members, and all the members of that one body, being many, are one body: so also is Christ.
13. For by one Spirit are we all baptized into one body, whether

we be Jews or Gentiles, whether we be bond or free; and have been all made to drink into one Spirit.

14. For the body is not one member, but many.
15. If the foot shall say, Because I am not the hand, I am not of the body; is it therefore not of the body?
16. And if the ear shall say, Because I am not the eye, I am not of the body; is it therefore not of the body?
17. If the whole body were an eye, where were the hearing? If the whole were hearing, where were the smelling?
18. But now hath God set the members every one of them in the body, as it hath pleased him.
19. And if they were all one member, where were the body?
20. But now are they many members, yet but one body.
21. And the eye cannot say unto the hand, I have no need of thee: nor again the head to the feet, I have no need of you.
22. Nay, much more those members of the body, which seem to be more feeble, are necessary:
23. And those members of the body, which we think to be less honourable, upon these we bestow more abundant honour; and our uncomely parts have more abundant comeliness.
24. For our comely parts have no need: but God hath tempered the body together, having given more abundant honour to that part which lacked:
25. That there should be no schism in the body; but that the members should have the same care one for another.
26. And whether one member suffer, all the members suffer with it; or one member be honoured, all the members rejoice with it.
27. Now ye are the body of Christ, and members in particular.
28. And God hath set some in the church, first apostles, secondarily prophets, thirdly teachers, after that miracles, then gifts of healings, helps, governments, diversities of tongues.
29. Are all apostles? are all prophets? are all teachers? are all workers of miracles? 30. Have all the gifts of healing? do all

speak with tongues? do all interpret?

31. But covet earnestly the best gifts: and yet shew I unto you a more excellent way.

Power Given By The Holy Ghost - Third (3rd) Level Of Christianity After Salvation

Acts 1 (KJV)

8. But ye shall receive power, after that the Holy Ghost is come upon you: and ye shall be witnesses unto me both in Jerusalem, and in all Judaea, and in Samaria, and unto the uttermost part of the earth.

Holy Ghost Brings Righteousness, Peace, Joy, And Hope

Romans 14 (KJV)

17. For the kingdom of God is not meat and drink; but righteousness, and peace, and joy in the Holy Ghost.
18. For he that in these things serveth Christ is acceptable to God, and approved of men.

Romans 15 (KJV)

13. Now the God of hope fill you with all joy and peace in believing, that ye may abound in hope, through the power of the Holy Ghost.

Holy Ghost's Temples - Christian Bodies

1 Corinthians 6 (KJV)

19. What? know ye not that your body is the temple of the Holy Ghost which is in you, which ye have of God, and ye are not your own?

20. For ye are bought with a price: therefore glorify God in your body, and in your spirit, which are God's.

Holy Ghost - Christian's Battle Axe (Not By Might And Not By Power)

Zechariah 4 (KJV)

1 And the angel that talked with me came again, and waked me, as a man that is wakened out of his sleep.
2. And said unto me, What seest thou? And I said, I have looked, And behold a candlestick all of gold, with a bowl upon the top of it, and his seven lamps thereon, and seven pipes to the seven lamps, which are upon the top thereof:
3. And two olive trees by it, one upon the right side of the bowl, and the other upon the left side thereof.
4. So I answered and spake to the angel that talked with me, saying, What are these, my lord?
5. Then the angel that talked with me answered and said unto me, Knowest thou not what these be? And I said, No, my lord.
6. Then he answered and spake unto me, saying, This is the word of the Lord unto Zerubbabel, saying, Not by might, nor by power, but by my spirit, saith the Lord of hosts.
7. Who art thou, O great mountain? before Zerubbabel thou shalt become a plain: and he shall bring forth the headstone thereof with shoutings, crying, Grace, grace unto it.
8. Moreover the word of the Lord came unto me, saying,
9. The hands of Zerubbabel have laid the foundation of this house; his hands shall also finish it; and thou shalt know that the Lord of hosts hath sent me unto you.
10. For who hath despised the day of small things? for they shall rejoice, and shall see the plummet in the hand of Zerubbabel with those seven; they are the eyes of the Lord, which run to and fro through the whole earth.

11. Then answered I, and said unto him, What are these two olive trees upon the right side of the candlestick and upon the left side thereof?
12. And I answered again, and said unto him, What be these two olive branches which through the two golden pipes empty the golden oil out of themselves?
13. And he answered me and said, Knowest thou not what these be? And I said, No, my lord.
14. Then said he, These are the two anointed ones, that stand by the Lord of the whole earth.

CHAPTER 44

Churches - Holy Spirit - Praise and Worship Song to Him

Holy Spirit, I praise You! Holy Spirit, I praise You! Holy Spirit, I praise You! I praise You, Holy Spirit! I praise You, Holy Spirit! I praise You, Holy Spirit!

Holy Spirit, I praise Your Holy Name! Holy Spirit, I praise Your Holy Name! Holy Spirit, I Praise Your Holy Name! I praise Your Holy Name, Holy Spirit! I praise Your Holy Name, Holy Spirit! I praise Your Holy Name, Holy Spirit!

Holy Spirit, I adore You! Holy Spirit, I adore You! Holy Spirit, I adore You! I adore You, Holy Spirit! I adore You, Holy Spirit! I adore You, Holy Spirit!

Holy Spirit, I love You! Holy Spirit, I love You! Holy Spirit, I love You! I love You, Holy Spirit! I love You, Holy Spirit! I love You, Holy Spirit!

Holy Spirit, Thank You,
For anointing me!
Thank You,
For being my battle axe!
Thank You,
For giving me Almighty God's Blessings!
Thank You,

For Your fellowship with me!
Thank you,
For healing my body!
Thank You,
For being my power!
Thank you,
For giving me Your Spiritual Gifts!
Praise Almighty God,
Jesus Christ, the Son, and The Holy Spirit, forever! Amen, Amen, and Amen!

CHAPTER **45**

Churches - Pastors and Preachers Under Sex Curses

It is unfortunate that not only are pastors guilty of fornication, adultery, incest and other sex acts outside of marriage, but many ministers in general are guilty as well. Many pastors have lost their positions because they were caught up in illegal and immoral sex acts. Many television evangelist and denominational heads have fallen into the traps of these sex curses including adultery, fornication, homosexuality and other immoral sex acts.

God Admonishes Us Not To Commit Adultery

Exodus 20 (KJV)

14. Thou shalt not commit adultery.
17. Thou shalt not covet thy neighbour's house, thou shalt not covet thy neighbour's wife, nor his manservant, nor his maidservant, nor his ox, nor his ass, nor any thing that is thy neighbour's.

God's Anger With The Jews' Acts of Fornication

Ezekiel 16 (KJV)

26. Thou hast also committed fornication with the Egyptians

thy neighbours, great of flesh; and hast increased thy whoredoms, to provoke me to anger.

Married Couples (Male and Female) - No Sex Outside Of Your Marriage

Exodus 20 (KJV)

14. Thou shalt not commit adultery.

Matthew 15 (KJV)

19. For out of the heart proceed evil thoughts, murders, adulteries, fornications, thefts, false witness, blasphemies:

Admonished To Abstain From Fornication

Acts 15 (KJV)

20. But that we write unto them, that they abstain from pollutions of idols, and from fornication, and from things strangled, and from blood.
29. That ye abstain from meats offered to idols, and from blood, and from things strangled, and from fornication: from which if ye keep yourselves, ye shall do well. Fare ye well.

Acts 21 (KJV)

25. As touching the Gentiles which believe, we have written and concluded that they observe no such thing, save only that they keep themselves from things offered to idols, and from blood, and from strangled, and from fornication.

Romans 1 (KJV)

29. Being filled with all unrighteousness, fornication, wickedness, covetousness, maliciousness; full of envy, murder, debate, deceit, malignity; whisperers,
30. Backbiters, haters of God, despiteful, proud, boasters, inventors of evil things, disobedient to parents,
31. Without understanding, covenantbreakers, without natural affection, implacable, unmerciful:

1 Corinthians 5 (KJV)

1. It is reported commonly that there is fornication among you, and such fornication as is not so much as named among the Gentiles, that one should have his father's wife.
9. I wrote unto you in an epistle not to company with fornicators:
10. Yet not altogether with the fornicators of this world, or with the covetous, or extortioners, or with idolaters; for then must ye needs go out of the world.
11. But now I have written unto you not to keep company, if any man that is called a brother be a fornicator, or covetous, or an idolater, or a railer, or a drunkard, or an extortioner; with such an one no not to eat.

Neither Adulterers, Nor Fornicators Will Go To Heaven

1 Corinthians 6 (KJV)

9. Know ye not that the unrighteous shall not inherit the kingdom of God? Be not deceived: neither fornicators, nor idolaters, nor adulterers, nor effeminate, nor abusers of themselves with mankind,
10. Nor thieves, nor covetous, nor drunkards, nor revilers, nor extortioners, shall inherit the kingdom of God.

CHAPTER 46

Churches - Pastors Are Babes in Christ

Most of these preachers can be characterized as dairy farmers because they are only providing milk or most of the time just empty milk bottles or pacifiers to their churches. They were never weaned from milk to meat in God's Holy Word. That is, they are still babes in Christ and need to be taught in God's word themselves.

1 Cor 3:1-3 (KJV) And I, brethren, could not speak unto you as unto spiritual, but as unto carnal, even as unto babes in Christ.

2. I have fed you with milk, and not with meat: for hitherto ye were not able to bear it, neither yet now are ye able.
3. For ye are yet carnal: for whereas there is among you envying, and strife, and divisions, are ye not carnal, and walk as men?

Heb 5:13 (KJV) "For every one that useth milk is unskilful in the word of righteousness: for he is a babe."

Heb 5:14 (KJV) "But strong meat belongeth to them that are of full age, even those who by reason of use have their senses exercised to discern both good and evil."

Their wisdom, knowledge and their understanding of God's word is quite lacking or non existent. Once a person has obtained the knowledge, wisdom and understanding in God's Word, he or she has been weaned or graduated from milk to what is called the meat in God's Word.

CHAPTER **47**

Churches - Pastors Not Called by Almighty God

There are false preachers and prophets in the churches today. Speaking from personal experiences, many of them are in the Baptist churches and they are full of them. Many are filling those position through their being called by the church body and not by God, Almighty. Many of these false preachers/prophets have taken on those position to fullfil their desires for careers, lucrative fringe benefits, retirement and/or other personal means which has nothing to do with the feeding of God's flock.

Just recently we attended a summer camp meetings where one of the speakers told us that a so-called pastor of a Presbyterian chuch shared with him that he had not accepted Jesus Christ as his personal Savior. He decided to go before his congregation where he told them that he had been pastoring for the past 25 years and that he had not accepted the Lord, Jesus Christ as his personal Savior. Well, after this false pastor finished his speech, approximately 90% of the congregation stood up and said that they weren't save either.

You see, the majority of the congregation can only reach the highest level of their leader. If he or she is highly anointed, then most of that congregation will be highly anointed as well. On the other hand if those so-called pastors aren't saved, then most of the congregation will remain unsaved as well. They are essentially false prophets. The blind leading the blind.

It is no telling how many souls around the world were lost and where precious souls are now being lost because of these false preachers, pastors, prophets and so-called ministers of God, Almighty. Taking on a position of a minister falsely representing God, Almighty is a very serious undertaking which puts these false representative's souls at serious risks and with the doors of their souls wide open to the wrath of God as well.

Mark 16:17 (KJV) "And these signs shall follow them that believe; In my name shall they cast out devils; they shall speak with new tongues;"

Mark 16:20 (KJV) "And they went forth, and preached every where, the Lord working with them, and confirming the word with signs following. Amen."

Signs. Greek definition. 4592. semeion, say-mi'-on; neut. of a presumed der. of the base of G4591; an indication, espec. cer. or supernat.:--miracle, sign, token, wonder.

2 Tim 3:5 (KJV) "Having a form of godliness, but denying the power thereof: **from such turn away**."

Many churches call or hire persons as their pastors, but often time, God never actually called those particular persons into the ministry as pastors. Simply put, they were the churches' choices, but not God's choices. Not all proclaiming or professing ministers are given a second calling to pastor. Some minister in the pulpits have received neither of the calls or anointings from God. Some are serving because of their desire to fulfill their desire for careers or easy vocations, but not necessary to do God's will. Additionally, churches sought those persons as their choices, mostly because those hooping and hollering preachers excited the emotions of them and their congregational audiences.

Rom 10:14 (KJV) "How then shall they call on him in whom they have not believed? and how shall they believe in him of whom they have not heard? and how shall they hear without a preacher?"

Rom 10:15 (KJV) "And how shall they preach, except they be sent? as it is written, How beautiful are the feet of them that preach the gospel of peace, and bring glad tidings of good things!"

One case in point is a story that was shared with me (Curtis) by a senior minister in our congregation. He told me about a pastor who had served in a local congregation for forty (40) years. He had been in the ministry for about fifty-five (55) years. The shocking fact is this pastor was never detected as not being saved. God said in Marks book of the bible that if it were possible, these false people shall deceive the very elect which are Christians. These people who made up that particular congregation were probably not Christians at all. Normally the spirituality of the congregation is no higher than that of their pastor. If there were Christians among that congregation, then somebody should have detected this demon a long time ago, but nobody did.

Mat 24:24 (KJV) "For there shall arise false Christs, and false prophets, and shall show great signs and wonders; insomuch that, if it were possible, they shall deceive the very elect."

This false pastor came forward on his own. He was essentially a false preacher and a false pastor whose spirits were both from out of hell and from Satan. I wonder how many lives were lost because of this foolishness? However, fortunately he came forward and repented to his congregation that he had never accepted the Lord, Jesus Christ as his personal Savior. He really told the church that he was never a saved person and that he was coming forward to accept Jesus Christ as his personal Savior.

I guess this particular person did all of the right things which satisfied the congregation and he said predominately all of the right words to the ears of that particular ignorant and spiritually unequipped congregation. Baptist churches are notorious for their unbelief, lack of knowledge, lack of wisdom, lack of understanding, and lack of spiritual discernment of God's Holy Word. It is sadly unfortunate that this lackadaisical attitude is still prevalent in many of our churches this very day.

Jer 3:15 (KJV) "And I will give you pastors according to mine heart, which shall feed you with knowledge and understanding."

Eph 4:11 (KJV) "And he gave some, apostles; and some, prophets; and some, evangelists; and some, pastors and teachers;"

Notice above: "PASTORS and TEACHERS". God equips those persons to be not only Shepards (leaders) for His flocks, but as equipped Teachers as well.

We often watch and cringe with sadness, unbelief, pity and dismay as some of these so called pastors attempt to unskillfully teach God's Word to their congregations. The congregation would ask questions which go unanswered or explained away as something else totally off the subject.

Eph 4:12 (KJV) "For the perfecting of the saints, for the work of the ministry, for the edifying of the body of Christ:"

I recently heard a so called pastor say, "I don't like preaching, but I like administrating". This really doesn't sound like a person called by God, Almighty to preach His work, does it?

Jer 10:21 (KJV) "For the pastors are become brutish, and have not sought the LORD: therefore they shall not prosper, and all their flocks shall be scattered."

CHAPTER **48**

Churches, Traditional Doctrine, Practices and Principles Curses

Many of these so called pastors are comfortably bent on traditional church practices and principles, but they are not rooted and grounded on the biblical principals of God's Word, His Bible. Most Baptist churches are operated on such books as the Hiscox Manuals, Pendleton Manuals and probably other secular manuals. Most are not based on sound biblical principals. You can even see with your physical eye that there are revolving doors to many of the churches. Many people join the churches, attend a few worship services, but drop out of sight or start church hopping in their attempts to satisfy their hunger for God's word.

Rom 10:14 (KJV) "How then shall they call on him in whom they have not believed? and how shall they believe in him of whom they have not heard? and how shall they hear without a preacher?"

Rom 10:15 (KJV) "And how shall they preach, except they be sent? as it is written, How beautiful are the feet of them that preach the gospel of peace, and bring glad tidings of good things!"

Some of these pastors have no desire to dig in and get their hands and their feet deep into God's Holy Word. Furthermore, they don't have the Spiritual discernment to understand what they are studying. When they can arouse the emotions of the congregation with a lot of hooping and hollering with no substance of meat within their words, they feel they are successful in proclaiming God's Word. Some will conclude their empty sermons with a proclamation, "The word of Lord, Amen?". Unfortunately, the congregation will respond with "Amen!" and then with hands clapping in applauding this ignorant speaker.

1 Tim 4:16 (KJV) "Take heed unto thyself, and unto the doctrine; continue in them: for in doing this thou shalt both save thyself, and them that hear thee."

1 Tim 6:3-5 (KJV) If any man teach otherwise, and consent not to wholesome words, even the words of our Lord Jesus Christ, and to the doctrine which is according to godliness; {4} He is proud, knowing nothing, but doting about questions and strifes of words, whereof cometh envy, strife, railings, evil surmisings, {5} Perverse disputings of men of corrupt minds, and destitute of the truth, supposing that gain is godliness: from such withdraw thyself.

Church traditions are clouds of plagues which have rained down curses over many of our churches. This has really stagnated or halted the Christian growth of their members where they have not advanced enough in their Christian walk to be weaned from milk to meat. Many of the so-called pastors are not at the level where they have been weaned from milk either.

Church traditions have ruled from generations to generations and is quite alive and well among our present day churches.

Isa 28:9 (KJV) "Whom shall he teach knowledge? and whom shall he make to understand doctrine? them that are weaned from the milk, and drawn from the breasts."

Isa 28:10 (KJV) "For precept must be upon precept, precept upon precept; line upon line, line upon line; here a little, and there a little:"

CHAPTER 49

Churches Cursed with Ignorance and Unbelief

Christians Don't Fully Represent Christ

Christians don't fully represent Christ's likeness in their daily walk with Him. Having the Holy Spirit within us is a great start towards the likeness of our Savior, Jesus Christ. But, there is more to it than just being filled with God's Holy Spirit. Before carpenters begin to build something, they must equip themselves with certain equipment, tools and supplies to effectively and efficiently perform their required tasks. Christians are required to have the necessary equipment, tools and supplies to do God's will also. To begin with their tasks, they must be like the Master Carpenter, Jesus Christ. Jesus had not only the anointing of the **Holy Spirit**, but He had the **Spirit of Wisdom**, the **Spirit of Understanding**, the **Spirit of Knowledge**, the **Spirit of Might**, the **Spirit of the Fear of God**, and the **Spirit of Counsel**.

Rev 1:4 (KJV) "John to the seven churches which are in Asia: Grace be unto you, and peace, from him which is, and which was, and which is to come; and from the seven Spirits which are before his throne;"

Acts 2:38 (KJV) "Then Peter said unto them, Repent, and be baptized every one of you in the name of Jesus Christ for the remission of sins, and ye shall receive the gift of the Holy Ghost."

HOLY - Greek 40. hagios, hag'-ee-os; from hagos (an awful thing) [comp. G53, H2282]; sacred (phys. pure, mor. blameless or religious, cer. consecrated):--(most) holy (one, thing), saint.

GHOST - 4151. pneuma, pnyoo'-mah; from G4154; a current of air, i.e. breath (blast) or a breeze; by anal. or fig. a spirit, i.e. (human) the rational soul, (by impl.) vital principle, mental disposition, etc., or (superhuman) an angel, daemon, or (divine) God, Christ's spirit, the Holy Spirit:--ghost, life, spirit (-ual, -ually), mind. Comp. 5590.

Isa 11:2 (KJV) "And the spirit of the LORD shall rest upon him, the spirit of wisdom and understanding, the spirit of counsel and might, the spirit of knowledge and of the fear of the LORD;"

WISDOM - Hebrew 2451. chokmah, khok-maw'; from H2449; wisdom (in a good sense):--skillful, wisdom, wisely, wit.

Prov 4:7-13 (KJV) Wisdom is the principal thing; therefore get wisdom: and with all thy getting get understanding. {8} Exalt her, and she shall promote thee: she shall bring thee to honour, when thou dost embrace her.

9. She shall give to thine head an ornament of grace: a crown of glory shall she deliver to thee.
10. Hear, O my son, and receive my sayings; and the years of thy life shall be many.
11. I have taught thee in the way of wisdom; I have led thee in right paths.
12. When thou goest, thy steps shall not be straitened; and when thou runnest, thou shalt not stumble.
13. Take fast hold of instruction; let her not go: keep her; for she is thy life.

UNDERSTANDING - Hebrew 998. biynah, bee-naw'; from H995;

understanding:--knowledge, meaning, X perfectly, understanding, wisdom.

COUNSEL - Hebrew - 6098. 'etsah, ay-tsaw'; from H3289; advice; by impl. plan; also prudence:--advice, advisement, counsel ([-lor]), purpose.

Prov 11:14 (KJV) "Where no counsel is, the people fall: but in the multitude of counsellors there is safety."

MIGHT - Hebrew 1369. gebuwrah, gheb-oo-raw'; fem. pass. part. from the same as H1368; force (lit. or fig.); by impl. valor, victory:--force, mastery, might, mighty (act, power), power, strength.

KNOWLEDGE - Hebrew 1847. da'ath, dah'-ath; from H3045; knowledge:--cunning, [ig-] norantly, know(-ledge), [un-] awares (wittingly).

FEAR - Hebrew 3374. yir'ah, yir-aw'; fem. of H3373; fear (also used as infin.); mor. reverence:-- X dreadful, X exceedingly, fear (-fulness).

CHAPTER **50**

Churches, Catholic Faith - Virgin Mary Neither Hears, Nor Answers Any Prayers

First of all the Virgin Mary was chosen to birth His Son, Jesus Christ. Mary was a chosen human who did not possess any special spirits as an intercessor, neither for her own family, nor for anybody else in this world or the world to come. Almighty God's Son, Jesus is not only our intercessor, but his earthy mother, Mary, as well. We are not to attempt to pray to Mary for anything. She neither sits on the right hand of Almighty God, nor does she sit on his left. Mary is not within the links of prayer chain. Our prayer includes Almighty God, The Father, Almighty God, The Son, and Almighty God, The Holy Spirit. The God Head only includes a Triune Spirit, a three (3) partition spirit, or three (3) heads in one, not four (4) heads in one.

Isaiah 53 (KJV)

> 12. Therefore will I divide him a portion with the great, and he shall divide the spoil with the strong; because he hath poured out his soul unto death: and he was numbered with the transgressors; and he bare the sin of many, and made intercession for the transgressors.

The God Head works in concert with each other. When a Christian attempts to pray, the Holy Spirit takes that prayer and intercedes with groaning that we can't utter, then our Savior, Jesus Christ receives those groans with interpretations and intercedes them on our behalf to the Father, Almighty God.

Romans 8 (KJV)

26. Likewise the Spirit also helpeth our infirmities: for we know not what we should pray for as we ought: but the Spirit itself maketh intercession for us with groanings which cannot be uttered.

There was a lady speaking on the News Network of CNN after she was rescued from being a prisoner in Bogota Columbia. I heard her say that she constantly prayed to the Virgin Mary for her release. Well, sister, unfortunately, your prayers weren't heard by you, neither were your prayers interceded by her. You were without a doubt, praying to the wrong person. Fortunately, somebody else's prayers got through and you have been freed by the grace of Almighty God and your Savior, Jesus Christ, your real Intercessor.

Mark 16 (KJV)

19. So then after the Lord had spoken unto them, he was received up into heaven, and sat on the right hand of God.

There is no mentioning of Mary sitting near or on the throne of Almighty God or with Jesus Christ, our Savior. Jesus is also Mary's Savior as well. She was a chosen vessel to give birth to our Divine Savior, Jesus Christ. She was not given any special anointings or authority after that.

CHAPTER 51

Churches, Christians - Allah (Muslims) Is Not Almighty God

Who the hell is Allah? We can't merely say, "Who the heaven is Allah?"

History tells us that the so-called prophet Muhammad concocted the name, "ALLAH" himself. This was his fictitious god. Among other things, he was a terrorist and a fornicator as he loved many women.

First, we know that Allah is not the God that we as Christians serve. We know that our God is three heads in one. He is not merely our Supreme being, but three spiritual persons, all wrapped-up in one glorious spiritual body.

Secondly, He can't be in Heaven since our God, Almighty is the only Supreme being in Heaven. Our God said that He will not share His Glory with nobody, nor will He give His praises to any graven images.

Isaiah 42 (KJV)

8. I am the Lord: that is my name: and my glory will I not give to another, neither my praise to graven images.

He also said that He is a jealous God.

Exodus 20 (KJV)

2. I am the Lord thy God, which have brought thee out of the land of Egypt, out of the house of bondage.
3. Thou shalt have no other gods before me.
4. Thou shalt not make unto thee any graven image, or any likeness of any thing that is in heaven above, or that is in the earth beneath, or that is in the water under the earth.
5. Thou shalt not bow down thyself to them, nor serve them: for I the Lord thy God am a jealous God, visiting the iniquity of the fathers upon the children unto the third and fourth generation of them that hate me;

Finally, those who believe in Allah also believe that the so-called Prophet Mohammed ascended into Heaven from Mecca (Saudi Arabia). This can't be true because Mohammed along with his many believers did not believe that Jesus Christ was the Son of God, neither did they believe that Jesus died for all of our sins. So, in essence, they did not believe in God the Father, God the Son, and God the Holy Spirit. Our God is a triune person, a three partition person. Since we are made in His image, we humans are triune persons and three partition persons as well. That is, we have a body, a soul and a spirit. Jesus Christ fills the spirit realm of our bodies. Ones who aren't saved through the blood of Jesus Christ, their spirits are filled by Satan.

Here is a thought, maybe Mohammed descended into hell and is sitting on the right side of Satan waiting to return to earth as the Anti-Christ when the time is right. Everyone is now wondering who that person maybe. So, Mohammed could that person who will make an appearance on the scene to earth, again.

Since Mohammed and his more than 1.6 billion followers don't accept Jesus as their personal Savior, they are lost in their sins. If they don't accept Jesus Christ as their personal savior or ask Jesus to come into their hearts, they are subject to eternal damnation with their final resting place in hell.

Our Great Master, Jesus Christ said that no one can come to His Father, God, Almighty without coming to Him first.

John 14 (KJV)

6. Jesus saith unto him, I am the way, the truth, and the life: no man cometh unto the Father, but by me.
7. If ye had known me, ye should have known my Father also: and from henceforth ye know him, and have seen him.

CHAPTER 52

Circumstances Beyond Our Control

Now, there are times when we think that we are prayed up, living a fairly righteous life, attend church regularly, giving a fair amount of donations or even committed to tithing in the church, but things happen out of our control. There could be a curse lurking around in our lives in which we aren't aware of. This is when we need to ask God's Holy Spirit to reveal to us this or those curse so they we may be cleansed of them. Ask the Holy Spirit to reveal to you each evil deed that you have done from your birth to the present. One biblical account that Satan has to ask God's permission to render troubles, conflicts, miseries and such on Christians is with Job, an uprighteous and perfect man of God. Satan went to God not only once, but at least twice to destroy Job as you will find in the following scriptures.

Satan's 1st Attempt To Destroy Job

Job 1:6 (KJV) "Now there was a day when the sons of God came to present themselves before the LORD, and Satan came also among them."

Job 1:7 (KJV) "And the LORD said unto Satan, Whence comest thou? Then Satan answered the LORD, and said, From going to and fro in the earth, and from walking up and down in it."

Job 1:8 (KJV) "And the LORD said unto Satan, Hast thou considered my servant Job, that there is none like him in the earth, a perfect and an upright man, one that feareth God, and escheweth evil?"

Job 1:9 (KJV) "Then Satan answered the LORD, and said, Doth Job fear God for nought?"

Job 1:10 (KJV) "Hast not thou made an hedge about him, and about his house, and about all that he hath on every side? thou hast blessed the work of his hands, and his substance is increased in the land."

Job 1:12 (KJV) "And the LORD said unto Satan, Behold, all that he hath is in thy power; only upon himself put not forth thine hand. So Satan went forth from the presence of the LORD."

Job 1:13 (KJV) "And there was a day when his sons and his daughters were eating and drinking wine in their eldest brother's house:"

Job 1:14 (KJV) "And there came a messenger unto Job, and said, The oxen were plowing, and the asses feeding beside them:" Job 1:15 (KJV) "And the Sabeans fell upon them, and took them away; yea, they have slain the servants with the edge of the sword; and I only am escaped alone to tell thee."

Job 1:16 (KJV) "While he was yet speaking, there came also another, and said, The fire of God is fallen from heaven, and hath burned up the sheep, and the servants, and consumed them; and I only am escaped alone to tell thee." Job 1:17 (KJV) "While he was yet speaking, there came also another,

Job 1:17 (KJV) "While he was yet speaking, there came also another, and said, The Chaldeans made out three bands, and fell upon the camels, and have carried them away, yea, and slain the servants with the edge of the sword; and I only am escaped alone to tell thee."

Job 1:18 (KJV) "While he was yet speaking, there came also another, and said, Thy sons and thy daughters were eating and drinking wine in their eldest brother's house:"

Job 1:19 (KJV) "And, behold, there came a great wind from the wilderness, and smote the four corners of the house, and it fell upon the young men, and they are dead; and I only am escaped alone to tell thee."

Satan's 2nd Attempt To Destroy Job

Job 2:1-7 (KJV) Again there was a day when the sons of God came to present themselves before the LORD, and Satan came also among them to present himself before the LORD.

2. And the LORD said unto Satan, From whence comest thou? And Satan answered the LORD, and said, From going to and fro in the earth, and from walking up and down in it.
3. And the LORD said unto Satan, Hast thou considered my servant Job, that there is none like him in the earth, a perfect and an upright man, one that feareth God, and escheweth evil? and still he holdeth fast his integrity, although thou movedst me against him, to **destroy him without cause**.
4. And Satan answered the LORD, and said, Skin for skin, yea, all that a man hath will he give for his life.
5. But put forth thine hand now, and touch his bone and his flesh, and he will curse thee to thy face.
6. And the LORD said unto Satan, Behold, he is in thine hand; but save his life.
7. So went Satan forth from the presence of the LORD, and smote Job with sore boils from the sole of his foot unto his crown.

John 10:10 (KJV) "The thief cometh not, but for to steal, and to kill, and to destroy: I am come that they might have life, and that they might have it more abundantly."

1 Pet 5:8-9 (KJV) Be sober, be vigilant; because your adversary the devil, as a roaring lion, walketh about, seeking whom he may devour: {9} Whom resist stedfast in the faith, knowing that the same afflictions are accomplished in your brethren that are in the world.

James 4:7 (KJV) "Submit yourselves therefore to God. Resist the devil, and he will flee from you."

Luke 10:19 (KJV) "Behold, I give unto you power to tread on serpents and scorpions, and over all the power of the enemy: and nothing shall by any means hurt you."

CHAPTER 53

Colony Collapse Disorder of Honey Bees - Lost Pollination to Crops

There is a serious problem with our honey bee colonies for not only in America, but around the world. Honey bees are disappearing at an alarming rate. Why should we be concerned, you ask? Well for starters the fruits and vegetables that we love to eat will not grow without the much needed pollination that the honey bees provide. Not only that, the honey bees won't be around to create honey combs and fill them with that sweet liquid that we call honey which is used to sweeten our coffees, our teas, our cakes, our pies and used in many recipes and mixtures.

We can call this particular phenomenon one of the sinful curses of plagues that we allowed to creep into our daily lives because of blatant sins.

Note: Please read Deut. Chapter 28 In Your Bible.

Colony Collapse Disorder

From Wikipedia, the free encyclopedia Jump to: navigation, search Semi-protected

Colony Collapse Disorder (or CCD) is a poorly understood phenomenon in which worker bees from a beehive or Western honey bee colony abruptly disappear. While such disappearances have occurred throughout the history of apiculture, the term 'Colony Collapse Disorder' was first applied to a drastic rise in the number of disappearances of Western honey bee colonies in North America in late 2006.[1]

European beekeepers observed a similar phenomenon in Belgium, France, the Netherlands, Greece, Italy, Portugal, and Spain,[2] and initial reports have also come in from Switzerland and Germany, albeit to a lesser degree.[3] Possible cases of CCD have also been reported in Taiwan since April 2007.[4]

The cause or causes of the syndrome are not yet understood. Some of the proposed causes include environmental change-related stresses,[5] malnutrition, pathogens (i.e., disease[6] including Israel acute paralysis virus[7][8]), mites, pesticides such as neonicotinoids or imidacloprid, genetically modified (GM) crops with pest control characteristics such as transgenic maize,[9][10], and migratory beekeeping.

Contents

Background

From 1971 to 2006, there was a dramatic reduction in the number of feral (wild) honeybees in the US (now almost absent);[11] and a significant, though somewhat gradual decline in the number of colonies maintained by beekeepers. This decline includes the cumulative losses from all factors such as urbanization, pesticide use, tracheal and Varroa mites, and commercial beekeepers retiring and going out of business. However, late in the year 2006 and in early 2007 the rate of attrition was alleged to have reached new proportions, and the term "Colony Collapse Disorder" was proposed to describe this sudden rash of disappearances.[1]

Limited occurrences resembling CCD have been documented as early as 1896,[6][12] and this set of symptoms has in the past several decades been given many different names (disappearing disease, spring dwindle, May disease, autumn collapse, and fall dwindle disease).[13] Most recently, a similar phenomenon in the winter of 2004/2005 occurred, and was attributed to Varroa mites (the "Vampire Mite" scare), though this was never ultimately confirmed. Nobody has been able to determine the cause of any past appearances of this syndrome. Upon recognition that the syndrome does not seem to be seasonally-restricted, and that it may not be a "disease" in the standard sense — that there may not be a specific causative agent — the syndrome was renamed.[14]

Symptoms

A colony which has collapsed from CCD is generally characterized by all of these conditions occurring simultaneously[15]:

- Complete absence of adult bees in colonies, with little or no build-up of dead bees in or around the colonies.
- Presence of capped brood in colonies. Bees normally will not abandon a hive until the capped brood have all hatched.
- Presence of food stores, both honey and bee pollen:
  - i. which are not immediately robbed by other bees
  - ii. which when attacked by hive pests such as wax moth and small hive beetle, the attack is noticeably delayed.

Precursor symptoms that may arise before the final colony collapse are:

- Insufficient workforce to maintain the brood that is present * Workforce seems to be made up of young adult bees * The Queen is present
- The colony members are reluctant to consume provided feed, such as sugar syrup and protein supplement.

Scale of the disorder

In the U.S., at least 24 different states[5][16] as well as portions of Canada[17] have reported at least one case of CCD. However, in many cases, beekeepers reporting significant losses of bees did not experience CCD, and a major part of the subsequent analysis of the phenomenon hinges upon distinguishing between true CCD losses and non-CCD losses.[18] In a survey of 384 responding beekeepers from 13 states, reporting the number of hives containing few or no bees in spring, only 23.8% met the specified criteria for CCD (that 50% or more of their dead colonies were found without bees and/or with very few dead bees in the hive or apiary).[18] In the US, despite highly variable anecdotal claims appearing in the media, the best documentation indicates that CCD-suffering operations had a total loss of 45% compared to the total loss of 25% of all colonies experienced by non-CCD suffering beekeepers in 2006-2007; it is further noted that non-CCD winter losses as high as 50% have occurred in some years and regions (e.g., 2000-2001 in Pennsylvania), though "normal" winter losses are typically considered to be in the range of 15-25%.[18]

There are also putative cases reported by the media from India, Brazil[19] and parts of Europe.[20] Since the beginning of the 1990s, France, Belgium, Italy, Germany, Switzerland, Spain, Greece, Slovenia and the Netherlands have been affected by honey bee disappearances, though this is not necessarily associated with CCD;[2] Austria and United Kingdom (where it has been dubbed the "Mary Celeste" phenomenon, after a ship whose crew disappeared in 1872[21]) have also reportedly been affected.[4] It is far from certain that all or any of these reported non-US cases are indeed CCD: there has been considerable publicity, but only rarely was the phenomenon described in sufficient detail. In Germany, for example, where some of the first reports of CCD in Europe appeared, and where — according to the German national association of beekeepers — 40% of the honey bee colonies died,[4] there has been no scientific confirmation; as of early May 2007, the German media were reporting that no confirmed CCD cases seemed to have occurred in Germany.[22]

Possible causes and research

The exact mechanisms of CCD are still unknown. One report indicates a strong but possibly non-causal association between the syndrome and the presence of the Israel acute paralysis virus.[8] Other factors may also be involved, however, and several have been proposed as causative agents; malnutrition, pesticides, pathogens, immunodeficiencies, mites, fungus, genetically modified (GM) crops, beekeeping practices (such as the use of antibiotics, or long-distance transportation of beehives) and electromagnetic radiation. Whether any single factor is responsible, or a combination of factors (acting independently in different areas affected by CCD, or acting in tandem), is still unknown. It is likewise still uncertain whether CCD is a genuinely new phenomenon, as opposed to a known phenomenon that previously only had a minor impact.

At present, the primary source of information, and presumed "lead" group investigating the phenomenon, is the Colony Collapse Disorder Working Group, based primarily at Penn State University. Their preliminary report pointed out some patterns, but drew no strong conclusions.[14] A survey of beekeepers early in 2007 indicates that most hobbyist beekeepers believed that starvation was the leading cause of death in their colonies, while commercial beekeepers overwhelmingly believed that invertebrate pests (Varroa mites, honey bee tracheal mites, and/or small hive beetles) were the leading cause of colony mortality.[18] A scholarly review in June 2007, similarly addressed numerous theories and possible contributing factors, but left the issue unresolved.[13]

In July 2007, the USDA released its "CCD Action Plan", which outlines a strategy for addressing CCD consisting of four main components:[23]

1. survey and data collection;
2. analysis of samples;

3. hypothesis-driven research; and,
4. mitigation and preventative action.

As of late 2007, there is still no consensus of opinion, and no definitive causes have emerged; the schedule of presentations for a planned national symposium on CCD, titled "Colony Collapse Disorder in Honey Bees: Insight Into Status, Potential Causes, and Preventive Measures," which is scheduled for December 11, 2007, at the meeting of the Entomological Society of America in San Diego, California, gives no indication of any major breakthroughs. [3]

Poor nutrition or malnutrition

One of the patterns reported by the group at Penn State was that all producers in a preliminary survey noted a period of "extraordinary stress" affecting the colonies in question prior to their die-off, most commonly involving poor nutrition and/or drought.[14] This is the only factor that all of the cases of CCD had in common in this report; accordingly, there is at least some significant possibility that the phenomenon is correlated to nutritional stress, and may not manifest in healthy, well-nourished colonies. This is similar to the findings of a later independent survey, in which small-scale beekeeping operations (up to 500 colonies) in several states reported their belief that malnutrition and/or weak colonies was the factor responsible for their bees dying, in over 50% of the cases, whether the losses were believed to be due to CCD or not.[18]

Some researchers have attributed the syndrome to the practice of feeding high fructose corn syrup (HFCS) to supplement winter stores. The variability of HFCS may be relevant to the apparent inconsistencies of results. European commentators have suggested a possible connection with HFCS produced from genetically modified corn.[3] If this were the sole factor involved, however, this should also lead to the exclusive appearance of CCD in wintering colonies being fed HFCS, but many reports of CCD occur in other contexts, with beekeepers who do not use HFCS.

Pathogens and immunodeficiency theories

Further information: Pathogen, immunodeficiency, and diseases of the honey bee

General

Some researchers have commented that the pathway of propagation functions in the manner of a contagious disease; however, there is some sentiment that the disorder may involve an immunosuppressive mechanism,[24] potentially linked to the aforementioned "stress" leading to a weakened immune system. Specifically, according to researchers at Penn State: "The magnitude of detected infectious agents in the adult bees suggests some type of immunosuppression." These researchers initially suggested a connection between Varroa destructor mite infestation and CCD, suggesting that a combination of these bee mites, deformed wing virus (which the mites transmit) and bacteria work together to suppress immunity and may be one cause of CCD.[25] This research group is reported to be focusing on a search for possible viral, bacterial, or fungal pathogens which may be involved.[14]

When a colony is dying, for whatever cause, and there are other healthy colonies nearby (as is typical in a bee yard), those healthy colonies often enter the dying colony and rob its provisions for their own use. If the dying colony's provisions were contaminated (by natural or man-made toxins), the resulting pattern (of healthy colonies becoming sick when in proximity to a dying colony) might suggest to an observer that a contagious disease is involved. However, it is typical in CCD cases that provisions of dying colonies are not being robbed, suggesting that at least this particular mechanism (toxins being spread via robbing, thereby mimicking a disease) is not involved in CCD.

Additional evidence that CCD might be an infectious disease came from the following observation: the hives of colonies that had died from CCD could be reused with a healthy colony only if they were first treated with DNA-destroying radiation.[8]

Varroa and Israel Acute Paralysis Virus

According to a 2007 article, the mites Varroa destructor remain the world's most destructive honey bee killer due in part to the viruses they carry, including Deformed Wing Virus and Acute bee paralysis virus, which have both been implicated in CCD.[25] Affliction with Varroa mites also tends to weaken the immune system of the bees. As such, Varroa have been considered as a possible cause of CCD, though not all dying colonies contain these mites.[26]

In September 2007, results of a large-scale statistical RNA sequencing study of afflicted and non-afflicted colonies were reported. RNA from all organisms in a colony was sequenced and compared with sequence databases to detect the presence of pathogens. The study used technology from 454 Life Sciences developed for human genome sequencing. All colonies were found to be infected with numerous pathogens, but only the Israel acute paralysis virus (IAPV) showed a significant association with CCD: the virus was found in 25 of the 30 tested CCD colonies, and only in one of the 21 tested non-CCD colonies.[8] Scientists pointed out that this association was no proof of causation, and other factors may also be involved in the disease or the presence of IAPV may only be a marker signifying afflicted colonies and not the actual causative agent. To prove causation, experiments are planned to deliberately infect colonies with the virus.[7]

The IAPV was discovered in 2004 and belongs to the Dicistroviridae. It causes paralysis in bees which then die outside of the hive. It can be transmitted by the mite Varroa destructor. These mites, however, were found in only half of the CCD colonies.[8]

The virus was also found in samples of Australian honey bees. Australian honey bees have been imported into the U.S. since 2004[7] and until recently it was thought possible that this is how the virus originally reached North America. Recent findings, however, reveal the virus has been present in American bees since 2002.[27][28]

Nosema

Some have suggested that the syndrome may be an inability by beekeepers to correctly identify known diseases such as European foulbrood or the microsporidian fungus Nosema. The testing and diagnosis of samples from affected colonies (already performed) makes this highly unlikely, as the symptoms are fairly well-known and differ from what is classified as CCD. A high rate of Nosema infection was reported in samples of bees from Pennsylvania, but this pattern was not reported from samples elsewhere.[14]

Mariano Higes, a scientist heading a team at a government-funded apiculture centre in Guadalajara, Spain, has reported that when hives of European honey bees were infected with Nosema ceranae, a recently described microsporidian fungus, the colonies were wiped out within eight days.[29] Higes has extrapolated from this research to conclude that CCD is caused by N. ceranae. Higes and his team have worked on this problem since 2000, and claim to have ruled out many other potential causes.[30][31] Various areas in Europe have reported this fungus, but no direct link to CCD has yet been established.[32][33] Highly preliminary evidence of N. ceranae was recently reported in a few hives in the Merced Valley area of California (USA).[34][35] The researcher did not, however, believe this was conclusive evidence of a link to CCD; "We don't want to give anybody the impression that this thing has been solved."[36] A USDA bee scientist has similarly stated, "while the parasite Nosema ceranae may be a factor, it cannot be the sole cause. The fungus has been seen before, sometimes in colonies that were healthy."[37]

Likewise, a Washington State beekeeper familiar with N. ceranae in his own hives discounts it as being the cause of CCD.[38] A study reported in September 2007 found that 100% of afflicted and 80% of non-afflicted colonies contained Nosema ceranae.[8]

The primary antibiotic used against Nosema is Fumagillin, which has been used in a German research project to reduce the microsporidian's impact, and is mentioned as a possible remedy by the CCDWG.[39]

Pesticides

Further information: Pesticide toxicity to bees

One of the more common general hypotheses concerns pesticides (or, more specifically, insecticides), though several studies have found no common environmental factors between unrelated outbreaks studied.

It is particularly difficult to evaluate pesticide contributions to CCD for several reasons. First, the variety of pesticides in use in the different areas reporting CCD makes it difficult to test for all possible pesticides simultaneously. Second, many commercial beekeeping operations are mobile, transporting hives over large geographic distances over the course of a season, potentially exposing the colonies to different pesticides at each location. Third, the bees themselves place pollen and honey into long-term storage, effectively meaning that there may be a delay of anywhere from days to months before contaminated provisions are fed to the colony, negating any attempts to associate the appearance of symptoms with the actual time at which exposure to pesticides occurred. Pesticides used on bee forage are far more likely to enter the colony via the pollen stores rather than via nectar (because pollen is carried externally on the bees, while nectar is carried internally, and may kill the bee if too toxic), though not all potentially lethal chemicals, either natural or man-made, affect the adult bees — many primarily affect the brood, but brood die-off does not appear to be happening in CCD. Most significantly, brood are not fed honey, and adult bees consume relatively little pollen; accordingly, the pattern in CCD suggests that if contaminants or toxins from the environment are responsible, it is most likely to be via the honey, as it is the adults that are dying (or leaving), not the brood.

One recently published view is that bees are falling victim to new varieties of nicotine-based pesticides;[40][41] beekeepers in Canada are also losing their bees and are blaming neonicotinoid pesticides. To date, most of the evaluation of possible roles of pesticides in CCD have relied on the use of surveys submitted by beekeepers, but it seems likely that direct testing of samples from affected colonies will be needed, especially given the possible role of systemic insecticides such as the neonicotinoid imidacloprid (which are applied to the soil and taken up into the plant's tissues, including pollen and nectar), which may be applied to a crop when the beekeeper is not present. The known effects of imidacloprid on insects, including honey bees, are consistent with the symptoms of CCD;[42] for example, the effects of imidacloprid on termites include apparent failure of the immune system, and disorientation.[43] In Europe the interaction of the phenomenon of "dying bees" with imidacloprid, has been discussed for quite some time now.[44][45][46] It was a study from the "Comité Scientifique et Technique (CST)" which was in the center of discussion recently, which led to a partial ban of imidacloprid in France (known as Gaucho), primarily due to concern over potential effects on honey bees.[47][48][49] Consequently when fipronil, a phenylpyrazole insecticide and in Europe mainly labeled "Regent", was used as a replacement, it was also found to be toxic to bees, and banned partially in France in 2004.[50] In February 2007, about forty French deputies, led by UMP member Jacques Remiller, requested the creation of a Parliamentary Investigation Commission on Overmortality of Bees, underlining that the honey production was decreasing by 1,000 tons a year for a decade. As of August

2007, no investigations were yet opened.[31] The imidacloprid pesticide Gaucho was banned, however, in 1999 by the French Minister of Agriculture Jean Glavany. Five other insecticides based on fipronil were also accused of killing bees. However, the scientific committees of the European Union are still of the opinion "that the available monitoring studies were mainly performed in France and EU-member-states should consider the relevance of these studies for the circumstances in their country."[51]

In 2005, a team of scientists led by the National Institute of Beekeeping in Bologna, Italy, found that pollen obtained from seeds dressed with imidacloprid contains significant levels of the insecticide, and suggested that the polluted pollen might cause honey bee colony death.[52] Analysis of maize and sunflower crops originating from seeds dressed with imidacloprid suggest that large amounts of the insecticide will be carried back to honey bee colonies.[53] Sub-lethal doses of imidacloprid in sucrose solution have also been documented to affect homing and foraging activity of honeybees.[54] Imidacloprid in sucrose solution fed to bees in the laboratory impaired their communication for a few hours.[55] Sub-lethal doses of imidacloprid in laboratory and field experiment decreased flight activity and olfactory discrimination, and olfactory learning performance was impaired.[56] However, no detailed studies of toxicity or pesticide residue in remaining honey or pollen in CCD-affected colonies have been published so far, so, despite the similarity in symptoms, no connection of neonicotinoids to CCD has yet been confirmed.

Antibiotics and miticides

Most beekeepers affected by CCD report that they use antibiotics and miticides in their colonies, though the lack of uniformity as to which particular chemicals are used[14] makes it seem unlikely that any single such chemical is involved. However, it is possible that not all such chemicals in use have been tested for possible effects on honey bees, and could therefore potentially be contributing to the CCD phenomenon.[13] Some reports indicate that organic beekeepers (who do not use antibiotics or miticides) are not affected by CCD, despite proximity to non-organic beekeepers that have been affected.[57]

Genetically modified crops (GMO)

Further information: Genetically modified organism

Potential effects on honey bees of gathering pollen and nectar from genetically modified (GM) crops that produce Bacillus thuringiensis (Bt) toxin have been investigated, and there is scant evidence of deleterious effects on bees visiting such crops. Corn (maize), the major such crop, is not a preferred plant for honey bees, although beekeepers who keep bees near corn fields state that "corn is an excellent source of pollen when in tassel".[40] Cotton, the second important Bt crop, is highly subject to bee visitation for nectar (pollen is only consumed if there is no other pollen available),[58] but there is no credible evidence of toxicity of GM cotton, other than that from insecticides used during bloom.

The Sierra Club Genetic Engineering Committee recently published a letter to Senator Thomas Harkin on the web.[9] They are of the opinion that "highly respected scientists believe that exposure to genetically engineered crops and their plant-produced pesticides merit serious consideration as either the cause or a contributory factor to the development and spread of CCD." Nine literature references which might support this theory are cited.[9]

The primary effect of Bt on insects is in the larval stage. Thus the studies on Bt-toxins and effects on honey bees originally concentrated more on larvae and their development. However, as pollen is an important part of bee bread, which is also food for adult bees, some beekeepers think that adult bees may be more affected by ingredients of pollen, because adult bees are something like a filter for larvae. And as the CCD phenomenon involves the disappearance of the adult bees, some think there could be a direct connection[59] despite the absence of symptoms in the larvae, and despite any evidence that the bees experiencing CCD have ever been exposed to GM crops.

In 2005, Bt maize, which has been commercially planted in the U.S. since 1996, accounted for 35% (106,400 km^2) of the total U.S. maize plantings. GM insect-resistant Bt cotton has also been grown commercially in the U.S. since 1996, and by 2005, was planted on 52% (28,000 km^2) of total cotton plantings.[60] According to David Hackenberg, former president of the American Beekeeping Federation, and who has been leading the publicizing of information concerning CCD, "beekeepers that have been most affected so far have been close to corn, cotton, soybeans, canola, sunflowers, apples, vine crops and pumpkins", though he personally attributes CCD to neonicotinoid pesticides applied to these crops. [40] Thus, some Bt plants may have been visited by honey bees that later exhibited CCD. However, similar massive bee die-offs (or disappearances) have been recorded for decades prior to the introduction of these crops,[6] and also "have occurred in Europe and areas of Canada where Bt crops were not grown."[61] According to the European Union's GMO Compass, Bt maize is grown in Spain, France, Czech Republic, Portugal, Germany and Slovakia [4][5]. Various documents relating to U.S. risk assessment studies on Bt in relation to honey bees are published on the United States Environmental Protection Agency (EPA) homepage for Biopesticides Registration Action Documents;[62][63][64] there is no indication that any of these studies found effects of Bt pollen on honey bees.
In 2004, the knowledge of GMO authorization agencies was mainly based on a comprehensive review of the scientific literature published in Bee World[65] which examined the effects of various commercialized and uncommercialized transgenes on honey bees. The review concludes that "evidence available so far shows that none of the GM plants currently commercially available have significant impacts on honey bee health." However, in 2005 a new publication

in the Journal Apidologie[66] indicated that foraging activity of bees fed with CRY1Ab may decline continuously through the treatment stages without any recovery between treatments (though in the treatment with CRY1Ab-enriched feed, no significant differences in bee mortality were found at different treatment stages). The European Union GMO Panel of the European Food Safety Authority (EFSA) did not share the view by the authors "that the above results were mainly CRY1Ab dependent." The Panel was of the opinion that "negative effects on bees are likely not directly associated with exposure to the CRY1Ab protein because of the design of the experiment and lack of simultaneous controls or replication.[67]

A research study conducted in Germany suggested that rather than having a direct effect, exposure to Bt maize pollen may weaken the adult bees' defense against Nosema, though in the absence of such an infection, there were no detectable effects: "When the trial was repeated the colonies were treated prophylactically with antibiotics to prevent re-infection...This indicates that healthy bee colonies are not impaired in any way by the toxin in any of the tested vital functions of colony size, foraging activity, brood care activity or development, even when exposed to extreme levels of Bt maize pollen over a period of six weeks."[68] However, if "the bee colonies happened to be infested with parasites (microsporidia), this infestation led to a reduction in the number of bees and subsequently to reduced broods.... This effect was significantly more marked in the Bt-fed colonies." It has further been suggested that "genetically modified corn may have altered the surface of the bee's intestines, sufficiently weakening the bees to allow the parasites to gain entry—or perhaps it was the other way around", though it was also noted "Of course, the concentration of the toxin was ten times higher in the experiments than in normal Bt corn pollen. In addition, the bee feed was administered over a relatively lengthy six-week period."[69] Other more recent studies have failed to show any adverse effects of Bt pollen on healthy bee colonies,[61] but the possibility that Bt pollen weakens already unhealthy colonies has not been explored.

The preliminary report of the Colony Collapse Disorder Working Group[6] concerning "Fall Dwindle Disease"[14] indicated that "all PA samples were found to have Nosema spores in their rectal contents. The sting gland of many examined bees was obviously scarred with distinct black "marks"; this type of pin-point melanization or darkening is indicative of an immune response to some sort of pathogen." If the bees in Pennsylvania were gathering Bt-toxin-containing corn pollen, it could potentially have interacted with Nosema and thus contributed to CCD in those colonies; however, there is no evidence that these colonies were gathering corn pollen at any point prior to their deaths, nor has it been reported that colonies afflicted by CCD elsewhere had been collecting corn pollen. Many of the colonies reported to be dying from CCD occur in locations where GM corn is not grown (at least in the United States; also, 5 of the 10 states with the greatest amount of corn production, including GM corn -Illinois, Indiana, Kansas, Missouri, and Nebraska -- have had no reported cases of CCD[16][13]), nor have bees from other areas outside of Pennsylvania been reported to be significantly infected by Nosema (e.g.,[14]).

In 2006 the "Committee on Status and Trends of Pollinators" of the United States National Research Council published a report on the "Status of Pollinators in North America".[70] It suggested that GMO, besides other factors, might contribute to pollinator decline because, according to one scientific review of "the small literature on this topic, ... in some cases, there are negative but sublethal effects attributable to consumption of transgenic pollens." The report goes on to say that, "These effects varied with the identity of the transgene and the amount of its expression, but in no case have any effects of transgenic crops on honey bee populations been documented."[71]

On March 28, 2007, the "Mid-Atlantic Apiculture Research and Extension Consortium"[72] published a new "Summary of Research on the Non-Target Effects of Bt Corn Pollen on Honeybees", which states that according to "a field study... (soon to be published in the bee journal Apidologie) there is no evidence thus far of any lethal or sub-lethal effects of the currently used Bt proteins on honey bees", and, specifically regarding the possible causal connections between Bt pollen and CCD, stated "While this possibility has not been ruled out, the weight of evidence reported here argues strongly that the current use of Bt crops is not associated with CCD."[61]

Bee rentals and migratory beekeeping

Further information: Beekeeping

Since US beekeeper Nephi Miller first began moving his hives to different areas of the country for the winter of 1908, migratory beekeeping has become widespread in America.

Bee rental for pollination is a crucial element of US agriculture, which could not produce anywhere near its current levels with native pollinators alone.[73] US beekeepers collectively earn much more from renting their bees out for pollination than they do from honey production.

Researchers are concerned that trucking colonies around the country to pollinate crops, where they intermingle with other bees from all over, helps spread viruses and mites among colonies. Additionally, such continuous movement and re-settlement is considered by some a strain and disruption for the entire hive, possibly rendering it less resistant to all sorts of systemic disorder.[74]

US bee rental travel extent

One major US beekeeper reports moving his hives from Idaho to California in January, then to apple orchards in Washington in March, to North Dakota two months later, and then back to Idaho by November -- a journey of several thousand kilometres. Others move from Florida to New Hampshire or to Texas; nearly all visit California for the almond bloom in January.

Beekeepers in Europe and Asia are generally far less mobile, with bee populations moving and mingling within a smaller geographic extent (although some keepers do move longer distances, it is much less common).

This wider spread and intermingling in the US has resulted in far greater losses from Varroa mite infections in recent years.[75]

Climate change

Some beekeepers think the culprit may be climate change, in which the earth as a whole is warming but regional and local temperatures may drop much lower or rise higher than normal. "Erratic weather patterns caused by global warming could play havoc with bees' sensitive cycles. A lot of northeastern U.S. beekeepers say a late cold snap is what did the damage to them this year" [6]. Indeed an unusually dry and warm winter prevented the flowering of many plants, "If there is not a common thread, such as a pathogen seen in many of the affected colonies, Professor Eric Mussen of UC Davis said he is convinced that a nutritional deficit helps explain how the honeybees were weakened by the smorgasbord of potential causes of death. That is because dry conditions, certainly in California, did not produce flowers in which bees find their required mix of pollens, he said ... 'In many situations the bees were weakened by not being able to get a nice mix of nutrients that they needed from the pollens, and I think that weakened them,' he said. 'Under those circumstances you can take all the other (causes), and there are plenty of them, and combine them together and down go the bees'" [7].

"Dry conditions in many parts of the country last fall reduced good nectar flow, so fewer good fall pollens were taken into colonies. 'Bees rely on fall pollens to rear a brood and take them through the winter. It was a hard fall, followed by a warm winter, and bees were out flying. There weren't any resources (food) out there, so the bees were burning up flight muscles'" [8]. "Well, you get this blast of hot temperature, which is about the time the flower buds are forming and the pollen grains are beginning to form. What does that do? You get sterile pollen. A beekeeper could look into the hive and say, "I've got all kinds of pollen in there and the bees disappeared." Well, right, you've got pollen grains, but do they have any nutrition in them? ... I think something happened at the end of last year in many places in the temperate climate around the world, not just here, and fouled up the bees' food supply. Unless somebody tells me differently, I'm blaming it on the weather ... for whatever reason, we are beginning to kind of move into a cycle where we are going to find more extremes than we used to have. The droughts may be hotter and longer, the storms and floods may be more severe. Things aren't going to be so nice in the future" [9]. In fact the first half of 2006 was the warmest on record in U.S.[10].

Some say that flowers are blooming earlier than in the past, "Climate change and earlier springs have also taken a toll. Plants like red maples and pussy willows, typically the first pollen sources for honeybees, have been blossoming weeks before the bees can fly in the spring, Conrad [author of Natural Beekeeping] said, so they miss out on that important source of pollen" [11]. Wayne Esaias, a NASA climatologist and beekeeper has been keeping tabs on the possible connection [12][13]. See also Bees, Pollination and Climate Change: A Guide to Selected Resources.

Electromagnetic radiation

Further information: Electromagnetic radiation and Mobile phone radiation and health

In April 2007, news of a University of Landau study appeared in major media, beginning with an article in The Independent that stated that the subject of the study was mobile phones and had related them to CCD.[76] Cellular phones were implicated by other media reports, but were in fact not covered in the study, and the researchers have since emphatically disavowed any connection between their research, cell phones, and CCD, specifically indicating that the Independent article had misinterpreted their results and created "a horror story".[77][78][79]

The 2006 University of Landau pilot study was looking for non-thermal effects of radio frequency ("RF") on honey bees (Apis mellifera carnica) and suggested that when bee hives have DECT cordless phone base stations embedded in them, the close-range electromagnetic field ("EMF") may reduce the ability of bees to return to their hive; they also noticed a slight reduction in honeycomb weight in treated colonies.[80] In the course of their study, one half of their colonies broke down, including some of their controls which did not have DECT base stations embedded in them.

The team's 2004 exploratory study on non-thermal effects on learning did not find any change in behavior due to RF exposure from the DECT base station operating at 1880-1900 MHz.[81]

Like the links to CCD from variants (herbicides, genetically modified crops, etc), the link of either cordless or cellular phones, cell towers, interference by the High Frequency Active Auroral Research Program (HAARP) or Ground Wave Emergency Network (GWEN) to CCD is speculative.

Possible effects

The phenomenon is particularly important for crops such as almond growing in California, where honey bees are the predominant pollinator and the crop value in 2006 was $1.5 billion. In 2000, the total U.S. crop value that was wholly dependent on honey bee pollination was estimated to exceed $15 billion.[82]

Honey bees are not native to the Americas, therefore their necessity as pollinators in the US is limited to strictly agricultural/ornamental uses, as no native plants require honey bee pollination, except where concentrated in monoculture situations—where the pollination need is so great at bloom time that pollinators must be concentrated beyond the capacity of native bees (with current technology).

They are responsible for pollination of approximately one third of the United States' crop species, including such species as almonds, peaches, soybeans, apples, pears, cherries, raspberries, blackberries, cranberries, watermelons, cantaloupes, cucumbers and strawberries. Many but not all of these plants can be (and often are) pollinated by other insects in small holdings in the U.S., including other kinds of bees, but typically not on a commercial scale. While some farmers of a few kinds of native crops do bring in honey bees to help pollinate, none specifically need them, and when honey bees are absent from a region, there is a presumption that native pollinators may reclaim the niche, typically being better adapted to serve those plants (assuming that the plants normally occur in that specific area).

However, even though on a per-individual basis, many other species are actually more efficient at pollinating, on the 30% of crop types where honey bees are used, most native pollinators cannot be mass-utilized as easily or as effectively as honey bees—in many instances they will not visit the plants at all. Beehives can be moved from crop to crop as needed, and the bees will visit many plants in large numbers, compensating via sheer numbers for what they lack in efficiency. The commercial viability of these crops is therefore strongly tied to the beekeeping industry.
Remedies

As of March 1, 2007 MAAREC offers the following tentative recommendations for beekeepers noticing the symptoms of CCD:[39]

1. Do not combine collapsing colonies with strong colonies.
2. When a collapsed colony is found, store the equipment

where you can use preventive measures to ensure that bees will not have access to it.

3. If you feed your bees sugar syrup, use Fumagillin.
4. If you are experiencing colony collapse and see a secondary infection, such as European Foulbrood, treat the colonies with Terramycin, not Tylan.

CHAPTER 54

Continuing in Your Ancestors' Curses and Sins

Generations after generations of families have continued in the sins of their forefathers and their ancestors. These curses have been effectively carried over to the destruction of Christians over and over again. One of our main problems is to accept the lie that we are destined or preordained to sicknesses, diseases, poverty, failure and such. I have actually heard people say that, "Well, we have to die from something". God, Almighty doesn't have His hand in such foolishness. He may have allowed these things to come on us, albeit through **ignorance** and **lack of knowledge**, it was our choice, not His. His will is for us to be in prosperity, be in good health, live abundantly in life with His abundance in grace.

1 Ki 9:6 (KJV) "But if ye shall at all turn from following me, ye or your children, and will not keep my commandments and my statutes which I have set before you, but go and serve other gods, and worship them:"

1 Ki 9:7 (KJV) "Then will I cut off Israel out of the land which I have given them; and this house, which I have hallowed for my name, will I cast out of my sight; and Israel shall be a proverb and a byword among all people:"

Exo 20:3-5 (KJV) Thou shalt have no other gods before me.

4. Thou shalt not make unto thee any graven image, or any likeness of any thing that is in heaven above, or that is in the earth beneath, or that is in the water under the earth:
5. Thou shalt not bow down thyself to them, nor serve them: for I the LORD thy God am a jealous God, visiting the iniquity of the fathers upon the children unto the third and fourth generation of them that hate me;

CHAPTER 55

Cremation Is Not the Final Episode of One's Life

Resurrection of The Dead Sinners

Revelation 20 (KJV)

11. And I saw a great white throne, and him that sat on it, from whose face the earth and the heaven fled away; and there was found no place for them.
12. And I saw the dead, small and great, stand before God; and the books were opened: and another book was opened, which is the book of life: and the dead were judged out of those things which were written in the books, according to their works.
13. And the sea gave up the dead which were in it; and death and hell delivered up the dead which were in them: and they were judged every man according to their works.
14. And death and hell were cast into the lake of fire. This is the second death.
15. And whosoever was not found written in the book of life was cast into the lake of fire.

Resurrection of The Dead Christians

1 Corinthians 15 (KJV)

51. Behold, I shew you a mystery; We shall not all sleep, but we shall all be changed,
52. In a moment, in the twinkling of an eye, at the last trump: for the trumpet shall sound, and the dead shall be raised incorruptible, and we shall be changed.
53. For this corruptible must put on incorruption, and this mortal must put on immortality.

CHAPTER **56**

Crimes, Black-On-Black - Philadelphia, PA's Curses

Black Murder Rate Tops The Nation In PA
Submitted by Mark Rosenkranz on June 5, 2007 - 7:25pm.

* News I just heard on a radio station that the black murder rate in PA is the highest in our nation. Is this true? Even if this happens not to be true, murder rates and crime in communities needs to come down NOW. There needs to be intervention from different agencies to deal with this terror.

* Mark Rosenkranz's blog

Philadelphia's murder rate on pace to be highest in 10 years : ...

Philadelphia's murder rate on pace to be highest in 10 years Eleven die over the weekend in disputes over drugs, disrespect.

Full story: The Morning Call Read the original story - Apr 24, 2007

Philadelphia, Pennsylvania is unfortunately called "Chocolate City" where many black people have congregated to live and reside. It is similar to the District of Columbia where over 600,000 black residents reside. The majority of the crime is black-on-black crime. There are rumors of black mofia establishments in those environments as well.

Philly seeks 10,000 black men to patrol streets

Philadelphia police chief Sylvester Johnson in a desperate move to stem violent crime has asked for 10,000 black men to volunteer to help patrol the cities streets. This desperate move comes after the ... more »

Philadelphia, PA

Black Men Rally Against Phila. Crime

"I grew up in the streets. I don't want my son to be subjected to the same thing"

Thousands of black men turned out Sunday to support a volunteer effort aimed at reducing violence in this crime-plagued city, lining up for several blocks to register.

Volunteers who join street patrols as part of the 'Call to Action: 10,000 Men, It's a New Day' campaign will not carry weapons or make arrests but will instead be trained in conflict resolution, organizers said.

'Nobody else is going to magically come into this community and get it done,' said real estate developer Abdur-Rahim Islam, a lead organizer.

Isaiah 34 (KJV)

5. For my sword shall be bathed in heaven: behold, it shall come down upon Idumea, and upon the people of my curse, to judgment.

Deuteronomy 28 (KJV)

15. But it shall come to pass, if thou wilt not hearken unto the voice of the Lord thy God, to observe to do all his commandments

and his statutes which I command thee this day; that all these curses shall come upon thee, and overtake thee:

16. Cursed shalt thou be in the city, and cursed shalt thou be in the field.
17. Cursed shall be thy basket and thy store.
18. Cursed shall be the fruit of thy body, and the fruit of thy land, the increase of thy kine, and the flocks of thy sheep.
19. Cursed shalt thou be when thou comest in, and cursed shalt thou be when thou goest out.
20. The Lord shall send upon thee cursing, vexation, and rebuke, in all that thou settest thine hand unto for to do, until thou be destroyed, and until thou perish quickly; because of the wickedness of thy doings, whereby thou hast forsaken me.

Romans 1 (KJV)

17. For therein is the righteousness of God revealed from faith to faith: as it is written, The just shall live by faith.
18. For the wrath of God is revealed from heaven against all ungodliness and unrighteousness of men, who hold the truth in unrighteousness;
19. Because that which may be known of God is manifest in them; for God hath shewed it unto them.
20. For the invisible things of him from the creation of the world are clearly seen, being understood by the things that are made, even his eternal power and Godhead; so that they are without excuse:
21. Because that, when they knew God, they glorified him not as God, neither were thankful; but became vain in their imaginations, and their foolish heart was darkened.
22. Professing themselves to be wise, they became fools,
23. And changed the glory of the uncorruptible God into an image made like to corruptible man, and to birds, and fourfooted beasts, and creeping things.

24. Wherefore God also gave them up to uncleanness through the lusts of their own hearts, to dishonour their own bodies between themselves:
25. Who changed the truth of God into a lie, and worshipped and served the creature more than the Creator, who is blessed for ever. Amen.
26. For this cause God gave them up unto vile affections: for even their women did change the natural use into that which is against nature:
27. And likewise also the men, leaving the natural use of the woman, burned in their lust one toward another; men with men working that which is unseemly, and receiving in themselves that recompence of their error which was meet.
28. And even as they did not like to retain God in their knowledge, God gave them over to a reprobate mind, to do those things which are not convenient;
29. Being filled with all unrighteousness, fornication, wickedness, covetousness, maliciousness; full of envy, murder, debate, deceit, malignity; whisperers,
30. Backbiters, haters of God, despiteful, proud, boasters, inventors of evil things, disobedient to parents,
31. Without understanding, covenantbreakers, without natural affection, implacable, unmerciful:
32. Who knowing the judgment of God, that they which commit such things are worthy of death, not only do the same, but have pleasure in them that do such.

CHAPTER 57

Crimes, Black-On-Black - Washington, DC's Curses

Washington, D.C. is unfortunately called "Chocolate City" where black people have congregated to live and reside. It is a population of over 600,000 black residents reside. The majority of the crime are black-on-black crime. There are rumors of many violent gangs in the city.

In 1992 there were more Black men in prison (583,000) than in college (537,000)(11)

- One out of every four Black men will go to prison in his lifetime(12) 30% of Black men aged 20-29 in Chicago were arrested in 1993(13)
- 42% of Black men aged 18-35 in Washington, D.C. were under some form of criminal justice control in 1992(14)
- 56% of Black men aged 18-35 in Baltimore were under some form of criminal justice control in 1992(15)

Isaiah 34 (KJV)

5. For my sword shall be bathed in heaven: behold, it shall come down upon Idumea, and upon the people of my curse, to judgment.

Deuteronomy 28 (KJV)

15. But it shall come to pass, if thou wilt not hearken unto the voice of the Lord thy God, to observe to do all his commandments and his statutes which I command thee this day; that all these curses shall come upon thee, and overtake thee:
16. Cursed shalt thou be in the city, and cursed shalt thou be in the field.
17. Cursed shall be thy basket and thy store.
18. Cursed shall be the fruit of thy body, and the fruit of thy land, the increase of thy kine, and the flocks of thy sheep.
19. Cursed shalt thou be when thou comest in, and cursed shalt thou be when thou goest out.
20. The Lord shall send upon thee cursing, vexation, and rebuke, in all that thou settest thine hand unto for to do, until thou be destroyed, and until thou perish quickly; because of the wickedness of thy doings, **whereby thou hast forsaken me**.

Romans 1 (KJV)

17. For therein is the righteousness of God revealed from faith to faith: as it is written, The just shall live by faith.
18. For the wrath of God is revealed from heaven against all ungodliness and unrighteousness of men, who hold the truth in unrighteousness;
19. Because that which may be known of God is manifest in them; for God hath shewed it unto them.
20. For the invisible things of him from the creation of the world are clearly seen, being understood by the things that are made, even his eternal power and Godhead; so that they are without excuse:
21. Because that, when they knew God, they glorified him not as God, neither were thankful; but became vain in their imaginations, and their foolish heart was darkened.

22. Professing themselves to be wise, they became fools,
23. And changed the glory of the uncorruptible God into an image made like to corruptible man, and to birds, and fourfooted beasts, and creeping things.
24. Wherefore God also gave them up to uncleanness through the lusts of their own hearts, to dishonour their own bodies between themselves:
25. Who changed the truth of God into a lie, and worshipped and served the creature more than the Creator, who is blessed for ever. Amen.
26. For this cause God gave them up unto vile affections: for even their women did change the natural use into that which is against nature:
27. And likewise also the men, leaving the natural use of the woman, burned in their lust one toward another; men with men working that which is unseemly, and receiving in themselves that recompence of their error which was meet.
28. And even as they did not like to retain God in their knowledge, God gave them over to a reprobate mind, to do those things which are not convenient;
29. Being filled with all unrighteousness, fornication, wickedness, covetousness, maliciousness; full of envy, murder, debate, deceit, malignity; whisperers,
30. Backbiters, haters of God, despiteful, proud, boasters, inventors of evil things, disobedient to parents,
31. Without understanding, covenantbreakers, without natural affection, implacable, unmerciful:
32. Who knowing the judgment of God, that they which commit such things are worthy of death, not only do the same, but have pleasure in them that do such.

CHAPTER **58**

Crimes, Excessive Imprisonments - Black Men Curses

The justice system in America is very blatant in its perpetrating excessive imprisonments, especially towards black men. Black men are likely to receive excessive imprisonments or jail times comparable to the same crimes that white men commit. White men are likely to receive far less punishments over black men. Most of the time, there are white men or white women sitting on the benches handing out those punishments. Also, most of the time there are a majority of white people sitting in judgement on the court's jury boxes. There has never been an equitable justice system in place for black people as a whole.

- In 1992 there were more Black men in prison (583,000) than in college (537,000)(11)
- One out of every four Black men will go to prison in his lifetime(12) * 30% of Black men aged 20-29 in Chicago were arrested in 1993(13)
- 42% of Black men aged 18-35 in Washington, D.C. were under some form of criminal justice control in 1992(14)
- 56% of Black men aged 18-35 in Baltimore were under some form of criminal justice control in 1992(15)

Unfortunately, our society is still inundated with much discrimination, much prejudices, and very much racism which is merely a sleeping giant in the white (Caucasian) race of people. Many still have that superior type of attitudes that they are better than other races of people is in fact a lie from hell. Black people are essentially thorns in their sides. Any perceived power they think that have will be perpetrated and directed towards all people of color, especially those of the black race. The legal system is one such power structure they use to leverage their arms of power. They make the rules and bend them as they so desire while legally perpetrating discriminations, prejudices, and racisms.

Prov 26:26 (KJV) "Whose hatred is covered by deceit, his wickedness shall be showed before the whole congregation."

Prov 26:27 (KJV) "Whoso diggeth a pit shall fall therein: and he that rolleth a stone, it will return upon him."

Ezek 35:11 (KJV) "Therefore, as I live, saith the Lord GOD, I will even do according to thine anger, and according to thine envy which thou hast used out of thy hatred against them; and I will make myself known among them, when I have judged thee.
Article by: The Committee to End the Marion Lockdown 3/27/95
The least controversial observation that one can make about American criminal justice today is that it is remarkably ineffective, absurdly expensive, grossly inhumane, and riddled with discrimination. The beating of Rodney King was a reminder of the ruthlessness and racism that characterize many big city police departments. But the other aspects of the justice system, especially sentencing practices and prison conditions, are every bit as harsh and unfair.(1) The Committee to End the Marion Lockdown (CEML) was founded in 1985 to fight against the brutality of the United States Penitentiary at Marion. In 1987, we wrote that by the year 2000 the U.S. might have 1,000,000 people in prison. At that time U.S. prisons held 561,000 people, and most of our friends thought the notion of 1,000,000 prisoners was foolish. In the Fall of 1994, the U.S. announced that it sent its millionth human being to prison in June,(2) more than five years sooner than the projection

that was considered foolish just a few years ago. What we would like to do in this paper is examine the growth of imprisonment in the U.S. We will then analyze the nature of crime, and then the relationship between crime and imprisonment. Since crime and imprisonment are in fact not closely related, we will conclude the article by discussing why the U.S. is sending so many people to prison.

IMPRISONMENT

In addition to a million people in prison there are those in jails (about 500,000), those on parole (about 600,000), those on probation (about 3,000,000) and those in juvenile facilities (about 100,000).(3) It is difficult to grasp the enormity of these numbers. For example, the number of people in prison would comprise the 9th largest city in the U.S. The number of people who are incarcerated in jails and prisons is greater than the number of people who live in 13 states.(4) The number of people under the control of the "criminal" "justice" system is almost two times larger than the number of people who live in Nicaragua, or Chicago. The number of people in the U.S. who were arrested last year (14,000,000) is much larger than the population of Cuba.

Placing a million human beings in prison is an extraordinary landmark, the number of prisoners today being about five times larger than it was 20 years ago. This growth has more than kept up with the population. Between 1925 (when official imprisonment statistics were first organized) and 1971, the imprisonment rate remained on the order of about 100 per 100,000. Then, in 1972, the imprisonment rate began to soar and is still soaring. Figure 1 shows this trend. Today the imprisonment rate is 373 (per 100,000 population), almost four times higher than it was in 1972.(5)

INTERNATIONAL COMPARISONS

In 1991 the Sentencing Project, an independent organization based in Washington D.C., issued a report authored by Marc Mauer, its assistant director, entitled "Americans Behind Bars: A Comparison of International Rates of Incarceration." (6) The report, which used data from 1989 and 1990, found that the U.S. had the highest incarceration rate in the world (426) compared to a distant second South Africa (333) and third, the Soviet Union (268).(7)

Incredibly, when the report was revised using data from one year later, the gap had widened,(8) and was wider still one year later. (9) In 1992 the U.S. had an incarceration rate of 519 compared to South Africa's rate of 368. Furthermore, in 1990 the incarceration rate for Black men in the U.S. was 3,109 compared to 729 for Black men in South Africa. In 1992 this differential had increased: the rates were, respectively, 3,822 and 851. Thus, in 1990 the incarceration rate for Black men in the U.S. was 4.3 times greater than the rate for Black men in South Africa. Two years later that ratio had increased to 4.5.

Table 1 provides some of the incarceration rates assembled by Mauer. Among other observations, it is interesting to note that the competition between Washington, D.C. and Moscow continues as the newly formed country of Russia has just overtaken the U.S. as the country with the highest imprisonment rate in the world.

Table 1. Incarceration Rates (Number of People in Prisons and Jails, per 100,000 Population) for Selected Countries, 1992-1993 (10)

Country	Rate of Incarceration
Australia	91
Mexico/ Belgium	71
Netherlands/Brazil	84
Portugal/Canada	116
Russia/Denmark	66
South/Africa	368
England/Wales	93

Sweden/France	84
Switzerland/Germany	80
United States/Italy	80
Thailand	

U.S. PRISONS -- IN BLACK AND WHITE

97 49 93 558
69 85 519
159

Consider the racial nature of imprisonment in the U.S.. Using U.S. Census and other estimates derived from the Bureau of Justice Statistics, we have calculated imprisonment rates (we are now using only people in prison for these calculations) as of June,1994. These are shown in Table 2.

Table 2. Imprisonment Rates in the United States, 1994

Group	Rate	Total
Compared to White Rate	2.1	373
White People	1.0	176
Hispanic People	3.9	686
Black People	8.5	1489

We can see from the table that Black people are 8.5 times more likely and that Hispanic people are 3.9 times more likely to go to prison than are White people.

Further examination of these statistics reveals the depth of their meaning. For example, if instead of the usual per 100,000 people, we employ percentages (per 100 people), we see that 1.489% of all Black people (and 0.176% of all White people) will be in prison at any given moment. Using census data we can calculate related figures: 3.0% of all Black males will be in prison on a given day in 1994 as will 6.0% of all Black men aged 18-44 and 7.6% of all Black men aged 25-29.

We can also consider some other research findings:

- In 1992 there were more Black men in prison (583,000) than in college (537,000)(11) * One out of every four Black men will go to prison in his lifetime(12) * 30% of Black men aged 20-29 in Chicago were arrested in 1993(13)
- 42% of Black men aged 18-35 in Washington, D.C. were under some form of criminal justice control in 1992(14)
- 56% of Black men aged 18-35 in Baltimore were under some form of criminal justice control in 1992(15)

THE NEW CRIME BILL

A new "crime" bill has just been passed by Congress. This bill will render the horrific numbers discussed above small by comparison. In addition to adding scores of new crimes punishable by the death penalty, the goals of this new "crime initiative" involve: placing 100,000 more police on the streets; increasing conviction rates; increasing the proportion of convictions resulting in imprisonment; requiring those imprisoned to serve at least 85% of their sentences ("truth in sentencing"); and incarcerating "three- time losers" for the rest of their lives.

Political scientists and criminologists have started to estimate the impact that this bill will have on imprisonment. John Irwin and James Austin, two criminologists who often prepare publications for the prestigious National Council on Crime and Delinquency, have estimated in their new book entitled 'It's About Time' (16) that a package of laws such as those included in the new crime bill would result in over 9 times as many people being imprisoned. Thus, if we multiply by 9 the 6.0%

noted above, we see that well over half of all Black men aged 18-44 would be in prison on any given day if all projected aspects of the new "crime initiative" are implemented. Irwin and Austin note similarly: "[The Crime Bill] would mean that most of the nation's 5.5 million black males aged 18-39 would be incarcerated."(17) Other estimates of the potential impact of the crime bill have suggested a smaller but still devastating impact.(18)

There is much that is speculative about this estimate, and that must remain so given the unfolding details of the new crime bill. Other specifics would have to be taken into consideration to refine the estimates above, such as estimating the impact of an aging prison population, determining how much of the "crime" bill will actually be funded, etc. Whatever these refinements, the numbers will remain staggering. Never before has any society at any time used imprisonment in this fashion. The impact that this will have on the Black community is difficult even to fathom.

FINANCES

Much has been written about the financing of the "criminal" "justice" system (CJS). Just a few figures here will suffice. Funding for the CJS has increased seven-fold over the past 20 years, from $10 billion to $74 billion a year, with $25 billion spent for incarceration. (19) This, however, is all spare change compared to what may follow, depending upon which aspects of the new crime bill are implemented. For example, it has been estimated that the "three-time loser" provision itself will cost $5.7 billion annually and require an additional $21 billion in prison construction costs.20 It has also been estimated that the crime bill could cost as much as an extra $351 billion over the next ten years.(21)

Since not many of us have this much money in our pockets, or even in our bank accounts, let's try to understand just how much it really is. It costs much more to send a person to prison for a year than it does to send that person to Harvard. In fact, it costs more to send a person to prison than it would to support a family of four. Interestingly, about 300,000 families of four or 1.2 million people could live for what it will cost just to implement the new three-time loser laws. Noting the surging hunger in the U.S., the Bread for the World Institute has just determined that $10 billion would be enough to expand the Women, Infants and Children (WIC) food program to assure that there were no longer any hungry people in this category.(22) This is less than two years of payments for the three-time loser law. Or, consider this. According to a report from the American Bar Association,(23) all the state taxes of 18 average taxpayers in Delaware are required to keep one person in prison for a year; and the money spent to build a prison in Wisconsin would pay for 11,000 children to attend Head Start.

CRIME
WHAT IS CRIME?

This is not as simple a question as it appears. For example, there is the street crime that breaks the law and that sometimes results in imprisonment. But most crime does not result in imprisonment, nor is it even considered crime. For example, domestic violence, or the battering of women, is almost never seen as a crime -- even though it is estimated that 3 4,000,000 women a year in the U.S. are battered by their mates.(24) Waging war is not considered criminal even though the war against Iraq murdered about 500,000 Iraqis. Denying people health care, food or housing also isn't a crime. And it is not a crime to manufacture and sell cigarettes, which each year kill 20 times as many people as guns. We make these points to emphasize that whatever the relationship between crime and imprisonment, it doesn't involve any of these issues.

HOW IS CRIME MEASURED?

There are two main ways that street crime is measured in the U.S.

The first is with the Uniform Crime Report (UCR). This is computed by adding together the major crimes that are reported to the police who in turn report to the F.B.I. who in turn publish the findings. The other measure of crime comes from the National Crime Victimization Survey (NCVS). About 20 years ago it became clear that only a proportion of crimes are actually reported to the police and that if we wanted a more accurate count, we would have to conduct scientific surveys of the population and ask people if they had been victims of crime. This is what the NCVS does.

Since the UCR and the NCVS measure crime in different ways, they present different views of crime. For example, the UCR only contains crimes that are reported to the police, by some estimates only 40% of the total. (In 1992 there were about 34,000,000 crimes reported to the NCVS and 13,000,000 to the UCR.)25 On the other hand, the NCVS does not include the crime murder (since its victim can't report it) nor crimes for which there is no reporting victim, like most drug-related crimes. Also not included are all white collar crimes, like the savings and loan frauds, and much more.

Let's look at each. But first let's look at murder since this is the easiest to measure and thus is the crime we know most about. About 25,000 people were murdered in the U.S. last year. As Figure 2 shows, the murder rate in the U.S. was about 10 (per 100,000 population) in 1930 and about 10 in 1990 -- almost no change at all in 60 years.26 Similarly, the murder rate in 1993 (9.3) was just about what it was in 1973 (9.4).(27)

HAS CRIME BEEN INCREASING?

Figures 3 and 4 show crime that is measured by the NCvs. As you can see, since 1973, when the NCVS was initiated,(28) the index of all NCVS crimes has decreased rather steadily while the violent crime index has stayed constant. Figures 5 and 6 show crime that is measured by the UCR, also since 1973. Here an uneven pattern of increases and decreases is present for all crimes while violent crimes increased steadily and dramatically.(29,30)

THE RELATIONSHIP BETWEEN CRIME AND IMPRISONMENT

Few matters are as clear as the answer to the question: Is there a relationship between crime and imprisonment?" Virtually everyone, from criminologists to wardens to social scientists to specially appointed task forces, answers the question the same way: "No." We would like to sketch just some of the arguments which illustrate this lack of relationship.

Let us consider the data presented above. We can see that over the past 20 years one measure of crime (the NCVS) has decreased by 26% and the other measure (the UCR) has increased about 47%, and the imprisonment rate has increased by 200%. In addition, consider the fact that the UCR (Figure 4) decreased from 1980 to 1985 and then increased about the same amount between 1985 and 1990. These changes took place while imprisonment rates spiralled equally upward during both of these intervals (Figure 1). When all of this is added together, it is clear that putting enormous numbers of people into prison has not reduced the crime rate. A recent report from the National Council on Crime and Delinquency(31) presents these data in a summary form that is reproduced here in Table 3.

Table 3. Changes in Correctional Populations Between 1980 and 1990.

Population	1980	1990	% Change
Probation	1,118,097	2,670,234	139
Jails	163,994	403,019	146
Prisons	329,821	771,243	134
Parole	220,438	531,403	141
Total	1,832,350	4,375,903	139
UCR Index Crimes	13,400,000	14,500,000	8

Consider the funnel effect, which demonstrates why most crimes don't even come into contact with the criminal justice system. Joan Petersilia, former president of the American Society of Criminology, and an employee of the conservative Rand Corporation, in an article entitled "Building More Prison Cells Won't Make a Safer Society," notes: "Of the approximately 34 million serious felonies in 1990, 31 million never entered the criminal justice system because they were either unreported or unsolved." Thus, she continues, only 10% of all crime ever entered the courts, about half of these resulted in convictions, and about a third of these resulted in imprisonment -- less than 2% of the total amount of crime.(32)

Over half of all murders are committed by people known to the victim. In addition, virtually all murder is committed in fits of passion that are immune to rational consideration of consequences. We are not saying that murderers should not be incarcerated. We are saying that incarceration will not prevent murders. Similarly, it has been demonstrated again and again that the death penalty does not deter murder. These latter observations are illustrated by the data in Figure 2, which shows that the murder rate has remained more-or-less constant over the past 60 years, through periods of little imprisonment and through periods of massive imprisonment; through periods of the use of the death penalty and through periods when the death penalty was not used.

Consider the question of supply. There is a virtually unlimited supply of people who will commit crimes associated with drugs. As soon as one person is removed from the labor market, another replaces him or her. Prisons will never be able to dent this supply.

Virtually all experts agree that prisons cause people to become even more deeply embedded in a life of crime. Recidivism rates are over 50% within three years in most states.(33,34)

The following comments are by people in the field who one would expect to be supportive of imprisonment. Thus their denials of the impact of imprisonment on crime merit attention:

- By a criminologist: "Incapacitation appears to have been only slightly more effective in averting crimes in the early 1980s than in the 1970s, despite a near doubling of the U.S. prison populations in less than ten years."(35)
- From the Correctional Association of New York: "The state's new policies have been staggeringly expensive, have threatened a crisis of safety and manageability in the prison system, and have failed to reduce the rate of crime or even stop its increase. After almost ten years of getting tough the citizens of New York are more likely to be victims of crime today than in 1971. Moreover, the largest rise in crime came at the end of the decade, during 1980-81, well after the introduction of more severe sentencing practices."(36)
- Even the Director of Corrections of Alabama understands this situation: "We're on a train that has to be turned around. It doesn't make any sense to pump millions and millions into corrections and have no effect on the crime rate."(37)
- From Robert Gangi, current Director of the Correction Association of New York: "Building more prisons to address crime is like building more graveyards to address a fatal disease."(38)
- One last study on this topic must be noted before moving ahead. Justice Fellowship, the organization founded by Chuck Colson (of Watergate infamy), commissioned a special report to determine how much prisons deterred crime. Their findings were so non-supportive of prisons that they were reduced to this sarcastic attack:

  » Incarceration rates are such a poor predictor of crime rates that researchers would find proximity [of states] to Canada more reliable. Eight of the 12 states that border on Canada rank in the bottom 20 in overall

> crime rates. Even alphabetical order is more reliable [than incarceration rates] when predicting crime rates: Three states among the first 15 alphabetically rank in the bottom two-fifths of crime rates.(39)

WHAT DOES IT ALL MEAN?

We have examined imprisonment, crime, and the relationship between the two. What can a reasonable person conclude?
Elliot Currie has written an insightful book on crime and imprisonment. (40) In this book, Currie poses the question why the U.S. keeps pumping billions of dollars into the CJS, which everyone, he acknowledges, knows doesn't work: "Ifwe know as much about crime as I think we do, why haven't we already acted on that knowledge more consistently and constructively."(41) In other words, Currie is asking why the U.S. continues to pursue imprisonment strategies that don't work. The only answer that Currie can find for his question is that the U.S. doesn't understand what the research is showing. This is an extraordinary answer which shows where liberals must wind up on such a question. Here is a system that is spending $74 billion a year and Currie thinks it acts the way it does because it cannot find someone to explain what the research is saying. Let us try another possible answer.

Currie and many others get stuck and can move no further because they assume that the purpose of the criminal justice system is to prevent crime. Consider a quote from another leading liberal in "criminal" "justice" reform, Norval Morris, a professor of law at the University of Chicago who has written excellent articles and books critiquing the CJS: "The whole law-and-order movement that we've heard so much about is, in operation, anti-black and anti-underclass. Not in plan, not in design, not in intent, but in operation."(42) Thus, also according to Morris, the direction of the CJS is an accident.
If liberal critics of the CJS would just turn the problem around and not ask why the CJS fails at its stated purpose but rather ask what

purposes a system like this could have, then they could find an answer. Let us examine Table 4 which presents the characteristics of the CJS that have been established above:

Table 4. Characteristics of the "Criminal" "Justice" System

- The process of mass incarceration started in 1972.
- The CJS spends many billions of dollars every year caging millions of people.
- The cages are filled with people of color, most of them Black.
  * The system does not prevent crime.
- The system does not rehabilitate people.
- We know of many other measures that would prevent crime.

We would suggest that a system with these characteristics might be seen, not as a crime prevention system, but as a system whose foremost purpose is to control of people of color. Remember what events preceded the growth in imprisonment that started in 1972. That year followed in the midst of the F.B.I.'s COINTELPRO program; the assassination of dozens of leaders of the Black Liberation Movement and the imprisoning of hundreds more; the assassination of George Jackson on August 21, 1971; and the rebellion at Attica on September 9 - 13, 1971. Then just a few months later, the imprisonment rate started to spiral upwards, and has not yet stopped doing so. Furthermore, 1972 was also the year that the first Control Unit was opened -- as one wing of the U.S. Penitentiary at Marion.

When this historical context is added to the statistics about crime and imprisonment and the rampant racism of U.S. society, it seems clear that the hypothesis that prisons are institutions for control of people of color is a far more viable one than the notion that prisons are an effort to prevent crime. In fact, the only support for the latter hypothesis would appear to be the assertions of some of those who run the prison system and politicians.

It seems worthwhile to elaborate on this point. There is no viable evidence that prisons prevent crime. There is an abundance of evidence, a small proportion of it presented above, that prisons don't and can't prevent crime. In addition, every serious analyses of the history of incarceration reveal the same historical thrust: prisons and other systems of punishment are for social control, not crime control. For example, in 1939 Rusche and Kirchheimer wrote a very important book showing that the systems of imprisonment throughout history were simply reflections of the economic systems that existed at given times. These systems were not about crime prevention; they were about the relations of production.(43) Foucault, in his seminal book, Discipline & Punish, has shown that the evolution of state punishment had little to do with crime and everything to do with the exertion of the state to maintain its power: " . . . one would be forced to suppose that the prison, and no doubt punishment in general, is not intended to eliminate offences, but rather to distinguish them, to distribute them, to use them"(44) or: "We are aware of all the inconveniences of prison, and that it is dangerous when it is not useless. And yet one cannot 'see' how to replace it. It is the detestable solution, which one seems unable to do without."(45)

CEML belives that one of the main functions of progressive struggle is to counter the prevailing ideology. If this is correct, then fighting to establish the real purpose of the "criminal" "justice" system is meaningful work. At the same time, it is not easy work, to say the least. Many progressive publications show no understanding of or interest in these issues. We in CEML have often posed the slogan "Not One More Cell," only to be opposed by other progressive people. When we have asked why they disagree, they note that crime is a serious problem and we have to offer some solutions. We couldn't agree more that crime is a serious problem, and that solutions are needed. But prisons have nothing to do with preventing crime. They haven't; they don't; and they can't -- ever. Until we all understand this and have the courage to put forward the notion that we need real solutions, not diversions which are nothing more than racist attacks on people of color, we will not be able to move our pursuits for a human society any further.

This gives us still one more reason to fight against law and order hysteria and the racist use of imprisonment in our society. Rather than devoting our resources and energies to proven failed strategies like the use of massive imprisonment, we should instead pursue those strategies which will build a truly human society and thus prevent crime. These strategies include struggling to eliminate white supremacy and poverty while building an economy that meets human needs rather than the desires of profiteers. Rather than creating a nation of prisons we should be allowing the emergence of a nation of human beings.

CHAPTER 59

Cyber Attacks on America by China and Russia

America has enemies all over the world due to its status of the world's super power. Additionally, America is hated for her stand with Israel, the Jewish/Hebrew nations. If she wants to continue to exist, then this is the road she must. Even Almighty God tells us that He will bless those who bless Israel and Jerusalem and curse those who curse Israel and Jerusalem, mainly the Jews. Many nations would like to see the demise of America by doing anything evil to her.

Genesis 12 (KJV)

1. Now the Lord had said unto Abram, Get thee out of thy country, and from thy kindred, and from thy father's house, unto a land that I will shew thee:
2. And I will make of thee a great nation, and I will bless thee, and make thy name great; and thou shalt be a blessing:
3. And I will bless them that bless thee, and curse him that curseth thee: and in thee shall all families of the earth be blessed.

U.S. Under Siege from Chinese, Russian Cyber-Attackers
Wednesday, April 8, 2009 6:52 PM

WASHINGTON - U.S. concerns about the potential for cyber-attacks on critical infrastructure extended to the American electrical power grid on Wednesday and experts pointed the finger anew at Chinese hackers, among others.

U.S. Homeland Security Secretary Janet Napolitano told reporters the power grid is vulnerable to potentially disabling computer attacks, while declining to comment on reports that an intrusion had taken place.

"The vulnerability is something that the Department of Homeland Security and the energy sector have known about for years," she said. "We acknowledge that ... in this world, in an increasingly cyber world, these are increasing risks."

Napolitano spoke after the Wall Street Journal reported that cyberspies had penetrated the U.S. electrical grid and left behind software programs that could be used to disrupt the system.

The Journal said the intruders have not sought to damage the power grid or other key infrastructure but could try during a crisis or war. The United States for several years has accused the Chinese and Russians, among others, of using cyber-attacks to try to steal American trade secrets, military secrets and
government secrets.

The Chinese have been particularly active, a former U.S. security official told Reuters.

"They are all over the place," said the official, who spoke on condition of anonymity. "They're getting into university systems, contractor systems, hacking government systems. There's no reason to think that the electrical system would be immune as well."

Eric Rosenbach, executive director for research at Harvard University's Kennedy School of Government's Belfer Center, said that if true, it showed that the Chinese and Russians are thinking strategically about how to either constrain the United States or inflict more damage if they ever felt they needed to do so.

'POTENTIAL WEAKNESS'

"I think that China recognizes if in a very strategic sense you want to ensure you have the ability to exploit another country's potential weakness or vulnerability but do it in a way that isn't confrontational or cause an international crisis, then this is a very good way of doing that," he said.

President Barack Obama, aware of the concerns about the vulnerability of infrastructure, has launched a cyber review that is expected to be completed in the coming weeks.

"The president takes the issue of cybersecurity very seriously, which is why he ordered a top-to-bottom review shortly after taking office," said White House spokesman Nick Shapiro.
He said the White House was not aware of "any disruptions to the power grid caused by deliberate cyber-activity here in the United States."

"The Department of Homeland Security works with industry to identify vulnerabilities and to help industry enhance the security of control system networks. The federal government is also working to ensure that security is built in as we develop the next generation of 'smart grid' networks," Shapiro said.

Mississippi Democratic Representative Bennie Thompson, chairman of the House of Representatives Homeland Security Committee, said he would introduce legislation to address the grid's vulnerability to cyber-attack.

"Our electric system is critical to our way of life, and we cannot afford to leave it vulnerable to attack. Our oversight indicates there is a significant gap in current regulation to effectively secure this infrastructure," he said.

The United States is not alone. CIA analyst Tom Donahue told a power-industry conference last year that "we have information from multiple regions outside the United States, of cyber-intrusion into utilities followed by extortion demands." The North American Electric Reliability Corp, the industry group with responsibility for grid reliability and security for the United States and Canada, said it was unaware of any cyber-attacks that have led to disruptions of electric service. The group has been working for several years with the industry to create and implement cybersecurity measures.
"NERC and industry leaders are taking steps in the right direction to improve preparedness and response to potential cyberthreats," the group said. "There is definitely more to be done."

American Electric Power Co spokeswoman Melissa McHenry said the utility takes security and reliability of the grid seriously.

"We long ago identified that there are numerous scans and probes of our networks from external sources and have put in place a very comprehensive multilayered security system to protect it from internal and external intrusion attempts," she said.

Still, she said, "We realize that there are no guarantees that you can always be completely safe from a cyber-attack. We continually monitor the effectiveness of our systems and seek to enhance them."

China Denies Cyber Attacks on U.S. Power Grid
Owen Fletcher, IDG News Service Apr 9, 2009 11:20 pm

Malware attacks from China and Russia designed to shut down the U.S. electrical grid in a time of war did not occur, China said Thursday.

"The incident of attacks on the U.S. electrical grid from China and Russia simply does not exist," Chinese foreign ministry spokeswoman Jiang Yu told reporters, according to a transcript of the briefing.

"We hope the concerned media will cautiously handle groundless statements and especially critiques against China."

Widespread intrusions by cyberspies in countries including China and Russia have infected the U.S. power grid with software that could be used to halt its operation, a Wall Street Journal report said this week, citing unnamed U.S. national security officials.

The newest allegations of Chinese cyberespionage follow long-standing concern that a coordinated attack on the U.S. power grid could cripple its operation.

China produces the majority of the world's malware but part of it could come from attackers in other countries, who often hide behind Chinese IP (Internet Protocol) addresses.

CHAPTER 60

Deacons Selected from Lay Membership in Churches

One of the serious mistakes churches make is to select lay members from their congregations to serve in the office as deacons. Biblically speaking, deacons are supposed to be selected from a select group of ministers (preachers). In most churches these ministers are referred to as associate ministers or associate pastors. This is the select group of people where deacons are selected from and not from the general congregation as a whole. These men and women should already have a call on their lives as preachers.

Let's take for example the office of Bishop. A person who desires to become a bishop should already be a professing preacher who is called to preach by God, Almighty. The biblical guidelines for the office of bishop applies equally for the office of deacon. Even simple logic will prove that these two offices have almost the same requirements for holy living as both offices are based initially upon divine calls of that person from God, Almighty. Even in the Temple where priest were the leaders, ministers under them had various functions within the Temple. Additionally, there were helpers to assist them and the priest.

Baptist churches have gone so far as discriminate against associate ministers or associate pastors by not including them in their Church Constitutions and By-Laws and by not allowing them to exercise the fruits of their calling within their home church. These so-called reigning deacons don't consider these minister as leaders in their churches simply because they aren't selected officials as they and the pastor. This is a great tragedy and a curse upon many churches mainly because God Almighty's anointed ones are being ignored. Present day deacon offices are similar to the offices that the Levites served as in the Tabernacle of the congregation under Aaron and his sons. Levites served in keeping the vessels and many other possessions of the Temple.

1 Chr 9:24 (KJV) "In four quarters were the porters, toward the east, west, north, and south."

1 Chr 9:25 (KJV) "And their brethren, which were in their villages, were to come after seven days from time to time with them."

1 Chr 9:26 (KJV) "For these Levites, the four chief porters, were in their set office, and were over the chambers and treasuries of the house of God."

1 Chr 9:27 (KJV) "And they lodged round about the house of God, because the charge was upon them, and the opening thereof every morning pertained to them."

1 Chr 9:28 (KJV) "And certain of them had the charge of the ministering vessels, that they should bring them in and out by tale."

1 Chr 9:29 (KJV) "Some of them also were appointed to oversee the vessels and all the instruments of the sanctuary, and the fine flour, and the wine, and the oil, and the frankincense, and the spices."

1 Chr 9:30 (KJV) "And some of the sons of the priests made the ointment of the spices."

1 Chr 9:31 (KJV) "And Mattithiah, one of the Levites, who was the firstborn of Shallum the Korahite, had the set office over the things that were made in the pans."

1 Chr 9:32 (KJV) "And other of their brethren, of the sons of the Kohathites, were over the showbread, to prepare it every sabbath."

1 Chr 9:33 (KJV) "And these are the singers, chief of the fathers of the Levites, who remaining in the chambers were free: for they were employed in that work day and night."

1 Chr 9:34 (KJV) "These chief fathers of the Levites were chief throughout their generations; these dwelt at Jerusalem."

Num 18:2-8 (KJV) And thy brethren also of the tribe of Levi, the tribe of thy father, bring thou with thee, that they may be joined unto thee, and minister unto thee: but thou and thy sons with thee shall minister before the tabernacle of witness.

3. And they shall keep thy charge, and the charge of all the tabernacle: only they shall not come nigh the vessels of the sanctuary and the altar, that neither they, nor ye also, die.
4. And they shall be joined unto thee, and keep the charge of the tabernacle of the congregation, for all the service of the tabernacle: and a stranger shall not come nigh unto you.
5. And ye shall keep the charge of the sanctuary, and the charge of the altar: that there be no wrath any more upon the children of Israel.
6. And I, behold, I have taken your brethren the Levites from among the children of Israel: to you they are given as a gift for the LORD, to do the service of the tabernacle of the congregation.
7. Therefore thou and thy sons with thee shall keep your priest's office for every thing of the altar, and within the veil; and ye shall serve: I have given your priest's office unto you as a service of gift: and the stranger that cometh nigh shall be put to death.

8. And the LORD spake unto Aaron, Behold, I also have given thee the charge of mine heave offerings of all the hallowed things of the children of Israel; unto thee have I given them by reason of the anointing, and to thy sons, by an ordinance for ever.

God only allowed them to serve from ages 25 to 50 years. After 50 years of age they could no longer serve in any capacity. However, they could minister after age 50.

Num 8:24 (KJV) "This is it that belongeth unto the Levites: from twenty and five years old and upward they shall go in to wait upon the service of the tabernacle of the congregation:"

Num 8:25 (KJV) "And from the age of fifty years they shall cease waiting upon the service thereof, and shall serve no more:"

Num 8:26 (KJV) "But shall minister with their brethren in the tabernacle of the congregation, to keep the charge, and shall do no service. Thus shalt thou do unto the Levites touching their charge."

Catholic churches guidelines for deacons are biblically based and are structured similar to the offices in the Temple. Deacons are actually members of the clergy who are responsible to and reports directly to the presiding priest. These deacons officiate marriages, funerals, wakes, they counsel members, they teach, preach and do whatever other functions are directed to them by the priest or his delegated official(s). In the Protestant denominational churches, the Senior Pastor or the Assistant Pastor would be the one to direct or dictate duties to these ministers. Preachers called by God Almighty should actually be deacons of churches, but not lay members from the congregation. It is no wonder churches are having so many problems when vacant pastoral positions are being filled with inept selection processes based on gut feelings, secular selection processes and not necessarily from any discernment from the Holy Spirit. Most deacons in the Protestant denominations are babes in Christ and really don't have the gift of discernment. Most deacons (lay membership) don't have the foggiest idea on what to look for when calling a preacher to lead them and their congregations. It is clear that this curse is rampart in many of our Protestant denominational churches

Phil 1:1 (KJV) "Paul and Timotheus, the servants of Jesus Christ, to all the saints in Christ Jesus which are at Philippi, with the bishops and deacons:"

Bishop. Greek definition. 1985. episkopos, ep-is'-kop-os; from G1909 and G4649 (in the sense of G1983); a superintendent, i.e. Chr. officer in gen. **charge of a (or the) church** (lit. or ig.):-- bishop, **overseer**.

Deacons/Deaconess. Greek definition. 1249. diakonos, dee-ak'-on-os; prob. from an obs. diako (to run on errands; comp. G1377); an attendant, i.e. (gen.) a waiter (at table or in other menial duties); spec. a Chr. **teacher and pastor** (techn. a deacon or deaconess):--**deacon, minister, servant**.

1 Tim 3:1-13 (KJV) This is a true saying, If a man desire the office of a bishop, he desireth a good work.

2. A bishop then must be blameless, the husband of one wife, vigilant, sober, of good behaviour, given to hospitality, apt to teach;
3. Not given to wine, no striker, not greedy of filthy lucre; but patient, not a brawler, not covetous;
4. One that ruleth well his own house, having his children in subjection with all gravity;
5. (For if a man know not how to rule his own house, how shall he take care of the church of God?)
6. Not a novice, lest being lifted up with pride he fall into the condemnation of the devil.

7. Moreover he must have a good report of them which are without; lest he fall into reproach and the snare of the devil.
8. Likewise must the deacons be grave, not double tongued, not given to much wine, not greedy of filthy lucre;
9. Holding the mystery of the faith in a pure conscience.
10. And let these also first be proved; then let them use the office of a deacon, being found blameless.
11. Even so must their wives be grave, not slanderers, sober, faithful in all things.
12. Let the deacons be the husbands of one wife, ruling their children and their own houses well.
13. For they that have used the office of a deacon well purchase to themselves a good degree, and great boldness in the faith which is in Christ Jesus.

CHAPTER **61**

Demonic Rituals, Designs, and Drawings Are Curses

I (Curtis) have a friend in church who shared with me that he had an acquaintance who had an occultic book of rituals. So, as he said that one day he was curious and decided to open up the book and try some of the rituals just to see if they worked or actually occur. To his surprise, he found that there was a certain ritual of chanting to make certain people that he selected to do certain things. He said that he tried that particular ritual once and it worked. He then tried it again on another person and it worked again. So, he then got scarred and stop doing the rituals. One big problem and a number of other problems came into his life when he tried to stop. All hell broke loose in his life and in his children's life.

Through Occultic Drawings

You can bring curses upon yourself and to your household by bringing occultic type drawings into your residence for displaying on walls, desks, furniture, fixtures or just merely possessing such items. Such items have already been cursed before you even took possession of them. If something looks weird to you or if you have any doubt that is of an evil source, don't touch it nor go near such items.

Acts 19:18-19 (KJV) And many that believed came, and confessed, and showed their deeds.

19. Many of them also which used curious arts brought their books together, and burned them before all men: and they counted the price of them, and found it fifty thousand pieces of silver.

Through The Spirit Realm Directly

If you are a part of occultic activities or if you are associated with someone who participates in occult activities, then you are subject to being cursed through the evil spirit realm. This can be done unbeknownst to you. If you take part in any satanic ritual, you have opened yourself to an unknown number of curses.

There is a case where a young man was encouraged to follow his friends after they told him they could make tables levitate or lift up off the floor without anybody touching it. Well, this young man was curious and he followed them to watch them make the table levitate. Later, this young man was found on the ground out of his mind. The parents took him home and they didn't know what was wrong with their son. Their son couldn't speak to them to tell them what he had done. Whatever they would position him on the bed, he would stay in that position all night. If they would lift his arm and hand, it would still be in the same position the next morning. They finally found out that their son was demon possessed. Fortunately, he was delivered from that demon and was back into his right mind again to explain what he had done. He was just merely a spectator looking for the wrong sign and wonder. In the process this young man trespassed on Satan's ground and his territorial rights, he was spiritually possessed with one of Satan's demons.

- Magical aspects of piercing:
- Abnormal ears piercing
- Nose piercing
- Lip piercing
- Tongue piercing

- Belly button (naval) piercing
- Flesh piercing
- Tattoos Leviticus 19:28. Ye shall not make any cuttings in your flesh for the dead, nor print any marks upon you: I am the Lord.
- Watching horror movies
- Watching Die Hard II movies
- Watching Vampire movies
- Tatoos
- Voodoo rituals
- Cultural rituals
- Horoscopes, using and leaning on
- Superstitions, leaning on
- Good luck charms (i.e, rabbit foot, crystals, etc.)
- Gambling games of chance (i.e., shooting craps, lotteries, etc.)
- Drunkards (habitual abuse of beer, wine, hard liquor and/or other alcoholic beverages)
- Possessing Sphinx (Egyptian Mythology) figurines, statues, toys, ceramic pieces, etc.
  1) Body of a lion, head of a man, ram, or hawk
  2) Winged monster having the head of a woman, and the body of a lion that destroyed all who could not answer its riddle
- Possessing Santa Claus clothing, uniforms with accessories, equipment, figurines, statues, toys, cards, etc.
- Playing with Ouija boards
- Wearing Hawaiian Leis (necklaces of flowers) around your neck
- Listening to country death songs
- Listening to hard rock music
- Listening to acid rock music
- Listening to gangster rap music
- Listening to backward mast music with demonic lyrics
- Chanting occult phrases and/or languages

- Participating in occult rituals
- Seeking out fortune tellers for advice and for other information
- Seeking out and calling psychic Telephone Hot lines
- Seeking out and communicating with psychics through the Internet and through various other means as well
- Seeking out and entering satanic web sites
- Seeking out and entering gothic web sites
- Seeking out advice from palm readers
- Seeking out advice from tarot card readers
- Participating in pornography schemes
- Playing power games of demonic influences
- Playing Nintendo games of demonic influence
- Playing Play Station games of demonic influence
- Playing Internet games of demonic influence
- Seeking out spiritualist (fortune teller, psychic, etc). Some use the title of "Reverend" with their names in order to gain the benefits that a church affords them under the law.
- Playing Dungeons and Dragons games
- Watching witchcraft, witch and/or warlock movies
- Participating in rituals to call up the dead (seances)
- Participating in Halloween parties (Satanic holiday)
- Dressing up in Halloween costumes and other attire in representing Halloween
- Habitually smoking crack cocaine, cocaine, hashish and other mind altering drugs to get high
- Habitually Shooting drugs in veins with needles to get high
- Habitually Sniffing drugs through the nose or mouth to get high
- Lighting candles and incense to demon gods or Satan
- Praying to Satan
- Fasting to Satan to obtain favors (lies) from him
- Rape victims (some are demonically traumatized or

possessed as a result of such experiences). I, (Curtis) have a young niece that this happened to at her very young age.

- Occultic drawings, art, designs, paintings, etc
- Yoga meditations and/or similar meditations
- Karate and other self defense rituals using mind over matter or related type techniques
- Praying to or seeking assistance from Mary (Jesus' earthly mother). These requests fall on the ears of Satan and his demons. Mary is not an intercessor, nor is she one to pray to.
- Rosary (necklaces of beads) and "Hail Mary" exclamations used in prayers
- Anointing oil use prohibited by many Churches

By The Use Of Personal Items

You can be cursed through your own personal items, even if they don't look like cursed items of such. Somebody can at will put curses on your personal items just because you looked at them the wrong way. So, you have to be very careful who you associate with or who you hang out with, so to speak. You can also be cursed with possession that you love more than human beings. If you believe your possessions and/or your wealth brings you much joy and success, then you are cursed. You need to reevaluate your lifestyle and your possession because this curse is simply destroying you. On the other hand, neither your possession, nor your wealth seem to bring you any joy and/or peace of mind. You are looking for all the right things, but all in all of the wrong places. First, set your priorities on Jesus Christ and everything else is secondary. There is nothing wrong with being wealthy and/or having many possessions, but know who is the head of your life, Jesus Christ, and keep Him there, always.

Through Cursed Gifts

An evil person can readily send you gifts in which they have cursed or have curses put on them. Since you are unaware that the gift is curse, you except it with open arms as a good gesture from the gift giver. On the other hand, if you have not had a good relationship with someone you know and all of a sudden they start sending you nice gifts, then you should be on alert for possibly cursed gifts.

CHAPTER 62

Discriminations, Prejudices, and Racism Curses

Almighty God hates racial discriminations, racial prejudices, racism perpetrated by any member of His human creation. As an example of his hatred for these evil curses, he took vengeance on one of his Prophetess by the name of Miriam, the sister of the Priest named Aaron who was the Spokesman for Moses. Moses married a black woman who was an Ethiopian woman. In their racist rage, they angered Almighty God. He told them to go out of the Tabernacle. He them directed his wrath upon Miriam.

Numbers 12 (KJV)

1. And Miriam and Aaron spake against Moses because of the Ethiopian woman whom he had married: for he had married an Ethiopian woman.
2. And they said, Hath the Lord indeed spoken only by Moses? hath he not spoken also by us? And the Lord heard it.
3. (Now the man Moses was very meek, above all the men which were upon the face of the earth.)
4. And the Lord spake suddenly unto Moses, and unto Aaron, and unto Miriam, Come out ye three unto the tabernacle of the congregation. And they three came out.
5. And the Lord came down in the pillar of the cloud, and

stood in the door of the tabernacle, and called Aaron and Miriam: and they both came forth.

6. And he said, Hear now my words: If there be a prophet among you, I the Lord will make myself known unto him in a vision, and will speak unto him in a dream.
7. My servant Moses is not so, who is faithful in all mine house.
8. With him will I speak mouth to mouth, even apparently, and not in dark speeches; and the similitude of the Lord shall he behold: wherefore then were ye not afraid to speak against my servant Moses?
9. And the anger of the Lord was kindled against them; and he departed.
10. And the cloud departed from off the tabernacle; and, behold, Miriam became leprous, white as snow: and Aaron looked upon Miriam, and, behold, she was leprous.
11. And Aaron said unto Moses, Alas, my lord, I beseech thee, lay not the sin upon us, wherein we have done foolishly, and wherein we have sinned.
12. Let her not be as one dead, of whom the flesh is half consumed when he cometh out of his mother's womb.
13. And Moses cried unto the Lord, saying, Heal her now, O God, I beseech thee.
14. And the Lord said unto Moses, If her father had but spit in her face, should she not be ashamed seven days? let her be shut out from the camp seven days, and after that let her be received in again.
15 And Miriam was shut out from the camp seven days: and the people journeyed not till Miriam was brought in again.
16. And afterward the people removed from Hazeroth, and pitched in the wilderness of Paran.

Unfortunately, racial discrimination, prejudices, and racism is alive and evil. Although there are blatant acts of these mentioned sins, there are also subtle acts that aren't so blatant or straight forward. There are many examples that I have experienced in my life time. Acts of discrimination, acts of prejudices, acts of racism are found in every aspect of our lives, from the lowest levels of our societies to the highest levels of our societies.

There are many hate groups: Klu Klux Klansman, Shin Heads, Black Panthers, White Supremacy groups, etc. The majority of those hate groups are perpetrated by white people which is quite sad as they are the majority of our populations.

I, Curtis, grew up in the rural farm areas in and near Augusta and Newport, Arkansas where racial discrimination, racial prejudices, certainly racism was the norm perpetrated by the white majority. This is not to say that all white people practiced these evil sins. There were a few white people who saw no color barriers, but the majority of them did.

There was one older couple who hired me to help out on their farm by driving their tractor and discing their farm land. Well to my surprise, when lunch time came, I went to the outside water faucet near the barn to wash up to eat my lunch from my greasy paper bag. Just I as finished washing up, the older gentlemen, "no, you are not going to eat out here. You are coming inside and eat with us." So, I put down my greasy lunch bag and went in with him. To my surprise, his wife had a table laid out with roast beef, chicken, vegetables, cakes and pies, all fit for a king. They sat me down at the head of the other end of the table and the older gentlemen sat at the other. He blessed the food and we ate, talked and ate. Well, we had already sat for about an hour and thought that I needed to get back to work. The older gentleman refused to let me go back to work because we kept on talking. He then pulled out his check book and paid me for a full day and told that I had helped him catch up with preparing his land. This sort of treatment towards black people by white people was not common. Normally, as long as black people stay in their so-called places, the two races would get along peacefully.

The Ku Klux Klansman are much a presence in those small country towns. From the lowest level of those societies to the highest level are members in this hate organization. Just to highlight a few, there are farmers, day laborers, store clerks, judges, lawyers, doctors, majors and various other business men and woman. There are a lot of evil sins perpetrated in a subtle or subdued way which is done in a way as not to bring attention to outside public audiences. Allow me to share some examples with you.

Newport, Arkansas. 1976 - An older gentleman by the name of Norman Alcorn, my step father's cousin had a farm in the Robinson Addition about 5 miles outside of the township of Newport. He divided some of his farm land into lots build houses on to sell to black families. He was attempting to provide lots at affordable prices because the lots sold by the white people were too expensive for the blacks to purchase. Unfortunately, Cousin Norman refused to sell to white people. Not long after his refusal to sell any lots to white people, someone set his house on fire while he and his wife were inside. He and his wife died from inhaling the smoke from the fire. There was a 5 gallon gas can found near the house that had been emptied. There was no investigation.

Augusta, Arkansas. Gibbs family of eight perished in their home when it was engulfed in flames in the rural areas of Revels, a community farm area outside of Augusta. It is said that the head of the household was a black man and the foremen on the farm. This caused some contentions with the white employees on the farm. They were upset that the white boss had put a black gentleman over them. Soon after that the Gibbs family perished in the fire.

I, Curtis, left home and joined the U.S. Army on April 26, 1965. I took my physical at recruiting station at Little Rock, Arkansas. After taking the oath of enlistment, we free that afternoon until the time came to board a bus to the airport for our flight to Shreveport, Louisiana and our subsequent bus ride to Fort Polk, Louisiana. I befriended two white guys who also enlisted that day as well. The gentlemen were Donald R. Rawls from Monroe, Louisiana, and the other gentleman was Hankins and I don't remember where he was from.. As we walked the streets of Little Rock, we came upon a pool hall. Rawls and Hankins decided that they wanted to play a few games of pool. They ask me to go with them. We entered the pool hall and went straight for the pool table. I stood at the far wall so I could watch them play pool. They were attempting to rack up the balls to play, when the bartender came from behind the bar directly to me. He allowed, "We don't serve your kind here!" Rawls and Hankins replied, "If you don't serve him, then you can't serve us!". We then departed the pool hall.

On the eve of my tour the 2nd Supply and Transportation Battalion in Munsani, Korea. I had appeared before several awards boards where I had won savings bonds, certificates and special days leaves and passes. It came time for me to appear before a promotion board. I passed the board for promotion. Normally, ones name would go a promotion list to wait for a slot to become available for promotion. Well after several tries to get my copy of the list with my name on it, the white sergeant in charge of the list intentionally delayed in producing a copy for me. I was due to leave in a few days and I never received the copy of the promotion list for my promotion at my next duty station. This was a very subtle attempt to deny me the promotion that I deserved and worked for.

During my tour at the 2nd Armored Division, S-4 Office (Division Supply), I was the senior clerk when a white gentleman arrived to our office. I was given the tasks of training him in the procedures and practices of our office. Our boss was a black man who was a Sergeant First Class (E-7). He had taught me well. Meanwhile a promotion board was scheduled. Not only was I eligible for promotion, but the new white clerk was eligible as well. So, I started teaching him what he should know to appear before a promotion board including our general orders, our chain of command, and current events the week of the promotion board. Well, both us appeared before the promotion board. The white gentleman was granted promotion, but I was denied. The Battalion Adjutant, a 1st Lieutenant lied and said that I missed a certain question, which I didn't. My boss pursued the matter even further. I received a called to report to the Adjutant. He sat me down told me to re-appear at the next promotion board and that he would make sure I would be promoted.

Newport, Arkansas. There was another black gentlemen who was a member of the NAACP Chapter and who voiced his opinion for the rights of the black citizens. Well, he had a new home built. To everybody's surprise, this house caught fire and burned up. The gentlemen's insurance company rebuilt his house. He continued to voice his opinion. To his surprise the second house caught fire and burned up. I believe this time the gentlemen moved out of the area.

Newport, Arkansas. I, Curtis, owned some property in Auvergne community which was about 8 miles from the township of Newport. It had a two-story house on it and two large lots. I was serving in the U.S. Army and the house was empty. I had a person who would occasionally mow the grass on the lots. Well at one point, the grass had grown up on the lots. My step father got word to me that threats were made to me that my house would be burned down if my grass was not cut. This was another example of the subtle threats of evil intents. Although there was an old barn about three buildings from my property with grass grown up all around it. It was owned by a white person.

Another incident among many others is that I wish to highlight was during my tour at Headquarters Landsouth, Verona, Italy. I was being processed for a Top Secret Clearance when a local investigator made a visit to me to question me and have me sign some documents. The documents were to give him unlimited access to any and all of my personal files. I really wanted to limit his access. So, I refused to sign those documents. Also, in answering his questions on my finances, I made a comment, "God is my witness!". The next thing I knew was that I was called to see First Sergeant Munoz and Brigadier General Benjamin Jones, my Executive Officer. They made an appointment for me to see a Psychiatrist, Dr. Iapolo at the military hospital at Vicenza, Italy. They handed me sealed envelope to take to the Psychiatrist. Fortunately, I was able to open the envelope to see what was in it. They had a problem with the phrase that I used, "God is my witness!". I made a copy of the form and closed the envelope up again. When I arrived for my appointment, I went to the doctor's office. He departed the office momentarily. When he returned, I had my head down praying. He aloowed, "Look at that!" referring to my praying. He did not examined me, questioned. He asked, "Do you want to go back to the states?". I replied, "No, we like it here in Italy!" He replied, "I bet you can't even pronounce my name. What is it?". I pronounce his name properly. Then he said, "I am going to recommend that you be transferred back to the states and treatment begin on you immediately. I was transferred immediately back to the U.S. at Fort Hood, Texas, all based upon a lie, discrimination, prejudice and racism. Subsequently, my security clearance was revoked, I was reclassified from being a Computer Programmer/Analyst back to a previous field, Technical Supply, Stock Control and Accounting Specialist. My career progression in the computer field in the U.S. Army was essentially destroyed. Discrimination, prejudices, and racism continued after I arrived at Fort Hood, Texas because of the stigma associated with losing my clearance as a senior non-commissioned officer.

No Human Is Inferior, Nor Superior To Another

The Prophet Isaiah put it quite bluntly, we are all unclean as filthy dirty rags in our spirits when we stand before our Maker, Almighty God. Satan is the father of lies and deception. His main purpose is to kill, steal and destroy. This is the primary goals of so-called white supremacy groups of white people who subscribe to such evil behavior.

Isaiah 64 (KJV)

6. But we are all as an unclean thing, and all our righteousnesses are as filthy rags; and we all do fade as a leaf; and our iniquities, like the wind, have taken us away.
7. And there is none that calleth upon thy name, that stirreth up himself to take hold of thee: for thou hast hid thy face from us, and hast consumed us, because of our iniquities.

Haggai 2 (KjV)

10. In the four and twentieth day of the ninth month, in the second year of Darius, came the word of the Lord by Haggai the prophet, saying,
11. Thus saith the Lord of hosts; Ask now the priests concerning the law, saying,
12. If one bear holy flesh in the skirt of his garment, and with his skirt do touch bread, or pottage, or wine, or oil, or any meat, shall it be holy? And the priests answered and said, No.
13. Then said Haggai, If one that is unclean by a dead body touch any of these, shall it be unclean? And the priests answered and said, It shall be unclean.
14. Then answered Haggai, and said, So is this people, and so is this nation before me, saith the Lord; and so is every work of their hands; and that which they offer there is unclean.

Matthew 23 (KjV)

27. Woe unto you, scribes and Pharisees, hypocrites! for ye are like unto whited sepulchres, which indeed appear beautiful outward, but are within full of dead men's bones, and of all uncleanness.
28. Even so ye also outwardly appear righteous unto men, but within ye are full of hypocrisy and iniquity.

Almighty God Created No Human As Common Or Unclean

Apostle Peter had to admonish Cornelius when he bowed down to him in reverence to his position as an Apostle. Even our positions or standing in society does not make us any better than anyone else.

Acts 10 (KJV)

25. And as Peter was coming in, Cornelius met him, and fell down at his feet, and worshipped him.
26. But Peter took him up, saying, Stand up; I myself also am a man.
27. And as he talked with him, he went in, and found many that were come together.
28. And he said unto them, Ye know how that it is an unlawful thing for a man that is a Jew to keep company, or come unto one of another nation; but God hath shewed me that I should not call any man common or unclean.

Now, Christians are admonished to love their enemies and do good to them.

Matthew 5 (KJV)

44. But I say unto you, Love your enemies, bless them that curse you, do good to them that hate you, and pray for them which despitefully use you, and persecute you;

CHAPTER 63

Divorced Couples Cursed - Deliverance Is Necessary

When a man and a woman are joined together in holy matrimony, their spirits are joined together as well. Their two separate spirits become one spirit. They are one in the same spirit.

One such experience with our marriage, my wife Carolyn (Carol) was pregnant with our youngest daughter, Vanessa while we were stationed at a U.S. Army Post called Fort Hood, Texas. Normally the wife would have morning sickness during her months of pregnancy. Guess what? Carol never had one day of morning sickness. Every morning before I went to work, I had morning sickness, basically around the same time every morning until she delivered Vanessa. Quite strange isn't it? Our one spirit was doing its thing.

Whether a man has abstained from having sex before he is married, or whether he had committed fornication or had sex with someone else before he was married, or whether he was a prostitute or whore or whether he committed an act or acts of adultery while in his marriage, all of those spirits are shared with his wife.

Whether a woman has abstained from having sex before she is married, or whether she had committed fornication or had sex with someone else before she was married, or whether she was a prostitute or whore or whether she committed an act or acts of adultery while she was in her marriage, all of those spirits are shared with her husband. Unfortunately, when these couples go their separate ways in a divorce arrangement, both take hefty bags of generational curses, other curses and inherited marital curses with them. Each of these individuals, their children, their grandchildren and their great grandchildren to the third and fourth generations, all need to be delivered from all of the generational curses and other curses including the curses of adultery and the curses of fornication. The divorced couple need to cut and sever each of themselves from all links to all bonds, all cords, all snares, and all ties to those marital curses or marriage curses by using the example prayer, titled, "Prayer To Deliver You From Generational Curses and Other Curses" in this book.

Matthew 19 (KJV)

1. And it came to pass, that when Jesus had finished these sayings, he departed from Galilee, and came into the coasts of Judaea beyond Jordan;
2. And great multitudes followed him; and he healed them there.
3. The Pharisees also came unto him, tempting him, and saying unto him, Is it lawful for a man to put away his wife for every cause?
4. And he answered and said unto them, Have ye not read, that he which made them at the beginning made them male and female,
5. And said, For this cause shall a man leave father and mother, and shall cleave to his wife: and they twain shall be one flesh?
6. Wherefore they are no more twain, but one flesh. What therefore God hath joined together, let not man put asunder.
7. They say unto him, Why did Moses then command to give a writing of divorcement, and to put her away?

8. He saith unto them, Moses because of the hardness of your hearts suffered you to put away your wives: but from the beginning it was not so.
9. And I say unto you, Whosoever shall put away his wife, except it be for fornication, and shall marry another, committeth adultery: and whoso marrieth her which is put away doth commit adultery.

CHAPTER 64

Drugs, Including Caffeine and Nicotine in Excess Can Be Harmful

Biblical Day Drugs Available: Strong Drinks And Wine

Prov 20:1 (KJV) "Wine is a mocker, strong drink is raging: and whosoever is deceived thereby is not wise."

Prov 21:17 (KJV) "He that loveth pleasure shall be a poor man: he that loveth wine and oil shall not be rich."

Prov 23:30 (KJV) "They that tarry long at the wine; they that go to seek mixed wine."

Prov 31:4 (KJV) "It is not for kings, O Lemuel, it is not for kings to drink wine; nor for princes strong drink:"

Prov 31:5 (KJV) "Lest they drink, and forget the law, and pervert the judgment of any of the afflicted."

Prov 31:6 (KJV) "Give strong drink unto him that is ready to perish, and wine unto those that be of heavy hearts."

Eccl 9:7 (KJV) "Go thy way, eat thy bread with joy, and drink thy wine with a merry heart; for God now accepteth thy works."

Eccl 10:19 (KJV) "A feast is made for laughter, and wine maketh merry: but money answereth all things."

Isa 5:11 (KJV) "Woe unto them that rise up early in the morning, that they may follow strong drink; that continue until night, till wine inflame them!"

Isa 5:12 (KJV) "And the harp, and the viol, the tabret, and pipe, and wine, are in their feasts: but they regard not the work of the LORD, neither consider the operation of his hands."

Isa 5:22 (KJV) "Woe unto them that are mighty to drink wine, and men of strength to mingle strong drink:"

Christians should be aware of less dangerous drug products that they can readily buy. These are not limited to coffee, tea, chocolate candy, chocolate products, cocoa, and soft drink products.

Note: A young man who professed to have been an employee of a nationally known coffee company gave us some advise about decaffeinated coffees. He said to be careful when you buy decaffeinated coffee. If it doesn't say that is "Naturally Decaffeinated" which is done with water, it was possibly decaffeinated with formaldehyde, an embalming type of substance normally used in mortuary firms in preserving dead bodies.

HARD DRUGS

Christians shouldn't become involved in hard drugs, except for medical purposes. Some of the drugs are readily available as marijuana, cocaine, crack cocaine, hashes, and many other drugs that are out on the streets of this world. It has been reported that children have found other habits in sniffing glue, paint thinner, gasoline, etc. Hard drugs can become seriously addictive through abuse or habitual use.

Drugs can also open doors in your life for Satan and his demons to take control of you, your mind and your body.

NICOTINE - TOBACCO PRODUCTS

Christians shouldn't become slaves to chewing tobacco, smoking cigarettes, smoking cigars, dipping snuff, or smoking tobacco products in pipes. NICOTINE is the addictive or habit forming drug found in tobacco products. As a result of using tobacco products, many people have acquired various cancer ailments in their mouths, throats, lungs and in other parts of their bodies. These are definitely tools that Satan (our enemy) uses to cripple Christians and even his own people (unbelievers) in the world. The enemy can only bind you if your back is bent. Your back is bent and bound over when you habitually use tobacco or nicotine products. You are then rendered slaves to nicotine products or its by-products.

Drug Abusers and/or Alcoholic Abusers Will Not Go To Heaven

I Cor 6:9 (KJV) Know ye not that the unrighteous shall not inherit the kingdom of God? Be not deceived: neither fornicators, nor idolaters, nor adulterers, nor effeminate, nor abusers of themselves with mankind,

I Cor 6:10 (KJV) Nor thieves, nor covetous, nor drunkards, nor revilers, nor extortioners, shall inherit the kingdom of God.

CHAPTER 65

Eating or Partaking of Other God's or Idol's Sacrificial Foods Is Strictly Prohibited

If you are invited to partake in a meal or snack where this food and/or beverages were prepared for sacrifices to idols and/or other gods, you should, neither touch, nor eat the food, nor consume the beverages, nor even touch the table setting or anything connected to that feast. Just depart those surroundings very quickly. Make very sure that you aren't there when the ritual of sacrifices ceremony begins.

1 Cor 8:4-6 (KJV) As concerning therefore the eating of those things that are offered in sacrifice unto idols, we know that an idol is nothing in the world, and that there is none other God but one.

5. For though there be that are called gods, whether in heaven or in earth, (as there be gods many, and lords many,)
6. But to us there is but one God, the Father, of whom are all things, and we in him; and one Lord Jesus Christ, by whom are all things, and we by him.

CHAPTER **66**

European (White) People Lack Original Hair and Skin Colors Through Their Ancestor, Gehazi

Scientific Researchers have determined that through their DNA analyst has proven that all races of people on earth have originated from with skin color and possibly that of a black skin color including the white (Caucasian) race of people.

There are some white (Caucasian) races of people who spew out their prejudices and racism of their purported superior racial standing at races of people other than their own. God never made any superior races of people. Black people of the African races aren't superior, white people of the Caucasian races aren't superior, nor are other races of people superior. God doesn't like racism or prejudices among the human races. Moses married an Ethiopian woman whose father was a Priest of God, Almighty. Aaron and his wife didn't like the fact that Moses married this black woman. Aaron's wife, Miriam was punished severely by God with leprosy until she became white as snow. This leprosy made her skin totally white in color and she did not have any dark color pigment in her skin. However, Miriam was later healed of this disease after her husband, Aaron prayed to God for her healing. There is another account of this in the bible which happened to a man and which followed his future generations as well. This man was named Gehazi who lied to his master, the Prophet Elisha. Gehazi was cursed with and received the leprosy that Naaman was previously plagued with and was healed of it by the Prophet Elisha.

2 Ki 5:27 (KJV) "The leprosy therefore of Naaman shall cleave unto thee, and unto thy seed for ever. And he went out from his presence a leper as white as snow."

The Prophet Elisha put the leprosy, not only on Gehazi, but on all of Gehazi's future generations as well including babies born today. Certain features, color of the skin and colors of the hair leads to the description of the generational skin color hair curses of the Caucasian race of people. This also gives credence to the leprosy color of this particular race of people. However, this doesn't mean that our white sisters and brothers are unclean with leprosy. Their hair and skin have the features identified with the features of leprosy. Lev 13:30-31 (KJV) Then the priest shall see the plague: and, behold, if it be in sight deeper than the skin; and there be in it a yellow thin hair; then the priest shall pronounce him unclean: it is a dry scall, even a leprosy upon the head or beard.

Yellow. Hebrew definition. 6669. tsahob, tsaw-obe'; from H6668; golden in color:--yellow.

31. And if the priest look on the plague of the scall, and, behold, it be not in sight deeper than the skin, **and that there is no black hair** in it; then the priest shall shut up him that hath the plague of the scall seven days:

    Lev 13:36-37 (KJV) Then the priest shall look on him: and, behold, if the scall be spread in the skin, the priest shall not seek for yellow hair; he is unclean.

37. But if the scall be in his sight at a stay, and that there is black hair grown up therein; the scall is healed, he is clean: and the priest shall pronounce him clean.

CHAPTER 67

Fat, Obese (Glutton) and Skinny Christians

Christians are among worldly people in being over weight or obese. Even though they may not be gluttons or greedy when they eat, they still find themselves in the obese or over weight category. Most have not been able to conquer those types of curses. On the other hand, there are those who love to eat and as a result, they become obese or over weight in the process. So, the best thing is eat and drink in moderation to help in conquering these curses.

Proverbs 23 (KJV)

21. For the drunkard and the glutton shall come to poverty: and drowsiness shall clothe a man with rags

The medical profession has determined through indices of overweight measured by "desirable" or "relative" weight. Life insurance tables of desirable weight are based on weights associated with the lowest mortality, among the insured population, who are predominantly upper middle class Caucasian individuals. Relative weight is calculated by dividing the patient's weight by a standard weight that is based on the patient's height, age and sex. [1]

Obesity is probably the world's oldest "METABOLIC DISORDER" where there is an imbalance between energy intake and energy expenditure and that is a curse on our bodies. That is, our bodies have slowed down in burning body fat causing fat to accumulate which adds not only inches, but pounds as well. It seems as though that everything we eat turns to fat. There is a formula to determine your "Body Mass Index" [2] to determine if you are obese or overweight as follows:

Weight (kg) = weight divided by 2.2 Height (meters) = height divided by 39.37

In the First Federal Obesity Clinical Guidelines (released June 1998), overweight was defined as a body mass index value between 25 and 29.9; and obesity was defined as a body mass index value greater than or equal to 30. **According to this report, an estimated 97 million adults in the United States are overweight or obese.**

"Malignant obesity" is a term now used to define persons 60% above desirable weight; this corresponds to an absolute excess of a minimum of 100 lbs. With this degree of obesity, there is a minimum doubling of the prevalences of all causes of morbidity and mortality. Weight reduction should be recommended for patients with BMIs equal to or above 27. Weight reduction is also desirable at all levels of obesity if the patient has concomitant diabetes, hypertension, heart disease or other cardiovascular risk factors.[1]

Obesity triggers other bodily curses including:

- Asthma
- Hypertension (High Blood Pressure)
- Diabetes (normally called Sugar Diabetes)
- Cardiovascular (Heart and Blood Vessel) Disease and Fat
- Distribution[2]

---

1 CLEVELAND, Posted 8:59 a.m. January 20, 1999 -- More Americans are fatter than ever

2 Obesity and Health--An Overview, http://www.quantumhcp.com/obesity.htm
2 Body Mass Index Calculation, http://www.mealformation.com/bmassidx.htm

- Cancer
- Endocrine Abnormalities
- Gall Bladder
- Pulmonary Abnormalities
- Arthritis
- Functional and Psychological Disorders

Skinny Christians

Some Christians are normally skinny or slim by nature and are not due to any type of eating disorders as explained below. These Christians don't fit into the categories listed below.

Anorexia

Anorexia is where you eat very little or nothing at all and bulimia is where you eat everything in the house then puke it up. Either way it can kill you or cause severe health problems.

Anorexia nervosa is a psychiatric diagnosis that describes an eating disorder characterized by low body weight and body image distortion. Individuals with anorexia often control body weight by voluntary starvation, purging, vomiting, excessive exercise, or other weight control measures, such as diet pills or diuretic drugs. It primarily affects young adolescent girls in the Western world and has one of the highest mortality rates of any psychiatric condition, with approximately 10% of people diagnosed with the condition eventually dying due to related factors. Anorexia nervosa is a complex condition, involving psychological, neurobiological, physiological and sociological components.

Bulimia

Bulimia is when a person gorges and then purges the food eaten via vomiting, laxatives and any other way to get rid of the food. They, too, can exercise to extremes.

Bulimia nervosa, more commonly known as bulimia, is an eating disorder. It is a psychological condition in which the subject engages in recurrent binge eating followed by an intentional purging. This purging is done in order to compensate for the excessive intake of the food and to prevent weight gain. Purging typically takes the form of vomiting; inappropriate use of laxatives, enemas, diuretics or other medication; excessive physical exercise, or fasting.The main criteria differences involve weight, as an anorexic must technically be classified as underweight (defined as a BMI < 18.5, though to be diagnosed with anorexia, the patient generally must have a BMI of less than 17.5). Typically an anorexic is defined by the refusal to maintain a normal weight by self-starvation. Another criteria which must usually be met is amenorrhea, the loss of her menstrual cycle not caused by the normal cessation of menstruation during menopause. Generally the anorexic does not engage in regular binging and purging sessions. In the rare instant that this is observed, in that the patient binges and purges as well as fails to maintain a minimum weight they are classified as a purging anorexic, due to the underweight criteria being met. Characteristically, those with bulimia nervosa feel more shame and out of control with their behaviors, as the anorexic meticulously controls her intake, a symptom that calms her anxiety around food as she feels she has control of it, naïve to the notion that it, in fact, controls her. For this reason, the bulimic is more likely to admit to having a problem.

What happens with both these situations is that the illness is the symptom of problems. Unfortunately, the symptom becomes the problem.

Both can be lifetime battles.

CHAPTER **68**

Females - Church Directed Head Coverings by Some Churches

Many churches strongly encourage and suggest that their females to wear head coverings as if it is a sin for them to not wear it. Head coverings don't make females any holier than females not wearing them. The actual words in biblical translations aren't what they appear to be at face value. The head covering is really a Jewish tradition and an ordinance for Jews to follow. The head in this sense means to seize or take hold of. Meaning that the woman's covering and her head is her husband. The husbands covering is Jesus Christ. However, the Churches covering for all of Christianity is Jesus Christ.

Head. Greek definition. 2776. kephale, kef-al-ay'; prob. from the prim. kapto (in the sense of seizing); the head (as the part most readily taken hold of), lit. or fig.:--head.

The reference which appears in the bible telling women to cover their head is not what it means in face value.

1 Cor 11:2 (KJV) "Now I praise you, brethren, that ye remember me in all things, and **keep the ordinances**, as I delivered them to you."

Ordinance. Greek definition. 3862. paradosis, par-ad'-os-is; from G3860; transmission, i.e. (concr.) a precept; spec. the **Jewish traditionary law**:--**ordinance, tradition**.

1 Cor 11:3 (KJV) "But I would have you know, that the head of every man is Christ; and the head of the woman is the man; and the head of Christ is God."

1 Cor 11:4 (KJV) "Every man praying or prophesying, having his head covered, dishonoureth his head." 1 Cor 11:5 (KJV) "But every woman that prayeth or prophesieth with her head uncovered dishonoureth her head: for that is even all one as if she were shaven."

1 Cor 11:6 (KJV) "For if the woman be not covered, let her also be shorn: but if it be a shame for a woman to be shorn or shaven, let her be covered." 1 Cor 11:7 (KJV) "For a man indeed ought not to cover his head, forasmuch as he is the image and glory of God: but the woman is the glory of the man." 1 Cor 11:7 (KJV) "For a man indeed ought not to cover his head, forasmuch as he is the image and glory of God: but the woman is the glory of the man."

1 Cor 11:8 (KJV) "For the man is not of the woman; but the woman of the man."

1 Cor 11:9 (KJV) "Neither was the man created for the woman; but the woman for the man."

1 Cor 11:10 (KJV) "For this cause ought the woman to have power on her head because of the angels."

1 Cor 11:11 (KJV) "Nevertheless neither is the man without the woman, neither the woman without the man, in the Lord." 1 Cor 11:12 (KJV) "For as the woman is of the man, even so is the man also by the woman; but all things of God."

1 Cor 11:7 (KJV) "For a man indeed ought not to cover his head, forasmuch as he is the image and glory of God: but the woman is the glory of the man."

1 Cor 11:8 (KJV) "For the man is not of the woman; but the woman of the man."

1 Cor 11:9 (KJV) "Neither was the man created for the woman; but the woman for the man." Christian females have been delegated the biblical authority: freedom, jurisdiction, liberties, rights and privileges of their own heads as the word "POWER" from 1 Corinthians 11:10 affords them with the exposition of the Greek definitions below. In reality, Christians are seeking to follow some of the Jewish ordinances and traditions which do not apply them. If females are in fact of the Jewish birth and faith, then this particular verse certainly applies to them.

1 Cor 11:10 (KJV) "For this cause ought the woman to have **power** on her head because of the angels."

Power. Greek definition. 1849. exousia, ex-oo-see'-ah; from G1832 (in the sense of ability); privilege, i.e. (subj.) force, capacity, competency, freedom, or (obj.) mastery (concr. magistrate, superhuman, potentate, token of control), delegated influence:--authority, jurisdiction, liberty, power, right, strength.

1 Cor 11:11 (KJV) "Nevertheless neither is the man without the woman, neither the woman without the man, in the Lord."

1 Cor 11:12 (KJV) "For as the woman is of the man, even so is the man also by the woman; but all things of God."

1 Cor 11:13 (KJV) "Judge in yourselves: is it comely that a woman pray unto God uncovered?" 1 Cor 11:14 (KJV) "Doth not even nature itself teach you, that, if a man have long hair, it is a shame unto him?"

Females' Hair Is Her Physical Covering

1 Cor 11:15 (KJV) "But if a woman have long hair, it is a glory to her: for her hair is given her for a covering."

CHAPTER **69**

Females - Churches Prohibit the Wearing of Pants

When the Bible specifically prohibited men from wearing clothes made for women, and prohibited women from wearing clothes made for men, neither pants, nor trousers or slacks were in existence at that particular time. Basically, everybody wore something similar to long robes or long dress like garments, even the men.

Trousers
From Wikipedia, the free encyclopedia

> Germanic trousers of the 4th century found in the Thorsberg moor, Germany
> Early use of trousers in France: a sans-culotte by Louis-Léopold Boilly.

Trousers (or pants in Canada, South Africa and the United States, and sometimes called slacks or breeches (sometimes pronounced [0brwt•vz])) are an item of clothing worn on the lower part of the body, covering both legs separately (rather than with cloth stretching across both as in skirts and dresses). Historically, as for the West, trousers have been the standard lower-body clothing item for males since the 16th century; by the late 20th century, they had become prevalent for females as well. Trousers are worn at the hips or waist, and may be held up by their own fastenings, a belt, or suspenders (braces). Leggings are form-fitting trousers of a clingy material, often knitted cotton and lycra.

Many of the Pentecostal and Apostolic Protestant denominational churches forbid or prohibit their females from wearing pants or trousers to their churches. There is nothing holy or unholy about whether females wear or not wear pants or trousers to church. It is simply a way of life. Now, if females choose to wear clothes which would portray them as males, then common sense should prevail. When females are mistakenly addressed as males because of the clothes that they wear, then maybe the wear of dresses would be appropriate.

Oftentimes females who wear their hair as short or shorter than that of men are mistakenly addressed by titles as males. I, (Curtis) was at the food court at Potomac Mills Mall at Dale City, Virginia to order some Chinese food. The young lady who ask me for my for my order had a deep voice, her hair was very short and she had on a short sleeve shirt and trousers. After I had ordered my meal she ask me if their was anything else and I said, "No sir!". She promptly replied, "No, ma'am". I apologized and responded that I was in the habit of saying, "No, sir!". This is true, but I also thought that she was a gentleman by her voice and her dress.

There is nothing wrong with females wearing their hair as short as men. However, there are certain ways barbers and beauticians can curt female's hair where they still retain the features of females. Usually when men's hair are cut short, there are certain razor lines given all around, except that in the back of the necks, they are squared. I have seen some females with the same squared neck resembling the males' hair cuts which has been around for a number of generations. On the other hand, female hair cuts are usually rounded or in a v-shaped fashion which normally reflects the female gender.

Deu 22:5 (KJV) "The woman shall not wear that which pertaineth unto a man, neither shall a man put on a woman's garment: for all that do so are abomination unto the LORD thy God."

1 Pet 3:3 (KJV) "Whose adorning let it not be that outward adorning of plaiting the hair, and of wearing of gold, or of putting on of apparel;"

1 Pet 3:4 (KJV) "But let it be the hidden man of the heart, in that which is not corruptible, even the ornament of a meek and quiet spirit, which is in the sight of God of great price."

In other words, good taste prevails as far as wearing male or female garments. This is not to say that females can't wear male garments, such as blue jeans, hats, tennis shoes, watches, jackets, trouser and so forth. Sometimes these particular types of attire are more suitable to some females for wear than the female designs. It is not that they are trying to imitate the features of the male gender, but that certain male styles of attire suits their tastes more than particular female designs. Men normally don't wear female designed clothes because of their feminine design types. Sometimes men are caught wearing female night robes and house slippers around the house, motel rooms, hotel rooms or various other places. This is more comical than wrong. Use your own discretion with good taste in such matters.

CHAPTER 70

Females - Churches Prohibit Them from Wearing of Makeup (Cosmetics)

Some churches are famous for putting their members in bondage, especially the Pentecostal and Apostolic Churches by prohibiting their females from wearing makeup. This is a form of bondage created by these churches and is thereby a curse. There is nothing in the Holy Bible prohibiting women from wearing makeup on their bodies. It certainly does not have any effect on their salvation, nor does it have any effect on ones service to God Almighty, Jesus Christ, the Son or the Holy Spirit. The bible doesn't expressly say that women shouldn't were makeup. It tells them that when they adorn themselves, they should do it with good taste which becomes women professing godliness with good works.

1 Tim 2:9 (KJV) "In like manner also, that women adorn themselves in modest apparel, with shamefacedness and sobriety; not with broided hair, or gold, or pearls, or costly array;"

1 Tim 2:10 (KJV) "But (which becometh women professing godliness) with good works."

This is not to say that women can't wear make-up. The use of various types of makeup should be applied with moderation as with anything else that goes in or on the body. It should be pleasant to look upon, rather than looking like a prostitute or woman of the night, so to speak.

CHAPTER 71

Females Wearing Makeup (Cosmetics) for the Wrong Reasons

There are women in the secular arena who portray themselves with enticing clothes and makeup in order to assist them in attracting their male customers for sexual encounters.

These women are known as prostitutes, call girls and/or women for hire for sex. This is where makeup and flashy clothes is used for the wrong purposes and is against good standards and Christian morals at best.

2 Ki 9:30 (KJV) "And when Jehu was come to Jezreel, Jezebel heard of it; and she painted her face, and tired her head, and looked out at a window."

Jer 4:30 (KJV) "And when thou art spoiled, what wilt thou do? Though thou clothest thyself with crimson, though thou deckest thee with ornaments of gold, though thou rentest thy face with painting, in vain shalt thou make thyself fair; thy lovers will despise thee, they will seek thy life."

Ezek 23:40 (KJV) "And furthermore, that ye have sent for men to come from far, unto whom a messenger was sent; and, lo, they came: for whom thou didst wash thyself, paintedst thy eyes, and deckedst thyself with ornaments,"

Jezebel was among other women who had no intentions of doing anything in a godly manner. She and they were bent on performing whoredom and prostitution. Jezebel paid a dear price with her physical life as with her spiritual life as well.

CHAPTER 72

Females Are Denied Positions as Ministers and Deacons in Some Churches

Some churches carry their secular discriminations, prejudices, and racism from the secular society to that of the spiritual society as well. These are surely demonic curses which have quenched the actions of Almighty God's Holy Spirit and thereby have blocked the spiritual growth of the Christians as well.

1 Tim 2:12 (KJV) "But I suffer not a woman to teach, nor to usurp authority over the man, but to be in silence."

Among other scriptures, the above scripture is one of the most widely misunderstood scriptures that men use to substantiate their claim that women should not usurp authority over men. First of all, the Apostle Paul is talking about a husband and a wife, not men in general. When you read that particular chapter, you will find out that he is referring to the "MAN" Adam and the "WOMAN" Eve as husband and wife. He is not talking about usurping (taking) authority over men in general. The word "USURP" means to take authority from something or someone. God placed man in the responsibility of authority over his family. This does not mean that man should exercise kingship over his wife. The man is responsible for the Christian upbringing of his family. There is nothing wrong with the woman running the house. She should have the option to consult her husband for assistance, leadership and guidance for the family's secular and Christian well-being.

Eph 5:21-25 (KJV) Submitting yourselves one to another in the fear of God.

22. Wives, submit yourselves unto your own husbands, as unto the Lord.
23. For the husband is the head of the wife, even as Christ is the head of the church: and he is the savior of the body.
24. Therefore as the church is subject unto Christ, so let the wives be to their own husbands in every thing.
25. Husbands, love your wives, even as Christ also loved the church, and gave himself for it;

Titus 2:5 (KJV) "To be discreet, chaste, keepers at home, good, obedient to their own husbands, that the word of God be not blasphemed."

Titus 2:6 (KJV) "Young men likewise exhort to be sober minded."

This does not mean that men should exercise kingship or lordship over their wives. God chose the male gender as the responsible party for his family. He wants to be able to point a finger at someone and He chose the husband. He placed this responsibility on our shoulders so that we would lead our families in Christian like manners. He merely did this because He made man first and that the woman was made for the man. In spite of our responsibilities of God's directed leadership in our families, we are to still lead in a democratic fashion. That is, we must not be dictators, but share in the leadership of our families. Our wives are Christians just as we are. By all means ask her opinions on matters concerning you and your family and especially if you are to make the final decision on a matter.

Look at Ephesians 5:21, specifically the word "SUBMIT". It means that the husband must subordinate himself to his wife, be subject to his wife, put under authority of his wife or obey his wife in a Christian like manner as his wife must subordinate herself to her husband, be subject to her husband, put under authority of her husband or obey him in Christian like manners. Meaning, they are equal in the leadership of the family and their Christian well being. Now when a wife feels that her decision is contingent on her husband's approval, then it falls on the husband to make a decision on behalf of the family. In other words, the husband will have the final decision in such complicated matters when it is deemed necessary. I tell my wife all of the time, "Use your own discretion!". She still consults me in the majority of the situations she is confronted with before she makes her decisions. Sometimes I get upset when I ask her to give me her opinion on something that I am confronted with and which could subsequently effect the family. She'll reply to me, "Do whatever you want, you know what is best!". I really don't always know what is best as I am of the human species also. I have certainly made some wrong decisions during my lifetime. That is one of our dilemmas as human beings.

I, (Curtis) watch with much concern as my fellow male brothers spew out their hatred in the form of prejudice towards our sisters in Christ. This includes no only older men, but this younger generation of males as well. Many of these men feel that the women should be under the men's feet, cook for them, wash their clothes, clean their houses and such other tasks that they feel are beneath them. Men are probably some of the most prejudice persons on earth. However, I have found that women aren't far behind this trend of prejudices. Men have this big egotistical, macho and self crowned kingship type attitude. Most men have the idea if we put woman in the pulpit they are usurping authority over men. This is simply not true. God, Almighty uses vessels no matter what the sexes are to proclaim His holy word. These vessels can be a male or a female. There is nothing sexist about being a vessel of honor for God. Neither your strength, your looks, your features, your height, your size, whether you are single, nor whether you are married or single have anything to do with your being a vessel of honor for God.

Women should be respected equally and on the same level as men as ministers and deacons. In the Baptist churches, men are ordained and placed on their deacon boards. In most of the Baptist churches, women are not ordained as deacons, but consecrated as deaconesses and placed on deaconess boards. In most the Baptist churches, females are not recognized as preachers of the gospel. These churches feel that God doesn't call women to preach. This is pure ignorance, prejudice and blatant hatred for women. God despises ignorance and hatred and He will not tolerate it by continuing to blink His eyes at these sinful attitudes of both men and women towards female preachers and deacons.

I, (Curtis) had watched our deacons with dismay and discuss when they were always requiring additional assistance during communion services which is regularly scheduled on the first Sunday of every month and other special occasions. Whenever they were short of servers which mainly included male deacons, they would ask some of us male preachers to assist them in serving. Well, I suggested to the Constitution and By-Laws Committee that they should use deaconess. I stressed to them that they deaconess should be treated with the same respect as deacons including the assisting in serving communion. I further recommended that the churches Constitution and By-Laws should be changed to reflect that change. Well, to my surprise since my recommendations are usually not respected, nor viewed as important, the Chairman of the deacon board who was also the chairman of the Constitution and By-Laws Committee did just that. He started using the deaconess in the serving of communion. The Chairman of the Deaconess Board said in a conversation to me, "Reverend Hall, you make a lot of recommendations to this church and they use them, but you never get the credit." I replied to her that God sees what I do and He will get all of the credit. My suggestion and recommendation to ordain females as deacons has yet to come to fruition. As a matter of fact, some members have left the church when women started sharing in the serving of communion. This is a classic case of generational ignorance and unbelief.

Acts 2:17 (KJV) "And it shall come to pass in the last days, saith God, I will pour out of my Spirit upon all flesh: and your sons and your daughters shall prophesy, and your young men shall see visions, and your old men shall dream dreams:" Acts 2:18 (KJV) "And on my servants and on my handmaidens I will pour out in those days of my Spirit; and they shall prophesy:"

Proof Of Female Preachers In Biblical Days

Acts 21:8 (KJV) "And the next day we that were of Paul's company departed, and came unto Caesarea: and we entered into the house of **Philip the evangelist**, which was one of the seven; and abode with him."

Acts 21:9 (KJV) "And the same man had **four daughters, virgins, which did prophesy**."

Exo 15:20 (KJV) "And **Miriam** the prophetess, the sister of Aaron, took a timbrel in her hand; and all the women went out after her with timbrels and with dances."

Judg 4:4 (KJV) "And **Deborah**, a prophetess, the wife of Lapidoth, she judged Israel at that time."

2 Ki 22:14 (KJV) "So Hilkiah the priest, and Ahikam, and Achbor, and Shaphan, and Asahiah, went unto **Huldah** the prophetess, the wife of Shallum the son of Tikvah, the son of Harhas, keeper of the wardrobe; (now she dwelt in Jerusalem in the college;) and they communed with her."

Neh 6:14 (KJV) "My God, think thou upon Tobiah and Sanballat according to these their works, and on the prophetess **Noadiah**, and the rest of the prophets, that would have put me in fear."

Isa 8:3 (KJV) "And I went unto the prophetess; and she conceived, and bare a son. Then said the LORD to me, Call his name Mahershalalhashbaz." Luke 2:36 (KJV) "And there was one **Anna**, a prophetess, the daughter of Phanuel, of the tribe of Aser: she was of a great age, and had lived with an husband seven years from her virginity;"

CHAPTER 73

Filthy Communications (i.e., Cursing, Foul and Bad Language) Are Forbidden

Some ministers are no different than some of the people in the world when they are approached in communicating to others. Some of them feel that in order for them to effectively express themselves, they have to use curse words. This is quite prevalent among persons who have served in the armed forces, especially the United States Army and the United States Marine Corp. It seems that every other word that proceeds out of their mouths are foul words of cursing in order to get their points across. I, (Curtis) have always said that such persons are saying what is in their hearts. If filth is in their hearts, then filth will come out. If clean communication is in their heart, then clean communication will proceed from their hearts. In the computer world, we have a saying "GIGO". Garbage In, Garbage Out!

Col 3:8 (KJV) "But now ye also put off all these; anger, wrath, malice, blasphemy, filthy communication out of your mouth."

Prov 23:7 (KJV) "For as he thinketh in his heart, so is he: Eat and drink, saith he to thee; but his heart is not with thee."

So, what is in someone's heart, that is what will come out of it. There is an old saying in the Computer Science field when talking about the data that goes into a computer's memory and it is: "GIGO", that is "Garbage In, Garbage Out". So, whatever is put in that computer's memory is what will be the output. Good data begets good output data, while bad input data will beget bad output data. This scenario applies to human beings as well. Think on great things and great things will proceed from your heart as well.

CHAPTER **74**

Fires, Wild & Droughts - California Curses

USA TODAY weather focus: "Winds worsen wildfire threat in Southern California"

California Wild Fires Force Nearly 1Million People From Their Homes

Climate change likely to increase fires

Witch Fire, Irvine Fire, San Diego Fire: "Looks Like End Of The World"

Post Chronicle
by Jack Ryan Witch Fire, Irvine Fire, Los Angeles Fire, South Orange County Fire, Ventura

Mass evacuation — California fires: 1,800 homes burned; 500,000 flee

Associated Press
Published: Oct. 24, 2007 12:30 a.m. MDT

Fire Information - National Fire News
12 Un-contained Large Fires Have Burned More Than 335,000 acres.
October 23, 2007

The fire situation in southern California remains critical where 12 uncontained large fires have burned more than 335,000 acres. Hundreds of homes and commercial buildings throughout the area have been damaged or destroyed. The Santa Ana winds continue to be a challenge as firefighters work to contain these blazes.

The state of California is plagued with a lack of rain, droughts and many fires. These fires have destroyed thousands of homes and properties, caused the deaths of people, caused over 1 million people to be evacuated from their homes because of potential threats to their lives from the raging fires. Bottom line: California has predominately forsaken and turned their backs on Almighty God. They are therefore, reaping the wrath of His anger.

Isaiah 34 (KJV)

5. For my sword shall be bathed in heaven: behold, it shall come down upon Idumea, and upon the people of my curse, to judgment.

Deuteronomy 28 (KJV)

15. But it shall come to pass, if thou wilt not hearken unto the voice of the Lord thy God, to observe to do all his commandments and his statutes which I command thee this day; that all these curses shall come upon thee, and overtake thee:
16. Cursed shalt thou be in the city, and cursed shalt thou be in the field.
17. Cursed shall be thy basket and thy store.

18. Cursed shall be the fruit of thy body, and the fruit of thy land, the increase of thy kine, and the flocks of thy sheep.
19. Cursed shalt thou be when thou comest in, and cursed shalt thou be when thou goest out.
20. The Lord shall send upon thee cursing, vexation, and rebuke, in all that thou settest thine hand unto for to do, until thou be destroyed, and until thou perish quickly; because of the wickedness of thy doings, whereby **thou hast forsaken me**.

Romans 1 (KJV)

17. For therein is the righteousness of God revealed from faith to faith: as it is written, The just shall live by faith.
18. For the wrath of God is revealed from heaven against all ungodliness and unrighteousness of men, who hold the truth in unrighteousness;
19. Because that which may be known of God is manifest in them; for God hath shewed it unto them.
20. For the invisible things of him from the creation of the world are clearly seen, being understood by the things that are made, even his eternal power and Godhead; so that they are without excuse:
21. Because that, when they knew God, they glorified him not as God, neither were thankful; but became vain in their imaginations, and their foolish heart was darkened.
22. Professing themselves to be wise, they became fools,
23. And changed the glory of the uncorruptible God into an image made like to corruptible man, and to birds, and fourfooted beasts, and creeping things.
24. Wherefore God also gave them up to uncleanness through the lusts of their own hearts, to dishonour their own bodies between themselves:
25. Who changed the truth of God into a lie, and worshipped and served the creature more than the Creator, who is blessed for ever. Amen.

26. For this cause God gave them up unto vile affections: for even their women did change the natural use into that which is against nature:
27. And likewise also the men, leaving the natural use of the woman, burned in their lust one toward another; men with men working that which is unseemly, and receiving in themselves that recompence of their error which was meet.
28. And even as they did not like to retain God in their knowledge, God gave them over to a reprobate mind, to do those things which are not convenient;
29. Being filled with all unrighteousness, fornication, wickedness, covetousness, maliciousness; full of envy, murder, debate, deceit, malignity; whisperers,
30. Backbiters, haters of God, despiteful, proud, boasters, inventors of evil things, disobedient to parents,
31. Without understanding, covenantbreakers, without natural affection, implacable, unmerciful:
32. Who knowing the judgment of God, that they which commit such things are worthy of death, not only do the same, but have pleasure in them that do them.

NBC Evening News for Wednesday, Jun 30, 1976
Headline: California / Drought and Fires Abstract:

(Studio) California suffers drought, brush fires and lack of water. REPORTER: David Brinkley

(Stinson Beach, California) There is talk of water rationing. [Watershed fire council D.F. HOOPER - says fire season predicted to be worst in 52 years] REPORTER: Frank Bourgholtzer

(Red Bluff, California) California fires usually the worst in fall. REPORTER: Frank Bourgholtzer

(Los Angeles, California) Smog is so bad that officials are trying to buy extra natural gas for area's inds. to reduce pollution. REPORTER: Frank Bourgholtzer

(California) Farmers feel effects of drought. Beaches shown. REPORTER: Frank Bourgholtzer

SAN DIEGO -- At least 500 homes and 100 businesses have been destroyed in a single San Diego County wildfire, officials announced Monday evening.

Evacuations ordered for 250,000 households there and thousands more in other areas of Southern California.

CHAPTER 75

Foods - Eggs and Peanut Products - Salmonella Poisonings

During the late 1940's, I, Curtis, my brother Joe, my step-father Jesse (Curly), and my mother (mama) Willie B, lived on a farm in Arkansas where we didn't have most of the modern appliances such as for example, a refrigirator. Moma had prepared us a delicious and sumptuous dinner which included an entre with chicken and dressing. When the meal was over she put the food away in the old ice box. This ice box was two-compartment appliance for storing ice and various foods. The top compartment housed the ice and the lower compartment which was much larger, housed the foods. The next day we had a repeat of that previous meal which was so delicious. To our surprise, daddy, myself, and my brother, Joe became sick with what they called back then "Ptomaine Poison" from eating the left-over chicken and dressing. The ice box did not keep the chicken and dressing cold enough for a second consumption. So, this is somewhat of the human side of our dilemma on earth. Now, as you will read below, there is a spiritual side as well. This side is known as a blessing or on the other hand, a curse. Almighty God, the Father in Heaven gives two promises: one is a blessing if we will obey His commandments, and another is a curse if we disobey His commandments.

Deuteronomy 11 (KJV)

26. Behold, I set before you this day a blessing and a curse;

27. A blessing, if ye obey the commandments of the Lord your God, which I command you this day:
28. And a curse, if ye will not obey the commandments of the Lord your God, but turn aside out of the way which I command you this day, to go after other Gods, which ye have not known.

HealthCentral.com
Health Sites

Salmonella Food Poisoning

WHAT YOU SHOULD KNOW

Salmonella (sal-muh-NEL-uh) is a type of bacteria often found in tainted food. The germs usually settle in your stomach and intestines and cause diarrhea.

Causes:

Salmonella infection usually stems from undercooked meat and poultry, raw eggs, or water containing live salmonella bacteria. Pet turtles and other animals can carry the bacteria. Infection can also spread from person-to-person.

Signs/Symptoms

Typical symptoms include watery or bloody diarrhea, stomach cramps, throwing-up, fever, headache, chills, sweats, fatigue, and lack of appetite.

Care

You will probably need medicine to treat your diarrhea. If the infection is severe, you may be given an antibiotic to fight it.

Risks

The greatest danger lies in loss of body fluids and salts (dehydration) from prolonged diarrhea. This can lead to shock and can be deadly, especially in infants and people over 60. If the bacteria get into the bloodstream, other parts of the body may become infected.

WHAT YOU SHOULD DO

- If you are taking antibiotics, continue to take them until they are all gone--even if you feel well. Always take medicine as directed. If you feel it is not helping, call your doctor. Do not quit taking it on your own.
- Rest in bed at least 3 days after your symptoms go away. You may get up to go to the bathroom. While in bed, move your legs a lot. This helps to prevent blood clots from forming.
- Use a heating pad or hot water bottle to help relieve stomach cramps.
- Drink plenty of liquids that have a lot of minerals and vitamins in them until the diarrhea stops. Then eat healthy, soft, bland foods such as bananas, rice, applesauce, and toast.
- To keep from getting another infection, cook all meat and poultry thoroughly. Do not eat dishes containing raw eggs.
- Follow directions on food labels on how to properly store and refrigerate foods known to be carriers of the salmonella bacteria.
- Wash your hands after handling uncooked foods and before handling cooked foods.

Call Your Doctor If...

- You have diarrhea, stomach cramps, fever, or a headache that last longer than a few days.
- You have a dry mouth; dry, wrinkled skin; dark urine, less urine than usual; dry eyes without tears; or if you feel sleepier

than usual. These are signs of the dehydration that can develop from prolonged diarrhea.

- You develop a rash, itching, or swelling of your abdomen (belly) or legs. This condition may be caused by your medicine.

Seek Care Immediately If...

- You can't drink fluids or keep food down.
- You have high temperature, yellow color to the skin or eyes, cough up blood, or worsening diarrhea.

CSPI REPORTS: Scrambled Eggs

How a broken food safety system let contaminated eggs become a national food poisoning epidemic

Elizabeth Dahl
Staff Attorney, Food Safety Program
Caroline Smith DeWaal Director, Food Safety Program
May 1997
Center for Science in the Public Interest

We gratefully acknowledge the assistance of Michael F. Jacobson, Lucy Alderton, Kimberly Loui, and Grace Ko in preparing this report. We also thank the experts in government and industry who reviewed drafts of the report.

The Center for Science in the Public Interest is a non-profit organization that focuses on food and nutrition policies. It is supported largely by the nearly one million subscribers to its Nutrition Action Healthletter.

Center for Science in the Public Interest 1875 Connecticut Avenue, NW, Suite 300 Washington, D.C. 20009-5728
332-9110

Table of Contents

Executive Summary

Eggs used to be safe. Parents, without worrying, could let their children lick the bowl after preparing cakes and cookies. Consumers, without fear, could eat raw or undercooked eggs in salad dressings, egg nog and stuffing. Sunny-side-up eggs with runny yolks were great with toast. Now those same cooking practices can lead to severe illness and even death, if the eggs are contaminated with Salmonella.

What happened to safe eggs? Why are eggs today associated with more food poisoning outbreaks than any other single food? Why are public health officials now urging us to eat only fully cooked shell eggs or to use pasteurized egg products?

The answers to those questions involve a complex story with

numerous plot twists: a biological adaptation that allowed bacteria to enter otherwise sterile eggs; federal agencies inspecting frequently to assure egg quality but never providing regulations adequate to ensure egg safety; and industry lobbyists dictating Congressional action.

The result is that eggs have become the number one contributor to food poisoning outbreaks in the nation, with annual consumer costs in the hundreds of millions of dollars. Hundreds, and possibly thousands, of people die every year from contaminated eggs.
The story began when a strain of Salmonella bacteria called enteritidis found its way first into the ovaries of chickens and then into their eggs. The problem was identified by federal disease detectives in the mid 1980s. The first farms producing contaminated eggs were all located in the northeastern U.S. and with quick action, the problem might have stopped there. But the numerous federal agencies with oversight responsibilities for eggs didn't act. Instead they competed with each other, stumbled over each other, and ultimately backed down in the face of industry pressure. Meanwhile, Salmonella enteritidis (SE) reached epidemic proportions.

Today, internally contaminated eggs are showing up from coast to coast. There is no way to tell without laboratory testing which eggs contain Salmonella and which ones are contamination-free. Grading programs run by the United States Department of Agriculture continuously check Grade A eggs for blood spots and yolk size, but have no controls for the harmful bacteria found in eggs. That responsibility falls to the Food and Drug Administration, which inspects egg plants an average of once every 10 years and merely recalls already-tainted food instead of preventing contaminated food from reaching the market. Consumers are generally unaware of the hazard and continue to eat raw and undercooked eggs, without realizing that such practices are risky.

Key Conclusions and Recommendations

The history of the federal government's failure to curb the SE epidemic illustrates the ineffectiveness of having multiple government agencies responsible for regulating the same food. The agencies were further hamstrung by a Congress that cut funding for a pilot control program just as it was beginning to show results and an industry that, except for producers in Pennsylvania, resisted attempts to prevent egg contamination on the farm.

Effective government action could have prevented many illnesses and deaths over the past twenty years and could prevent countless future unnecessary tragedies. To protect consumers from the hazards of SE, we recommend the following steps.

- FDA should mandate that egg producers implement on-farm Hazard Analysis and Critical Control Point (HACCP) programs to control SE. The SE control programs should be modeled after the successful Pennsylvania Egg Quality Assurance Program. The programs should include testing of manure and eggs. That testing should be monitored by FDA.
- Shell egg plants should be inspected for safety at least several times per year. These inspections should verify that plants only accept eggs from farms with SE testing programs in place and should ensure that eggs from infected flocks are diverted to pasteurization plants.
- FDA and FSIS should act quickly to implement science-based regulations mandating egg refrigeration at 41 degrees F during transportation and storage. Temperature requirements should be standardized across all the government agencies that regulate food, including the state and local governments responsible for enforcing temperatures at the retail level. Retailers and consumers should be informed that eggs should be kept refrigerated.

- Until the egg industry has effective programs in place to control SE, consumers must be warned that they risk illness from eating raw or undercooked eggs. FDA should mandate that the following label be placed on the tops of egg cartons: "Caution: Eggs may contain illness-causing bacteria. Do not eat raw. Cook until yolk is firm."
- FDA's Food Code should recommend that restaurants and other establishments not pool unpasteurized eggs unless they are cooked immediately.
- Food safety responsibility for eggs should be consolidated under the clearly defined authority of one of the two food safety agencies, either FSIS or FDA. Clear jurisdiction is needed to avoid agency competition and miscommunication.
- Congress should significantly increase funding for FDA's food safety functions and should fully fund FSIS's and FDA's efforts to address SE in eggs. President Clinton's request for additional funding for food safety is an important step in ensuring that these agencies can adequately protect the public health.

Introduction

Eggs, once considered a safe food, have become increasingly contaminated over the last 15 years by a strain of Salmonella bacteria known as Salmonella enteritidis, or SE. While Salmonella sometimes is present on the outside of egg shells, no one ever thought the inside of eggs could be contaminated by bacteria. It was a surprise when government scientists first linked human illness from SE to internally contaminated eggs in 1986.

Since the early 1980s, the SE problem in shell eggs (fresh eggs purchased in cartons) has ballooned out of control. The Centers for Disease Control and Prevention (CDC) reported five times as many SE cases in 1995 as in 1980. (See Figure 1.) By 1994, SE caused an estimated 200,000 to one million human cases of salmonellosis each year. Contaminated eggs cause at least 80 percent of these illnesses, according to data from CDC.

Illness from SE can be fatal to the elderly, children, and those with weakened immune systems. The SE bacteria caused more reported deaths between 1988 and 1992 than any other foodborne pathogen. Hundreds or even thousands of people die from eating SE-tainted eggs each year.

SE is responsible for the lion's share of food poisoning illnesses, about a third of all food poisoning outbreaks where the cause is known. (See Figure 2.) The estimated annual cost of illness from SE ranges from $118 million to $767 million.

The magnitude of the current SE crisis was not inevitable. Before 1984, SE outbreaks were largely confined to one geographical area, the northeastern United States. The problem spread to the mid-Atlantic states in the late 1980s. In 1992, a government-supported control program began in Pennsylvania that required testing of hens and cleaning of poultry houses. This program showed promise in reducing the number of food poisonings from SE. However, federal support for that program was discontinued in 1995, and no nationwide program has ever been implemented.

The government response to SE-tainted eggs has been inadequate and ineffective. When Salmonella showed up on the outside of egg shells in the 1970s, government programs helped to curb the problem. Unfortunately, no similar programs were developed to stop the internal contamination of eggs with SE. A number of factors have contributed to the federal government's failure to control the SE epidemic: overlapping and unclear lines of jurisdiction between different government agencies; inter-agency competition; lack of support from Congress; and a lack of urgency among health officials.

Among other absurdities, a system has developed in which shell eggs are monitored continuously for quality and cleanliness by a federal marketing agency, but are inspected for microbiological and chemical contamination by the leading federal food safety agency only once every ten years, on average. Egg product plants (plants that produce liquid, frozen or powdered egg products) are inspected continuously by yet a third agency.

SE Has Increased Throughout the Nation

Between 1980 and 1995, the number of SE cases reported in the U.S. increased by more than fivefold. SE, which had been present in low levels, began growing out of control in the northeastern United States and then steadily increased across the country.

By 1984, SE began appearing in larger numbers outside the Northeast. (See Figures 3 and 4 and Appendix.) By 1986, the year CDC first linked SE to consumption of raw and undercooked eggs that were internally contaminated, the incidence of SE in the Northeast had increased more than sixfold over 1976 levels. While the number of cases of illness leveled off in the Northeast between 1990 and 1994, cases in the Rocky Mountain region doubled and cases in the Pacific region quadrupled during that same time period. In 1994, California accounted for about a quarter of the nation's laboratory-confirmed cases of SE. A USDA survey showed that the frequency of SE isolates in unpasteurized liquid eggs nearly doubled in the northeastern and western U.S. between 1991 and 1995.

To make matters worse, a more virulent form of SE, known as SE phage type 4, has appeared in five SE outbreaks in California and has also appeared in Utah, Arizona and Nevada. Although scientists do not yet know why, this new type causes five times as many human salmonellosis cases as other types of SE in the regions where it appears. In Europe, phage type 4 has become the predominant form of SE.

Even though CDC data in 1986 clearly documented the increase in the number of human illnesses from SE, federal food safety officials allowed SE to continue to spread around the country, resulting in millions of illnesses and thousands of deaths over the past 10 years. (See Table 1.) The federal government partially funded and pilot-tested an SE control program from 1992 to 1995 in Pennsylvania. However, this program did not develop into a comprehensive, nationally coordinated approach to testing for and controlling SE. Instead, in 1995, at the urging of the egg industry, Congress cut the federal funding for this program and prohibited USDA employees from working on the SE problem.

Table 1. A Ten-Year History: How a Tiny Food-borne Bacteria Outsmarted the Federal Government SE Increases Throughout the Nation Year Federal Government Fails to Act Almost 6,000 SE food poisonings reported for the year

After an outbreak sickens 3,000, CDC identifies eggs as a source of SE food poisoning USDA decides not to establish a mandatory SE control program

Almost 8,500 SE food poisonings reported for the year

FDA and USDA simultaneously develop competing SE control programs

USDA begins control program targeted only at flocks that have been identified as the cause of human illness through tracebacks

Congress passes law requiring egg refrigeration; USDA never enforces it

USDA, Pennsylvania government, and industry begin voluntary pilot program

Over 10,000 reported SE food poisonings for the year

Congress cuts funding for successful pilot program and for traceback program, at egg industry request

Consumers Are at Risk of Illness from SE in Eggs

SE is found inside eggs laid by otherwise healthy hens that are infected by the bacteria. It is estimated that one out of every 10,000 eggs, or about 4.5 million eggs each year, are infected with SE. Consumers have no way of knowing which eggs are infected. The SE bacteria multiply inside eggs that are not properly refrigerated (to an internal temperature of 45 degrees F.) As few as 10 to 100 SE organisms may be enough to cause illness in elderly people, children, and the immuno-compromised.

The elderly residents of nursing homes are especially at risk of death from SE: 85 percent of reported deaths from SE between 1988 and 1992 were from this group. SE infection causes flu-like symptoms, such as diarrhea, abdominal pain, nausea, fever and chills, and can have more serious complications, such as rheumatoid arthritis, meningitis, kidney or heart disease, and death.

Thorough cooking of eggs will kill the bacteria. However, many common egg-preparation practices are not sufficient to kill SE. Some high-risk practices include:

- serving eggs "sunny side up," lightly poached, soft-boiled, or any other style where the yolk is still runny
- preparing French toast with an egg coating that is not thoroughly cooked
- using raw eggs in cookie dough or cake batter which is eaten before cooking
- using raw eggs in salad dressing, such as Caesar salad or homemade mayonnaise

- using raw eggs in eggnog
- using lightly cooked eggs in desserts, such as meringue and tiramisu

Another high-risk practice common in restaurants, nursing homes, and other institutions is pooling eggs in a large container after breaking and before cooking them. One SE-positive egg can contaminate dozens of others. This practice can result in major outbreaks of human illness if the pooled eggs are allowed to remain too long at room temperature and then are not fully cooked.

A recent government survey found that about half of all consumers surveyed had eaten undercooked eggs in the past year. Although the SE problem in eggs has been fully documented for more than ten years, this survey, combined with the increase in human illnesses, demonstrates that both industry and government have failed to sufficiently inform consumers about the risk of consuming undercooked eggs.

Government's Inadequate Response Allowed the SE Problem to Grow Out of Control

As many as 45 percent of all egg-laying flocks in the U.S. are now infected with SE, according to government estimates. Yet the spread of SE throughout the nation could have been stopped, or at least substantially slowed, years ago with appropriate government intervention. Control of SE is possible when government, with the cooperation of producers, demonstrates a commitment to eliminating the human health risk of this pathogen. In Sweden, for example, only five SE-infected flocks have been identified in the entire country since 1987. The Swedish government has a rigorous control program directed at all types of Salmonella in both laying hens and broilers. The program requires testing of laying flocks at least three times during their lives, with destruction of all flocks that are found to be SE-positive.

By contrast, the U.S. government failed to take effective action when confronted with evidence of human illness from SE-contaminated eggs. Any one of the following steps could have substantially cut today's high level of SE infections:

- Rigorous, regularly scheduled testing and sanitation requirements on the farm could have identified SE-positive flocks and forced producers to clean up their henhouses.
- Regulators could have required eggs from SE-positive flocks to be sent to pasteurization plants instead of allowing them to be sold as shell eggs. Inspection at egg packing plants could have verified compliance.
- Refrigeration requirements to minimize the growth of SE during transportation and storage could have been enforced.
- Consumers could have been warned through labels of the risk of eating raw or undercooked eggs.
- Instead, the federal agencies that share responsibility for regulation of eggs and the egg industry made only minimal and sometimes counterproductive efforts to stop SE. A confusing array of laws, regulations, and voluntary programs divides responsibility among four federal agencies:
- U.S. Department of Agriculture's Food Safety and Inspection Service (FSIS), which continuously inspects egg product (pasteurized liquid or powdered egg) plants;
- USDA's Agricultural Marketing Service (AMS), which provides voluntary shell egg grading services and inspects shell egg plants four times a year for cleanliness and quality control;
- USDA's Animal and Plant Health Inspection Service (APHIS), which is responsible for preventing the spread of animal disease; and
- the U.S. Department of Health and Human Services' Food and Drug Administration (FDA), which is responsible for keeping adulterated food out of the marketplace, preventing the spread of communicable diseases from animals to people, and for

inspecting all food products other than meat, poultry, and some egg products.

- In addition, state governments may inspect poultry houses, egg packing and processing plants, and retail establishments such as restaurants and supermarkets.

This crazy quilt of jurisdiction over eggs led to government inaction and inefficiency in the face of the emerging SE problem. The government agencies failed to take effective action at any of four key steps in egg production where SE could have been controlled: (1) on the farm; (2) at the packing and processing plants; (3) during transportation; or (4) at the retail level. The agencies were also hindered by Congress, which failed to establish clear jurisdiction for egg safety in one federal agency and placed the concerns of egg producers over public health.

Failing to Stop SE on the Farm: The Agencies Compete Rather than Cooperate

The response of both FDA and USDA to reports of increasing numbers of SE food poisoning traced to eggs was to compete with each other, rather than to cooperate to solve the problem. Although the two agencies at first worked together during discussions about the problem, they did not cooperate in developing a solution.

The two agencies were initially unsure who had jurisdiction over infected laying flocks. APHIS is responsible for preventing the spread of communicable diseases among poultry and other domestic animals. However, FDA also has broad authority under the Public Health Service Act to make and enforce regulations to prevent the spread of communicable diseases from animals to humans. Further, the Food, Drug and Cosmetic Act gives FDA authority to prevent "adulterated" foods from entering interstate commerce. These two laws give FDA the power to recall eggs produced by infected flocks or to require them to be diverted to pasteurization plants.

In 1987, USDA officials decided not to establish a mandatory SE control program out of fear that the government would have to reimburse infected flock owners for substantial losses from the destruction of their flocks. Ironically, in the early 1980's, USDA spent at least $60 million to combat an outbreak of Avian Influenza, a virus that affects poultry but poses no human health threat, by destroying flocks and reimbursing owners. In contrast to USDA's approach, Canada's federal government requires destruction of laying flocks that are linked to human illnesses from SE, with full compensation to the producers. To date, the SE problem in Canada has remained comparatively small.

In August 1988, APHIS and FDA approved an industry-developed voluntary SE control program, but took no regulatory action. When it became clear that the voluntary SE control program was not slowing the spread of SE, a disagreement emerged between the two agencies as to how to solve the problem. FDA urged a mandatory program, while APHIS wanted to continue with the voluntary program.
For a period of time in 1989, FDA and APHIS were actually simultaneously developing competing mandatory SE control programs. Rather than working cooperatively, FDA officials were unwilling to discuss their proposed plan, which required testing of all laying flocks in the U.S., with APHIS. FDA publicly announced the plan before sharing it with APHIS.

In December 1989, to the surprise of FDA officials, APHIS announced a mandatory SE control program that targeted only flocks already implicated in SE food poisoning incidents. FDA then withdrew its stronger plan and supported APHIS's plan.

A Slow and Ineffective Program to Trace Human SE Illnesses Back to the Farm

APHIS's plan targeted only those flocks to which human illness could be traced. Rather than sampling a large number of flocks to determine how widespread the problem was, the agency adopted a purely reactive approach, waiting until illnesses and deaths occurred before taking any regulatory action.

APHIS's SE control regulations, issued in 1991, applied to laying flocks whose eggs were implicated in SE food poisoning incidents, or that included hens from already-identified infected breeder flocks. Once a flock was identified as meeting one of those two conditions, the regulations required testing of manure and equipment from the laying houses, and of the internal organs of chickens. Chickens or eggs from those flocks could not be moved out of state (unless the eggs were sent to pasteurization plants) until extensive testing, including tests of the hens' internal organs and the poultry houses, show the complete absence of SE. The regulations place no limits on marketing eggs from contaminated flocks within a state.

The effectiveness of the tough-sounding regulations depended on successful tracing of human illness from SE back to the farm. In 1990, 19 outbreaks were traced back to flocks under the program, a success rate of 86%. By 1993, the success rate had declined to 14% (three of 21 outbreaks). The program was criticized for slow and redundant tracebacks. The average traceback took four months from the time of an outbreak until the decision was made to test a suspected flock. The tracebacks were so slow in part because APHIS refused to accept traceback work that had already been completed by state agencies.

APHIS's relationship with the states was not the only weakness in the program. APHIS also failed to work cooperatively with FDA. In one example, APHIS conducted an investigation of an outbreak of SE food poisoning in New York. The investigation implicated a Pennsylvania chicken flock, which tested positive for SE. However, APHIS waited almost a month before notifying FDA of the test results. By then, it was too late for FDA to find and recall eggs from the infected flock that had already been shipped to market and consumers were unnecessarily exposed to SE.

Though the regulations remain in place, APHIS no longer does tracebacks from SE food poisoning incidents to implicated flocks. Responsibility for the traceback program shifted to another USDA agency, FSIS, under the USDA Reorganization Act of 1994. One year later, in 1995, Congress cut funding for the program at the behest of industry groups. Since that time, the traceback function has been taken over by the FDA. As of December 1996, FDA had undertaken four traceback investigations.

The Pennsylvania Pilot Program: A Successful Control Program Is Abandoned

In April 1992, USDA began a voluntary pilot program to control SE in Pennsylvania with the help of egg producers and state government agencies. The goal was to reduce SE contamination in shell eggs in Pennsylvania, a state that had been particularly hard hit by SE. The program contained the following requirements for producers:

- Chicks for layer flocks had to be obtained from breeder flocks that were monitored for SE.
- Manure samples from layer flocks were required to be regularly tested for SE. All testing was to be monitored by a neutral third party.
- Where testing of eggs showed that some were positive for SE, all eggs from that flock were diverted to pasteurization plants. Before the eggs from that flock could be sold as shell eggs again, a total of 4,000 eggs over eight weeks had to test negative for SE.
- Biosecurity programs (programs to prevent bacteria from being carried into poultry houses from outside sources) and rodent control measures for layer houses had to be implemented.

- Eggs were to be kept refrigerated at all times.

USDA was supposed to monitor the program's requirement that eggs from contaminated flocks be diverted to pasteurization plants. USDA's Office of Inspector General found that USDA was failing in this regard. There were no shipping controls in place to ensure that eggs from infected flocks went to pasteurization plants. Two pasteurization plants were also selling fresh shell eggs, unaware that they were receiving eggs from known SE-positive flocks.

Even without full enforcement by USDA, the Pennsylvania program apparently reduced the incidence of SE in the flocks. When the program was implemented in 1992, multiple manure and other samples were taken from the houses of 70 laying flocks. In 1992, 38 percent of laying houses had at least one SE positive sample, but by 1995, only 13 percent of flocks had a positive SE sample. In 1992, 23 percent of all the samples taken tested positive for SE, down to only 3.2 percent of samples in 1995. Human illness from SE in the market area for Pennsylvania eggs (New York, New Jersey, and Pennsylvania) also decreased between 1992 and 1995. A team of 15 scientists from federal and state government agencies attributed at least part of this decrease to the Pennsylvania program and recently recommended that the interventions in the Pennsylvania program be implemented by all egg producers.

Despite the apparent success of the program, in 1995, Congress cut $3 million in funding for USDA's SE control task force, which included all funding for the Pennsylvania pilot program, after lobbying by the egg industry. USDA employees were prohibited from spending any time on the program. The program, now called the Pennsylvania Egg Quality Assurance Program, is still operating on a voluntary basis in Pennsylvania, and about 85 percent of the state's producers participate. However, without federal involvement, the plan will not be expanded nationwide.

Failing to Stop SE at the Packing and Processing Stage: No Inspection for Safety

The spread of SE could have been slowed by more stringent inspection at the packing and processing level. Eggs that came from SE-infected flocks should have been diverted to pasteurization plants, rather than sold as shell eggs. Eggs that came from geographical areas with known high SE rates should have been sampled to determine if they contained SE.

Nevertheless, although three agencies have responsibility for inspecting eggs during processing, no government agency has been monitoring eggs for SE. In fact, even when USDA knew of SE-infected flocks in Pennsylvania, it continued to allow some eggs from these flocks to be marked "Grade A" and sold in supermarkets.

FDA occasionally inspects shell egg- packing plants and is responsible for moni-toring whether eggs are contaminated with SE. However, FDA's inspection resources are so limited that it inspects most food manufacturing plants under its jurisdiction an average of only once every ten years. (See Figure 5.) Ironically, USDA inspects egg plants much more frequently, but does not check for SE contamination.

USDA, through its Agricultural Marketing Service (AMS), provides a voluntary grading program for shell eggs that is paid for by participating producers. Approximately 40 percent of the nation's shell egg producers participate. The program grades eggs for quality, but does not inspect eggs to determine whether they are free of microbial contaminants such as SE. Participating egg-packing plants are inspected for sanitation and proper washing of eggs.

AMS is also responsible for the Shell Egg Surveillance Program. AMS inspectors visit shell egg plants four times a year to ensure that dirty eggs, cracked eggs, and eggs with blood spots are properly disposed of and are not sold to consumers in cartons. However, this program does not include testing eggs for SE and diversion of infected eggs to pasteurization plants.

Until November 1995, AMS was also responsible under the Egg Products Inspection Act for inspection of egg product plants, plants that produce liquid, frozen, or powdered egg products. While these products are generally pasteurized and pose little threat from SE, under the Act, AMS provided continuous safety inspection of egg product plants. Congress shifted the inspection of egg products to USDA's FSIS effective May 1995 and now FSIS conducts continuous inspection in these plants. In contrast, there is no continuous inspection in shell egg plants, or any safety inspection at all beyond FDA's infrequent visits.

Failing to Stop the Growth of SE During Transportation and Storage: Inadequate and Unenforced Refrigeration Requirements

Refrigeration requirements are a key element of any SE control program. If SE is present inside the eggs, refrigeration can help prevent the SE organisms from multiplying. To prevent SE growth, eggs should be refrigerated at an internal temperature of 45 degrees F or lower from the time they leave the farm until they reach the supermarket. However, the government agencies have been unable to provide a cohesive strategy for regulation of refrigeration temperatures during transportation and storage.

The way eggs are processed means that they often leave packing plants warmer than room temperature. They are washed in hot water, immediately placed in cartons, stacked in pallets of several dozen cartons, and then, frequently, shrink-wrapped in plas-tic. These industry practices make it difficult to cool eggs sufficiently, especially those eggs at the center of a pallet of cartons.

By a 1991 amendment to the Egg Products Inspection Act, Congress required USDA to issue regulations mandating that eggs be held under refrigeration at an ambient temperature of 45 degrees F after packing and during transportation. Ambient temperature refers to the tem-perature of the air in the area where the eggs are, not to the eggs' internal temperature.

Both USDA and FDA were given enforcement authority under this amendment. Although an internal temperature, rather than an ambient temperature, of 45 degrees F is necessary to prevent the growth of SE, many observers agree that the ambient temperature standard would be better than the complete absence of a temperature requirement, which is the current situation. After they leave the plants, eggs in some states can legally be shipped, stored, and displayed in supermarkets at room temperature.

In October 1992, USDA issued a proposed rule requiring storage and transportation of eggs at an ambient temperature of 45 degrees F, but never finalized it. FSIS, which was given responsibility for implementing the law when egg safety functions were transferred from APHIS to FSIS, believed that the ambient temperature at which eggs are kept is not the relevant factor in assuring the safety of eggs and declined to enforce the requirement.

Since 1992, USDA has never mandated either the 45 degree F ambient temperature or the scientifically superior internal temperature standard for the egg industry. To further complicate matters, yet another USDA agency has a conflicting temperature requirement based on quality, not safety considerations. The AMS voluntary grading service requires an ambient temperature of 60 degrees F or less in egg handling and storage areas. About 40 percent of the egg industry participates in this program.

The 1991 amendment also gave authority to FDA to ensure that food manufacturing establishments, institutions, and restaurants comply with the ambient 45 degrees F requirement. FDA does not inspect many of these facilities and has failed to enforce the Congressional mandate.

Failing to Warn Consumers of SE in Eggs at Supermarkets and Restaurants

Since the government has not taken steps on the farm, during processing, or during transportation and storage to prevent SE outbreaks, the last opportunity to prevent illness is to warn consumers not to eat raw or undercooked eggs. A warning label on egg cartons informing purchasers how to protect themselves could have prevented many illnesses and deaths. A government survey recently found that half of all consumers had eaten undercooked eggs in the last year. Despite this, the federal agencies have not taken critically needed steps to warn consumers of the risk of SE.

FDA, the agency with the legal authority to require egg carton labels, has required warning labels on foods with a far smaller public health impact than SE-tainted eggs, such as low-calorie protein products (60 deaths) and iron-containing products (3,210 illnesses and two deaths). Yet FDA has not taken the simple step of requiring a label on egg cartons, which could help to prevent the 200,000 to one million illnesses from SE each year.

In contrast, USDA issued a regulation requiring safe-handling labels on meat and poultry sold in supermarkets shortly after the 1993 Jack in the Box outbreak caused by tainted hamburger. Those labels have provided valuable information to consumers. One survey has shown that 66 percent of all respondents and 70 percent of parents with children under the age of 12 have noticed the safe-handling instructions. Another survey found that six out of 10 shoppers surveyed were aware of the safe-handling labels and that 43 percent of these shoppers had changed their meat and poultry handling practices as a result. The surveys show that labeling can be an effective way to provide food safety information to consumers.

FDA has also been ineffective in advising restaurants and other establishments on safe egg handling. FDA delayed for years publication of an updated version of its food safety recommendations for restaurants (known as the Food Code), so that safe-handling guidelines for eggs were not included until 1993. In the 1993 Food Code, FDA recommended that eggs (along with all other perishable foods) be refrigerated at an ambient temperature of 41 degrees F or lower. FDA also recommended that eggs be cooked to at least 145 degrees F, or that pasteurized egg products be used for uncooked foods or for highly susceptible populations. No warning against pooling eggs was included. FDA recommended that restaurants provide a consumer warning about the risk of eating undercooked animal foods, but no suggested language was provided, and the recommen-dation has been adopted by only a few states.

Both FDA and USDA's FSIS provide safe egg cooking advice to consumers. However, this information is generally available only upon request from the agencies. The recommendation given out on USDA's safe food-handling hotline is to cook eggs until the white is firm and the yolk is just beginning to set (and is no longer runny).

Conclusion and Recommendations

The history of the federal government's failure to curb the SE epidemic illustrates the ineffectiveness of having multiple government agencies responsible for regulating the same food. Instead of providing additional food safety protection, the numerous agencies charged with regulating eggs actually hindered each other in stopping the SE problem. The agencies did not identify which of them was responsible for controlling SE in eggs; they competed with each other instead of cooperating; and, when faced with decisions about how to regulate to solve the problem, chose the least protective approach. The agencies were further hamstrung by a Congress that cut funding for a control program just as it was beginning to show results and an industry that, except for producers in Pennsylvania, resisted attempts to prevent SE contamination on the farm.

Effective government action could have prevented many illnesses and deaths over the past twenty years and could prevent countless future unnecessary tragedies. To protect consumers from the hazards of SE, we recommend the following steps.

- FDA should mandate that egg producers implement on-farm Hazard Analysis and Critical Control Point (HACCP) programs to control SE. The SE control programs should be modeled after the successful Pennsylvania Egg Quality Assurance Program. The programs should include manure and egg testing that is monitored by FDA. (If the vitally needed HACCP programs are not required, producers who implement FDA-monitored voluntary programs should be allowed to inform consumers of their programs through the use of a special label or symbol on egg cartons.
- Shell egg plants should be inspected for safety several times per year. These inspections should include verification that a testing program is in place to assure that eggs from infected flocks are diverted to pasteurization plants.
- FDA and FSIS should act quickly to implement science-based regulations mandating egg refrigeration at 41 degrees F during transportation and storage. Temperature requirements should be standardized across the government agencies that regulate food, including the state and local governments responsible for enforcing temperatures at the retail level. Eggs should not be left unrefrigerated at any time.

- Until the egg industry has effective programs in place to control SE, consumers must be warned that they face the risk of illness from eating raw or undercooked eggs. FDA should mandate that the following warning notice be placed on the lids of egg cartons: "Caution: Eggs may contain illness-causing bacteria. Do not eat raw. Cook until yolk is firm." The notice should be designed and positioned to maximize visibility and consumer compliance.
- FDA's Food Code should recommend that restaurants and other establishments not pool unpasteurized eggs unless they are cooked immediately.
- Jurisdiction for food safety scattered among different agencies impairs protection of the public's health, results in duplication of efforts, inhibits needed actions, and wastes government resources. Until food safety functions are consolidated into a single federal food agency, the safety regulation of each food product, such as eggs, should fall under the clearly defined authority of one of the two primary food safety agencies, either FSIS or FDA. Clear jurisdiction is needed to avoid agency competition and miscommunication.
- Congress should significantly increase funding for FDA's food safety functions and should fully fund FSIS's and FDA's efforts to address SE in eggs. President Clinton's recent announcement of additional funding for food safety is an important step in ensuring that these agencies can adequately protect the public health.

FDA: 'Postpone' eating foods containing peanut butter

By Elizabeth Weise, USA TODAY

The Food and Drug Administration says Americans should "postpone" eating cookies, crackers, candy and ice cream that contain peanut butter or peanut paste while the agency works to establish which products are tainted with the strain of salmonella typhimurium which has sickened 474 people nationwide and is implicated in six deaths.

"Product specific information will become available in the next few days," says Stephen Sundlof, director of FDA's Center for Food Safety and Applied Nutrition.

While snack products are potentially contaminated, supermarket peanut butter is not.

It appears that the only peanut butter linked to the outbreak was an institutional brand sold in 5 to 50 pounds tubs to schools, hospitals and nursing homes under the King Nut and Parnell's Pride label. It was never sold at the retail level and is not available at supermarkets and grocery stores, FDA says.

As for products that might contain the tainted peanut butter and peanut paste, FDA is encouraging companies that bought from the Peanut Corporation of America's Blakely, Ga., plant to inform consumers their products might be contaminated.

Tests by the Georgia Dept. of Agriculture found peanut butter from the plant tested positive for salmonella, but tests to determine if that salmonella is an exact DNA match to the outbreak strain are still ongoing.

The agency is asking companies that make peanut butter or paste containing products that aren't linked to products from the Georgia plant also make that known to the public.

For the FDA's up-to-date list of affected products, visit: www.fda.gov/oc/opacom/hottopics/salmonellatyph.html#recalls

The list of items affected by the salmonella-tainted peanut butter from the plant rose substantially Friday night when the Kellogg Company added 12 new items to its list, including select snack-size packs of Famous Amos Peanut Butter Cookies and Keebler Soft Batch Homestyle Peanut Butter Cookies.

Kellogg said the products "have the potential to be contaminated with salmonella."

"The actions we are taking today are in keeping with our more than 100-year commitment to providing consumers with safe, high-quality products," said David Mackay, president and CEO, Kellogg Company.

Kellogg is one of 85 companies which bought peanut butter and peanut paste produced in the Georgia plant.

PCA Friday expanded its recall of peanut butter and peanut paste made at the plant to include all peanut butter produced on or after August 8, 2008 and all peanut paste produced on or after September 26, 2008.

The peanut butter was sold in containers ranging in size from five to 1,700 pounds. The peanut paste was sold in sizes ranging from 35 pounds to tanker containers, the company said in a release. Peanut paste consists of ground, roasted peanuts and is used as an ingredient in cookies, crackers, cereals and ice creams, says FDA's Sundlof.

Supermarkets nationwide worked Friday and Saturday to remove potentially tainted products.

A spokesperson for Wal-Mart said the Bentonville-Ark.-company had contacted each of its stores so they immediately can "pull and hold" the crackers.

Costco pulled the Kellogg crackers off store shelves Tuesday night even before Kellogg had made its announcement, says Craig Wilson, Costco's vice president of food safety.

There was an empty gap Saturday on the shelves of the Marsh grocery store in Brownsburg, Ind., where several varieties of Keebler snack crackers with peanut butter fillings had been removed.

Dan Fredrickson, manager of the Woodman's Food Market in Madison, Wis. says he thought his shelves were empty because his supplier recently stopped shipping the product. But he said in any recall, he said his store acts quickly.

"It's off the shelves as soon as we are notified," Fredrickson says.

In Colorado, managers at several Fort Collins-area King Soopers and Safeway grocery stores said they received the recall notice Thursday and immediately pulled the crackers from their shelves.

Ron Freeman, chief financial officer for Asheville, N.C.-based Ingles markets says all the Keebler and Austin products placed on hold were taken off its shelves on Thursday.

"We pulled them all as soon as realized they were being recalled," he said.

West Des Moines- based Hy-Vee Inc. is holding the products until they receive more information about them.

The firm will "err on the side of caution. When something like this is not easily identified, we like to act in the best interest of our customers," says Chris Friesleben, director of communications.

That extends even to the firm's bakery items, she says." We have peanut butter cookies and other things we bake, and we're not even making those anymore in our bakery plant. We're going to suspend production for awhile."

Grocery stores in Mountain Home, Ark., have pulled the Austin and Keebler brand of peanut butter crackers off there shelves and some stores were offering customer refunds of the products.

"As soon as a recall is issued, we send it out to the stores," says Jim Wieland, director of pricing at Harps and Price Cutter Food Stores at its general office in Springdale, Ark.

For the full Kellogg list, see www.fda.gov/oc/po/firmrecalls/kellogg201_09.html

CHAPTER 76

Foods - Vegetarian Diets - Influenced by Evil Seducing Spirits

Many people believe that the vegetarian diet is a healthier diet without eating meat. Some Christians, including the 7th Day Adventist Denomination Churches believe that back in the Book of Genesis the diet was the vegetarian diet. That was correct at that particular time, but after the flood, God commanded us to eat meat. Even during the preparations for certain battles, the men were commanded to eat meat for strength

The following verse is where some churches get their confusions from and they are still stuck in the periods of time from the Garden of Eden to the flood. They have yet to go past the events of the flood.

Genesis 3 (KJV)

18. Thorns also and thistles shall it bring forth to thee; and **thou shalt eat the herb of the field**;

My youngest sister converted from being a Baptist to a 7th Day Adventist. She married a young man of her faith who was an Elder in the Church. They visited us in the Summer of 2006. He was quite adamant in trying to get us to convert to the 7th Day Adventist Denomination. He would take scriptures, turn them around to suit his way of thinking. I tried to be nice to him, but finally told him in an abrupt way that I was not going to change. I further explained to him about what God said to Peter about calling his food common or unclean in the scriptures below. He tried to twist the scriptures around with another scripture which talks about common and unclean men. I then told him that he was referencing two different subjects. God did not tell Peter to slay and eat men. The young Elder was quite confused in his erroneous teachings of the bible.

After the great flood that destroyed all of man-kind accept Noah and his family and the animals and fowls which Almighty God told him to take into the Ark, God allowed us to start eating meat, fowls, crawling things or anything that we so desired, except the flesh of humans:

Genesis 9 (KJV)

2. And the fear of you and the dread of you shall be upon every beast of the earth, and upon every fowl of the air, upon all that moveth upon the earth, and upon all the fishes of the sea; into your hand are they delivered.
3. Every moving thing that liveth shall be meat for you; even as the green herb have I given you all things.
4. But flesh with the life thereof, which is the blood thereof, shall ye not eat.

Almighty God has re-emphasized the fact that we could eat meat in the New Testament books of the bible as well.

Acts 11 (KJV)

1. And the apostles and brethren that were in Judaea heard that the Gentiles had also received the word of God.
2. And when Peter was come up to Jerusalem, they that were of the circumcision contended with him,

3. Saying, Thou wentest in to men uncircumcised, and didst eat with them.
4 But Peter rehearsed the matter from the beginning, and expounded it by order unto them, saying,
5. I was in the city of Joppa praying: and in a trance I saw a vision, A certain vessel descend, as it had been a great sheet, let down from heaven by four corners; and it came even to me:
6. Upon the which when I had fastened mine eyes, I considered, and saw fourfooted beasts of the earth, and wild beasts, and creeping things, and fowls of the air.
7. And I heard a voice saying unto me, Arise, Peter; slay and eat.
8 But I said, Not so, Lord: for nothing common or unclean hath at any time entered into my mouth.
9. But the voice answered me again from heaven, What God hath cleansed, that call not thou common.
10. And this was done three times: and all were drawn up again into heaven.

One of the key issues was that he and my sister were vegetarians and they thought they were following God's commandment back in Genesis. They never came up to the flood, nor did they come up to the New Testament were God, Almighty had to explain to Peter that nothing he made was uncommon, nor unclean to eat.

1 Timothy 4 (KJV)

1. Now the Spirit speaketh expressly, that in the latter times some shall depart from the faith, giving heed to seducing spirits, and doctrines of devils;
2. Speaking lies in hypocrisy; having their conscience seared with a hot iron;
3. Forbidding to marry, and commanding to abstain from

meats, which God hath created to be received with thanksgiving of them which believe and know the truth.

4. For every creature of God is good, and nothing to be refused, if it be received with thanksgiving:
5. For it is sanctified by the word of God and prayer.

Even when we are just having a little snack, we should bless Almighty God and give him thanks for what we are about to consume in our bodies, whether we are in a fast food store, restaurant, dining facility, at home, at the mall or wherever we intend to consume our snacks or our meals.

CHAPTER 77

Fornication - Sexual Intercourse Between Un-Married Couples

Unfortunately, evil thoughts of fornication or sexual intercourse comes from what is already in one's heart. People are predominately evil from birth. They have to be taught to be better persons and to live good Christian lives.

Matthew 15 (KJV)

> 19. For out of the heart proceed evil thoughts, murders, adulteries, fornications, thefts, false witness, blasphemies:

There are at least a couple of analogies that males use to satisfy their consciences and they are:

1. Analogy - "Why buy the cow when the milk is free!", meaning, "Why get married, when the sex is free!".
2. Analogy - "You should test drive an automobile before you buy it!", meaning, "You should try out the sex before you get married!".

This type of thinking is not only disrespectful coming from that particular person, but it is also disrespectful towards their mate as well. Not only that but both of them are in danger of burning in hell as well. Children must be taught at their earliest ages of comprehension and understanding concerning the dangers having sexual intercourse before they are married.

Abstain From Having Sexual Intercourse Until Marriage

Acts 15 (KJV)

20. But that we write unto them, that they abstain from pollutions of idols, and from fornication, and from things strangled, and from blood.
29. That ye abstain from meats offered to idols, and from blood, and from things strangled, and from fornication: from which if ye keep yourselves, ye shall do well. Fare ye well.

Acts 21 (KJV)

25. As touching the Gentiles which believe, we have written and concluded that they observe no such thing, save only that they keep themselves from things offered to idols, and from blood, and from strangled, and from fornication.

Consequences From Refusing To Retain Almighty God In Your knowledge

Romans 1 (KJV)

28. And even as they did not like to retain God in their knowledge, God gave them over to a reprobate mind, to do those things which are not convenient;
29. Being filled with all unrighteousness, fornication, wickedness, covetousness, maliciousness; full of envy, murder, debate, deceit, malignity; whisperers,
30. Backbiters, haters of God, despiteful, proud, boasters, inventors of evil things, disobedient to parents,

31. Without understanding, covenantbreakers, without natural affection, implacable, unmerciful:
32. Who knowing the judgment of God, that they which commit such things are worthy of death, not only do the same, but have pleasure in them that do them.

Your Body Is For Almighty God, Not For Fornication

1 Corinthians 6 (KJV)

13. Meats for the belly, and the belly for meats: but God shall destroy both it and them. Now the body is not for fornication, but for the Lord; and the Lord for the body.

Fornication Is Sin Against The Body

1 Corinthians 6 (KJV)

18. Flee fornication. Every sin that a man doeth is without the body; but he that committeth fornication sinneth against his own body.

Gays, Homosexuals, Transexuals. Nor Fornicators Will Not Go To Heaven

1 Corinthians 6 (KJV)

9. Know ye not that the unrighteous shall not inherit the kingdom of God? Be not deceived: neither fornicators, nor idolaters, nor adulterers, nor effeminate, nor abusers of themselves with mankind,
10. Nor thieves, nor covetous, nor drunkards, nor revilers, nor extortioners, shall inherit the kingdom of God.

Advice To Abstain From Fornication

1 Corinthians 7

1. Now concerning the things whereof ye wrote unto me: It is good for a man not to touch a woman.
2. Nevertheless, to avoid fornication, let every man have his own wife, and let every woman have her own husband.
3. Let the husband render unto the wife due benevolence: and likewise also the wife unto the husband.
4. The wife hath not power of her own body, but the husband: and likewise also the husband hath not power of his own body, but the wife.
5. Defraud ye not one the other, except it be with consent for a time, that ye may give yourselves to fasting and prayer; and come together again, that Satan tempt you not for your incontinency.
6. But I speak this by permission, and not of commandment.
7. For I would that all men were even as I myself. But every man hath his proper gift of God, one after this manner, and another after that.
8. I say therefore to the unmarried and widows, It is good for them if they abide even as I.

Better To Marry, Than To Burn

9. But if they cannot contain, let them marry: for it is better to marry than to burn.
10. And unto the married I command, yet not I, but the Lord, Let not the wife depart from her husband:
11. But and if she depart, let her remain unmarried, or be reconciled to her husband: and let not the husband put away his wife.
12. But to the rest speak I, not the Lord: If any brother hath a

wife that believeth not, and she be pleased to dwell with him, let him not put her away.

13. And the woman which hath an husband that believeth not, and if he be pleased to dwell with her, let her not leave him.
14. For the unbelieving husband is sanctified by the wife, and the unbelieving wife is sanctified by the husband: else were your children unclean; but now are they holy.
15. But if the unbelieving depart, let him depart. A brother or a sister is not under bondage in such cases: but God hath called us to peace.
16. For what knowest thou, O wife, whether thou shalt save thy husband? or how knowest thou, O man, whether thou shalt save thy wife?
17. But as God hath distributed to every man, as the Lord hath called every one, so let him walk. And so ordain I in all churches.
18. Is any man called being circumcised? let him not become uncircumcised. Is any called in uncircumcision? let him not be circumcised.
19. Circumcision is nothing, and uncircumcision is nothing, but the keeping of the commandments of God.
20. Let every man abide in the same calling wherein he was called.
21. Art thou called being a servant? care not for it: but if thou mayest be made free, use it rather.
22. For he that is called in the Lord, being a servant, is the Lord's freeman: likewise also he that is called, being free, is Christ's servant.
23. Ye are bought with a price; be not ye the servants of men.
24. Brethren, let every man, wherein he is called, therein abide with God.
25. Now concerning virgins I have no commandment of the Lord: yet I give my judgment, as one that hath obtained mercy of the Lord to be faithful.

26. I suppose therefore that this is good for the present distress, I say, that it is good for a man so to be.
27. Art thou bound unto a wife? seek not to be loosed. Art thou loosed from a wife? seek not a wife.
28. But and if thou marry, thou hast not sinned; and if a virgin marry, she hath not sinned. Nevertheless such shall have trouble in the flesh: but I spare you.
29. But this I say, brethren, the time is short: it remaineth, that both they that have wives be as though they had none;
30. And they that weep, as though they wept not; and they that rejoice, as though they rejoiced not; and they that buy, as though they possessed not;
31. And they that use this world, as not abusing it: for the fashion of this world passeth away.
32. But I would have you without carefulness. He that is unmarried careth for the things that belong to the Lord, how he may please the Lord:
33. But he that is married careth for the things that are of the world, how he may please his wife.
34. There is difference also between a wife and a virgin. The unmarried woman careth for the things of the Lord, that she may be holy both in body and in spirit: but she that is married careth for the things of the world, how she may please her husband.
35. And this I speak for your own profit; not that I may cast a snare upon you, but for that which is comely, and that ye may attend upon the Lord without distraction.
36. But if any man think that he behaveth himself uncomely toward his virgin, if she pass the flower of her age, and need so require, let him do what he will, he sinneth not: let them marry.
37. Nevertheless he that standeth stedfast in his heart, having no necessity, but hath power over his own will, and hath so decreed in his heart that he will keep his virgin, doeth well.

38. So then he that giveth her in marriage doeth well; but he that giveth her not in marriage doeth better.
39. The wife is bound by the law as long as her husband liveth; but if her husband be dead, she is at liberty to be married to whom she will; only in the Lord.
40. But she is happier if she so abide, after my judgment: and I think also that I have the Spirit of God.

23,000 People Perished Because Of Fornication

1 Corinthians 10 (KJV)

8. Neither let us commit fornication, as some of them committed, and fell in one day three and twenty thousand.

Divine Punishments In Store For Fornicators

2 Corinthians 12 (KJV)

21. And lest, when I come again, my God will humble me among you, and that I shall bewail many which have sinned already, and have not repented of the uncleanness and fornication and lasciviousness which they have committed.

Evil Works Of The Flesh Includes Fornication

Galatians 5 (KJV)

19. Now the works of the flesh are manifest, which are these; Adultery, fornication, uncleanness, lasciviousness,
20. Idolatry, witchcraft, hatred, variance, emulations, wrath, strife, seditions, heresies,
21. Envyings, murders, drunkenness, revellings, and such like:

of the which I tell you before, as I have also told you in time past, that they which do such things shall not inherit the kingdom of God.

22. But the fruit of the Spirit is love, joy, peace, longsuffering, gentleness, goodness, faith,
23. Meekness, temperance: against such there is no law.
24. And they that are Christ's have crucified the flesh with the affections and lusts.
25 If we live in the Spirit, let us also walk in the Spirit.
26. Let us not be desirous of vain glory, provoking one another, envying one another.

Saints, Flee From Fornication

Ephesians 5 (KJV)

1. Be ye therefore followers of God, as dear children;
2. And walk in love, as Christ also hath loved us, and hath given himself for us an offering and a sacrifice to God for a sweetsmelling savour.
3. But fornication, and all uncleanness, or covetousness, let it not be once named among you, as becometh saints;
4. Neither filthiness, nor foolish talking, nor jesting, which are not convenient: but rather giving of thanks.

The Wrath Of Almighty God Punishes Fornicators

Colossians 3 (KJV)

1. If ye then be risen with Christ, seek those things which are above, where Christ sitteth on the right hand of God.
2. Set your affection on things above, not on things on the earth.
3. For ye are dead, and your life is hid with Christ in God.
4. When Christ, who is our life, shall appear, then shall ye also appear with him in glory.

5. Mortify therefore your members which are upon the earth; fornication, uncleanness, inordinate affection, evil concupiscence, and covetousness, which is idolatry:
6. For which things' sake the wrath of God cometh on the children of disobedience:

It Is Almighty God's Will That You Abstain From Fornication

1 Thessalonians 4 (KJV)

3. For this is the will of God, [even] your sanctification, that ye should abstain from fornication:

Example Of Almighty God's Vengeance On Fornicators

Jude 1 (KJV)

7. Even as Sodom and Gomorrha, and the cities about them in like manner, giving themselves over to fornication, and going after strange flesh, are set forth for an example, suffering the vengeance of eternal fire.

Jesus Christ, Our Savior Is Against Fornication

Revelation 2 (KJV)

14. But I have a few things against thee, because thou hast there them that hold the doctrine of Balaam, who taught Balac to cast a stumblingblock before the children of Israel, to eat things sacrificed unto idols, and to commit fornication.

CHAPTER 78

Gay Men and Women (Homosexuals & Transsexuals) Are Abominations to Almighty God

There are many gay men and gay women who believe their sexual choices homosexuality is normal and a way of normal life. Well, it is not normal. It is actually a generational curse in their bloodline who spans back at least three (3) to four (4) generations. Now, fortunately these generational curses can be broken if the perspective desire for such to be done. That means that they must be delivered from those curses which then set them free to live normal lives.

However, many homosexuals are so blinded that they desire to stay in those conditions and live out their lives in the same as well. Almighty did not intend for Steve to be married to Stephen, nor did He intend for Mary to be married to Margarita. Almighty God told Adam and Eve to be fruitful and multiply. He did not mean for two (2) women to marry and multiply, nor did He intend for two (2) men to marry and multiply, either. Same sexes don't have the power to reproduce.

Transsexuals who have changed their sex organs to that of the opposite sex is really in the same category as homosexuals. They are also an abomination to Almighty God. Almighty God created us in His own image and likeness. He did not tell us to change our sex organs because He was satisfied how He first created us.

Believe it or not, there are homosexual ministers proclaiming to be men or women of God. God doesn't call homosexuals into His ministry. Homosexuality is an abomination to Him. People who have chosen the life of homosexuality is not only ridiculed by the world for their choice in their sexual orientation, but by God as well. He allows them to pay or be punished for their errors through a number curses on earth such as the Aids viruses and other sexual contracted diseases. There are those who are not only homosexuals (same sex), but as heterosexuals (opposite sex, male and female) as well.

Rom 1:26-27 (KJV) For this cause God gave them up unto vile affections: for even their women did change the natural use into that which is against nature:

27. And likewise also the men, leaving the natural use of the woman, burned in their lust one toward another; men with men working that which is unseemly, and receiving in themselves that recompense of their error which was meet.

Lev 18:22 (KJV) Thou shalt not lie with mankind, as with womankind: it is abomination.

CHAPTER **79**

Generational (Bloodline) Inherited Curses

You are probably saying to yourself that you haven't touched any cursed thing or object, you don't follow demonic fads, you are not a member of any masonic lodge, Eastern Star or Shriner organizations, but you feel you are defeated, your prayers are not being answered, you are sick and can't get well, and on top of all of that, you need a break through with your finances. Well, the problem could be that you have inherited curses from your ancestors' sins. Even if you have ask God to forgive your every sin and which He has, you could be suffering from the effects of the sins of your ancestors which brought curses upon them, their children and their future generations as well.

Exo 20:5 (KJV) "Thou shalt not bow down thyself to them, nor serve them: for I the LORD thy God am a jealous God, **visiting the iniquity of the fathers upon the children unto the third and fourth generation of them that hate me;**"

Deu 30:19 (KJV) "I call heaven and earth to record this day against you, that I have set before you life and death, blessing and cursing: therefore choose life, that both thou and thy seed may live:"

I, (Curtis) was raised by my step father whose family is inundated, that is they are flooded or overwhelmed with the curse of diabetes. Well, to my knowledge, there was no history of diabetes in my paternal father's family. Although, my mother is not a diabetic, but her family is also flooded with the curse of diabetes as well. So, as you can see, I have curses coming in from at least three to five directions: my father, my step father, and my mother's family including curses that I received from serving in Viet Nam (Agent Orange and Buddhist Monks Curses). These curses of diabetes have also followed me. This diabetes effected just about every major organ of my body. However, God is gradually healing me. I was supposed to be going blind in one and legally blind in the other eyes. I have had six (6) laser surgeries on both eyes, but both eyes deteriorated anyway. My left eye is doing fine and getting better on a daily basis. I was legally blind in my right eye, but the vision in this eye is getting better every day as well. I am standing on God's promises for a full and complete recovery. You need to understand that you can inherit curses not only from your immediate families, but your step parents and their families, adopted parents and/or those children that you adopt by the mere fact of your association with them. You will probably not know what manner of curses these adopted children bring with them as they inherited them from their ancestors and/or their blood families. On the other hand, you will probably not know what curses you and your family are sharing with your adopted children. So, there is a two-edged sword here where curses cut both ways.

CHAPTER **80**

Giving Credit to Self Instead of Almighty God

Christians who are anointed vessels of God, Almighty to do His will of teachings, preachings, healings, miracles, prophecies and all of the gifts of the Holy Spirit are subject to curses from Him when they are out of His will. Anointed ones of God are held to very high standards in following His word and are not to be taken lightly in any sense of God's word. Moses and Aaron found that out in their lives. When the children of Israel reached the wilderness, they complained that neither they, nor their animals have any to eat, nor did they have anything water to drink. So, Moses and Aaron went to the tabernacle and went down on their faces to pray to God for water. God's glory appeared as a cloud in the tabernacle where He told Moses what to do with his rod to get water for the children of Israel.

Num 20:7 (KJV) "And the LORD spake unto Moses, saying,"

Num 20:8 (KJV) "Take the rod, and gather thou the assembly together, thou, and Aaron thy brother, and speak ye unto the rock before their eyes; and it shall give forth his water, and thou shalt bring forth to them water out of the rock: so thou shalt give the congregation and their beasts drink."

Num 20:9 (KJV) "And Moses took the rod from before the LORD, as he commanded him."

Mose's And Aaron's Sin Of Rebellion

You'll see in Numbers 20:10 where Moses and Aaron committed their sins against God, Almighty. They gave themselves credit and honor instead of God for giving the water to the children of Israel. They were only vessels in which God chose to use in providing water to His people. We must understand that we must give God all of the credit, glory, honor, respect, praises and worship for His awesome power and His glorious Glory and blessings. We can't take credit for anything.

Num 20:10 (KJV) "And Moses and Aaron gathered the congregation together before the rock, and he said unto them, Hear now, ye rebels; must we fetch you water out of this rock?"

Num 20:11 (KJV) "And Moses lifted up his hand, and with his rod he smote the rock twice: and the water came out abundantly, and the congregation drank, and their beasts also."

God Cursed Moses And Aaron

Neither Moses, nor Aaron were blessed to cross over from the wilderness to the glorious land of promise which God had given the children of Israel. Their acts of sin had brought down curses upon them. When we commit a sin, we must immediately ask God for forgiveness. If you commit a sin against another human, you must immediately ask that person for forgiveness. It matters not whether that person forgives you or not. Ask him or her anyway and then ask God to forgive you.

Num 20:12 (KJV) "And the LORD spake unto Moses and Aaron, Because ye believed me not, to sanctify me in the eyes of the children of Israel, therefore ye shall not bring this congregation into the land which I have given them."

Num 20:13 (KJV) "This is the water of Meribah, because the children of Israel strove with the LORD, and he was sanctified in them."

God Cursed Aaron To Death

Aaron had another sin on him as well as the sin of prejudice which included his wife Miriam. They were prejudice against the Ethiopian wife of Moses which angered God. They didn't like it that Moses married an Ethiopian as his wife. This really angered God mightily. God struck Aaron's wife with the curse of leprosy. Aaron prayed to God for his wife and she was healed. However, Aaron prayed to Moses instead of God for the same sin that he committed. So, God had not forgiven him for this sin, nor did He forgive them of the sin of unbelief against His word for the blessings of water from the rock at Meribah.

Num 20:24 (KJV) "Aaron shall be gathered unto his people: for he shall not enter into the land which I have given unto the children of Israel, because ye rebelled against my word at the water of Meribah."

Num 20:25 (KJV) "Take Aaron and Eleazar his son, and bring them up unto mount Hor:"

Num 20:26 (KJV) "And strip Aaron of his garments, and put them upon Eleazar his son: and Aaron shall be gathered unto his people, and shall die there."

Num 20:27 (KJV) "And Moses did as the LORD commanded: and they went up into mount Hor in the sight of all the congregation."

Aaron's garments were in fact anointed coverings as high priests were required to wear in the Tabernacle of God. These were garments as well as under garments specifically designed by God. Although Aaron's last two (2) sons were priests, they were under him and Moses who higher orders of priest in the Tabernacle of God.

Num 20:28 (KJV) "And Moses stripped Aaron of his garments, and put them upon Eleazar his son; and Aaron died there in the top of the mount: and Moses and Eleazar came down from the mount."

Num 20:29 (KJV) "And when all the congregation saw that Aaron was dead, **they mourned for Aaron thirty days, even all the house of Israel.**"

CHAPTER **81**

Giving Honor to Satan or Demon Gods Is Prohibited

One big mistake that a Christian can do is to honor Satan and/or his demon gods. These are little gods of someone else's religion other than Christianity. These could be Jehovah's Witnesses, Moslem religions, Buddhist and various other non Christian religions. The name Jehovah is the national name that Jews use when they refer to God, Almighty. So, as you can see, Satan is a counterfeit who stole that name as well. Sometimes we feel that we don't want to hurt somebody's feeling by disrespecting the god they serve. Our God said that we should not have no other gods before him. But, if our forefathers had other gods before Him, He will PUNISH the children for their father's sins even up to the 3rd and 4th generations that hate Him. So, you see, even if we have other gods in our lives and we die without breaking or severing the ties to those gods, then our children, their children and their children's children will have to pay for our sins. These sins take on a snowball effect if we haven't taken these curses from us.

Exo 20:3-5 (KJV) Thou shalt have no other gods before me.

4. Thou shalt not make unto thee any graven image, or any likeness of any thing that is in heaven above, or that is in the earth beneath, or that is in the water under the earth:
5. Thou shalt not bow down thyself to them, nor serve them:

> for I the LORD thy God am a jealous God, **visiting the iniquity of the fathers upon the children unto the third and fourth generation of them that hate me;**

Well, you say, "I don't hate God!". But in fact you do because you are not loving Him with all of your heart as He requires us to do. When you give honor to another god, you aren't totally in love with God, Almighty.

Mark 12:30 (KJV) "And thou shalt love the Lord thy God with all thy heart, and with all thy soul, and with all thy mind, and with all thy strength: this is the first commandment." Mark 12:31 (KJV) "And the second is like, namely this, Thou shalt love thy neighbour as thyself. There is none other commandment greater than these."

One key note of discernment and wisdom is when you are talking to someone with whom you feel is not of the Christian faith and they tell you that we are all serving the same god. Ask them one question similar to this, "Do you believe that Jesus Christ is the Son of God, Almighty and that He is our Savior?". If they say, no, then the case is closed. They will probably go on to tell you that Jesus was a good prophet just like any of other prophet or words to that effect. They are certainly serving other gods. If they can't honor Jesus Christ, our personal Savior, then they certainly cannot honor God, Almighty in heaven.

John 5:23 (KJV) "That all men should honour the Son, even as they honour the Father. He that honoureth not the Son honoureth not the Father which hath sent him."

CHAPTER 82

Global Warming and Climate Changes Are Man-Made Myths

Global Warming or climate change is a phenomenon created by humans, who by the way have no type of power to change the set seasons or climates this small planet call earth. Only Almighty God can make those changes.

Genesis 1 (KJV)

14. And God said, Let there be lights in the firmament of the heaven to divide the day from the night; and let them be for signs, and for **seasons**, and for days, and years:

Genesis 8 (KJV)

22. While the earth remaineth, seedtime and harvest, and cold and heat, and summer and winter, and day and night shall not cease.

Psalms 104 (KJV)

19. **He appointed the moon for seasons:** the sun knoweth his going down.

Daniel 2 (KJV)

21. And he **changeth the times and the seasons:** he removeth kings, and setteth up kings: he giveth wisdom unto the wise, and knowledge to them that know understanding:

Deuteronomy 11

13. And it shall come to pass, if ye shall hearken diligently unto my commandments which I command you this day, to love the Lord your God, and to serve him with all your heart and with all your soul,
14. That I will give you the rain of your land in his due season, the first rain and the latter rain, that thou mayest gather in thy corn, and thy wine, and thine oil.
15. And I will send grass in thy fields for thy cattle, that thou mayest eat and be full.

Matthew 16 (KJV)

2. He answered and said unto them, When it is evening, ye say, It will be fair weather: for the sky is red.
3. And in the morning, It will be foul weather to day: for the sky is red and lowring. O ye hypocrites, ye can discern the face of the sky; but can ye not discern the signs of the times?

The sins of the world have a devastating effect on world conditions which allows Almighty God to withdraw His blessings of suitable climate conditions for living and for planting, harvesting and consumption as our needs arises. However, we are so blatant in perpetrating sin for we are tremendously lacking in good moral Chiristian values towards humanity. Below is just a sampling of what can cause climate change:

- Allowing capital punishment to be carried out in states around the U.S.
- Allowing abortions to be performed.
- Allowing states to take prayer out of the schools.
- Directing and allowing immigration reform with underlying racism, prejudices, and the fear of political takeover is at the root of their decisions as they are themselves White European American Immigrates with the exception of Native Americans (Indians).
- unjust imprisonments of minorities with numbers far greater than those of White European Americans who are the majority U.S. Citizens.
- Oklahoma bombing of a federal building by a home-grown terrorist.
- Shoe bombing airplane home-grown terrorist.
- Anthrax and other deadly chemicals through U.S. Postal Services by home-grown terrorists.
- School massacres by home-grown terrorist such as what happened at Columbine, Virginia Tech and other schools across the United States of America.

Governors can also bring curses to their states:

- By allowing the execution/capital punishment of convicted humans which results in the death of these humans. These Governors/Leaders will now have human blood on their hands, whether they actually participated in the executions or not.
- Also who allowing abortions to be performed in their states, legally.
- By directing schools to take prayer out of their classrooms and school buildings.

These sins bring on many curses not only upon their citizens, but to their lands as well.

King Saul was a nation's leader in the below mentioned scriptures depicts what can happen when a leader has the zeal to commit war against another nation, thereby causing blood to be upon his or her hands and their households, as well as the Continent, the State or the Nation(s) that they lead or rule. Any discrepancies in the cosmic phenomenons over the earth cannot be modified or changed by man at his own will.

2 Samuel 21 (KJV)

1. Then there was a famine in the days of David three years, year after year; and David inquired of the Lord. And the Lord answered, It is for Saul, and for his bloody house, because he slew the Gibeonites.
2. And the king called the Gibeonites, and said unto them; (Now the Gibeonites were not of the children of Israel, but of the remnant of the Amorites; and the children of Israel had sworn unto them: and Saul sought to slay them in his zeal to the children of Israel and Judah.)
3. Wherefore David said unto the Gibeonites, What shall I do for you? and wherewith shall I make the atonement, that ye may bless the inheritance of the Lord?
4. And the Gibeonites said unto him, We will have no silver nor gold of Saul, nor of his house; neither for us shalt thou kill any man in Israel. And he said, What ye shall say, that will I do for you.
5. And they answered the king, The man that consumed us, and that devised against us that we should be destroyed from remaining in any of the coasts of Israel,
6. Let seven men of his sons be delivered unto us, and we will hang them up unto the Lord in Gibeah of Saul, whom the Lord did choose. And the king said, I will give them.
7. But the king spared Mephibosheth, the son of Jonathan the son of Saul, because of the Lord's oath that was between them, between David and Jonathan the son of Saul.

8. But the king took the two sons of Rizpah the daughter of Aiah, whom she bare unto Saul, Armoni and Mephibosheth; and the five sons of Michal the daughter of Saul, whom she brought up for Adriel the son of Barzillai the Meholathite:
9. And he delivered them into the hands of the Gibeonites, and they hanged them in the hill before the Lord: and they fell all seven together, and were put to death in the days of harvest, in the first days, in the beginning of barley harvest.

CHAPTER **83**

Graven (i.e., Demonic, Idol Figurine) Images, Paintings, and Drawings - Burn with Fire to Completely Destroy Them

Many people are unaware that they can bring curses into their homes, offices or other working environments unbeknownst to them. Just to name a few:

- Buddhist type statues or what-nots.
- Items used in satanic rituals.
- Ouija Boards.
- Witchcraft or wicca type materials.
- Worship items from other religions.
- Gifts from other religions and/or occultic organizations.
- Geisha girl (Japanese prostitutes) dolls or figures.

Deuteronomy 7 (KJV)

25. The graven images of their gods shall ye burn with fire: thou shalt not desire the silver or gold that is on them, nor take it unto thee, lest thou be snared therein: for it is an abomination to the Lord thy God.
26. Neither shalt thou bring an abomination into thine house, lest thou be a cursed thing like it: but thou shalt utterly detest it, and thou shalt utterly abhor it; for it is a cursed thing.

CHAPTER **84**

Gulf War Veterans Syndromes - Post-War - Mental Illnesses

U.S. soldier kills five other soldiers in Baghdad
May 14, 10:16 PM

Sgt. Russell killed five of his fellow soldiers at Camp "Liberty."

Last Monday, Sergeant John M. Russell shot five of his fellow U.S. soldiers at Camp Liberty in Baghdad. This is the worst case of soldier-on-soldier violence in the six-year history of the Iraq War. Sgt. Russell had been ordered to undergo counseling for stress and battle related causes:

"Sergeant Russell, 44, of the 54th Engineering Battalion, based in Bamberg, Germany, has been charged with five counts of murder and one count of aggravated assault in the shooting, said Maj. Gen. David Perkins, a spokesman for the military in Iraq.

The dead included an Army officer and a Navy officer on the clinic staff, and three enlisted soldiers who were at the clinic."

This incident is terribly tragic, and my thoughts and prayers are with the families of the victims and the shooters'.

One of the worst things about this terrible incident is watching the "talking heads" on CNN and FOX News struggle with how this could have possibly happened, even with the Army's "stress clinics" constantly monitoring him. Doesn't the U.S. Army take care of its proud soldiers? Sgt. Russell's incident reveals a great truth about war, and also about the empire we insist on maintaining: our soldiers are nothing more than pawns to be shuffled around, and when incidents like these occur, the news and the military are quick to dismiss these incidents by "troubled" and "stressed" soldiers as totally "isolated." Except they aren't isolated. Though barely discussed, remember when a U.S. soldier tossed a hand grenade into his fellow soldiers' tent, killing a number of them, near the beginning of the Iraq War? Or when several U.S. soldiers tortured, beat, and humiliated innocent Iraqis at Abu Ghraib? Or when numerous veterans come home and beat their spouses, rob stores, are in crippling pain, and can't sleep from unimaginable nightmares and terrible memories?

This is not an attack on our soldiers, who fight bravely and honorably with the incredibly difficult tasks they are given. It's an attack on the inherent messiness and cruelty of war and the chickenhawks who send them to fight and die.

War is the most unpredictable, evil, cruel, messy, bloody, dehumanizing and scarring thing that governments engage in, and we wonder why soldiers break under this stress. Our soldiers are asked to kick in doors with God knows what behind them, drive vehicles under the constant threat of IEDs, bomb villages indiscriminately from 20,000 feet in the air, shoot people on command, and must do this with bravery, courage, and honor. Soldiers are raised by their parents to be good citizens; to not steal, kill, and to love their neighbor. Yet when we put them in a uniform, they are ordered to go against these basic, decent instincts.

What are we doing to our soldiers? We are numbing them to the murder of human life and punishing them if they protest. Actually, it's not WE who do it; it is our giant and reckless government that asks them to slaughter, pillage, and torture, and if they're lucky they get a pretty, shiny medal; if they're not so lucky, they come home limbless, shell-shocked, or in body bags.

Our soldiers' lives and minds are the consequences of our global empire, an empire that touches every corner of the globe (and is now continuing to grow with Obama pulling the war levers). Cowardly criminal chickenhawks like Obama, Cheney, and Bush (and the "men" who cheered these wars on) send younger, better men into their imperial adventures, and wrap themselves in the flag (and the classic: "support the troops") when their war games are criticized.
I support the troops, which is why I want them home as soon as possible. This war is unnecessary; you soldiers never are.

Mental Illnesses Appear Common Among Veterans Returning From Iraq And Afghanistan

ScienceDaily (Mar. 13, 2007) — Almost one-third of returning veterans who received health care at Veterans Affairs facilities between 2001 and 2005 were given a mental health or psychosocial diagnosis, according to a report in the March 12 issue of Archives of Internal Medicine, one of the JAMA/Archives journals.

See also:

Health & Medicine
- Mental Health Research
- Chronic Illness
- Health Policy

Mind & Brain
- Mental Health
- Depression
- Disorders and Syndromes

Reference
- Gulf War syndrome

- Post-traumatic stress disorder
- Psychological trauma
- Personality disorder

Ads by Google
Advertise here

Psychiatric Disorders
Get Assessment Tools & Info On Psychiatric Disorders - For Doctors
www.wyethneuroscience.com

Ptsd Statistics
Top 7 Sites For Post Traumatic Stress Disorder. Ranked and Ready.
post-traumatic-stress.net

Pending VA Medical Claim?
Dr. Bash, Empathetic to Your Needs Helps Veterans Receive Benefits
www.VeteransMedAdvisor.com

Prepare to be Shocked
Millions have already taken this amazing test. What's your RealAge?
www.RealAge.com

Depression Signs & Help
Find Information About Depression & Possible Treatments in Our Listing.
SignDepression.com

Some reports have suggested that soldiers returning from Operations Enduring Freedom and Iraqi Freedom, the most recent military efforts in Iraq and Afghanistan, experience high rates of substance abuse, post-traumatic stress disorder (PTSD) and other mental health conditions, according to background information in the article.

In these operations, the most sustained ground combat since the Vietnam era, "the majority of military personnel experience high-intensity guerilla warfare and the chronic threat of roadside bombs and improvised explosive devices," the authors write. "Some soldiers endure multiple tours of duty, many experience traumatic injury and more of the wounded survive than ever before." These veterans are eligible for two years of free health care related to their military service through the Department of Veterans Affairs (VA).

Karen H. Seal, M.D., M.P.H., and colleagues at the University of California, San Francisco, and San Francisco VA Medical Center examined data from a VA database including 103,788 veterans of these operations who were first seen at VA facilities between Sept. 30, 2001, and Sept. 30, 2005. About 13 percent were women, 54 percent were younger than age 30, close to one-third were minorities and almost one-half were veterans of the National Guard or Reserves rather than full-time military personnel.

A total of 32,010 (31 percent) received mental health and/or psychosocial diagnoses, including 25,658 (25 percent) who received mental health diagnoses (56 percent of whom had two or more diagnoses). The most common such diagnosis was PTSD; the 13,205 veterans with this disorder represented 52 percent of those receiving mental health diagnoses and 13 percent of all the veterans in the study. "Mental health diagnoses were detected soon after the first VA clinic visit (median of 13 days), and most initial mental health diagnoses (60 percent) were made in non-mental health clinics, mostly primary care settings," the authors write. "The youngest group of Operations Enduring Freedom and Iraqi Freedom veterans (age, 18 to 24 years) were at greatest risk for receiving mental health or post-traumatic stress disorder diagnoses compared with veterans 40 years or older."

About 29 percent of veterans returning from Iraq and Afghanistan have enrolled in VA health care, a high rate compared with 10 percent of Vietnam veterans. This and the relatively short period of time between the first VA clinic visit and diagnosis with a mental health condition suggest an opportunity to intervene early to diagnose and treat mental health concerns, the authors note. "Our results signal a need for improvements in the primary prevention of military service-related mental health disorders, particularly among our youngest service members," they conclude. "Furthermore, early detection and evidence-based treatment in both VA and non-VA mental health and primary care settings is critical in the prevention of chronic mental illness, which threatens to bring the war back home as a costly personal and public health burden."

(Arch Intern Med. 2007;167:476-482. Available pre-embargo to the media at http://www.jamamedia.org.)

Editor's Note: This study was funded by a VA Health Services Research and Development Career Development Award and a grant from the VA Seattle Epidemiological Research and Information Center. Please see the article for additional information, including other authors, author contributions and affiliations, financial disclosures, funding and support, etc.

CHAPTER **85**

Gulf War Veterans Syndromes and Post-War Suicides

The results of war, humanity-to-humanity is devastating to the body, soul and spirit of humanity. When, I, Curtis was stationed at 2d Armored Division, Fort Hood, Texas, they had a motto, "Hell On Wheels". Well, war is not only hell on wheels, but hell in the air, hell on the ground, and hell to the atmosphere as a whole. Anytime that our human elements are linked to any spirits of war, it sets up hell on humanity.

When leaders of any continent on earth declares war and sends its citizens into that war, they could or not have the blessings of Almighty God in Heaven on their side. If Almighty God is on their side, then so be it, but if He is not, then that leader has blood on his or her hand. A petition for repentance and forgiveness is then in order for that leader.

The most important key element of humanity and our troops sent into war is the power and strength of spirituality with that link to Devine power to heaven. I feel that 99.99 percent of Chaplains are not equipped, nor anointed to impart or disseminate any anointing of the Spirit to our troops. Many Chaplains are well educated, of high ranks in their branch of service, but not spiritually anointed as ones called and anointed by Almighty God. Ministry is not a vocation as such, but a calling.

Preachers Must Be Called By Almighty God

Romans 10 (KJV)

13. For whosoever shall call upon the name of the Lord shall be saved.
14. How then shall they call on him in whom they have not believed? and how shall they believe in him of whom they have not heard? and how shall they hear without a preacher?
15. And how shall they preach, except they be sent? as it is written, How beautiful are the feet of them that preach the gospel of peace, and bring glad tidings of good things!
16. But they have not all obeyed the gospel. For Esaias saith, Lord, who hath believed our report?

Ephesians 4 (KJV)

11. And he gave some, apostles; and some, prophets; and some, evangelists; and some, pastors and teachers;
12. For the perfecting of the saints, for the work of the ministry, for the edifying of the body of Christ:

Warnings Against Leaders Of Nations Who Obey Not Almighty God!

Exodus 5 (KJV)

1. And afterward Moses and Aaron went in, and told Pharaoh, Thus saith the Lord God of Israel, Let my people go, that they may hold a feast unto me in the wilderness.
2. And Pharaoh said, Who is the Lord, that I should obey his voice to let Israel go? I know not the Lord, neither will I let Israel go.
3. And they said, The God of the Hebrews hath met with us:

let us go, we pray thee, three days' journey into the desert, and sacrifice unto the Lord our God; lest he fall upon us with pestilence, or with the sword.

Almighty God's Wrath Against Humanity

Exodus 9 (KJV)

15. For now I will stretch out my hand, that I may smite thee and thy people with pestilence; and thou shalt be cut off from the earth.
16. And in very deed for this cause have I raised thee up, for to shew in thee my power; and that my name may be declared throughout all the earth.

Over 150,000 veterans have put their names in the American Legion's database according to spokesmen for the organization.

Iraq invades Kuwait

When Iraq invaded Kuwait, the United States government acted quickly. Ships were dispatched to the Persian Gulf and oil prices shot up as an oil embargo was placed against Iraq. The U.S. Government told us that Saddam Hussein was poised to invade the neighboring countries, including Saudi Arabia, and the worlds oil supply was threatened. George Bush launched operation "Desert Shield" in which a coalition of many nation's armies gathered in the deserts of Saudi Arabia bordering Iraq and Kuwait. We believed the threat to Iraq's other neighbors was real and demanded immediate action!

Public support for "Desert Shield" was tremendous. George Bush enjoyed some of his highest popularity ratings. The threat of Iraq's army to the world's oil supply was rarely questioned, though Russian spy satellite photos contradicted the reported threat. The cover-up of Russia's satellite photos was determined to be one of the Most Censored News Stories of 1991 by Sonoma State University in it's annual report on censorship. This was just the beginning of U.S. deception surrounding the Gulf War.

U.S. warns of Iraqi weapons

Iraq boasted the worlds 4th largest army, topped off with the fabled "Republican Guard", Saddam Hussein's elite battle-hardened troops. It was widely know that Iraq had used chemical weapons on Iran during the Iran-Iraq war and had used them again to crush uprisings among the Kurds of northern Iraq. Chemical weapons "sensors" were installed at military bases in Saudi Arabia. Troops, newspeople and Isrealis drilled on what to do in the event of a chemical weapons attack.

The hysteria surrounding the threat of chemical weapons was contageous. The chemical weapons "sensors" produced frequent false alarms, that occassionally led to panic. Complete investigations of the many false alarms failed to produce any evidence of chemical weapons, but troops, newspeople and Isrealis donned thier gas masks at every false alarm. It was believed that Iraq's "SCUD" missiles might include chemical weapons in addition to standard explosives, but no such missiles were ever found.

- Why was Saddam holding back?
- Did he have missiles capable of deliverying chemical weapons? If he did, he managed to keep them well hidden after the war. Not until June 10th, 1998 was there any evidence of missles capable of carrying chemical weapons. The evidence was found among the ruins of weapons sites by inspectors, but no evidence has been found of such weapons being used. Some Iraqi missiles may have had VX nerve gas, a chemical deadly in even very minute amounts.
- Did he have an even more insidious weapon, perhaps a

biological weapon? If he did, no evidence of such a weapon has been acknowledged by UN weapons inspectors in Iraq. High ranking defectors from Saddam's army claim that he was stockpiling Anthrax, a deadly biological agent.

- Did he have nuclear weapons capabilities? All the evidence to date indicates Iraq was working on nuclear weapons, but did not have them yet. Iraq's nuclear program has (hopefully) been completely dismantled by UN inspectors.

The War Begins, "Desert Storm"

The coalition of national armies, after assembling in Saudi Arabia, took a few shots from SCUD missiles fired from Iraq. When troops started moving into Iraq and Kuwait from Saudi Arabia, Saddam Hussein's "army" turned tail and tried to get out of Kuwait with everything they could carry. The Iraqi "Republican Guard" stayed safely back, far from the fighting. Several hundred U.S. troops died in the brief battle, and ten's of thousands of Iraqis died. Many, if not most, of the U.S. deaths were the result of "friendly fire". Iraq's army may have been poised to invade Saudi Arabia, but they were mostly Iraqi teenagers recruited for the war, who simply surrendered if given the opportunity. The worlds forth largest army stood no chance against the United States, let alone the combined might of the world. It turned out to be so easy, the U.S. actually made a profit. Kuwait was safely restored to it's former government, and it got a bunch of new oil fields in formerly disputed border areas as well. The job may only have been easy in the first gulf war because it was never satisfactorily completed.

Troops return home

With the worlds forth largest army dissolved, and nothing between coalition troops and the Iraqi capital, George Bush decided to end the war and bring the troops home. UN weapons inspectors converged on Iraq and the coalition armies dispersed. George Bush experienced his highest ratings ever, perhaps the highest of any U.S. President in history in the aftermath of the Gulf War.

Perhaps the most hyped war in history was now over. It was almost certainly the war most orchestrated for the media. All the troops had been drilled for months in preparation for a tremendous battle and possibly chemical and biological weapons. Suddenly it was over. They were sent home and returned to thier normal everyday lives. Memories of the threat of chemical and biological weapons lingered.

Years pass before rumors begin to surface - a veteran who suddenly died for no known cause - a veteran who developed an enormous tumor - a veteran who's new child is severely malformed. The threat of chemical and biological weapons returns to everyones waking memory. Perhaps this is the cause of all these illnesses!

Gulf War Syndrome is Born!

The threat seemed real enough. If it could be demonstrated that Gulf War veterans are suffering from the effects of chemical or biological weapons, they might have grounds for some restitution from the United States government, or perhaps the Iraqi government. Organizations began to form in response to rising concern over the plight of Gulf War veterans.

Some place the number of U.S. citizens who took part in the Gulf War at over 1 million. Official Pentagon numbers only show a total of 697,000, but they may not include non-military members. 45,000, about 6 percent of Gulf War veterans have reported an ailment they believe is linked to their service. The Pentagon found that 85 percent had ailments or diseases with known causes not linked to the Gulf War.

Further Defense Department research is focusing on the 15 percent, slightly less than 1 percent of all Gulf War veterans, whose ailments could not be diagnosed. Their problems included headache and memory loss, fatigue, sleep disorders, and intestinal and respiratory ailments. These have come to be known as the symptoms of Gulf War Syndrome

What are the symptoms?

Symptoms of Gulf War Illnesses (according to the American Legion)

- Chronic Fatigue
- Signs and symptoms involving skin (including skin rashes and unusual hair loss)
- Headache
- Muscle pain
- Neurologic signs or symptoms (nervous system disorders which could manifest themselves in numbness in one's arm, for instance)
- Neuropsychological signs or symptoms (including memory loss)
- Signs or symptoms involving upper or lower respiratory system
- Sleep disturbances
- Gastrointestinal signs or symptoms (including recurrent diarrhea and constipation)
- Cardiovascular signs or symptoms
- Menstrual disorders

Post-War Vet Suicides May Exceed Combat Deaths From The Wars
May 05, 2008 3:54 PM

At the American Psychiatric Association's annual meeting in Washington, Thomas Insel, director of the National Institute of

Mental Health in Bethesda, Md., told reporters ``it's quite possible that the suicides and psychiatric mortality of this war could trump the combat deaths."

He referred to an April 2008 study by the Rand Corporation that found that almost 20 percent of US veterans back from Iraq and Afghanistan have symptoms of post traumatic stress disorder or major depression. Only a little more than half, however, have sought treatment. 1.6 million troops have so far served in those two wars.

Army Suicides Highest in 26 Years
By PAULINE JELINEK
The Associated Press
Thursday, August 16, 2007; 2:54 AM

WASHINGTON -- Army soldiers committed suicide last year at the highest rate in 26 years, and more than a quarter did so while serving in Iraq and Afghanistan, according to a new military report.

The report, obtained by The Associated Press ahead of its scheduled release Thursday, found there were 99 confirmed suicides among active duty soldiers during 2006, up from 88 the previous year and the highest number since the 102 suicides in 1991 at the time of the Persian Gulf War.

The suicide rate for the Army has fluctuated over the past 26 years, from last year's high of 17.3 per 100,000 to a low of 9.1 per 100,000 in 2001.

Last year, "Iraq was the most common deployment location for both (suicides) and attempts," the report said.

The 99 suicides included 28 soldiers deployed to the two wars and 71 who weren't. About twice as many women serving in Iraq and Afghanistan committed suicide as did women not sent to war, the report said.

Preliminary numbers for the first half of this year indicate the number of suicides could decline across the service in 2007 but increase among troops serving in the wars, officials said.

The increases for 2006 came as Army officials worked to set up a number of new and stronger programs for providing mental health care to a force strained by the longer-than-expected war in Iraq and the global counterterrorism war entering its sixth year.

Failed personal relationships, legal and financial problems and the stress of their jobs were factors motivating the soldiers to commit suicide, according to the report.

"In addition, there was a significant relationship between suicide attempts and number of days deployed" in Iraq, Afghanistan or nearby countries where troops are participating in the war effort, it said. The same pattern seemed to hold true for those who not only attempted, but succeeded in killing themselves.

There also "was limited evidence to support the view that multiple ... deployments are a risk factor for suicide behaviors," it said.

About a quarter of those who killed themselves had a history of at least one psychiatric disorder. Of those, about 20 percent had been diagnosed with a mood disorder such as bipolar disorder and/or depression; and 8 percent had been diagnosed with an anxiety disorder, including post traumatic stress disorder _ one of the signature injuries of the conflict in Iraq.

Firearms were the most common method of suicide. Those who attempted suicide but didn't succeed tended more often to take overdoses and cut themselves.

In a service of more than a half million troop, the 99 suicides amounted to a rate of 17.3 per 100,000 _ the highest in the past

26 years, the report said. The average rate over those years has been 12.3 per 100,000.

The rate for those serving in the wars stayed about the same, 19.4 per 100,000 in 2006, compared with 19.9 in 2005.

The Army said the information was compiled from reports collected as part of its suicide prevention program _ reports required for all "suicide-related behaviors that result in death, hospitalization or evacuation" of the soldier. It can take considerable time to investigate a suicide and, in fact, the Army said that in addition to the 99 confirmed suicides last year, there are two other deaths suspected as suicides in which investigations were pending.

Associated Press reporter Lolita C. Baldor contributed to this report from Washington.

On the Net:
Defense Department: http://www.defenselink.mil

CHAPTER **86**

Halloween - Celebrating and Embracing Evil Curses

Our heavenly father, Almighty God is a jealous God who does not share His Glory with no one else and not with any of those little gods whom the world serves. He wants us to worship and serve him as the only God without wavering. Halloween is a traditional form of honoring, serving and worshiping other gods which is prohibited.

Exodus 20 (KJV)

1. And God spake all these words, saying,
2. I am the Lord thy God, which have brought thee out of the land of Egypt, out of the house of bondage.
3. Thou shalt have no other gods before me.
4. Thou shalt not make unto thee any graven image, or any likeness of any thing that is in heaven above, or that is in the earth beneath, or that is in the water under the earth.
5. Thou shalt not bow down thyself to them, nor serve them: for I the Lord thy God am a jealous God, visiting the iniquity of the fathers upon the children unto the third and fourth generation of them that hate me;

WHAT IS HALLOWEEN REALLY ALL ABOUT?

Written by: Unknown
Source: CCN

WHAT IS HALLOWEEN REALLY ALL ABOUT???

Have you ever thought about this? Have you ever asked yourself, "Who in the world ever thought of the idea of walking around in weird costumes, trick-or-treating, and/or putting a carved-out pumpkin in your window?"

You will agree with me that Halloween is really one of the strangest days in the year, is it not? Perhaps you wonder how the celebration of such a day ever got started. In this pamphlet I would like to answer this question for you!

WHERE AND WHEN DID THE HALLOWEEN CUSTOMS ORIGINATE?

The many customs we have today in relation to Halloween have their origin in the religious practices of the Romans and the Druids, therefore dating back many centuries. The Romans worshipped various gods, and on October 31, a special feast was held in honor of Pomona, goddess of the fruit trees. Later the Druids, an ancient order of Celtic priests in Britain, made this feast an even more extensive celebration by also honoring Samhain, lord of the dead. This was normally done on November 1 and it was therefore decided to conveniently honor both Pomona and Samhain on October 31 and November 1.

These Druids believed that on the night before November (October 31), Samhain called together wicked souls or spirits which had been condemned to live in the bodies of animals during the year which had just transpired. Since they were afraid of these spirits, they chose October 31 as a day of sacrifice to their gods, hoping they would protect them. They really believed that on this day they were surrounded by strange spirits, ghosts, witches, fairies, and elves, who came out to hurt them. In addition to this, they also believed that cats were holy animals, as they considered them to represent people who lived formerly, and as punishment for evil deeds were reincarnated as a cat. All this explains why witches, ghosts, and cats are part of Halloween today.

Trick-Or-Treat And Jack-O-Lanterns Traditions

The custom of trick-or-treating and the use of "jack-o'-lanterns" comes from Ireland. Hundreds of years ago, Irish farmers went from house to house, begging for food, in the name of their ancient gods, to be used at the village Halloween celebration. They would promise good luck to those who gave them food, and made threats to those who refused to give. They simply told the people, "You treat me, or else I will trick you!"

The apparently harmless lighted pumpkin face of "jack-o'-lantern" actually is an old Irish symbol of a damned soul. A man named Jack was supposed to be unable to enter heaven due to his miserliness, and unable to enter hell because he had played practical jokes on the devil. As a result, he was condemned to wander over the earth with his lantern until judgment day (i.e., the end of the world). The Irish were so afraid that they would receive an identical plight, that they began to hollow out pumpkins and place lighted candles inside to scare away evil spirits from their homes.

WHEN DID THE CELEBRATION OF HALLOWEEN, AS WE KNOW IT TODAY, BEGIN?

During the Middle Ages (about 600 years ago), the Roman Catholic Church at that time, decided to make the changeover from pagan religion to Christianity a bit easier, and therefore allowed the new converts to maintain some of their pagan feasts. It was agreed, however, that from now on they would be celebrated as "Christian" feasts. So instead of praying to their heathen gods, they would now pray to, and remember the death of saints. For this reason the church decided to call November 1 the "Day of All Saints," and the mass to be celebrated on that day "Alhallow mass." In consequence of this, the evening prior to this day was named, "All Hallowed Evening," which subsequently was abbreviated as "Halloween." In spite of this effort to make October 31 a "holy evening," all the old customs continued to be practiced, and made this evening anything but a holy evening!

HALLOWEEN TODAY

You would have to agree with me that also today Halloween is most definitely not a holy evening!! This annual event is far from the harmless, innocent tradition it is promoted to be. Many dread this "holy" evening as they think what could happen to them, their property, and/or their children! Consistent with its historical roots, this evening is characterized by fear, and frequently arouses dormant fears in many. The fear generated by this event is symbolic of the fear which plagues so many in our modern, morally bankrupt world. It is a gripping fear for an unknown and very threatening future, a fear caused by a gnawing, inner emptiness

Almighty God has many curses in store for those who serve or celebrate other gods. There are many curses He is warning us about and we should not take them lightly. Many people believe that these traditional celebrations including Halloween are harmless and that it is a time to have fund and unwind so to speak. It is to the contrary. People who continue to celebrate Halloween are putting bodies, their souls and certainly their spirits in grave danger of eternal damnation. Even while they live here on this earth, they will reap Almighty God's wrath through His curses as outlined below.

Deuteronomy 28 (KJV)

14. And thou shalt not go aside from any of the words which I command thee this day, to the right hand, or to the left, to go after other gods to serve them.
15. But it shall come to pass, if thou wilt not hearken unto the voice of the Lord thy God, to observe to do all his commandments and his statutes which I command thee this day; that all these curses shall come upon thee, and overtake thee:
16. Cursed shalt thou be in the city, and cursed shalt thou be in the field.
17. Cursed shall be thy basket and thy store.
18. Cursed shall be the fruit of thy body, and the fruit of thy land, the increase of thy kine, and the flocks of thy sheep.
19. Cursed shalt thou be when thou comest in, and cursed shalt thou be when thou goest out.
20. The Lord shall send upon thee cursing, vexation, and rebuke, in all that thou settest thine hand unto for to do, until thou be destroyed, and until thou perish quickly; because of the wickedness of thy doings, whereby thou hast forsaken me.
21. The Lord shall make the pestilence cleave unto thee, until he have consumed thee from off the land, whither thou goest to possess it.
22. The Lord shall smite thee with a consumption, and with a fever, and with an inflammation, and with an extreme burning, and with the sword, and with blasting, and with mildew; and they shall pursue thee until thou perish.
23. And thy heaven that is over thy head shall be brass, and the earth that is under thee shall be iron.
24. The Lord shall make the rain of thy land powder and dust: from heaven shall it come down upon thee, until thou be destroyed.
25. The Lord shall cause thee to be smitten before thine

enemies: thou shalt go out one way against them, and flee seven ways before them: and shalt be removed into all the kingdoms of the earth.

26. And thy carcase shall be meat unto all fowls of the air, and unto the beasts of the earth, and no man shall fray them away.
27. The Lord will smite thee with the botch of Egypt, and with the emerods, and with the scab, and with the itch, whereof thou canst not be healed.
28. The Lord shall smite thee with madness, and blindness, and astonishment of heart:
29. And thou shalt grope at noonday, as the blind gropeth in darkness, and thou shalt not prosper in thy ways: and thou shalt be only oppressed and spoiled evermore, and no man shall save thee.
30. Thou shalt betroth a wife, and another man shall lie with her: thou shalt build an house, and thou shalt not dwell therein: thou shalt plant a vineyard, and shalt not gather the grapes thereof.
31. Thine ox shall be slain before thine eyes, and thou shalt not eat thereof: thine ass shall be violently taken away from before thy face, and shall not be restored to thee: thy sheep shall be given unto thine enemies, and thou shalt have none to rescue them.
32. Thy sons and thy daughters shall be given unto another people, and thine eyes shall look, and fail with longing for them all the day long; and there shall be no might in thine hand.
33. The fruit of thy land, and all thy labours, shall a nation which thou knowest not eat up; and thou shalt be only oppressed and crushed alway:
34. So that thou shalt be mad for the sight of thine eyes which thou shalt see.
35. The Lord shall smite thee in the knees, and in the legs, with a sore botch that cannot be healed, from the sole of thy foot unto the top of thy head.

36. The Lord shall bring thee, and thy king which thou shalt set over thee, unto a nation which neither thou nor thy fathers have known; and there shalt thou serve other gods, wood and stone.
37. And thou shalt become an astonishment, a proverb, and a byword, among all nations whither the Lord shall lead thee.
38. Thou shalt carry much seed out into the field, and shalt gather but little in; for the locust shall consume it.
39. Thou shalt plant vineyards, and dress them, but shalt neither drink of the wine, nor gather the grapes; for the worms shall eat them.
40. Thou shalt have olive trees throughout all thy coasts, but thou shalt not anoint thyself with the oil; for thine olive shall cast his fruit.
41. Thou shalt beget sons and daughters, but thou shalt not enjoy them; for they shall go into captivity.
42. All thy trees and fruit of thy land shall the locust consume.
43. The stranger that is within thee shall get up above thee very high; and thou shalt come down very low.
44. He shall lend to thee, and thou shalt not lend to him: he shall be the head, and thou shalt be the tail.
45. Moreover all these curses shall come upon thee, and shall pursue thee, and overtake thee, till thou be destroyed; because thou hearkenedst not unto the voice of the Lord thy God, to keep his commandments and his statutes which he commanded thee:
46. And they shall be upon thee for a sign and for a wonder, and upon thy seed for ever.
47. Because thou servedst not the Lord thy God with joyfulness, and with gladness of heart, for the abundance of all things;
48. Therefore shalt thou serve thine enemies which the Lord shall send against thee, in hunger, and in thirst, and in nakedness, and in want of all things: and he shall put a

yoke of iron upon thy neck, until he have destroyed thee.

49. The Lord shall bring a nation against thee from far, from the end of the earth, as swift as the eagle flieth; a nation whose tongue thou shalt not understand;

50. A nation of fierce countenance, which shall not regard the person of the old, nor shew favour to the young:

51. And he shall eat the fruit of thy cattle, and the fruit of thy land, until thou be destroyed: which also shall not leave thee either corn, wine, or oil, or the increase of thy kine, or flocks of thy sheep, until he have destroyed thee.

52. And he shall besiege thee in all thy gates, until thy high and fenced walls come down, wherein thou trustedst, throughout all thy land: and he shall besiege thee in all thy gates throughout all thy land, which the Lord thy God hath given thee.

53. And thou shalt eat the fruit of thine own body, the flesh of thy sons and of thy daughters, which the Lord thy God hath given thee, in the siege, and in the straitness, wherewith thine enemies shall distress thee:

54. So that the man that is tender among you, and very delicate, his eye shall be evil toward his brother, and toward the wife of his bosom, and toward the remnant of his children which he shall leave:

55. So that he will not give to any of them of the flesh of his children whom he shall eat: because he hath nothing left him in the siege, and in the straitness, wherewith thine enemies shall distress thee in all thy gates.

56. The tender and delicate woman among you, which would not adventure to set the sole of her foot upon the ground for delicateness and tenderness, her eye shall be evil toward the husband of her bosom, and toward her son, and toward her daughter,

57. And toward her young one that cometh out from between her feet, and toward her children which she shall bear: for she shall eat them for want of all things secretly in the siege

and straitness, wherewith thine enemy shall distress thee in thy gates.

58. If thou wilt not observe to do all the words of this law that are written in this book, that thou mayest fear this glorious and fearful name, The Lord Thy God;
59. Then the Lord will make thy plagues wonderful, and the plagues of thy seed, even great plagues, and of long continuance, and sore sicknesses, and of long continuance.
60. Moreover he will bring upon thee all the diseases of Egypt, which thou wast afraid of; and they shall cleave unto thee.
61. Also every sickness, and every plague, which is not written in the book of this law, them will the Lord bring upon thee, until thou be destroyed.
62. And ye shall be left few in number, whereas ye were as the stars of heaven for multitude; because thou wouldest not obey the voice of the Lord thy God.
63. And it shall come to pass, that as the Lord rejoiced over you to do you good, and to multiply you; so the Lord will rejoice over you to destroy you, and to bring you to nought; and ye shall be plucked from off the land whither thou goest to possess it.
64. And the Lord shall scatter thee among all people, from the one end of the earth even unto the other; and there thou shalt serve other gods, which neither thou nor thy fathers have known, even wood and stone.
65. And among these nations shalt thou find no ease, neither shall the sole of thy foot have rest: but the Lord shall give thee there a trembling heart, and failing of eyes, and sorrow of mind:
66. And thy life shall hang in doubt before thee; and thou shalt fear day and night, and shalt have none assurance of thy life:
67. In the morning thou shalt say, Would God it were even!

and at even thou shalt say, Would God it were morning! for the fear of thine heart wherewith thou shalt fear, and for the sight of thine eyes which thou shalt see.

68. And the Lord shall bring thee into Egypt again with ships, by the way whereof I spake unto thee, thou shalt see it no more again: and there ye shall be sold unto your enemies for bondmen and bondwomen, and no man shall buy you.

CHAPTER 87

Harry Potter Phenomenon - Following This Demonic Fad Is Strictly Forbidden

Trying to be hip or cool by following certain fads will open the door of your life for curses to be placed upon your life. There are some young men who have their hair cut down close to their scalp with a sort of pony tail left on the rear of their heads. That particular pony tail is a fashion fad and is thereby a DEMONIC FAD and you guest it, a curse. People who constantly listening to hard rock music, acid rock and/or any music with demonic lyrics is a doorway for curses to be place upon your life. Rock groups singing such lyrics are already cursed, even those rappers of demonic lyrics as well. You should stay away from such fads. Not only that, but you should stay away from people who love to listen to such trash. If you listen to and purchase this trash, you are cursed with curses. Now, we wonder what is wrong with our children. They are in fact cursed children.

Exo 23:2 (KJV) "Thou shalt not follow a multitude to do evil; neither shalt thou speak in a cause to decline after many to wrest judgment:"

3 John 1:11 (KJV) "Beloved, follow not that which is evil, but that which is good. He that doeth good is of God: but he that doeth evil hath not seen God."

Lev 19:26-28 (KJV) Ye shall not eat any thing with the blood: neither shall ye use enchantment, nor observe times.

27. Ye shall not round the corners of your heads, neither shalt thou mar the corners of thy beard.
28. Ye shall not make any cuttings in your flesh for the dead, nor print any marks upon you: I am the LORD.

One of the major fades being perpetrated throughout the world is the Harry Potter demonic phenomenon from Europe. Many books and movies have been made and distributed worldwide to ignorant and innocent individuals, groups and families worldwide in massive numbers.

Harry Potter
From Wikipedia, the free encyclopedia

Harry Potter is a heptalogy of fantasy novels written by English author J. K. Rowling. The books chronicle the adventures of the eponymous adolescent wizard Harry Potter, together with his best friends Ron Weasley and Hermione Granger. The story is mostly set at Hogwarts School of Witchcraft and Wizardry, an academy for young wizards and witches. The central story arc concerns Harry's conflict against the evil wizard Lord Voldemort, who killed Harry's parents in his quest to conquer the wizarding world.

Since the release of the first novel Harry Potter and the Philosopher's Stone in 1997, which was retitled Harry Potter and the Sorcerer's Stone in the United States, the books have gained immense popularity, critical acclaim and commercial success worldwide.[2] The series has spawned films, video games and Potter-themed merchandise. As of April 2007, the first six books in the seven book series have sold more than 325 million copies[3] and have been translated into more than 64 languages.[4] The seventh and last book in the series, Harry Potter and the Deathly Hallows, was released on 21

July 2007.[5] Publishers announced a record-breaking 12 million copies for the first print run in the U.S. alone.[6]

The success of the novels has made Rowling the highest-earning novelist in history.[7] English language versions of the books are published by Bloomsbury in the United Kingdom, Scholastic Press in the United States, Allen & Unwin in Australia and Raincoast Books in Canada.

Thus far, the first five books have been made into a series of motion pictures by Warner Bros. The sixth, Harry Potter and the Half-Blood Prince, is set to begin filming in September 2007, and has a scheduled release of 21 November 2008.

CHAPTER **88**

Hatred, Jealousy, Envy, and the Unspoken Words of the Same

Having hatred in your heart for someone is certainly a curse which can keep you from going to heaven. The bible tells us love our brothers and sisters as we love ourselves. We can't get into heaven with hatred in our hearts not in the least. Jealousy is also a big stumbling block which God, Almighty simply hates and it is a curse that will take us down and allow the enemy to constantly attack us. The unspoken word is what we harbor or what we have in our heart for someone without speaking it or saying it with our speech. This is something evil that we keep inside of us and it eats at the core of our souls. This is certainly a big doorway for Satan and/or demons to come into our lives and reek havoc as they wish. A prime example are the shootings which occurred at Columbine High School, Littleton, Colorado. Those teenagers had hatred and jealousy in the hearts with revenge as well. There were also suicidal tendencies which were carried out and as we later found out, unspoken words in their hearts as well. Their shootings were coupled with their attempt to bomb the entire school. So, as we can see from these occurrences, there were a host of curses in these teens lives. You can best believe that there are some curses in the bloodline of their families as well. With that in mind, Columbine High School is certainly contaminated with numerous curses. Among other schools, including the ones at Jonesboro, Arkansas are heavily cursed as well.

1 John 3:14 (KJV) "We know that we have passed from death unto life, because we love the brethren. He that loveth not his brother abideth in death."

Song 8:6 (KJV) "Set me as a seal upon thine heart, as a seal upon thine arm: for love is strong as death; jealousy is cruel as the grave: the coals thereof are coals of fire, which hath a most vehement flame."

James 3:10 (KJV) "Out of the same mouth proceedeth blessing and cursing. My brethren, these things ought not so to be."

Prov 23:7 (KJV) "For as he thinketh in his heart, so is he: Eat and drink, saith he to thee; but his heart is not with thee."

Prayer Against Your Adversaries And Enemies Who Hate You

Psalms 109 (KJV)

1. Hold not thy peace, O God of my praise;
2. For the mouth of the wicked and the mouth of the deceitful are opened against me: they have spoken against me with a lying tongue.
3. They compassed me about also with words of hatred; and fought against me without a cause.
4. For my love they are my adversaries: but I give myself unto prayer.
5. And they have rewarded me evil for good, and hatred for my love.
6. Set thou a wicked man over him: and let Satan stand at his right hand.
7. When he shall be judged, let him be condemned: and let his prayer become sin.
8. Let his days be few; and let another take his office.
9. Let his children be fatherless, and his wife a widow.

10. Let his children be continually vagabonds, and beg: let them seek their bread also out of their desolate places.
11. Let the extortioner catch all that he hath; and let the strangers spoil his labour.
12. Let there be none to extend mercy unto him: neither let there be any to favour his fatherless children.
13. Let his posterity be cut off; and in the generation following let their name be blotted out.
14. Let the iniquity of his fathers be remembered with the Lord; and let not the sin of his mother be blotted out.
15. Let them be before the Lord continually, that he may cut off the memory of them from the earth.
16. Because that he remembered not to shew mercy, but persecuted the poor and needy man, that he might even slay the broken in heart.
17 As he loved cursing, so let it come unto him: as he delighted not in blessing, so let it be far from him.
18 As he clothed himself with cursing like as with his garment, so let it come into his bowels like water, and like oil into his bones.
19. Let it be unto him as the garment which covereth him, and for a girdle wherewith he is girded continually.
20. Let this be the reward of mine adversaries from the Lord, and of them that speak evil against my soul.
21. But do thou for me, O God the Lord, for thy name's sake: because thy mercy is good, deliver thou me.
22. For I am poor and needy, and my heart is wounded within me.
23. I am gone like the shadow when it declineth: I am tossed up and down as the locust.
24. My knees are weak through fasting; and my flesh faileth of fatness.
25. I became also a reproach unto them: when they looked upon me they shaked their heads.
26. Help me, O Lord my God: O save me according to thy mercy:

27. That they may know that this is thy hand; that thou, Lord, hast done it.
28. Let them curse, but bless thou: when they arise, let them be ashamed; but let thy servant rejoice.
29. Let mine adversaries be clothed with shame, and let them cover themselves with their own confusion, as with a mantle.
30. I will greatly praise the Lord with my mouth; yea, I will praise him among the multitude.
31. For he shall stand at the right hand of the poor, to save him from those that condemn his soul.

CHAPTER **89**

Hurricanes, Katrina - Louisiana and Mississippi Curses

The underlying causes of these sins are the sins of the people in these states. Some people, however will just put the blame on nature. That is part of the causes, but Satan will take those natural causes and increase them to reek havoc with humanity. Remember, Satan comes, but to "KILL, STEAL and DESTROY".

Effect of Hurricane Katrina on New Orleans
From Wikipedia, the free encyclopedia

The effect of Hurricane Katrina on New Orleans, Louisiana was catastrophic and long-lasting. As the center of Katrina passed east of New Orleans on August 29, 2005, winds were in the Category 2 range, and tidal surge was equivalent to about a Category 3 hurricane. Though the most severe portion of Katrina missed the city, the storm surge caused more than 50 breaches in drainage canal levees and also in navigational canal levees and precipitated the worst engineering disaster in US history. [1]

By August 31, 2005, eighty percent of New Orleans was flooded, with some parts under 15 feet of water. Most of the city's levees designed and built by the United States Army Corps of Engineers were breached, including the 17th Street Canal levee, the Industrial Canal levee, and the London Avenue Canal floodwall. These breaches are responsible for at least two-thirds of the flooding according to a June 2007 report by the American Society of Civil Engineers. [2]

Ninety percent of the residents of southeast Louisiana were evacuated in the most successful evacuation of a major urban area in the nation's history. Despite this, many remained (mainly the elderly and poor). The Louisiana Superdome was used as a designated "refuge of last resort" for those who remained in the city. The city flooded due primarily to the failure of the federally built levee system. Many who remained in their homes had to swim for their lives, wade through deep water, or remain trapped in their attics or on their rooftops.

The disaster had major implications for a large segment of the population, economy and politics of the entire United States. It has prompted a Congressional review of the Army Corps of Engineers and the near total failure of the federally built flood protection system which experts agree should have protected the city's inhabitants from Katrina's surge. Katrina has also stimulated significant research in the academic community into urban planning, real estate finance, and economic issues in the wake of a natural disaster

Effect of Hurricane Katrina on Mississippi

From Wikipedia, the free encyclopedia

Hurricane Katrina's winds and storm surge reached the Mississippi coastline on the afternoon of August 28, 2005,[1][2] beginning a two-day path of destruction through central Mississippi; by 10 a.m. CDT on August 29, 2005, the eye of Katrina began travelling up the entire state, only slowing from hurricane-force winds at Meridian near 7 p.m. and entering Tennessee as a tropical storm.[3] Many coastal towns of Mississippi (and Louisiana) had already been obliterated, in a single night.[4] Hurricane-force winds reached coastal Mississippi by 2 a.m.[1] and lasted over 17 hours, spawning 11 tornadoes (51 in other states[2]) and a 28-foot (9 m) storm surge[2] flooding 6-12 miles (10-

19 km) inland. Many, unable to evacuate,[5] survived by climbing to attics or rooftops, or swimming to higher buildings and trees. Afterward, over 235 people died in Mississippi, and all counties in Mississippi were declared disaster areas, 49 for full federal assistance

These curses are the results of these people disobeying Almighty God and not adhering to His commands. He promised curses to them who will not take heed to follow His mighty commands on this earth. Almighty God is not as patient as He used to be. He is taking vengeance on wrong doers almost immediately.

Isaiah 34 (KJV)

5. For my sword shall be bathed in heaven: behold, it shall come down upon Idumea, and upon the people of my curse, to judgment.

Deuteronomy 28 (KJV)

15. But it shall come to pass, if thou wilt not hearken unto the voice of the Lord thy God, to observe to do all his commandments and his statutes which I command thee this day; that all these curses shall come upon thee, and overtake thee:
16. Cursed shalt thou be in the city, and cursed shalt thou be in the field.
17. Cursed shall be thy basket and thy store.
18. Cursed shall be the fruit of thy body, and the fruit of thy land, the increase of thy kine, and the flocks of thy sheep.
19. Cursed shalt thou be when thou comest in, and cursed shalt thou be when thou goest out.
20. The Lord shall send upon thee cursing, vexation, and rebuke, in all that thou settest thine hand unto for to do, until thou be destroyed, and until thou perish quickly; because of the wickedness of thy doings, whereby ***thou hast forsaken me***.

Romans 1 (KJV)

17. For therein is the righteousness of God revealed from faith to faith: as it is written, The just shall live by faith.
18. For the wrath of God is revealed from heaven against all ungodliness and unrighteousness of men, who hold the truth in unrighteousness;
19. Because that which may be known of God is manifest in them; for God hath shewed it unto them.
20. For the invisible things of him from the creation of the world are clearly seen, being understood by the things that are made, even his eternal power and Godhead; so that they are without excuse:
21. Because that, when they knew God, they glorified him not as God, neither were thankful; but became vain in their imaginations, and their foolish heart was darkened.
22. Professing themselves to be wise, they became fools,
23. And changed the glory of the uncorruptible God into an image made like to corruptible man, and to birds, and fourfooted beasts, and creeping things.
24. Wherefore God also gave them up to uncleanness through the lusts of their own hearts, to dishonour their own bodies between themselves:
25. Who changed the truth of God into a lie, and worshipped and served the creature more than the Creator, who is blessed for ever. Amen.
26. For this cause God gave them up unto vile affections: for even their women did change the natural use into that which is against nature:
27. And likewise also the men, leaving the natural use of the woman, burned in their lust one toward another; men with men working that which is unseemly, and receiving in themselves that recompence of their error which was meet.
28. And even as they did not like to retain God in their

knowledge, God gave them over to a reprobate mind, to do those things which are not convenient;

29. Being filled with all unrighteousness, fornication, wickedness, covetousness, maliciousness; full of envy, murder, debate, deceit, malignity; whisperers,
30. Backbiters, haters of God, despiteful, proud, boasters, inventors of evil things, disobedient to parents,
31. Without understanding, covenantbreakers, without natural affection, implacable, unmerciful:
32. Who knowing the judgment of God, that they which commit such things are worthy of death, not only do the same, but have pleasure in them that do them.

CHAPTER 90

Ignorance and Unbelief Are Rampant in Churches

Ignorance is so rampart in today's churches where many church goers and some of the so called leaders within the churches believe that miracles, power, prophecy and healing with the power of oil anointing left with biblical day prophets. Many Christians often mix and confuse spiritual gifts with fruits of the Spirit and their physical or acquired gifts (talents). Fruits of the Spirit comes with the indwelling of the Holy Spirit. On the other hand the Gifts of the Spirit are where the Holy Spirit's actions are manifested or working in chosen vessel who are in fact Christians. These are not talents which are confused with spiritual gifts. Talents can be called our physical skills where most of the time we study and learn such talents. While on the other hand, gifts of the spirit are given by God, Almighty through His Holy Spirit.

1 Corinthians 12 (KJV)

1. Now concerning spiritual gifts, brethren, I would not have you ignorant.
2. Ye know that ye were Gentiles, carried away unto these dumb idols, even as ye were led.
3. Wherefore I give you to understand, that no man speaking by the Spirit of God calleth Jesus accursed: and that no man can say that Jesus is the Lord, but by the Holy Ghost.

4. Now there are diversities of gifts, but the same Spirit.
5. And there are differences of administrations, but the same Lord.
6. And there are diversities of operations, but it is the same God which worketh all in all.
7. But the manifestation of the Spirit is given to every man to profit withal.
8. For to one is given by the Spirit the word of wisdom; to another the word of knowledge by the same Spirit;
9. To another faith by the same Spirit; to another the gifts of healing by the same Spirit;
10. To another the working of miracles; to another prophecy; to another discerning of spirits; to another divers kinds of tongues; to another the interpretation of tongues:
11. But all these worketh that one and the selfsame Spirit, dividing to every man severally as he will.
12. For as the body is one, and hath many members, and all the members of that one body, being many, are one body: so also is Christ.
13. For by one Spirit are we all baptized into one body, whether we be Jews or Gentiles, whether we be bond or free; and have been all made to drink into one Spirit.
14. For the body is not one member, but many.
15. If the foot shall say, Because I am not the hand, I am not of the body; is it therefore not of the body?
16. And if the ear shall say, Because I am not the eye, I am not of the body; is it therefore not of the body?
17. If the whole body were an eye, where were the hearing? If the whole were hearing, where were the smelling?
18. But now hath God set the members every one of them in the body, as it hath pleased him.
19. And if they were all one member, where were the body?
20. But now are they many members, yet but one body.
21. And the eye cannot say unto the hand, I have no need of thee: nor again the head to the feet, I have no need of you.

22. Nay, much more those members of the body, which seem to be more feeble, are necessary:
23. And those members of the body, which we think to be less honourable, upon these we bestow more abundant honour; and our uncomely parts have more abundant comeliness.
24. For our comely parts have no need: but God hath tempered the body together, having given more abundant honour to that part which lacked:
25. That there should be no schism in the body; but that the members should have the same care one for another.
26. And whether one member suffer, all the members suffer with it; or one member be honoured, all the members rejoice with it.
27. Now ye are the body of Christ, and members in particular.
28. And God hath set some in the church, first apostles, secondarily prophets, thirdly teachers, after that miracles, then gifts of healings, helps, governments, diversities of tongues.
29. Are all apostles? are all prophets? are all teachers? are all workers of miracles?
30. Have all the gifts of healing? do all speak with tongues? do all interpret?
31. But covet earnestly the best gifts: and yet shew I unto you a more excellent way.

CHAPTER 91

Incest (Sex With Relatives) Is Strictly Forbidden

Many people have sexually abused some of their own relatives. Fathers and mothers have abused their children by having sexual intercourse with them. Even some children have gone as far as having sex with their step-parents or step-parents having sex with their step-children. We are admonished to not have sex with none of our relatives.

Lev 18:6-23 (KJV) None of you shall approach to any that is near of kin to him, to uncover their nakedness: I am the LORD.

7. The nakedness of thy father, or the nakedness of thy mother, shalt thou not uncover: she is thy mother; thou shalt not uncover her nakedness.
8. The nakedness of thy father's wife shalt thou not uncover: it is thy father's nakedness.
9. The nakedness of thy sister, the daughter of thy father, or daughter of thy mother, whether she be born at home, or born abroad, even their nakedness thou shalt not uncover.
10. The nakedness of thy son's daughter, or of thy daughter's daughter, even their nakedness thou shalt not uncover: for theirs is thine own nakedness.
11. The nakedness of thy father's wife's daughter, begotten of thy father, she is thy sister, thou shalt not uncover her

nakedness.

12. Thou shalt not uncover the nakedness of thy father's sister: she is thy father's near kinswoman.
13. Thou shalt not uncover the nakedness of thy mother's sister; for she is thy mother's near kinswoman.
14. Thou shalt not uncover the nakedness of thy father's brother, thou shalt not approach to his wife: she is thine aunt.
15. Thou shalt not uncover the nakedness of thy daughter in law: she is thy son's wife; thou shalt not uncover her nakedness.
16. Thou shalt not uncover the nakedness of thy brother's wife: it is thy brother's nakedness.
17. Thou shalt not uncover the nakedness of a woman and her daughter, neither shalt thou take her son's daughter, or her daughter's daughter, to uncover her nakedness; for they are her near kinswomen: it is wickedness.
18. Neither shalt thou take a wife to her sister, to vex her, to uncover her nakedness, beside the other in her life time.
19. Also thou shalt not approach unto a woman to uncover her nakedness, as long as she is put apart for her uncleanness.
20. Moreover thou shalt not lie carnally with thy neighbour's wife, to defile thyself with her.
21. And thou shalt not let any of thy seed pass through the fire to Molech, neither shalt thou profane the name of thy God: I am the LORD.
22. Thou shalt not lie with mankind, as with womankind: it is abomination.

CHAPTER **92**

Infidel (Denying One's Own Responsibilities) - Denying Child Support/Household Support

One of the biggest problems that we face in America is the lack of parental child support as well as adequate support of ones household. Many spouses are strapped with the responsibilities of attempting to support their fathers alone while the other spouse provides little or no support to his/her family or household. The majority of time, women are left holding the bag to support their children and their household without any resources coming from thier spouse or mate. There are some men supporting their children and their households whithout their spouses are mates assistance as well. The Bible terms these kinds of people as worst than Infidels.

Many men and women have shirked their responsibilities of financially, physically, and morally supporting their families and/or ones under their guardianship. It is so bad that local and county governments have to search for those worst than infidels and seize their money through employment garnishments, jail time and other feasible actions to recoup funds that they owe.

1 Timothy 5 (KJV)

8. But if any provide not for his own, and specially for those of his own house, he hath denied the faith, and is worse than an infidel.

CHAPTER **93**

Involvement with Cursed Things

Easter Bunnies And Egg Hunting

During the Easter holiday season, Christians along with the secular part of our society are caught up in the commercialization of purchasing so-called Easter dresses, suits, stuffed bunnies, live rabbits, Easter candy, hen eggs (mostly boiled and colored) and much more.

Easter egg hunting rituals is unfortunately a fad and a tradition of many generations of families. This is a common occurance in churches who associate Easter egg hunting as an Easter celebration on church grounds or other properties for their children. Neither does the rabbit, nor does the chicken egg have anything to do the death and glorious resurrection of Jesus Christ. There are no associations whatsoever in the world's Easter tradition.

Although Easter celebration is not found in the Holy Bible, it is a day set aside by Christians to commemorate the death and resurrection of our Lord and Savior, Jesus Christ. There are no bunnies or boiled plain eggs or colored eggs anywhere in this world to commemorate our Savior's death and resurrection. It is merely a fad and a tradition concocted by Satan to have not only the world, but to have Christians to inconspicuously celebrate him and to redirect most of the emphasis from the Master's celebrated death and resurrection. Satan has cunningly crafted an avenue of commercialism, that is with a string of retail outlets selling so-called Easter attire (Easter Frocks), Easter regalia, new suits, dresses, hats, shoes and many other things related to the Easter seasons. Retail stores and outlets usually do quite well during this particular season. Consumer spending increases while retail store profits increase as well.

Christians are not only in spiritual bondage, but in financial bondage as well. Christian's credit cards can and will make them slaves to the lender, the bank. Not only can credit card bills make us slaves to the lender, but time payments on other loans have the same effect as well.

Proverbs 22 (KJV)

7. The rich ruleth over the poor, and the borrower is servant to the lender.

Santa (Satan) Claus And Christmas

Santa Claus is actually Satan in disguise. Santa in its unscrambled word form is nicely spelled to represent Satan. In other words, Santa Claus inconspicuously represents Satan. There is no correlation between Santa Claus and the birth of our Lord and Savior, Jesus Christ. The giver of all gifts are from our Master, Jesus Christ. No man on earth can beat the Master giving. As a matter of fact, our Master's Father and our Father owns everything. So, how can man beat them giving?

Ho, ho, ho! Merry Christmas says the demon Santa Claus as he belts out his supposedly joyous and jolly exclamation of Christmas cheers. He is really saying "Woe, woe, woe! Have a Misery or sorrowful Christmas with troubles and afflictions! This is really the counterfeit of God Almighty's word of "Ho" which means woe. God is using the word "Ho" as an exclamation of warning that He was about to do something to His people or for them because sorrow, misery, afflictions, trouble and/or grief was about to befriend them. Zec 2:6 (KJV) "Ho, ho, come forth, and flee from the land of the north, saith the LORD: for I have spread you abroad as the four winds of the heaven, saith the LORD."

Ho. Hebrew definition. 1945. howy, hoh'ee; a prol. form of H1930 [akin to H188]; oh!:--ah, alas, **ho**, O, **woe.**

Woe. Webster's definition. 1. Great sorrow; grief; misery, 2. A cause of sorrow; affliction; trouble.

Hebrew definition of Woe. 3759. ouai, oo-ah'ee; a prim. exclamation of grief: "woe":--alas, woe.

Christmas trees and ornaments are traditionally displayed in Christian's homes, businesses, place of work, churches and many other places for their recognition in the spirit of Christmas celebrations so to speak. Christmas trees and the accessories used in the decorations of them have nothing whatsoever to do with the celebration of our Lord and Savior's birth. The purchasing of trees and decorations are additional expenses which are also sources of slavery or bondage of Christians.

Bringing Cursed Things Into Home/Office

One of the seemingly harmless things that we can do is to unknowingly bring cursed objects into our homes, offices and merely into our presence. These can be what appears to be beautiful things such as paintings, statues, games, videos: Walt Disney's Fantasia (Masterpiece), Aladdin (Classic), Beauty and the Beast (Classic), music CDs, audio and video music tapes such as the recordings of a Mormon cult called The Mormon Tabernacle Choir, records and many other objects. Buddhist objects, geisha girl (oriental prostitutes) figurines/dolls/ art designs/chop sticks/paintings, and/

or other cursed objects, Masonic objects and anything connected with the masonic lodges, Eastern Stars, Shriner organizations, just to name a few are all curses which plague Christians. Anything made and possibly cursed by its maker/owner who serves other gods.
Josh 6:18 (KJV) "And ye, in any wise keep yourselves from the accursed thing, lest ye make yourselves accursed, when ye take of the accursed thing, and make the camp of Israel a curse, and trouble it."

Through Handling Unholy Things

If we just handle a cursed object and immediately bring a curse into our lives without one iota of knowledge that we have done so. God doesn't even want us to touch any cursed thing or object. Just touching a cursed thing has the same effect as intentionally and physically bringing curses into our lives.

Josh 7:11 (KJV) "Israel hath sinned, and they have also transgressed my covenant which I commanded them: for they have even taken of the accursed thing, and have also stolen, and dissembled also, and they have put it even among their own stuff."
2 Cor 6:17 (KJV) "Wherefore come out from among them, and be ye separate, saith the Lord, and touch not the unclean thing; and I will receive you,"

CHAPTER **94**

Israel and America vs. Their Enemies

Just a word of thought before we get into the land dilemma of the Jews, there is one interesting bit of information about who will judge the Jewish nation after the end times events occur subsequent to the return of Jesus Christ. The twelve Jewish Disciples of Jesus Christ have twelve (12) thrones in heaven which is already prepared for them to occupy and judge the Jewish nation.

Twelve (12) Disciples Will Judge The Twelve (12) Tribes Of Israel

Matthew 19 (KJV)

28. And Jesus said unto them, Verily I say unto you, That ye which have followed me, in the regeneration when the Son of man shall sit in the throne of his glory, ye also shall sit upon twelve thrones, judging the twelve tribes of Israel.

When I was growing up in St. Louis, Missouri and various towns in Arkansas, I constantly heard negative statements about Jewish people from grown-ups in my respective neighbor. They would constantly talk about who possibly owned most of the real estate and businesses that they normally patronized. They would say things like, "The Jews owned everything in our neighborhood!".

Their summations were probably true as Almighty God because He promised them if they would obey His commandments, He prosper them in all their ways, that other blessings, He would bless them to be lenders and not borrowers.

President Obama is attempting to encourage Israel to give over some of its lands to Palestine so they can establish a statehood. Even if Israel did give part of their promised lands to Palestine, there will still be no peace until Almighty Jesus Christ, our Savior returns. The President is essentially on a defeating role in his attempts in encouraging Israel to part with it promised lands. The president and his Secretary of State are both ignorant of the promises that Almighty God have made to Israel. Biblical principles in the Holy Scriptures must be adhered to and followed without fail.

Jews - Lenders, Not Borrowers

Deuteronomy 28

1. And it shall come to pass, if thou shalt hearken diligently unto the voice of the Lord thy God, to observe and to do all his commandments which I command thee this day, that the Lord thy God will set thee on high above all nations of the earth:
2. And all these blessings shall come on thee, and overtake thee, if thou shalt hearken unto the voice of the Lord thy God.
3. Blessed shalt thou be in the city, and blessed shalt thou be in the field.
4. Blessed shall be the fruit of thy body, and the fruit of thy ground, and the fruit of thy cattle, the increase of thy kine, and the flocks of thy sheep.
5. Blessed shall be thy basket and thy store.
6. Blessed shalt thou be when thou comest in, and blessed shalt thou be when thou goest out.

7. The Lord shall cause thine enemies that rise up against thee to be smitten before thy face: they shall come out against thee one way, and flee before thee seven ways.
8. The Lord shall command the blessing upon thee in thy storehouses, and in all that thou settest thine hand unto; and he shall bless thee in the land which the Lord thy God giveth thee.
9. The Lord shall establish thee an holy people unto himself, as he hath sworn unto thee, if thou shalt keep the commandments of the Lord thy God, and walk in his ways.
10. And all people of the earth shall see that thou art called by the name of Lord; and they shall be afraid of thee.
11. And the Lord shall make thee plenteous in goods, in the fruit of thy body, and in the fruit of thy cattle, and in the fruit of thy ground, in the land which the Lord sware unto thy fathers to give thee.
12. The Lord shall open unto thee his good treasure, the heaven to give the rain unto thy land in his season, and to bless all the work of thine hand: and ***thou shalt lend*** unto many nations, and ***thou shalt not borrow***.
13. And the Lord shall make thee the head, and not the tail; and thou shalt be above only, and thou shalt not be beneath; if that thou hearken unto the commandments of the Lord thy God, which I command thee this day, to observe and to do them:

America Must Support Israel And The Jews

If America is to be blessed and continue to stand as a nation, she must support Israel at all cost. If it takes using destructive force against Israel's enemies who are attacking them, then America must do what it takes to accomplish the same. Our blessings as a whole is dependent upon our supporting Israel without failure.

Genesis 12 (KJV)

3. And I will bless them that bless thee, and curse him that curseth thee: and in thee shall all families of the earth be blessed.

Michael, The Warring Archangel (Chief Angel)Stands Watch Over Israel

The leaders of Iran and other haters of the Jews and Israel are threatening to destroy the existence of Israel and its Jewish people. When it gets to a point that Israel and/or Jerusalem can't defend itself and with no help available, Michael, the Archangel, who is also called the great prince will stand up and fight the war for Israel. Michael is Almighty God's war angel.

Daniel 12 (KJV)

1. And at that time shall Michael stand up, the great prince which standeth for the children of thy people: and there shall be a time of trouble, such as never was since there was a nation even to that same time: and at that time thy people shall be delivered, every one that shall be found written in the book.

American Ignorantly Supports Palestine's Desired Statehood In Israel

Unfortunately, America is putting its citizens in a dilemma in that she supports Israel on the one hand and also supports the desires of Palestine to create their statehood on land that God has promised to the Jews forever. The are seven (7) regions in the Middle-East which the promised lands of the 12 Tribes of Jacob (Israel). The seven (7) Ancient regions of Israel's promised lad are as follows:

Question: "What is the land that God promised to Israel?"

Answer: In regards to the land that God has promised Israel,

Genesis 15 (KJV)

18. In the same day the Lord made a covenant with Abram, saying, Unto thy seed have I given this land, from the river of Egypt unto the great river, the river Euphrates:

Genesis 15:18 declares, "To your descendants (Abraham's) I give this land, from the river of Egypt to the great river, the Euphrates."

God later confirms this promise to Abraham's son Isaac, and Isaac's son Jacob (whose name was later changed to Israel). When the Israelites were about to invade the promised land, God reiterated the land promise, as recorded in

Joshua 1:4, "Your territory will extend from the desert to Lebanon, and from the great river, the Euphrates — all the Hittite country — to the Great Sea on the west."

Joshua 1 (KJV)

4. From the wilderness and this Lebanon even unto the great river, the river Euphrates, all the land of the Hittites, and unto the great sea toward the going down of the sun, shall be your coast.

With Genesis 15:18 and Joshua 1:4 in mind, the land God gave to Israel included everything from the Nile river in Egypt to Lebanon (North to South) and everything from the Mediterranean Sea to the Euphrates River (West to East). So, what land has God stated belongs to Israel? All of the land modern Israel currently possesses, plus all of the land of the Palestinians (the West Bank and Gaza), plus some of Egypt and Syria, plus all of Jordan, plus some of Saudi Arabia and Iraq. Israel currently possesses only a fraction of the land God has promised.

7 Nations of Ancient Canaan (Israel)

Here is another promise that God gave to Israel concerning their enemies who come against them, such as Russia, Iran, Iraq and many others:

Deuteronomy 7 (KJV)

22. And the Lord thy God will put out those nations before thee by little and little: thou mayest not consume them at once, lest the beasts of the field increase upon thee.
23. But the Lord thy God shall deliver them unto thee, and shall destroy them with a mighty destruction, until they be destroyed.
24. And he shall deliver their kings into thine hand, and thou shalt destroy their name from under heaven: there shall no man be able to stand before thee, until thou have destroyed them.
25. The graven images of their gods shall ye burn with fire: thou shalt not desire the silver or gold that is on them, nor take it unto thee, lest thou be snared therein: for it is an abomination to the Lord thy God.
26. Neither shalt thou bring an abomination into thine house, lest thou be a cursed thing like it: but thou shalt utterly detest it, and thou shalt utterly abhor it; for it is a cursed thing.

CHAPTER **95**

Israel's Promised Lands - No to Palestinian Statehood in Israel's Promised Lands

President Obama is attempting to encourage Israel to give over some of its lands to Palestine so they can establish a statehood. Even if Israel did give part of their promised lands to Palestine, there will still be no peace until Almighty Jesus Christ, our Savior returns. The President is essentially on a defeating role in his attempts in encouraging Israel to part with it promised lands. The president and his Secretary of State are both ignorant of the promises that Almighty God have made to Israel. Biblical principles in the Holy Scriptures must be adhered to and followed without fail.

Just a word of thought before we get into the land dilemma of the Jews, there is one interesting bit of information about who will judge the Jewish nation after the end times events occur subsequent to the return of Jesus Christ. The twelve Jewish Disciples of Jesus Christ have twelve (12) thrones in heaven which is already prepared for them to occupy and judge the Jewish nation.

Twelve (12) Disciples Will Judge The Twelve (12) Tribes Of Israel

Matthew 19 (KJV)

28. And Jesus said unto them, Verily I say unto you, That ye

> which have followed me, in the regeneration when the Son of man shall sit in the throne of his glory, ye also shall sit upon twelve thrones, judging the twelve tribes of Israel.

The United States of America must support Israel at all cost or else our livelihood and mere existence will be in jeopardy. God said that whoever blesses Israel, He will bless, but whoever curses Israel will be cursed:

Genesis 12 (KJV)

3. And I will bless them that bless thee, and curse him that curseth thee: and in thee shall all families of the earth be blessed.

Dr. Condolezza Rice, Secretary of State is way off base on the issue of negotiating the transfer of land from Israel to Palestine. Actually, Palestine is already on part of Israel's land which Almighty God had already promised them as spelled out in the Biblical scriptures below:

Yishai, Rice divided on economic meeting

JERUSALEM, Oct. 14 (UPI) -- Israeli Industry, Trade and Labor Minister Eli Yishai's call for a Palestinian economic meeting has been rejected by U.S. Secretary of State Condoleezza Rice.

When the two met in Jerusalem Sunday, Yishai expressed displeasure with the current political climate in the Palestinian National Authority and said only an economic conference could unite the region behind Palestinian President Mahmoud Abbas, Ynetnews reported.

"Today we have a Palestinian Authority with two heads. It is impossible to sign an agreement with only 40 percent of the Palestinian people," he told Rice. "We need a real reinforcement, rather than a virtual one. Only an economic conference can bolster Abu Mazen."

Yet Rice rejected that motion, instead saying the upcoming Annapolis conference will serve as a forum for core issues and direct negotiations for the troubled region.

"I am convinced that the ***Palestinians need an independent country***," Rice said. "The Annapolis conference will discuss the core issues, but the negotiations will be held in a direct manner."

Question: "What is the land that God promised to Israel?"

Answer: In regards to the land that God has promised Israel,

Genesis 15 (KJV)

18. In the same day the Lord made a covenant with Abram, saying, Unto thy seed have I given this land, from the river of Egypt unto the great river, the river Euphrates:

Genesis 15:18 declares, "To your descendants (Abraham's) I give this land, from the river of Egypt to the great river, the Euphrates." God later confirms this promise to Abraham's son Isaac, and Isaac's son Jacob (whose name was later changed to Israel). When the Israelites were about to invade the promised land, God reiterated the land promise, as recorded in

Joshua 1:4, "Your territory will extend from the desert to Lebanon, and from the great river, the Euphrates — all the Hittite country — to the Great Sea on the west."

Joshua 1 (KJV)

4. From the wilderness and this Lebanon even unto the great river, the river Euphrates, all the land of the Hittites, and unto the great sea toward the going down of the sun, shall be your coast.

With Genesis 15:18 and Joshua 1:4 in mind, the land God gave to Israel included everything from the Nile river in Egypt to Lebanon (North to South) and everything from the Mediterranean Sea to the Euphrates River (West to East). So, what land has God stated belongs to Israel? All of the land modern Israel currently possesses, plus all of the land of the Palestinians (the West Bank and Gaza), plus some of Egypt and Syria, plus all of Jordan, plus some of Saudi Arabia and Iraq. Israel currently possesses only a fraction of the land God has promised.

Here is another promise that God gave to Israel concerning their enemies who come against them, such as Russia, Iran, Iraq and many others:

Deuteronomy 7 (KJV)

22. And the Lord thy God will put out those nations before thee by little and little: thou mayest not consume them at once, lest the beasts of the field increase upon thee.
23. But the Lord thy God shall deliver them unto thee, and shall destroy them with a mighty destruction, until they be destroyed.
24. And he shall deliver their kings into thine hand, and thou shalt destroy their name from under heaven: there shall no man be able to stand before thee, until thou have destroyed them.
25. The graven images of their gods shall ye burn with fire: thou shalt not desire the silver or gold that is on them, nor take it unto thee, lest thou be snared therein: for it is an abomination to the Lord thy God.
26 Neither shalt thou bring an abomination into thine house, lest thou be a cursed thing like it: but thou shalt utterly detest it, and thou shalt utterly abhor it; for it is a cursed thing.
1. When the Lord thy God shall bring thee into the land

whither thou goest to possess it, and hath cast out many nations before thee, the Hittites, and the Girgashites, and the Amorites, and the Canaanites, and the Perizzites, and the Hivites, and the Jebusites, seven nations greater and mightier than thou;

7 Nations of Ancient Canaan (Israel)

Canaanites, Amorites, Hittites, Jebusites, Hivites, Perrizites, and Girgashites.

CHAPTER **96**

Jehovah's Witnesses (Satan's Occult Organization) Is Not a Church

The Lord, Almighty God's name Jehovah represents a number of names, none of which is a representation by the occult, Jehovah's Witnesses. They don't represent the God that Christians serve. Our Jehovah has the following names and meanings as listed below:

Note: Not all biblical scriptures are referenced. Some of the suffixes of the Jehovah names are found in the Hebrew translations. However, there are several in the English language of the Bible (i.e., Jehovahnissi, Jehovahshalom and Jehovah without suffixes).

22. Jehovah-rapha/Jehovah-rophe (the Lord who heals) - (Exodus 15:22-26)
23. Jehovah-nissi (the Lord our banner) - (Exodus 17:15)
24. Jehovah-Shalom (the Lord our peace) - (Jude 16:24)
25. Jehovah-ra-ah/Jehovah-Roth (the Lord my shepherd) - (Psalms 23)
26. Jehovah-tsidkenu (the Lord our righteousness) - (Jeremiah 23:5-6, 33:16)
27. Jehovah-shammad/Jehovah-Shammah (the Lord is present) - (Ezekiel 48:15) 7)

7. Jehovah-Elohim (the Lord God) - (Genesis 2:4, Jude 5:3)
8. Jehovah Sabaoth (the Lord of hosts) - (Isaiah 1:24, Psalms 46:7)
9. Jehovah-Jireh (the Lord will provide) - (Genesis 22:14)

10. Jehovah-M'Kaddesh (the Lord who Sanctifies) - (Levicticus 20:8)

Jehovah's Witnesses (Satan's Witnesses) are bent on their idea that they believe that all souls die and there is no after life, nor do they believe there is an eternal life in heaven that the Bible promises to all believers of Jesus Christ.

Christians must understand that our souls never die. All souls belong to God, Almighty who made us. Even when we die in Christ, our souls live on. Contrary to popular beliefs of various cults who represent themselves as churches including the CULT, Jehovah's Witnesses. Jehovah's Witnesses will point out to Christians that their bibles claim in black and white that their souls dies. The particular scripture in which they famously like to use is:

Ezekiel 18:4 (KJV), "Behold, all souls are mine, as the soul of the father, so also the souls of the son is mine: THE SOUL THAT SINNETH, IT SHALL DIE."

As we explore the Hebrew translation of the word "soul" and the Greek translation of the word "soul", you'll see why although spelled the same, they are distinctively defined with different meanings.

HEBREW WORD "SOUL". Let's explore the Hebrew translation for the word "soul".

Soul. Hebrew definition. H5315. nephesh, neh'-fesh; (from H5314; naphash, naw-fash'; a prim. root: to breathe) prop. a breathing creature, i.e. animal or (abstr.) vitality; used very widely in a lit., accommodated or fig. sense (bodily or mental):--any, appetite, beast, body, breath, creature (person).

There are many other definitions that can be included, but the breathing creature in which we are referring to is a person's body and the breath it needs in order to live. In the above scripture both the body and breath are referred to as the soul. Let's take a look at the phrase "The soul that sinneth, it shall die". Now, wouldn't you agree that the breath in itself can't sin? With breath in our bodies, we can sin. So then, when we have done a portion of sinning, we are prone to die, wouldn't you agree again? Here is another scenario about the livelihood of breath for us to consider. If one person sinned and if the Jehovah's claim was true, then all of us including every living creature would be dead because breath would be dead. So, as you see, the definition of this particular soul refers to the physical body and not our breath. However, the breath can leave an individual body, but still reside in other living bodies. In essence the soul (breath) never dies.

One case in point is when the Prophet Elijah was summoned to the bedside of a child with whom his breath left him resulting in his death. As you can recall above in Ezekiel 18:4 where God said that all souls were His. Elijah knew this and prayed to God and ask Him to let that child's soul (breath) come into him again. The child's soul did come into him again and he did live again.

1 King 17:21-22 (KJV), "21) And he stretched himself upon the child three times, an cried unto the Lord, and said, O Lord my God, I pray Thee, let this child's soul come into him again.

22. And the Lord heard the voice of Elijah; and the soul of the child came into him again, and he revived."

There was no death on that child's soul (breath) whatsoever. It had merely returned to the owner, God Almighty.

GREEK WORD "SOUL". Matthew 10:28 (KJV), "And fear not them which kill the body, but are not able to kill the soul: but rather fear Him which is able to destroy both soul and body in hell."

Let's explore the Greek translation for the word "soul" in this particular scripture.

Soul. Greek definition. G5590. psuche, psoo-khay; from G5594, i.e. (by impl.) spirit, thus distinguished on the one hand from G4151, which is the rational and IMMORTAL SOUL.

Let's see what definition Webster's dictionary have the word "Immortal". Immortal (im mort'l) adj. 1. Not mortal; deathless; living or lasting forever.

Here you'll find that the soul is a spirit which man, neither can kill, nor can he destroy it. The soul doesn't die as the Jehovah's Witnesses occult would have you believe.

So as you can readily see, death comes to the soul (body), but not the soul (spirit). You can also see how Satan uses his deceptive meanings for words spelled exactly alike, but with two completely different meanings. We can now conclude that the spiritual soul lives forever and never dies.

Moses And Elias After Their Long Deaths Talked To Jesus

Matthew 17 (KJV)

1. And after six days Jesus taketh Peter, James, and John his brother, and bringeth them up into an high mountain apart,
2. And was transfigured before them: and his face did shine as the sun, and his raiment was white as the light.
3. And, behold, there appeared unto them Moses and Elias talking with him.

Many People Rose From Their Graves After Jesus' Resurrection

Matthew 27 (KJV)

50. Jesus, when he had cried again with a loud voice, yielded up the ghost.
51. And, behold, the veil of the temple was rent in twain from the

top to the bottom; and the earth did quake, and the rocks rent;

52. And the graves were opened; and many bodies of the saints which slept arose,
53. And came out of the graves after his resurrection, and went into the holy city, and appeared unto many.

A Poor Man Goes To Heaven And A Rich Man Goes To Hell

Luke 16 (KJV)

19. There was a certain rich man, which was clothed in purple and fine linen, and fared sumptuously every day:
20. And there was a certain beggar named Lazarus, which was laid at his gate, full of sores,
21. And desiring to be fed with the crumbs which fell from the rich man's table: moreover the dogs came and licked his sores.
22. And it came to pass, that the beggar died, and was carried by the angels into Abraham's bosom: the rich man also died, and was buried;
23. And in hell he lift up his eyes, being in torments, and seeth Abraham afar off, and Lazarus in his bosom.
24. And he cried and said, Father Abraham, have mercy on me, and send Lazarus, that he may dip the tip of his finger in water, and cool my tongue; for I am tormented in this flame.
25. But Abraham said, Son, remember that thou in thy lifetime receivedst thy good things, and likewise Lazarus evil things: but now he is comforted, and thou art tormented.
26. And beside all this, between us and you there is a great gulf fixed: so that they which would pass from hence to you cannot; neither can they pass to us, that would come from thence.
27. Then he said, I pray thee therefore, father, that thou wouldest send him to my father's house:

28. For I have five brethren; that he may testify unto them, lest they also come into this place of torment.
29. Abraham saith unto him, They have Moses and the prophets; let them hear them.
30. And he said, Nay, father Abraham: but if one went unto them from the dead, they will repent.
31. And he said unto him, If they hear not Moses and the prophets, neither will they be persuaded, though one rose from the dead.

When Jesus Christ was on the cross being crucified to death, He looked up towards Heaven and gave up his Spirit to His Father, Almighty God.

Luke 23 (KJV)

46. And when Jesus had cried with a loud voice, he said, Father, into thy hands I commend my spirit: and having said thus, he gave up the ghost.

Another such case was when Stephen was being stoned to death, he looked up towards heaven and saw Jesus Christ on the right side of Almighty God and he requested that Jesus receive his spirit as well.

Acts 7 (KJV)

59. And they stoned Stephen, calling upon God, and saying, Lord Jesus, receive my spirit.
60. And he kneeled down, and cried with a loud voice, Lord, lay not this sin to their charge. And when he had said this, he fell asleep.

CHAPTER 97

Jews - Original Bloodline from Black African People of Ethiopia, Africa

Black African People Have Lost Their Identity As Black African Jews

It is very interesting that over many centuries, Black Africans have lost their history of Black African Jews. They are presently known as Black Africans or as in the United States of America, African Americans. Additionally, there are other black people around the world such as Haitians and blacks in other countries around the world.

Unfortunately, the Jews from the Twelve Tribes of Israel who live in Israel don't recognize Black Africans as Black African Jews. There are however, two (2) groups of Jews: Black African Jews and the Jews established from the Twelve Tribes of Israel by Almighty God. The Twelve Tribes of Israel were established due to the hardness of their hearts, their un-beliefs of the Holy Scriptures, and their denying the coming of our Lord and Savior, Jesus Christ. We will however, explore the Holy Scriptures in this chapter.

Amos 9 (KJV)

7. Are ye not as children of the Ethiopians unto me, O children of Israel? saith the Lord. Have not I brought up Israel out of

the land of Egypt? and the Philistines from caphtor, and the Syrians from Kir?

1. The Original Jews and Hebrews Were Black Africans
2. Noah's Grand Sons, Ham's Sons Were Black African Jews: Shem, Cush, And Japheth

In mapping out the offspring down to Noah, note that Genesis 5:32 clearly states that he was 500 years old when he begat three sons, namely Shem, Ham, and Japheth - triplets. Then in Genesis 7:6, it says Noah was 600 years old when the floods came, which shows that only one year had elapsed since these births. This verse alone shows that Shem, Ham, and Japheth were born in Noah's 500th year of life, and Genesis 6:9 reads, "These are the generations of Noah." The word for generation in Hebrew is "hdlwt towldah to-led-aw" which means genealogy or birth. This verse shows that Noah's genes had not been racially mixed at that point but had come straight down, and that is why God said that he was perfect in his generations.

Noah And His Wife, Namah Later Birth Children Of Different Races Of People

Some scholars would like you to believe that Shem, Ham and Japheth, born of the same father Noah and mother Namah, (or through another wife much later), gave birth to three different races of children.

Genesis 10:6 continues, "and the sons of Ham (Sudan); Cush (Ethiopia), Mizraim (Egypt), Phut (Carthage / Libya), and Canaan," - who was cursed and settled outside of Africa in the region of the so-called "Middle East." The family is traced through the Bible in an unbroken chain to David, who then violates the law by marrying a Canaanite, which was something that was strictly forbidden by God, who in Genesis 24:3-4 issued a command not to marry outside one's own kindred so as not to damage the perfect genealogy or the holy seed.

David however violated that law and sinned by marrying outside his tribe, as can be deduced from the description found in Song of Solomon: 4 which changes from Negro to Mulatto, as a result of the unholy mixture. "Thou art fair, thy hair is as a flock of goats," which means straight and wavy, not like a sheep which is woolly and Nappy. Verse 2: "lips like scarlet," meaning reddish. The description continues in 5:10: "my beloved is white and ruddy," and verse 14 says, "his belly is as bright Ivory." As you can see, since David committed the sin of inter-marrying among the Canaanites as explained in the book of Ezra 9:1-2, the holy seed was infected and could no longer travel down through Solomon.

But Solomon, who had set up Jerusalem, had an older brother named Adonijah (1 Kings 1:5) by David through a Negroid wife, Haggith. Adonijah was denied his birthright and was put into exile, but he then set up the kingdom of Judea to preserve the holy seed or tribe of Judah. Eventually, Solomon and his band forced these tribes that fell under Judah namely Dina, Asher, Dan, Benjamin, and Issachar, to migrate through Yemen into Ethiopia, spreading northward back into their original homelands in Africa. However, some of the tribal members stayed behind and set up Nazareth, Magdella and Galilee, to mention a few, which to this day still have Negroes.

Mary of Magdalene, Martha, and Lazarus Are Revealed Through Their DNA To Have Been Black African Jews

Modern Egyptians 1890 Current research has unmistakably revealed through DNA tests taken from the tombs containing the names and bodies of Mary of Magdalene, Martha, and Lazarus, that the people of the village of Magdella where they lived, were in fact Negroes.

1. Jesus Christ With His Black, Kinky And Wooly Hair Was A Black African Jew
2. Original Black Jews (Hebrew-Israelites) As A Nation, With 1.1 Million Hebrews Slain By White Roman Soldiers

Clearly the original Biblical Jews and Hebrews were a Black African people from the line of Ham, and many of them still are, especially in northern Africa. These Black Jews were ruthlessly persecuted by the white man (Romans). Jesus, a Black Jew born during this time, had predicted that Jerusalem would be overthrown, the Temple would be destroyed, and the Black Hebrews would be scattered abroad. (Matt. 24:2,15-21, Luke 21: 5-6, 20-24).

Modern Egyptians, Roman (White) Soldiers Ended The Black African Jewish Nation

The Roman-Jewish War in A.D. 66 marked the peak of this persecution and also the end of the original Black Jews (Hebrew-Israelites) as a nation, with 1.1 million Hebrews slain, causing the entire lake of Galilee to turn red with blood and become littered with corpses. Millions of original Black Jews fled to Africa seeking to avoid destruction, but centuries later, their descendants were captured and sold into slavery in the Americas and the Caribbean bound in chains by cruel slave-traders.

Ancient Israelite from Roman times Black Israelite immigrants from northern and eastern Africa merged with indigenous groups in western Africa to become the Fulani of Futa Jalon, Bornu, Kamen, and Lake Chad. They also formed the parent-stock of groups such as the Ashanti, the Hausa, the B'nai Ephraim, and the Mavumbu or Ma-yomba. However, each of these groups suffered massive population decreases during the Atlantic slave trade, while others were completely eliminated. This is an image of an ancient Israelite from the Roman period.

One of the facts scripture provides about Israel is in connection to their physical appearance, which is described as resembling the sons of Ham (Khawm). Ham (Khawm) means Black, hot and burnt. Israel is being compared to Ham's first born son Cush or Ethiopia in Amos 9: "are you not as children of the Ethiopians unto me, o children of

Israel?" God calls the Israelites children of the Ethiopians, who are a known Black people. If ancient Israel were a white skinned people, it would have made more sense to compare them to another white skinned nation such as the Romans, Greeks or gentiles.

But the scriptures clearly compared Israel to a Black skinned people because Israel was and is a Black nation, being indistinguishable from native Egyptians and Ethiopians. Even Paul was mistaken for an "Egyptian" but declared himself to be a "Jew." (Acts 21:37-39, 22: 2,3)

Ethiopian Hebrews Moreover, ancient secular historians like Tacitus agreed on the physical appearance of the Hebrews, stating that it was the common opinion among the Romans that the Jews "were an Ethiopian race."

Tacitus also remarked that the Hebrews were Egyptians who left Egypt during a disease outbreak. In Roman times, Palestinian-Israelites were classified among Black Africans because it was practically impossible to differentiate between them.

The name Hebrew was inherited through Abraham, ancestor of the Hebrews, who dwelt in the land of Ethiopia-Canaan. (Gen. 13:18, 14:13, 1Chron.11:3-6). There were two tribes, Benjamin and Judah of the Ethiopian-Canaanite-Israelites that had inherited the name "Jew". (2 Kings 16:6; 18:26, 28; 25:25). See also (Josh 15:20, 54; 18:21; 28).

Black African Jews Are Called Sheep And Other Races Are Called Goats, The Gentiles

The term Jews and Gentiles covers all the people on the earth. "Jew" in a metaphorical sense represents all Negroes who are symbolically called Sheep, and the title Gentile represents all straight haired people, who are symbolically referred to as Goats (Rom. 9:24; Dan. 8:20-21).

John 10:27. "My sheep hear my voice and I know them and they follow me."

Matt 25:33. "And He shall set the sheep on His right hand, but the goats on the left."

According to Gen. 9:25, Ham's son Canaan received a curse, which caused all their lands, identity, and language to be given to the Israelites through Abraham (Gen. 12:5-7).

Genesis 9:25-27: "And he said, Cursed be Canaan; a servant of servants shall he be unto his brethren. And he said, blessed be the God of Shem; and Canaan shall be his servant. God shall enlarge [Ham], and he shall dwell in the tents of Shem; and Canaan shall be his servant.

Genesis 12:5-7: "And Abram took Sarai his wife, and Lot his brother's son, and all their substance that they had gathered, and the souls that they had gotten in Haran; and they went forth to go into the land of Canaan; and into the land of Canaan they came. And Abram passed through the land unto the place of Sichem, unto the plain of Moreh. And the Canaanite was then in the land. And JAH appeared unto Abram, and said, Unto thy seed will I give this land: and there builded he and altar unto JAH, who appeared unto him."

Ham's other son Japheth also had sons as stated in Gen:10, and their sons intermixed and produced a foreign race into the Negro Race (verse 5) known as the Gentiles or Goyim, which means Heathens. They are referred to as the people of Javan, Japheth's son which is translated as "Ionia" or "Greece." So the Greeks, according to the Bible, were the original Gentiles or nation other than the holy seed or chosen people.

God warns the Gentiles not to boast against the natural branches

(Negroes), unless they (Gentiles), from the wild olive tree, are taken out of the natural olive tree that symbolizes the Negro family, (Rom. 11:16-25).

All the preceding information provides ample proof that the ancient Israelites were a Black nation, but further proof is being provided to show that they were a Black skinned people from the beginning of their history, starting with the Patriarch Abraham, the father of the Hebrew Israelite nation. (Genesis 14:13)

Abraham was a native from Ur of the Chaldeans (Genesis 11:31), which is the country of Iraq. Archaeological discoveries have proven beyond doubt that the earliest inhabitants of southern Mesopotamia were members of the Negroid branch of humanity.

According to Sir Godfrey Higgins a reliable English archaeologist, Freemason and Fellow of the Society of Antiquaries, "The Chaldeans were originally Negroes." Professor Rudolph Windsor also writes, "The Chaldeans and the other People of that region were Jet Black in their complexion."

In that region the average temperature is 125 degrees, so this meant that the people from that part of the world needed to have large amounts of melanin in their skin to absorb the ultra violet radiation from the sun, which would confirm that they had to be a very dark skinned people. So, for Abraham to have come from that region of the world, he would have had very dark, Black-skin.

Black Iraquis_Basra This is borne out by those soldiers who are currently fighting in Iraq near the area that Abraham came from. Some of the white soldiers are being so badly burnt by the rays of sun that they could hardly walk, and very often have to use a special covering for protection.

They have also reported that the natives there are very Black and resemble afro-Americans. In other words, most of the people from the Iraqi town of Basra are Black skinned and look like present day Africans.

This is what Dr. Charles S. Finch III, M.D. had to say on the subject, "we know from the fate of albinos all over Africa that unprotected skin (light skin) is subject to grotesque, disfiguring cancers that are soon fatal." "Melanin is the substance that gives the skin a dark brown or Black pigment by absorbing ultra violet radiation and scattering the ions produced in order to protect the skin from cancer".

To continue, Biblical history relates that the descendants of Abraham, namely Jacob (Israel) and his twelve sons and their wives, 70 in all, migrated from Canaan to Egypt, and during their sojourn, the Children of Israel multiplied from a family of 70 to a nation of well over 2 million people by the time of the Exodus.

This massive number of people in such a short space of time could only have been achieved through intermarriage between the family of Jacob and the native Black Egyptian population.

Each one of Jacob's sons became a tribal nation which made up the greater nation of Israel. They were Reuben, Dan, Simeon, Gad, Levi, Asher, Judah, Naphtali, Zebulon, Joseph, Issachar and Benjamin.

All of Ham's four sons and their descendants, the Ancient Egyptians, Ethiopians, Somalis, Canaanites and so on, settled in and around the continent of Africa, including the so called Middle East which is also a part of the African Continent.

The Israelites are descendants of Noah's other son Shem through Abraham, who is the father of Isaac who is the father of Jacob who had the twelve sons mentioned above, who are the ancestors of the Israelite nation.

In the story of Joseph and his time in Egypt, he became Jacob's favorite son, and this created jealousy among his other brothers, ultimately resulting in him being sold as a slave to some Egyptians by Arab merchants.

Over a period of time, Joseph became Governor of Egypt and second in command to Pharaoh. There was a famine in Canaan where Jacob and his other sons lived. Meanwhile, Pharaoh had a dream which Joseph interpreted, that foretold of a coming famine, giving Egypt the opportunity to make preparations by storing food. As a result, Jacob sent ten of his sons to Egypt to buy bread, and when they came to Egypt, they were brought before Joseph who had immediately recognized his brothers, but they, on the other hand, did not recognize him. (Genesis 42:1-8).

Movie_Joseph Since the biblical Egyptians were a Black-skinned people, and not white like the person portraying Joseph in this picture, there can be no doubt that Joseph was also Black, because if he were white as over half the world's Jews are today, his brothers would have easily recognized him from among the Black skinned Egyptians, or be at least curious to find out why a white Hebrew was ruling in Egypt. But his brothers simply thought Joseph was just another native Egyptian.

Furthermore, in Genesis 50: 7-11, all the Hebrews are described as looking like the ancient Egyptians as seen after Jacob died, and all the Hebrews and Egyptians went down to the land of Canaan to bury him. (Genesis 49:29-30).

Verses 7-8, "states that all the elders of Pharaoh's house and all the elders of the land of Egypt along with all the Hebrews, went down." Verse 9 says, "It was a very great company."

Verse 11 says, that the Canaanites saw the funeral procession and proclaimed, "this is a grievous mourning to the Egyptians".

It was a mixed gathering of both Hebrews and Egyptians going to bury a Hebrew, yet the Canaanites identified both groups as Egyptians simply because the Canaanites saw a great number of Black-skinned people who all looked like the native Egyptians. In short, they mistook these Hebrews for Egyptians.

If the Hebrews were a white people, as we have been led to believe, the Canaanites who were familiar with both the Hebrews and Egyptians would have acknowledged them by saying something like, "this is a grievous mourning to the Hebrews and Egyptians," since white Hebrews would have stuck out among Black Egyptians.

More evidence can be gathered from the story of Moses. After the Hebrew population in Egypt grew rapidly years after the death of Joseph, his brothers, and the generation that had entered Egypt, they were no longer seen as friendly neighbours but as hostile enemies by the Egyptians who decided to enslave them. Because of their phenomenal population growth, the Egyptian Pharaoh issued a decree that all Hebrew males under the age of two would be killed (Exodus 1).

Moses was a Hebrew by birth from the tribe of Levi (Exodus 2:1-3) but he spent 40 years in the House of Pharaoh (Acts 7:23), raised as his grandson from an infant at the time when Pharaoh had declared that all Hebrew males be killed at birth, (Exodus 2: 6, 10). If Pharaoh were a Black-skinned descendant of Khawm / Ham and the Israelites were white, how could Moses secretly survive in the house of Pharaoh among Black-skinned Egyptians for 40 years masquerading as Pharaoh's grandson without being discovered? Moses would also have to be Black-skinned to pull that off. In the same way a Canaanite could not tell the difference between the Hebrews and the Egyptians, neither could Pharaoh make that distinction, otherwise Moses would certainly have been killed.

Seti 1 wall painting Rameses II It is claimed that the Pharaoh who was on the throne of Egypt at the time of Moses' birth, was Pharaoh Seti I on the left, and the father of Rameses II - the pharoah of oppression - on the right.

Moreover, after giving the decree himself to kill all Hebrew males, how could Pharaoh face or rule over his people if he knowingly had a white Hebrew baby living under his nose with all the rights and privileges as his own family? Moses could only have survived for 40 years in the palace of Pharaoh because he was a Black man just as the Egyptians were. So just as Joseph's brothers could not tell the Hebrews apart from the Egyptians, neither could Pharaoh.

Hollywood's version of Pharoah This image shows Hollywood's misinformation about how the Hebrews and ancient Egyptians used to look in the movie "The Ten Commandments." This image is supposed to be Pharaoh Seti I.

Much later Moses had killed an Egyptian whom he saw maltreating a Hebrew. This forced him to flee from Egypt for his life because Pharaoh had heard about the incident and wanted him to kill him. (Exodus 2:12-15). Moses fled to the land of Midian (Saudi Arabia), and after chasing away some shepherds who were bullying seven girls, he helped them to water their flock. The sisters related what took place to their father upon returning home, remarking that an Egyptian had saved them and watered their flock. (Exodus 2:16-19). Here, Moses is being described as a Black-skinned descendant of Ham, an Egyptian.

King Tut statue

There is a statue of King Tut as a boy, which was discovered in his tomb among many of his treasures in Egypt during an archaeological excavation in 1922.

The newly reconstructed image of King Tut which was featured on a Discovery Channel program. The image was put together from the skeleton of the King using forensic science and sophisticated computer programs. The facial reconstructions of King Tutankhamen based on CT scans of his mummy have produced images remarkably similar to the young pharaoh's ancient portraits, and even bears a strong resemblance to the golden mask of King Tut found in his tomb.

King Tut and the Egyptians of biblical times were a Black people, as can be seen in the pictures. The Truth can no longer be hidden.

Queen Nefertiti

There is also a newly reconstructed image from the skeleton of the ancient Egyptian Queen Nefertiti, one of the most famous queens of Egypt. The same methods used to reconstruct King Tut were used to create this image of Queen Nefertiti, revealing also that she was indeed a Black skinned woman.

Further evidence that Moses was Black-skinned is found in Exodus 4:6-7 where God is showing miracles to him so he can prove to the children of Israel that he was sent by God. God instructs Moses to put his hand in his bosom, and when he takes it out, it is leprous, white as snow.

If Moses were already white-skinned, what would have been the spectacle of turning his skin from white to white? But, since Moses and the rest of the Hebrews were a Black skinned people, this would have been a very powerful miracle to turn the Black skin on his hand to the opposite colour which is white.

In verse 7 God told Moses to put his hand back into his bosom, and when he takes it out, it turns as his other flesh, clearly showing that the rest of his skin colour had to be other than white or the opposite of white, that is, Black. Look at another of Hollywood's version of Moses.

From what history has revealed concerning the physical appearance of the Hebrews, it is clear that this Hollywood depiction of Moses is extremely inaccurate, and could only be viewed as racist distortion.

In Verse 8 God says that if the Israelites do not believe in the first sign of Moses' rod turning into a serpent, then they will believe in the second sign which was the changing of his skin from Black to white. God is clearly stating how powerful the second sign is, that it will make a believer out of the stiff necked Israelites.

Exodus 4: 8 reads, "And it shall come to pass, if they will not believe thee, neither hearken to the voice of the first sign, that they will believe the voice of the latter sign."

Closer depiction of Moses

On the other hand, according to the scriptures, history and archaeology, this image provides a more truthful depiction of what the Hebrew Prophet Moses would have looked like physically.

In Numbers:12:1, Miriam and Aaron, the sister and brother of Moses spoke out against him because he had married an Ethiopian woman, not because she was Black, but because she was of another nation. This behaviour angered God who then turned Miriam, a Black woman leprous, white as snow, that is, from Black to white. Again, if Miriam, a Hebrew, were white, what would have been the punishment or curse in turning a white person white instead of Jet Black as was claimed to be the case with Canaan's curse before the truth was revealed, dispelling that nonsense?

It is an established fact that the Bible always mentioned leprosy in the context of the skin turning white because of a disease, or in relationship to some specific wrong doing. If Israel were a white skinned people in ancient times, why does the scriptures only speak of them as turning white or becoming white with leprosy in reference to their skin colour?

In one case it was incitement to rebellion by Miriam, Moses' sister as in Num. 12:10. "And when the cloud had departed from above the Tabernacle, suddenly Miriam became leprous, as white as snow."

In another case it was sacrilege by Uzziah, king of Judah. 2 Chron. 26:19. "Then Uzziah became furious, and he had a censor in his hand to burn incense; and while he was angry with the priests, leprosy broke out on his forehead."

Then it was covetousness on the part of Gehazi, a servant of the prophet Elisha that caused him to become cursed and transformed to white for lying to Elisha, after taking money and gifts from Naaman, the captain of the Syrian Army. (2 Kings 5:27). "Therefore the leprosy of Na'aman shall cling to you and to your descendants forever. Then Gehazi went from Elisha's presence and he was leprous, as white as snow.

Paul

Acts 21:37-39, states that the apostle Paul was being led into a castle by a chief captain. Paul spoke to the chief in Greek, asking permission to speak with him. The chief captain was shocked to learn that Paul spoke Greek and asks Paul, "are not you that Egyptian?" to which Paul responded, "I am a man of Israel (Hebrew)."

In order for the chief captain to mistake Paul, a Hebrew, for a Black-skinned Egyptian, Paul had to look like an Egyptian, which, as scripture shows, was the case with the whole nation of Israel. Paul had to inform the chief captain he was an Israelite, so once again it is clear from the scriptures that it was hard to physically identify a Hebrew from an Egyptian.

Acts 21:37, "And as Paul was to be led into the castle, he said unto the chief captain, May I speak unto thee? Who said, Canst thou speak Greek?"

38 "Art not thou that Egyptian, which before these days madest an uproar, and leddest out into the wilderness four thousand men that were murderers?"

39 "But Paul said, I am a man of Israel (Hebrew) of Tarsus, a city in Cilicia, a citizen of no mean city: and, I beseech thee, suffer me to speak unto the people."

White Jesus

Another example is seen in the story of Joseph, Mary (Miriam) and Jesus (Yahshua), who were told to flee into Africa, not for military protection since at that time Egypt was a Roman province under Roman control, but because Egypt was still a Black country populated by Black people. So Joseph, Miriam and Yahshua would have been just another Black-skinned family among other Negroes, seeing that they had fled to Egypt for the purpose of hiding from Herod who was seeking to kill Yahshua. If Yahshua and the rest of the Hebrews looked like those pictures of the Christian Christ which portray Him as a long haired, white skinned blond with blue eyes, it would have been difficult for Him and His family to hide among Black Egyptians without being spotted. But since both the Hebrews and the Egyptians were Black, it would have been hard to recognize a Hebrew family from among the Black Egyptians.

For more confirmation regarding the colour of the ancient Israelites, read Acts 13:1 which says, "Now there were in the church that was at Antioch certain prophets and teachers; as Barnabas, and Simeon that was called Niger, and Lucius of Cyrene, and Manaen."

In Greek and Latin the word Niger means Black (skinned) and it is still used today when referring to Negroes and Moors. Cyrene is a city in Libya, North Africa, and historians and scholars both agree that Cyrene was a Black area heavily populated by Black skinned-people during Biblical times. Cyrene is also the place where Simon, the Black man who helped Yahshua carry His cross came. (Matt. 27:32, Mark 15:21, Luke 23:26).

But, bear in mind that the Hebrews were not dealing with any other people or racial group at that time, other than scattered Israel. Acts 11:19 says, "Now they which were scattered abroad upon the persecution that arose about Stephen travelled as far as Phenice and Cyprus, and Antioch, preaching the word to none but the Hebrews only".

This was before the apostles' ministries to the Gentiles at large started, so why were these "Black" men there if the Hebrews were a white people? They were Hebrews, just like Paul who was also there with them in the church in Antioch. Remember Paul was mistaken for a "Black" Egyptian. Niger and Lucius were prophets and teachers, and as the scripture teaches, all the prophets and teachers were Hebrews - Black.

Based on the evidence presented, it should be clear that Jesus' disciples, relatives, prophets, teachers, and associates like Mary of Magdalene were all Negroes.

Rastafari in dread locks Also, in many places throughout scriptures, references are made about the Israelites who wore their hair in long locks just like this Jamaican Rastafarian.

Numbers 6:5, "All the days of the vow of his separation there shall no razor come upon his head: until the days be fulfilled, in the which he separateth himself unto the Lord, he shall be holy, and shall let the locks of the hair of his head grow."

Judges 16:13, "And Delilah said unto Samson, Hitherto thou hast mocked me, and told me lies: tell me wherewith thou mightest be bound. And he said unto her, if thou weavest the seven locks of my head with the web."

19 "And she made him sleep upon her knees; and she called for a man, and she caused him to shave off the seven locks of his head; and she began to afflict him, and his strength went from him."

Ancient Egyptian in locks False depiction of Samson Nappy hair in its natural state is like the wool of a lamb. If a Black person does not cut or comb his/her hair it will eventually lock together forming huge matt's all over his/her head, and will produce seven or more locks similar to what Samson had. Samson never cut his hair, but allowed it to grow leaving it unkempt until it grew into locks.

If Samson the Israelite were a white skin person with white hair texture, then his hair would have grown long and straight without locking together, since it is very uncommon for a white person to get locks naturally. According to the scriptures Samson had seven locks which shows that Samson the Israelite was a Black man.

Jesus in early Roman church Jesus is called the Lamb of God according to the Bible, with His Woolly, Nappy, kinky hair being compared to lamb's wool, and His feet to the colour of burnt brass with a likeness resembling jasper and sardine stone, which are generally brownish stones. This image of Jesus was found in a church in Rome around AD 530.

These truths have been grossly neglected, suppressed, and distorted throughout most European and American historical texts, which are usually flavoured with race prejudice and hatred. Modern history books deliberately de-emphasize and leave out the history of kingdoms founded by the ten tribes of Israel such as Phoenicia, Carthage, Scythia, and Parthia for example, while at the same time, advance in a most eloquent manner, the histories of non Black empires.

The main vision was to convert everything that was African into a European structure, and then provide us with a fabricated history about ourselves and the world. So they sacked, looted and burnt the libraries in Egypt [Africa], Mesopotamia [Africa], and Ethiopia [Africa], and paralleled to the growth of the counterfeit, philosophical, Greco-Roman speculations and distortions, the original African truths were subtly replaced by myths based on these "new" European "revelations." This has continued over the centuries with Greece and Rome spreading propaganda, followed by Germany and England, with America eventually coming on board, to help enhance the de-Africanization of our history, culture and truths.

So for over 200 years, white scholars and historians, seeking to discredit African legacy, have been removing Black people from Egypt, Egypt from Africa and Africa from world history, teaching that Egypt is in the Near East, the Middle East, the Mediterranean and even the Fertile Crescent, while calculatingly refusing to enlighten the world that Egypt is and always has been on the Africa Continent.

So naturally when Europeans finally gained complete control of the African scriptures and perfected the printing press, an organized scheme to apply the concept of racial distinction within the African Family was initiated, in order to suppress and eliminate the truth of the African Bible.

White publishers have been controlling everything written and taught about Africa, even publishing books which taught that the Ancient

Egyptians were a white race. But as soon as Black people began to publish their own work and promote their own history, all of a sudden the white world became interested in setting Black people straight, insisting that the Ancient Egyptians were neither Black nor white, but more like the Arabs of today. The truth is, the Arabs invaded Egypt long after the Ancient Egyptian civilization had collapsed and faded away by the 7th Century AD, therefore they have no more claim or connection to Ancient Egypt than the Europeans have to Ancient America.

Fortunately, there are at present enough highly researched works by Black historians that can challenge the Eurocentric revisions of history and correct the erroneous views pertaining to the ethnic identity of the Hebrews/Africans.

So who are these white Jews?

Then if the original Jews were Black, where did these Caucasians who call themselves Jews come from? There are two main types of white Jews, the Edomites and the Khazars. The Edomites are the descendants of Esau, who was born ruddy (red) and hairy. This describes the white man who is all shades of red, and hairy, according to Gen. 25:25; "And the first came out red all over like an hairy garment; and they called his name Esau."

Esau was the albino, fraternal twin brother of Jacob, who was the father of the original Black Israelites. Rom 9:13 states, "As it is written, Jacob have I loved, but Esau have I hated."

The white Edomites and Black Israelites were constantly in conflict with each other, in fact, the Edomites fought the Black Jews in the Roman-Jewish War, but later in history, the Edomites (Idumeans) were conquered and forced to become Jews.

These so called Jewish people are the descendants of Esau's grandson Amalek, who, around 730-740 AD, were converted to the laws and statutes of Judaism, thus becoming Jews, but this group was not a descendant from the house of Israel either.

Their flourishing empire which extended from the Black Sea to the Caspian, and from the Caucasus to the Volga, was located between two major superpowers, the Eastern Roman Empire in Byzantium (Christianity), and the followers of Muhammad (Islam). The Khazar empire, representing a third force, could only maintain its political and ideological independence if it neither accepted Christianity nor Islam, since they did not want to become subordinate to either the authority of the Roman Emperor, or the Caliph of Baghdad.

For that reason, the Khazar king embraced the Jewish faith and ordered his subjects to do the same, which is how Judaism became the official state religion of the Khazars who now make up 90% of the so-called Jews of today. They were circumcised and started to use Jewish names. They also studied the Torah and Talmud, spoke and wrote in Hebrew, observed Hanukkah, Pesach and the Sabbath, and had synagogues and rabbis.

So as a political ploy they all converted to Judaism during the Middle Ages, and use a corrupted form of Judaism to hide behind, while continuing their treachery right into modern times. The Khazars have labelled themselves Zionists and "Jews" to deceive the world in furthering their own plans for global and political conquest. The Political Program for World Dominion is wrapped neatly in the cloak of religion.

But the Khazars nurtured a desire to possess a national Jewish motherland, an idea which took the shape of a Messianic type movement in the form of a Jewish Crusade, a movement first promoted by Solomon Ben Duji, a Khazar Jew, who then proceeded to communicate with all Jews from neighbouring nations. The intention was to forcibly suppress the Palestinian people.

The Khazars programmed themselves into believing that they were entitled to Palestinian land which they have never owned nor possessed through any right of ancestry, a land their ancestors have never occupied before. But with the help of a decision by United Nations in 1947 to divide up Palestine, the Khazars proclaimed themselves to be the State of Israel, and proceeded to randomly confiscate the territory belonging to those who had legally owned and occupied it for thousands of years. So, through a violation of their own charter, the United Nations were responsible for the dispossession of more than 4,000,000 Palestinians, in order to create a nation that did not have any ancestral nor existing rights whatsoever to that piece of land.

According to Arthur Koestler, a "Jew," such right "is not based on the hypothetical origins of the Jewish people, nor on the mythological covenant of Abraham with God; it is based on international law."

Not one Khazar had an ancestor who had ever set foot in the Holy Land, either from the beginning of time, or in Old Testament history, yet they sought support for their armed insurrections in Palestine.

According to Koestler, it was no "accident" or "coincident" that the Khazars chose Talmudism from the three prominent religions of that day: Islam, Christianity and Talmudism. Talmudism if you recall, is nothing more than Pharisaism, and remember what Jesus said to the Pharisees: "You are of your father, the Devil."

In Revelation 2:9 and 3:9, he said he knows the blasphemy of those calling themselves Jews and are not, clearly identifying that there are those impersonating Judaism who are Europeans by descent.

Rev 2:9, "I know the blasphemy of them which say they are Jews, and are not, but are the synagogue of Satan."

Rev 3:9, "Behold, I will make them of the synagogue of Satan, which say they are Jews, and are not, but do lie; behold, I will make them to come and worship before thy feet, and to know that I have loved thee."

Groups like the Khazars, Edomites and other racial groups make up what is modern Jewry today, although the Black Hebrew-Israelites are the real descendants of ancient Israel, a fact that is not well known by many, and is a well kept secret.

The Hebrew-Israelites are not known to the world as true Israel because of slavery and scattering, and some scholars, teachers and ministers even teach that God has cast them away, but God said, "I have chosen thee, and have not cast thee away." (Isa. 41:9). (Rom:11).

Information gathered from Jewish documents on "The Secret Relationship between Blacks and Jews" by the Nation of Islam, reveals the massive Jewish involvement in the Atlantic slave trade, but even though the children of Israel went into captivity, a remnant had returned as predicted.

These "Jewish" slave-sellers were most likely not real Jews but Khazars or counterfeit Jews, the hated, white Khazars who have usurped the real Jews. The Khazars learnt all they could from the real Hebrews before usurping and selling them into slavery, then taking over in their place.

Historians now recognize that the majority of eastern so-called Jews are really Khazars who have no Semitic roots at all. They are impostors, but well-suppressed knowledge is emerging about this war-like tribe of whites that rose to power in Eastern Europe who were hated even by the other whites they conquered, due to their severe, exploitative treatment of them.

These historical records make it abundantly clear that the majority of white European Jewry are not Hebrews in the biological sense but are the descendants of converts to Judaism during the Greco-Roman and Mediaeval periods. Professor Roland B. Dixon states emphatically that "The great majority of all Jews (Ashkenazi) to-day are 'Semites' only in speech, and their true ancestry goes back not so much to Palestine and Arabia as to the uplands of Anatolia, Armenia, the Caucasus, and the steppes of Central Asia, and their nearest relatives are still to be found in these parts to-day."

Caucasian Jews are clearly not the lineal descendants of Abraham, Isaac, and Jacob, nor do they constitute a separate race but rather a religious fraternity which adheres to the ethnic tradition of a people whose origins are inextricably linked to Black Africa.

So the majority of these Jews in the world who are of Eastern European descent, signifies that their ancestors did not come from the Jordan but from the Volga, not from Canaan but from the Caucasus once believed to be the cradle of the Aryan race; and that genetically they are more closely related to the Hun, uigur, and Magyar tribes than to the seed of Abraham, Isaac, and Jacob".

However, all Jews (Hebrews) that lived in Europe were not Khazar coverts, although 90% of them were. There were still some original Africans who lived in the environs of the Caucasus, in addition to others who had migrated to the Black Sea long before there was a Caucasian.

False representations of ancient Egyptians The Khazars who lived throughout Europe quickly became the new models for religious icons and images created during the middle ages. They had reasons to misrepresent the truth so as to develop white supremacy which they reinforced by inserting pictures of Caucasians throughout the Bible, on religious calendars, and by producing lily-white television programmes and religious movies. As a result, this present generation of both Black and white simply assumes, without any evidence whatsoever, that the ancient Hebrews were white, even though the original icons which portrayed the Hebrew Israelites, depicted them as Negroid.

These whitened images of the true Israelites may also have surfaced as the result of attitudes and racial prejudices displayed towards the Black Moors and other Blacks who ruled throughout Europe at different times.

Remember that in 193 AD, Septimius Severus, a Black man, descendant of the Phoenicians, and general in the Roman army who was aided by the Black men under his command, conquered Rome during the Dark or Middle Ages, and took control of Europe which was once held by whites, placing that power into the hands of the Blacks. So from that point onwards, Black people began to rule in different parts of Europe at different times during the Middle Ages. As a consequence, European hatred and resentment for Blacks stemmed from this action, as explained by David MacRitchie. "The Black giants of the Welsh, and other tales, are hateful and horrid. The Welsh Black Oppressor and the "Black Knight of Lancashire" are fierce tyrants, the cruel foes of all white people."

As a result, anything in opposition to European ideas or belief was then negatively linked to the colour Black, and even today we are still fed these negative images and statements related to the colour Black, such as Black Monday, Blackmail, Black sheep, Black day and Black Friday to list a few. Even the idea that sin is also Black implicitly leads to the misconception that God is white, therefore Satan must be Black.

Yet the Black man, now rejected because of his black skin and Woolly, Nappy hair, is the very race that gave the world its arts, sciences, use of speech, and even those civil and religious systems that still govern the universe today.

So it should be made clear that a colonial education will completely destroy a people's belief in their names, heritage, languages, ability, unity, and ultimately in themselves, as they seek to distance themselves from their heritage, erroneously striving to identify with all that is foreign or alien because of the brain/whitewashing.

By the way, the word "Semite" originates from the Latin prefix semi which means half Black and half white or mulatto, though Black is still dominant genetically speaking. The Semitic came into being as a result of crossbreeding between the Black inhabitants of the holy land and the white northern invaders. While many Semites like the Jews and gypsies have mixed so much with whites that they have forgotten or simply deny their African roots, racism or white supremacy will not let them forget this no matter how light-skinned they become, as evidenced by Hitler who mandated their destruction after they were classified as a non-white people originating in Africa. The very word gypsy means out of Egypt.

According to the scriptures, the Lord will call his people from the North, South, East and West to return them to Israel. Many in most of the political, Zionist and Christian circles believed this took place in 1947 when Israel, a land without people, for a people without a land, became sovereign, but this calling is yet to take place, so Black people wake up, re-learn your history, and serve your one true God.

The prophecy of Ezekiel: 37 talks about the spiritual resurrection of the people of Israel, who will be perpetually betrothed to their God in truth and in righteousness.

Blacks in the Bible

HAM
(Black-Hot)

Genesis 5:32; 6:10; 7:13; 9:18-22 10:1; 10:5-6; 10:20
Deut. 7:1; 11:23
1 Chron. 1:4-8
Nahum 3:9
Habekkuk 3:7

Ham's four sons were named Cush, Mizraim, Phut and Canaan. There was much controversy about the curse of Ham. The idea that Ham was cursed with a Black skin pigmentation is false. This probably originated as a Catholic misrepresentation. The Bible mentions nothing about his skin changing colour.

The curse only specified that his descendants (through his youngest son Canaan), would have to be temporarily servants of Ham's brothers Shem and Japeth. This did not include Cush, Mizraim or Phut.

Ham was created Black. He was the paternal ancestor of Ethiopia, Egypt, Libya, Tunisia, and many African tribes. He was also the patriarch of Southern Arabia, Crete, Cyprus, the Hittite Empire of Asia Minor, a part of Israel, and the Black Americans. These peoples can all be referred to as "Hamites". The Bible in the Book of Psalms refers to Egypt as "The Land of Ham". (Psalms 78:51; 105:23-27; and 106:19-23).

CUSH

(Blackness) Ham's eldest son.

Genesis 10:6-8
1 Chron. 1:8-10
2 Chron. 21:16
Jeremiah 13:23
Habekkuk 3:7
Acts 8:27

Cush was Ham's firstborn son and the grandson of Noah. He is regarded as the ancestor of the Cushites, the Black tribes in the region south of Egypt.

Cush's six sons were named Seba, Havilah, Sabtah, Raamah, Sabtechah, and Nimrod. When God confounded their language at Babylon, Cush gathered his family and traveled south, settling in Africa. He lived in the northeast part of Africa, while his brother Mizraim dwelt nearby in what we now call Egypt.

Cush is sometimes called, The Father of Ethiopia. The ancient name for Ethiopia was Cushi, meaning land of Cush.

Historically there were three types of Ethiopians. The northern type Ethiopian had wooly hair, while their southern cousins had straight hair but there was no genetic difference between these the woolly "Afro's" which was a blessing as it helped shield their heads from the fierce rays of the hot equatorial sun. The Bible mentions a third people called, "Arabian Ethiopians" who were the descendants of Cush who lived in Midian.

NIMROD

(Brave) Cush's youngest son.

Genesis 10:8-10; 11:3-9
1 Chron. 1:10

Nimrod was the son of Cush, grandson of Ham, and the great-grandson of Noah. In Genesis 10:9 he is called "the mighty hunter before God". Although his name is mainly associated with hunting, Nimrod was a mighty conqueror, and a powerful King in the region near the juncture of the Tigris and Euphrates rivers.

Nimrod achieved legendary status as the first empire-builder and the first man to design and build an architectural project, a gigantic tower or "Zigarot" so that man might be able to climb up to heaven.

This tower was built in a city called Babel, which was the starting-point of his empire. He received the required help from the families of Shem and Japeth. God was not pleased, so He confounded their speech so they would not be able to communicate among themselves.

In Micah 5:5-6, Babalon is noted to be the region of Nimrod. Many scholars agree with this and further identify Nimrod as the Babalonian Hero-diety named "Marduk" or "Merodach".

ZIPPORAH
(Beauty) Moses's wife.

Exodus 2:21-22; 4:25-26; 18:2-4
Numbers 12:1
Jeramiah 13:23

Zipporah was an Ethiopian woman, the daughter of a priest of Midian called Jethro, but also known as Hobab or Reuel. He was also the chief of a clan known as Kenites, part of a tribe called Midianites, desert nomads of the northern Sinai peninsula.

Zipporah met Moses during his exile from Egypt, a fugative from a murder charge. She went with her seven sisters to draw water for their father's flock but they were harrassed by herdsmen.

Moses was kind to the women, drove off the bullies, and helped the girls perform further chores. Their father was so impressed with Moses's good manners that he demonstrated his regard for the young hero by giving him Zipporah for a wife.

She bore Moses two sons, named Gershom and Eliezar. The marriage lasted but there were some harsh disagreements between them. One of the conflicts can be attributed to the ritual practice of circumcising their sons. Zipporah was not ready for this, as it was not a custom among her people, and seemed to her to be a barbarous act. Eventually, Moses managed to persuade her that this was an important religious ceremony relating to God's covenant, and she introduced the practice to her tribe.

GERSHOM & ELIEZER
1st & 2nd sons of Moses

Exodus 2:21-22; 4:25; 18:2-4
Judges 18:30

1 Chron. 23:14-17; 24:20; 26:24-25
Habekkuk 3:7

Gershom and Eleizar were the sons of Moses and Zipporah the Cushite. They were born in Midian during their father's fourty-year refuge from Egypt.

Moses named Eleizar (means God is help) in thanksgiving for his deliverance from the wrath of Pharoah. When Moses returned to Egypt to free his enslaved people, his sons did not follow him, but remained in Arabia with their mother and grandfather. They later joined their father after the Exodus from Egypt.

DELILAH
(Poor)

Judges 16:4-20
1 Chron. 1:8-12

Delilah was a Philistine woman who lived in the valley of Sorek. She used her glamorous beauty and feminine wiles to charm Samson into revealing the secret of his great strength. She was a Black woman from the blood line of Mizraim, who also was an ancestor of the Philistines.

SOLOMON
(Peaceful)

Genesis 10:15
2 Sam. 5:14; 12:10-24
1 Kings 1:37-39; 3:5-13; 4:32-34; 11:1; 21:7; 23:13; 24:13; 25:16
2 Chron. 1:13; 2:1; 30:26; 33:7; 35:34
Song of Solomon
Nehamiah 12:45; 13:26

Jeremiah 52:20
Matt. 1:6-7

Solomon was David's tenth son and the successor to his throne. His mother was Bathsheba, the beautiful Black Hittite woman who was a descendant of Ham's forth son, Canaan.

JEZEBEL

Genesis 10:6-15
1 Kings 16:31; 18:4-19; 19:1-2; 21:5-21
2 Kings 9:7-37
1 Chron. 1:13

Jezebel was a beautiful Black woman from Tyre of the Phoenicians (or Zidonians). She was also notoriously evil and the wife of King Ahab of Israel.

Jezebel was the daughter of King Ethball of Tyre, and an ardent worshipper of Baal (or Moloch). She was Queen of Zidon during her father's reign as high priest and king. She was persuasive and very energetic, especially when she wanted things to go her way.

When a proposal of marriage came from King Ahab of Israel, she accepted it, and became his wife and Queen of Israel. This also allowed her to import the Baal cult of paganism into Israel.

QUEEN OF SHEBA

(Oath)

Genesis 10:7
1 Kings 10:1-13
2 Chron. 9:1-12
Matt. 12:42
Luke 11:31

The Queen of Sheba was a royal Black woman from the southern part of the Arabian kingdom. She was from the lineage of Ham's grandson Sheba. After the confusion of tongues at Babel, some of the children of Ham journeyed to the southern part of Arabia and farther south.

Jesus Christ called her by the title of "The Queen of the South" as recorded in, Matthew 12:42 and Luke 11:31.

THE WISE MEN KASPAR, MELCHIOR & BALTHEZAR
Matthew 2:1

The three wise men were Magi or Persian (Arabic) Kings. The sign that they were following was a bright heavenly manifestation, a rare conjunction of the planets Venus, Jupiter, and Saturn.

They believed that Jesus was in some way connected with their culture, and if He were from the Ishmaelian line, rather than the Davidic, this might explain why the lighter-skinned Jews wouldn't allow his family into their nice clean inns.

SIMON THE CYRENE
From North Africa
Matt. 27:32
Mark 15:21
Luke 23:26
Acts 6:9
Romans 16:4-13

Simon was the Black man who helped Jesus carry His cross to Mount Calvary during the crucifixion. He was probably visiting Israel during the trial and crucifixion, because Black Hebrews had their own synagogue in Jerusalem.

SIMEON CALLED NIGER AND LUCIUS THE CYRENE

Acts 6:9; 13:1; 15:1
Romans 15:1; 16:21

Lucius and Simeon were two chosen men of God, both teachers and Prophets of a Church in Antioch. Lucius was from Cyrene which is in the northern part of Africa. Like Simon the Cyrene, he also was a supporter of the Black Hebrew synagogue located in Jerusalem.

Simeon, called Niger was also an African, but from a different area, that which lies along the river Niger. It was these two Africans who ordained both Barnabus and Saul, under the ministry of the Holy Spirit.

[Grimaldi] [Ancient Mexico] [Chinese Dynasties] [African MOORS] [Hannibal] [Black Seminoles] [Origin of White Man] [Black Gods] [Buddha] [JESUS] [Hercules] [Superman]

PLEASE FEEL FREE TO SUBMIT YOUR VIEWS OR COMMENTS ABOUT THIS SITE. REFER IT TO YOUR FRIENDS!!!.

CHAPTER 98

Judge People by Almighty God's Words in His Holy Bible

During a CNN newscast on February 15, 2008 hosted by Mr. Wolf Blitzer was interviewing celebrities concerning their choices of candidates running for President of the United States, Mr. Charles Barkley, a famous basketball player said that he was "Pro Choice" and "Pro Gay" or words to that effect. He went on to say that some socalled Christian tend to cast judgement without the right to do such towards women having abortions and the gay (homosexuality) movements. Almighty God has already made judgements against such secular movements, they are both abominations to Him or despised by Him. Mr. Barkley, I pray, trust and hope that you first, come to Jesus Christ in salvation, attempt to read and understand the Bible and only judge others with Almighty God's written word. God's word, the Bible is the judge for all men. This is a guide and tool for judging all men until the Master Judge, God Almighty appears to judge all men during the end-time events.

Most people of the secular world really don't understand the meaning in the Bible, "Judge Not". As sinners, we don't have the authority to judge others on our own abilities or authorities as such. However, as Christians and Trustees of Almighty God's written word, we can judge anybody by His word with understanding of those words. Christians do have the God given right to rebuke, admonish, correct those who are Christians as well as those who are sinners (secular world).

Matthew 7

1. Judge not, that ye be not judged.
2. For with what judgment ye judge, ye shall be judged: and with what measure ye mete, it shall be measured unto you.
3. And why beholdest thou the mote that is in thy brother's eye, but considerest not the beam that is in thine own eye?
4. Or how wilt thou say to thy brother, Let me cast out the mote out of thine eye; and lo, the beam is in thine own eye?
5. Thou hypocrite, cast out first the beam out of thine own eye; and then shalt thou see clearly to cast out the mote out of thy brother's eye.
6 Give not that which is holy unto the dogs, neither cast your pearls before the swine, lest haply they trample them under their feet, and turn and rend you.
7. Ask, and it shall be given you; seek, and ye shall find; knock, and it shall be opened unto you:
8. for every one that asketh receiveth; and he that seeketh findeth; and to him that knocketh it shall be opened.
9. Or what man is there of you, who, if his son shall ask him for a loaf, will give him a stone;
10. or if he shall ask for a fish, will give him a serpent?
11. If ye then, being evil, know how to give good gifts unto your children, how much more shall your Father who is in heaven give good things to them that ask him?
12. All things therefore whatsoever ye would that men should do unto you, even so do ye also unto them: for this is the law and the prophets.
13. Enter ye in by the narrow gate: for wide is the gate, and broad is the way, that leadeth to destruction, and many are they that enter in thereby.
14. For narrow is the gate, and straitened the way, that leadeth unto life, and few are they that find it.
15. Beware of false prophets, who come to you in sheep's clothing, but inwardly are ravening wolves.

16. By their fruits ye shall know them. Do men gather grapes of thorns, or figs of thistles?
17. Even so every good tree bringeth forth good fruit; but the corrupt tree bringeth forth evil fruit.
18. A good tree cannot bring forth evil fruit, neither can a corrupt tree bring forth good fruit.
19. Every tree that bringeth not forth good fruit is hewn down, and cast into the fire.
20. Therefore by their fruits ye shall know them.
21 Not every one that saith unto me, Lord, Lord, shall enter into the kingdom of heaven; but he that doeth the will of my Father who is in heaven.
22. Many will say to me in that day, Lord, Lord, did we not prophesy by thy name, and by thy name cast out demons, and by thy name do many mighty works? 23. And then will I profess unto them, I never knew you: depart from me, ye that work iniquity.
24. Every one therefore that heareth these words of mine, and doeth them, shall be likened unto a wise man, who built his house upon the rock:
25. and the rain descended, and the floods came, and the winds blew, and beat upon that house; and if fell not: for it was founded upon the rock.
26. And every one that heareth these words of mine, and doeth them not, shall be likened unto a foolish man, who built his house upon the sand:
27. and the rain descended, and the floods came, and the winds blew, and smote upon that house; and it fell: and great was the fall thereof.
28. And it came to pass, when Jesus had finished these words, the multitudes were astonished at his teaching:
29. for he taught them as one having authority, and not as their scribes.

The problem with judging someone is when the judgement is based upon preconceived actions, knowledge and/or reputations of someone and not based upon biblical principles in God's word.

John 7 (KJV)

24. Judge not according to appearance, but judge righteous judgment.

As with judges who sit on court benches are have responsibilities to Almighty God. Their responsibilities to judge is not to man, but to Him. Likewise, when a Christian person render a judgement to someone, it must be by Almighty God's written word. It cannot be by their on intuitions or their own ideas in judgement.

2 Chronicles 19 (KJV)

6. and said to the judges, Consider what ye do: for ye judge not for man, but for Jehovah; and he is with you in the judgment.

CHAPTER **99**

Kennedy's Tragedies Resulted from Bloodline Generational Curses

Unfortunately, the Kennedy family is plagued with generations of curses spanning over many of their generations. It seems as though each of their generations inherits the curses from previous generations. This curse is deep in their bloodlines which needs to be broken, loosed and all ties severed in order for them to be set free. They will have to go back behind their great grand parents' generations to clear up those curses or else the curses will continue with the present generation as well as their future generations.

Exodus 20 (KJV)

1. And God spake all these words, saying,
2. I am the Lord thy God, which have brought thee out of the land of Egypt, out of the house of bondage.
3. Thou shalt have no other gods before me.
4. Thou shalt not make unto thee any graven image, or any likeness of any thing that is in heaven above, or that is in the earth beneath, or that is in the water under the earth.
5. Thou shalt not bow down thyself to them, nor serve them: for I the LORD thy God am a jealous God, visiting the iniquity of the fathers upon the children unto the ***third and fourth generation*** of them that hate me;

CNN.com - "The Tragic Kennedy's" and "Kennedy Misfortune At A Glance"

The Virginia Pilot newspaper, "The Kennedy Curse"

John F., Jr. and wife, Carolyn Bessette were Killed.

John F. Kennedy, Jr's., his wife, Carolyn Bessette Kennedy's and her sister, Lauren Bessette's disappearance in a small plane (Piper Saratoga II) off the Atlantic Coast is the latest in a string of high-profile misfortunes that have torn apart a family -- and often a nation as well.

1941: Rosemary institutionalized.

Rosemary Kennedy, the oldest daughter of Joseph and Rose Fitzgerald Kennedy, is institutionalized because of retardation and failed lobotomy. After the operation, she no longer recognized her father She's now 80 years old.

1944: Joseph, Jr. killed.

Joseph P. Kennedy Jr., a Navy pilot stationed in Great Britain, the oldest son of Joseph and Rose Fitzgerald Kennedy, was killed in a plane crash while he was on a dangerous secret mission, flying a plane full of explosives in 1944 during World War II. He was 29.

1948: Kathleen dies.

Kathleen Kennedy, the fourth Kennedy child and daughter of Joseph and Rose, was flying from Paris to Cannes with Lord Peter Fitzwilliam, whom she intended to marry, when their De Havilland crashed in severe weather. Both were killed in the plane crash. She was 28.

1961: Joseph P., the family patriarch, suffered a debilitating stroke just a few months after his son, John F. Kennedy, was inaugurated as president. He lived until 1969, but never recovered.

1963: Patrick dies.

President John F. Kennedy's son Patrick Bouvier Kennedy was born nearly six weeks premature on August 7, 1963. He dies two days later.

1963: JFK assassinated.

John F. Kennedy, the second Kennedy child of Joseph and Rose and 35th president of the United States, was assassinated by Lee Harvey Oswald in Dallas on November 22, 1963. He was 46.

1964: Edward M. in a plane crash.

Edward M. Kennedy, the youngest Kennedy son and JFK's brother, is critically injured with a broken back in plane crash; an aide, Edward Moss, is killed. Five years later, he drives a car off a bridge on Massachusetts' Chappaquiddick Island after a party. Aide Mary Jo Kopechne is later found dead in submerged car.

1968: Bobby assassinated

Robert F. Kennedy, the third Kennedy child and JFK's brother, who was running for president, was shot by Sirhan Sirhan, just after claiming victory in the California primary in Los Angeles on June 5, 1968. He died twenty hours later. He was 42.

1969: A passenger drowned.

On the night of July 18-19, 1969, Edward M. Kennedy flew to Martha's Vineyard to sail in a regatta and to attend a party with several women who had been Robert's campaign aides. He left with one of them , Mary Jo Kopechne. He drove off a bridge on Chappaquiddick island and she drowned.

1973: A passenger paralyzed.

Joseph Kennedy, Robert's son, is involved in a car accident that leaves a female passenger paralyzed for life.

1973: Edward, Jr., cancer strikes.

Edward and Joan Kennedy's son, Edward Jr., has his right leg amputated because of cancer on November 18, 1973. He recovered and is now a lawyer in New Haven, Conn..

1984: David dies of drug overdose.

Robert and Ethel Kennedy's troubled son, David dies of a drug overdose on April 25, 1984 in a hotel near the family vacation home in Palm Beach, Florida. He had been watching his father on television in 1968 when Robert Kennedy was shot. He was 28.

1986: Patrick sought rehabilitation.

Edward Kennedy's son Patrick -- now a congressman -- seeks treatment for cocaine addiction as a teen-ager.

1991: William's Acquittal of rape charges.

William Kennedy Smith, JFK's nephew, is accused of raping a woman at the family's Palm Beach estate; he is acquitted later that year.

1997: Michael killed in a skiing trip.

Robert and Ethel Kennedy's son Michael, who was accused of having an affair with his family's teen-age baby sitter, is killed in a bizarre skiing accident when he skied into a tree while playing a game of ski football at Aspen, Colorado. His young est sister, Rory, who had planned to marry on Saturday, unsuccessfully gave him mouth-to-mouth resuscitation. He was 39.

2008 Edward Kennedy's cancer diagnosis shocks the nation

May 20: News that Sen. Edward Kennedy has been diagnosed with a cancerous brain tumor sent shockwaves across the country.

NBC's Andrea Mitchell reports. Nightly News

CHAPTER **100**

Lacking in Knowledge, Wisdom and Understanding in Some Churches

Our churches are embedded with hidden curses of ignorance and unbelief. We as Christians are quite ignorant of the things which God, Almighty has proclaimed to us as being **UNCLEAN** and **UNHOLY** such as things that are idols and other gods.

Ezek 44:23 (KJV) "And they shall teach my people the difference between the holy and profane, and cause them to discern between the unclean and the clean."

This IGNORANCE has bred monsters of CURSES. Our biggest problems lie in the fact that many so called pastors (not called by God to Pastor any churches) don't have the knowledge, wisdom nor do they have the understanding to even begin to teach about these things.

Just because a person is selected to serve as a pastor of a local church doesn't mean that God, Almighty had anything to do with the selection process. Many church members believe that once the majority of them make their final selection, then God, Almighty has shown His favor toward them in their selection.

Hosea 4:6 (KJV) "My people are destroyed for lack of knowledge: because thou hast rejected knowledge, I will also reject thee, that thou shalt be no priest to me: seeing thou hast forgotten the law of thy God, **I will also forget thy children**."

Isa 28:9 (KJV) "Whom shall he teach knowledge? and whom shall he make to understand doctrine? them that are weaned from the milk, and drawn from the breasts."

CHAPTER **101**

Lacking in Spiritual Discernment of Some Christians

Rev 2:20 (KJV) "Notwithstanding I have a few things against thee, because thou sufferest that woman Jezebel, which calleth herself a prophetess, to teach and to seduce my servants to commit fornication, and to eat things sacrificed unto idols."

Many Christians are far lacking in spiritual discernment in our churches. Spiritual discernment is one of the blessed gifts God gives us through His Holy Spirit. If you are a babe in Christ, then you will not possess any of the Spiritual gifts. You are, however, filled with God's Holy Spirit, but His Holy Spirit's gifts are not active in your life. You can't speak in another language as the Spirit gives you utterance. You can't even pray in the Spirit to God, Almighty as the Spirit gives you utterance. This is all because you never reached the next level of growth in your spirituality where the mystery of spiritual power lies. Let's put it like this; If you had a car for transportation and your first step was to get it with everything being powered such as windows, doors, windshield wipers, including the engine. You next step in providing yourself a mode of travel is to have this car to provide one of its power blessing to transport you. In order for you to access the engine power of that car, you will have to turn the key on to start the engine which is where the power is to move the vehicle. A number of things will happen once that engine is running. Power is at your disposal. Christians are similar to the car. We have the power at our disposal which is the Holy Spirit, but many of us don't possess the keys to access the power that we need the most. These keys are in the form of Spiritual gifts. We need to move to the next level of our Christianity and seek God for one of the gifts that we desire. Churches really need the blessed gift for discernment of spirits, otherwise they are cursed and defeated.

1 Cor 12:8-10 (KJV) For to one is given by the Spirit the word of wisdom; to another the word of knowledge by the same Spirit;

9. To another faith by the same Spirit; to another the gifts of healing by the same Spirit;
10. To another the working of miracles; to another prophecy; **to another discerning of spirits**; to another divers kinds of tongues; to another the interpretation of tongues:

Heb 5:14 (KJV) "But strong meat belongeth to them that are of full age, even those who by reason of use have their senses exercised to discern both good and evil."

Solomon was a king who walked with God. King Solomon didn't ask for riches, nor did he ask for long life. As a king, he wanted to lead his people with more wisdom, knowledge and understanding which would provide him with the discernment to judge adequately between right and wrong in dealing with his people. God was pleased with King Solomon for seeking discernment. This gift of discernment of spirits should be on the top of your list for spiritual gifts. God, Almighty delights in our seeking more wisdom, knowledge and understanding which will help to provide us with better or enhanced understanding in the discernment of spirits, both good and evil.

1 Ki 3:9 (KJV) "Give therefore thy servant an understanding heart to judge thy people, that I may discern between good and bad: for who is able to judge this thy so great a people?"

1 Ki 3:10 (KJV) "And the speech pleased the Lord, that Solomon had asked this thing."

1 Ki 3:11 (KJV) "And God said unto him, Because thou hast asked this thing, and hast not asked for thyself long life; neither hast asked riches for thyself, nor hast asked the life of thine enemies; but hast asked for thyself understanding to discern judgment;"

CHAPTER **102**

Laws Are Made for the Unrighteous People

Although, Christians are under the dispensation of Grace, sinners are under the dispensation of Law in the Bible. Meaning that they will be judged without the benefit of salvation through Jesus Christ who covers His own by His saving blood. When a sinner violates even one of the laws, them they have violated all of them. They will be punished accordingly. They will be condemned and sentenced to hell fire and damnation throughout eternally.

1 Timothy 1(KJV)

8. But we know that the law is good, if a man use it lawfully;
9. Knowing this, that the law is not made for a righteous man, but for the lawless and disobedient, for the ungodly and for sinners, for unholy and profane, for murderers of fathers and murderers of mothers, for manslayers,
10. For whoremongers, for them that defile themselves with mankind, for menstealers, for liars, for perjured persons, and if there be any other thing that is contrary to sound doctrine;
11. According to the glorious gospel of the blessed God, which was committed to my trust.

CHAPTER **103**

Lawsuits Against Fellow Christians Are Forbidden

On many of the court sessions on the television, many of the people profess to be Christians bringing lawsuits on not only other Christians, but on their relatives as well. We have seen mothers bringing lawsuits against some of their children and we have seen children bringing lawsuits against their parents or other relatives. Some Christians have brought lawsuits against their neighbor Christians as well. Many are probably wondering why their prayers are never answered. Forgiveness is the key. They must have forgiveness in their heart and actually ask Almighty God to first, forgive themselves, then ask Him to forgive that person whom that is at odds with the Christian. Then you must attempt to reconcile your differences and come to a friendly solution without taking that person to a secular court for so-called retribution or pay back, so to speak.

Attempt To Reconcile Your Differences, First

Matthew 5 (KJV)

23. Therefore if thou bring thy gift to the altar, and there rememberest that thy brother hath ought against thee;
24. Leave there thy gift before the altar, and go thy way; first be reconciled to thy brother, and then come and offer thy gift.

25. Agree with thine adversary quickly, whiles thou art in the way with him; lest at any time the adversary deliver thee to the judge, and the judge deliver thee to the officer, and thou be cast into prison.

Forgiveness Is Necessary For Prayers To Be Answered

Mark 11 (KJV)

25. And when ye stand praying, forgive, if ye have ought against any: that your Father also which is in heaven may forgive you your trespasses.
26. But if ye do not forgive, neither will your Father which is in heaven forgive your trespasses.

CHAPTER 104

Laziness and Procrastination Admonishments and Advices

A lazy person and a person who habitually procrastinates will lose many blessings from God. He doesn't like laziness, nor does He like wastefulness. House cleaning is a prime example of laziness and procrastination. Many men and women are guilty of not being diligent in keeping their houses in a state of cleanliness and in order.

Parents who constantly practice and display an attitude of laziness and procrastination will instill this in the rearing and upbringing of their children. This is normally a generational curse which is past on from generation to generation. There will be less and less of prosperity, but more and more of poverty from these two evils.

Lazy is the synonym for sloth (ful). Webster's definition. A). Disinclination to action or labor. B) Spiritual apathy and inactivity

Slothful. Hebrew definition. 7423. remiyah, rem-ee-yaw'; from H7411; remissness, treachery:--deceit (-ful, -fully), false, guile, **idle, slack, slothful**.

Procrastination. Webster's definition. To put off intentionally and habitually. To put off intentionally the doing of something that should be done. Synonym is to delay.

Prov 12:24 (KJV) "The hand of the diligent shall bear rule: but the slothful shall be under tribute."

Prov 12:27 (KJV) "The slothful man roasteth not that which he took in hunting: but the substance of a diligent man is precious."

Prov 15:19 (KJV) "The way of the slothful man is as an hedge of thorns: but the way of the righteous is made plain."

Prov 18:9 (KJV) "He also that is slothful in his work is brother to him that is a great waster."

Prov 19:15 (KJV) "Slothfulness casteth into a deep sleep; and an idle soul shall suffer hunger." Prov 19:24 (KJV) "A slothful man hideth his hand in his bosom, and will not so much as bring it to his mouth again."

Prov 21:25 (KJV) "The desire of the slothful killeth him; for his hands refuse to labour." Prov 21:25 (KJV) "The desire of the slothful killeth him; for his hands refuse to labour."

Prov 24:30 (KJV) "I went by the field of the slothful, and by the vineyard of the man void of understanding;" Prov 24:31 (KJV) "And, lo, it was all grown over with thorns, and nettles had covered the face thereof, and the stone wall thereof was broken down."

Eccl 10:18 (KJV) "By much slothfulness the building decayeth; and through idleness of the hands the house droppeth through." God commands us to be diligent in speed, in being careful and in making haste in our affairs as is defined as our business.

Rom 12:11 (KJV) "Not slothful in business; fervent in spirit; serving the Lord;"

Business. Greek definition. 4710. spoude, spoo-day'; from G4692; "speed", i.e. (by impl.) despatch, eagerness, earnestness:--business, (earnest) care (-fulness), diligence forwardness, haste.

CHAPTER 105

Leaders Chosen by People Are Not Necessarily Almighty God's Choices

Often times people select leaders to certain offices (congress, senate, pastors, governors, mayors, presidents, etc) by their so-called gut feelings, gender, race or intuitions. Their choices are not always consistent with the will of Almighty God. Many Christians are not lead by Almighty God's Holy Spirit as they ought to be.

Some years ago, I, Curtis, was given a revelation and a prophecy about my spiritual life by a Prophet of an Apostalic Denominational Church and by an Elder of a Pentecostal Denominational Church. The Elder and I were in Augusta, Arkansas where I had Eulogized my grandmother. We had gone to his car where he wanted to show me some Melaleuca products. All of a sudden he turned around and got my attention. He said, "God is telling me that He is calling you to become a Pastor!". I replied, "Would you repeat that with my wife present?". So,, he did. He further said, "You will pastor where you are or some place else". At that particular time, our Church, First Mount Zion Baptist Church, Dumfries, Virginia where we were also members where seeking a new pastor. Our sitting pastor was up in age and certainly not preaching God's Word. Since I had a pastoral call on my life, I along with another young preacher, also applied for the position. Our applications were returned to us because we did not have the required credentials of a doctoral degree in our credits. One young man was presented to the congregation with a doctoral degree, irrespective of his lack of spiritual enlightenment or lack of a spiritual calling by Almighty God as both a preacher and pastor. This selected pastor was merely the church's choice and not Almighty God's choice. Without a doubt, I know that I was Almighty God's choice for their pastor. I had already given them a vision (23-27 page booklet) for the rebuilding of the sanctuary (2,000 seat), their present home.

My wife and attended a church service in Stafford, Virginia where we received a prophecy from Prophet Walker from an Apostalic Denominational Church. Here what Prophet Walker told us. "God is telling me that you need to make a transition from where you are attending. He says that there are factions there who are attempting to destroy your anointing.". So, my wife and I took Prophet Walker as word and resigned our membership with First Mount Zion Baptist Church, Dumfries, Virginia.

This is one example where people selected their own pastor without asking Almighty God for whom His choice might be. Another typical example in the bible is when the people wanted a king of their own, they wanted a man named Saul. However, Almighty God's choice for a king was David. God gave the people their choice for a king, then He put that king to a test. He failed the test, then God selected His choice for king, King David as you will see in the following scriptures.

People's (Not God's) Choice For A King, King Saul

1 Samuel 8 (KJV)

4. Then all the elders of Israel gathered themselves together, and came to Samuel unto Ramah,
5. And said unto him, Behold, thou art old, and thy sons walk not in thy ways: now make us a king to judge us like all the nations.

6. But the thing displeased Samuel, when they said, Give us a king to judge us. And Samuel prayed unto the Lord.
7. And the Lord said unto Samuel, Hearken unto the voice of the people in all that they say unto thee: for they have not rejected thee, but they have rejected me, that I should not reign over them.

1 Samuel 12 (KJV)

1. And Samuel said unto all Israel, Behold, I have hearkened unto your voice in all that ye said unto me, and have made a king over you.

Almighty God Puts King Saul To A Test Which He Fails

1 Samuel 15 (KJV)

1. Samuel also said unto Saul, The Lord sent me to anoint thee to be king over his people, over Israel: now therefore hearken thou unto the voice of the words of the Lord.
2. Thus saith the Lord of hosts, I remember that which Amalek did to Israel, how he laid wait for him in the way, when he came up from Egypt.
3. Now go and smite Amalek, and utterly destroy all that they have, and spare them not; but slay both man and woman, infant and suckling, ox and sheep, camel and ass.
4. And Saul gathered the people together, and numbered them in Telaim, two hundred thousand footmen, and ten thousand men of Judah.
5. And Saul came to a city of Amalek, and laid wait in the valley.
6. And Saul said unto the Kenites, Go, depart, get you down from among the Amalekites, lest I destroy you with them: for ye shewed kindness to all the children of Israel, when they came up out of Egypt. So the Kenites departed from among the Amalekites.

7. And Saul smote the Amalekites from Havilah until thou comest to Shur, that is over against Egypt.
8. And he took Agag the king of the Amalekites alive, and utterly destroyed all the people with the edge of the sword.
9. But Saul and the people spared Agag, and the best of the sheep, and of the oxen, and of the fatlings, and the lambs, and all that was good, and would not utterly destroy them: but every thing that was vile and refuse, that they destroyed utterly.
10. Then came the word of the Lord unto Samuel, saying,
11. It repenteth me that I have set up Saul to be king: for he is turned back from following me, and hath not performed my commandments. And it grieved Samuel; and he cried unto the Lord all night.
12. And when Samuel rose early to meet Saul in the morning, it was told Samuel, saying, Saul came to Carmel, and, behold, he set him up a place, and is gone about, and passed on, and gone down to Gilgal.
13. And Samuel came to Saul: and Saul said unto him, Blessed be thou of the Lord: I have performed the commandment of the Lord.
14. And Samuel said, What meaneth then this bleating of the sheep in mine ears, and the lowing of the oxen which I hear?
15. And Saul said, They have brought them from the Amalekites: for the people spared the best of the sheep and of the oxen, to sacrifice unto the Lord thy God; and the rest we have utterly destroyed.
16. Then Samuel said unto Saul, Stay, and I will tell thee what the Lord hath said to me this night. And he said unto him, Say on.
17. And Samuel said, When thou wast little in thine own sight, wast thou not made the head of the tribes of Israel, and the Lord anointed thee king over Israel?

18. And the Lord sent thee on a journey, and said, Go and utterly destroy the sinners the Amalekites, and fight against them until they be consumed.
19. Wherefore then didst thou not obey the voice of the Lord, but didst fly upon the spoil, and didst evil in the sight of the Lord?
20. And Saul said unto Samuel, Yea, I have obeyed the voice of the Lord, and have gone the way which the Lord sent me, and have brought Agag the king of Amalek, and have utterly destroyed the Amalekites.
21. But the people took of the spoil, sheep and oxen, the chief of the things which should have been utterly destroyed, to sacrifice unto the Lord thy God in Gilgal.
22. And Samuel said, Hath the Lord as great delight in burnt offerings and sacrifices, as in obeying the voice of the Lord? Behold, to obey is better than sacrifice, and to hearken than the fat of rams.
23. For rebellion is as the sin of witchcraft, and stubbornness is as iniquity and idolatry. Because thou hast rejected the word of the Lord, he hath also rejected thee from being king.
24. And Saul said unto Samuel, I have sinned: for I have transgressed the commandment of the Lord, and thy words: because I feared the people, and obeyed their voice.
25. Now therefore, I pray thee, pardon my sin, and turn again with me, that I may worship the Lord.
26. And Samuel said unto Saul, I will not return with thee: for thou hast rejected the word of the Lord, and the Lord hath rejected thee from being king over Israel.
27. And as Samuel turned about to go away, he laid hold upon the skirt of his mantle, and it rent.
28. And Samuel said unto him, The Lord hath rent the kingdom of Israel from thee this day, and hath given it to a neighbour of thine, that is better than thou.
29. And also the Strength of Israel will not lie nor repent: for he is not a man, that he should repent.

30. Then he said, I have sinned: yet honour me now, I pray thee, before the elders of my people, and before Israel, and turn again with me, that I may worship the Lord thy God.
31. So Samuel turned again after Saul; and Saul worshipped the Lord.
32. Then said Samuel, Bring ye hither to me Agag the king of the Amalekites. And Agag came unto him delicately. And Agag said, Surely the bitterness of death is past.
33. And Samuel said, As thy sword hath made women childless, so shall thy mother be childless among women. And Samuel hewed Agag in pieces before the Lord in Gilgal.
34. Then Samuel went to Ramah; and Saul went up to his house to Gibeah of Saul.
35. And Samuel came no more to see Saul until the day of his death: nevertheless Samuel **mourned for Saul: and the Lord repented that he had made Saul king over Israel.**

Almighty God Selects His Choice To Be King, King David

David was the Apple of God's eye. He did everything that God commanded him to do and more. When God told him to do something, he did it completely as he was told to do it. David was one of Almighty God's warriors on earth. When God told him to destroy a nation of people, he did just that. As a matter of fact, our Master, Jesus Christ came from that particular bloodline.

1 Samuel 16 (KJV)

1. And the Lord said unto Samuel, How long wilt thou mourn for Saul, seeing I have rejected him from reigning over Israel? fill thine horn with oil, and go, I will send thee to Jesse the Bethlehemite: for I have provided me a king among his sons.
2. And Samuel said, How can I go? if Saul hear it, he will kill

me. And the Lord said, Take an heifer with thee, and say, I am come to sacrifice to the Lord.

3. And call Jesse to the sacrifice, and I will shew thee what thou shalt do: and thou shalt anoint unto me him whom I name unto thee.

4. And Samuel did that which the Lord spake, and came to Bethlehem. And the elders of the town trembled at his coming, and said, Comest thou peaceably?

5. And he said, Peaceably: I am come to sacrifice unto the Lord: sanctify yourselves, and come with me to the sacrifice. And he sanctified Jesse and his sons, and called them to the sacrifice.

6. And it came to pass, when they were come, that he looked on Eliab, and said, Surely the Lord's anointed is before him.

7. But the Lord said unto Samuel, Look not on his countenance, or on the height of his stature; because I have refused him: for the Lord seeth not as man seeth; for man looketh on the outward appearance, but the Lord looketh on the heart.

8. Then Jesse called Abinadab, and made him pass before Samuel. And he said, Neither hath the Lord chosen this.

9. Then Jesse made Shammah to pass by. And he said, Neither hath the Lord chosen this.

10. Again, Jesse made seven of his sons to pass before Samuel. And Samuel said unto Jesse, The Lord hath not chosen these.

11. And Samuel said unto Jesse, Are here all thy children? And he said, There remaineth yet the youngest, and, behold, he keepeth the sheep. And Samuel said unto Jesse, Send and fetch him: for we will not sit down till he come hither.

12. And he sent, and brought him in. Now he was ruddy, and withal of a beautiful countenance, and goodly to look to. And the Lord said, Arise, anoint him: for this is he.

13. Then Samuel took the horn of oil, and anointed him in the midst of his brethren: and the Spirit of the Lord came upon

David from that day forward. So Samuel rose up, and went to Ramah.

14. But the Spirit of the Lord departed from Saul, and an evil spirit from the Lord troubled him.
15. And Saul's servants said unto him, Behold now, an evil spirit from God troubleth thee.
16. Let our lord now command thy servants, which are before thee, to seek out a man, who is a cunning player on an harp: and it shall come to pass, when the evil spirit from God is upon thee, that he shall play with his hand, and thou shalt be well.
17. And Saul said unto his servants, Provide me now a man that can play well, and bring him to me.
18. Then answered one of the servants, and said, Behold, I have seen a son of Jesse the Bethlehemite, that is cunning in playing, and a mighty valiant man, and a man of war, and prudent in matters, and a comely person, and the Lord is with him.
19. Wherefore Saul sent messengers unto Jesse, and said, Send me David thy son, which is with the sheep.
20. And Jesse took an ass laden with bread, and a bottle of wine, and a kid, and sent them by David his son unto Saul.
21. And David came to Saul, and stood before him: and he loved him greatly; and he became his armourbearer.
22. And Saul sent to Jesse, saying, Let David, I pray thee, stand before me; for he hath found favour in my sight.
23. And it came to pass, when the evil spirit from God was upon Saul, that David took an harp, and played with his hand: so Saul was refreshed, and was well, and the evil spirit departed from him.

CHAPTER 106

Leaders on All Continents and All Over the World Bring Curses upon Their Lands

Our leaders, such as kings, queens, presidents, prime ministers and other such top leaders can by merely as results of their orders, directors and/or their approvals, either directly or indirectly, can in effect cause curses upon their lands. Unfortunately, our leaders, such as our Presidents and our Governors have in essence effected the cause of curses upon our lands as for examples:

1. Presidents: Directed wars against Viet Nam, Afghanistan, Iraq and other nations around the world which includes, but limited to the following curses:

- Afghanistan, Iraq and other wars where our troops serve have resulted in many human deaths of America's due to the directions of our leaders,
- Soldiers returning home with mental diseases,
- Soldiers committing suicide,
- Viet Nam military deaths and Viet Nam Veterans contracted Agent Orange resulting in many diseases including Diabetes and many other diseases with many veteran deaths.
- 911 attack on America with the destruction of the Twin-Towers at New York with many human deaths, the attack on the Pentagon with many human deaths, and the attempted attacks on our Nation's Capitol and the White House.

- Hurricane Katrina with resulted human deaths in Louisiana, Mississippi and other surrounding States.
- Droughts, wild fires, tornados and other disasters around the U.S. including those which regularly occur in California and other states are other noticeable curses.
- Global Warming or climate change is a phenomenon created by humans, who by the way have no type of power to change the set seasons or climates this small planet call earth. Only Almighty God can make those changes.

Genesis 1 (KJV)

14. And God said, Let there be lights in the firmament of the heaven to divide the day from the night; and let them be for signs, and for ***seasons***, and for days, and years:

Genesis 8 (KJV)

22. While the earth remaineth, seedtime and harvest, and cold and heat, and summer and winter, and day and night shall not cease.

Psalms 104 (KJV)

19. ***He appointed the moon for seasons***: the sun knoweth his going down.

Daniel 2 (KJV)

21. And ***he changeth the times and the seasons***: he removeth kings, and setteth up kings: he giveth wisdom unto the wise, and knowledge to them that know understanding:

Deuteronomy 11

13. And it shall come to pass, if ye shall hearken diligently unto my commandments which I command you this day, to love the Lord your God, and to serve him with all your heart and with all your soul,
14. That I will give you the rain of your land in his due season, the first rain and the latter rain, that thou mayest gather in thy corn, and thy wine, and thine oil.
15. And I will send grass in thy fields for thy cattle, that thou mayest eat and be full.

Matthew 16 (KJV)

2. He answered and said unto them, When it is evening, ye say, It will be fair weather: for the sky is red.
3. And in the morning, It will be foul weather to day: for the sky is red and lowring. O ye hypocrites, ye can discern the face of the sky; but can ye not discern the signs of the times?

- By allowing capital punishment to be carried out in states around the U.S.
- By allowing abortions to be performed.
- By allowing states to take prayer out of the schools.
- Directing and allowing immigration reform with underlying racism, prejudices, and the fear of political takeover is at the root of their decisions as they are themselves White European American Immigrates with the exception of Native Americans (Indians, original Americans).
- unjust imprisonments of minorities with numbers far greater than those of White European Americans who are the majority U.S. Citizens.
- Oklahoma bombing of a federal building by a home-grown terrorist.

- Shoe bombing airplane home-grown terrorist.
- Anthrax and other deadly chemicals through U.S. Postal Services by home-grown terrorists.
- School massacres by home-grown terrorist such as what happened at Columbine, Virginia Tech and other schools across the United States of America.
- By allowing the performance of gay (homosexual), same sex marriages of persons which are abominations to Almighty God.
- By allowing the performance of civil union marriages of gay (homosexuals), same sex persons which are abominations to Almighty God.
- By denying off-shore drilling and other drilling for oil and natural gas. At least two (2) states: Arkansas and Louisiana are sitting on rivers of oil and natural gas resources, but no one is sounding the alarm of these natural resources on America's own lands.

2. Governors can also bring curses to their states:

- By allowing the execution/capital punishment of convicted humans which results in the death of these humans. These Governors/Leaders will now have human blood on their hands, whether they actually participated in the executions or not.
- Also who allowing abortions to be performed in their states, legally.
- - California's and Massachuset's Governors - By Allowing the performance of gay (homosexual), same sex marriages of persons which are abominations (hatred) of Almighty God.
- By allowing the performance of civil union marriages of gay (homosexuals), same sex persons which are abominations (hatred) of Almighty God.
- By directing schools to take prayer out of their school classrooms and school buildings.

These sins bring on many curses not only upon their citizens, but to their lands as well.

King Saul in the below mentioned scriptures depicts what can happen when a leader has the zeal to commit war against another nation, thereby causing blood to be upon his or her hands and their households.

2 Samuel 21 (KJV)

1. Then there was a famine in the days of David three years, year after year; and David inquired of the Lord. And the Lord answered, It is for Saul, and for his bloody house, because he slew the Gibeonites.
2. And the king called the Gibeonites, and said unto them; (Now the Gibeonites were not of the children of Israel, but of the remnant of the Amorites; and the children of Israel had sworn unto them: and Saul sought to slay them in his zeal to the children of Israel and Judah.)
3. Wherefore David said unto the Gibeonites, What shall I do for you? and wherewith shall I make the atonement, that ye may bless the inheritance of the Lord?
4. And the Gibeonites said unto him, We will have no silver nor gold of Saul, nor of his house; neither for us shalt thou kill any man in Israel. And he said, What ye shall say, that will I do for you.
5. And they answered the king, The man that consumed us, and that devised against us that we should be destroyed from remaining in any of the coasts of Israel,
6. Let seven men of his sons be delivered unto us, and we will hang them up unto the Lord in Gibeah of Saul, whom the Lord did choose. And the king said, I will give them.
7. But the king spared Mephibosheth, the son of Jonathan the son of Saul, because of the Lord's oath that was between them, between David and Jonathan the son of Saul.

8. But the king took the two sons of Rizpah the daughter of Aiah, whom she bare unto Saul, Armoni and Mephibosheth; and the five sons of Michal the daughter of Saul, whom she brought up for Adriel the son of Barzillai the Meholathite:
9. And he delivered them into the hands of the Gibeonites, and they hanged them in the hill before the Lord: and they fell all seven together, and were put to death in the days of harvest, in the first days, in the beginning of barley harvest.

King David's Sins Caused 70,000 Deaths

2 Samuel 24 (KJV)

Almighty God Commanded King David To Number Israel

1. And again the anger of the Lord was kindled against Israel, and he moved David against them to say, Go, number Israel and Judah.

King David Disobeyed Almighty God And Numbered The Tribes, Instead

2. For the king said to Joab the captain of the host, which was with him, Go now through all the tribes of Israel, from Dan even to Beersheba, and number ye the people, that I may know the number of the people.
3. And Joab said unto the king, Now the Lord thy God add unto the people, how many soever they be, an hundredfold, and that the eyes of my lord the king may see it: but why doth my lord the king delight in this thing?
4. Notwithstanding the king's word prevailed against Joab, and against the captains of the host. And Joab and the captains of the host went out from the presence of the king, to number the people of Israel.

5. And they passed over Jordan, and pitched in Aroer, on the right side of the city that lieth in the midst of the river of Gad, and toward Jazer:
6. Then they came to Gilead, and to the land of Tahtimhodshi; and they came to Danjaan, and about to Zidon,
7. And came to the strong hold of Tyre, and to all the cities of the Hivites, and of the Canaanites: and they went out to the south of Judah, even to Beersheba.
8. So when they had gone through all the land, they came to Jerusalem at the end of nine months and twenty days.
9. And Joab gave up the sum of the number of the people unto the king: and there were in Israel eight hundred thousand valiant men that drew the sword; and the men of Judah were five hundred thousand men.
10. And David's heart smote him after that he had numbered the people. And David said unto the Lord, I have sinned greatly in that I have done: and now, I beseech thee, O Lord, take away the iniquity of thy servant; for I have done very foolishly.
11. For when David was up in the morning, the word of the Lord came unto the prophet Gad, David's seer, saying,
12. Go and say unto David, Thus saith the Lord, I offer thee three things; choose thee one of them, that I may do it unto thee.
13. So Gad came to David, and told him, and said unto him, Shall seven years of famine come unto thee in thy land? or wilt thou flee three months before thine enemies, while they pursue thee? or that there be three days' pestilence in thy land? now advise, and see what answer I shall return to him that sent me.
14. And David said unto Gad, I am in a great strait: let us fall now into the hand of the Lord; for his mercies are great: and let me not fall into the hand of man.

Israel Suffered Pestilences Which Killed 70,000 Souls

15. So the Lord sent a pestilence upon Israel from the morning even to the time appointed: and there died of the people from Dan even to Beersheba seventy thousand men.
16. And when the angel stretched out his hand upon Jerusalem to destroy it, the Lord repented him of the evil, and said to the angel that destroyed the people, It is enough: stay now thine hand. And the angel of the Lord was by the threshingplace of Araunah the Jebusite.
17. And David spake unto the Lord when he saw the angel that smote the people, and said, Lo, I have sinned, and I have done wickedly: but these sheep, what have they done? let thine hand, I pray thee, be against me, and against my father's house.
18. And Gad came that day to David, and said unto him, Go up, rear an altar unto the Lord in the threshingfloor of Araunah the Jebusite.
19. And David, according to the saying of Gad, went up as the Lord commanded.
20. And Araunah looked, and saw the king and his servants coming on toward him: and Araunah went out, and bowed himself before the king on his face upon the ground.
21. And Araunah said, Wherefore is my lord the king come to his servant? And David said, To buy the threshingfloor of thee, to build an altar unto the Lord, that the plague may be stayed from the people.
22. And Araunah said unto David, Let my lord the king take and offer up what seemeth good unto him: behold, here be oxen for burnt sacrifice, and threshing instruments and other instruments of the oxen for wood.
23. All these things did Araunah, as a king, give unto the king. And Araunah said unto the king, The Lord thy God accept thee.
24. And the king said unto Araunah, Nay; but I will surely buy it

of thee at a price: neither will I offer burnt offerings unto the Lord my God of that which doth cost me nothing. So David bought the threshingfloor and the oxen for fifty shekels of silver.

25. And David built there an altar unto the Lord, and offered burnt offerings and peace offerings. So the Lord was intreated for the land, and the plague was stayed from Israel.

CHAPTER **107**

Liars and False Accuseres - Doomed for Hell's Fire and Brimstone

I, (Curtis) have had my share of experiences with lying preachers and deacons. It is quite shocking to know that some of these liars are pastors and some are ministers of the gospel, so they say. They will readily tell lies which will fit their situations at those specific times. This is their way of covering up their rear ends when the situation gets too hot for them to handle.

Prov 17:4 (KJV) "A wicked doer giveth heed to false lips; and a liar giveth ear to a naughty tongue."

1 John 2:4 (KJV) "He that saith, I know him, and keepeth not his commandments, is a liar, and the truth is not in him."

Col 3:9 (KJV) "Lie not one to another, seeing that ye have put off the old man with his deeds;"

Rev 21:8 (KJV) "But the fearful, and unbelieving, and the abominable, and murderers, and whoremongers, and sorcerers, and idolaters, and all liars, shall have their part in the lake which burneth with fire and brimstone: which is the second death."

CHAPTER **108**

Living on Unclean or Cursed Houses and Lands Are Dangerous

If you know that you are in fact living on unclean or cursed land, then you in fact have brought a curse on yourself, your family and quite possibly curse on your future generations to come. Examples, say that the land you are living on: was previously lived on or owned by Satanist, human and/or animal sacrifices had been conducted on the property, fortune teller(s) occupied the property, Satanist held their meetings on the property, masons and/or Eastern Stars held their meetings there, Jehovah's Witnesses held their meetings there, Moslems held there meetings there, and/or any other such meetings or gatherings of religions and gods dedicated to Satan. Your mere association with the land will bring curses into your lives.

Living In Unclean Or Cursed Housing

Unfortunately many people are presently living in unclean housing such as just plain drug houses, crack cocaine housing, prostitute housing, housing for crime figures, murders, thieves and the like. These are all sources of curses. Washington, D.C. is a city with prime examples of cursed housing. The crime rate is quite high where it is mostly black on black crime with murders, fire arms shootings, stabbings, highjackings, burglaries, robberies and other such crimes against humanity. But, Washington, D.C. is a huge curse all by itself. These curses are not only across all human boundaries, but are at the seat of power in our nations Capital city. You will see in a later chapter as we deal with the plagues of curses with demonic symbolic street designed overtones in Washington, D.C..

One author thinks that black on black crime in Washington, D.C. is an inherited curse from Africa. Nonsense, the majority of blacks living the United States of America didn't come from Africa. However, there may be some native Africans living in and around Washington, D.C. who have brought many generational curses with them to America. Many black people are characterized and stigmatized as African Americans were born right here in America for centuries. Many are mixed with native Indians, Caucasians, Asians, as well as many other races and Nationalities of people. Black people probably share in wider and diverse group of bloodlines in the American mixing bowl than any other race of people. With this in mind, blacks share in a wider and diverse amount of curses from these varied races and Nationalities. Now, some things may have been carried over from generation to generation, but the bottom line is that our Nations Capital city is cursed with normally unseeable curses which are not likely to be seen through our normal senses or our naked eye. The city is designed with demonic symbolism with distinct Masonic touches to it. We will explain this later in another chapter.

1 Ki 9:7 (KJV) "Then will I cut off Israel out of the land which I have given them; and this house, which I have hallowed for my name, will I cast out of my sight; and Israel shall be a proverb and a byword among all people:"

Exo 20:3-5 (KJV) Thou shalt have no other gods before me.

4. Thou shalt not make unto thee any graven image, or any likeness of any thing that is in heaven above, or that is in the earth beneath, or that is in the water under the earth:
5. Thou shalt not bow down thyself to them, nor serve them: for I the LORD thy God am a jealous God, visiting the iniquity of the

fathers upon the children unto the third and fo Deuteronomy 28 (KJV)

Deuteronomy 28 (KJV)

14. And thou shalt not go aside from any of the words which I command thee this day, to the right hand, or to the left, to go after other gods to serve them.
15. But it shall come to pass, if thou wilt not hearken unto the voice of the Lord thy God, to observe to do all his commandments and his statutes which I command thee this day; that all these curses shall come upon thee, and overtake thee:
16. Cursed shalt thou be in the city, and cursed shalt thou be in the field.
17. Cursed shall be thy basket and thy store.
18. Cursed shall be the fruit of thy body, and the fruit of thy land, the increase of thy kine, and the flocks of thy sheep.
19. Cursed shalt thou be when thou comest in, and cursed shalt thou be when thou goest out.
20. The Lord shall send upon thee cursing, vexation, and rebuke, in all that thou settest thine hand unto for to do, until thou be destroyed, and until thou perish quickly; because of the wickedness of thy doings, whereby thou hast forsaken me.
21. The Lord shall make the pestilence cleave unto thee, until he have consumed thee from off the land, whither thou goest to possess it.
22. The Lord shall smite thee with a consumption, and with a fever, and with an inflammation, and with an extreme burning, and with the sword, and with blasting, and with mildew; and they shall pursue thee until thou perish.
23. And thy heaven that is over thy head shall be brass, and the earth that is under thee shall be iron.
24. The Lord shall make the rain of thy land powder and dust:

from heaven shall it come down upon thee, until thou be destroyed.

25. The Lord shall cause thee to be smitten before thine enemies: thou shalt go out one way against them, and flee seven ways before them: and shalt be removed into all the kingdoms of the earth.
26. And thy carcase shall be meat unto all fowls of the air, and unto the beasts of the earth, and no man shall fray them away.
27. The Lord will smite thee with the botch of Egypt, and with the emerods, and with the scab, and with the itch, whereof thou canst not be healed.
28. The Lord shall smite thee with madness, and blindness, and astonishment of heart:
29. And thou shalt grope at noonday, as the blind gropeth in darkness, and thou shalt not prosper in thy ways: and thou shalt be only oppressed and spoiled evermore, and no man shall save thee.
30. Thou shalt betroth a wife, and another man shall lie with her: thou shalt build an house, and thou shalt not dwell therein: thou shalt plant a vineyard, and shalt not gather the grapes thereof.
31. Thine ox shall be slain before thine eyes, and thou shalt not eat thereof: thine ass shall be violently taken away from before thy face, and shall not be restored to thee: thy sheep shall be given unto thine enemies, and thou shalt have none to rescue them.
32. Thy sons and thy daughters shall be given unto another people, and thine eyes shall look, and fail with longing for them all the day long; and there shall be no might in thine hand.
33. The fruit of thy land, and all thy labours, shall a nation which thou knowest not eat up; and thou shalt be only oppressed and crushed alway:
34. So that thou shalt be mad for the sight of thine eyes which thou shalt see.

35. The Lord shall smite thee in the knees, and in the legs, with a sore botch that cannot be healed, from the sole of thy foot unto the top of thy head.
36. The Lord shall bring thee, and thy king which thou shalt set over thee, unto a nation which neither thou nor thy fathers have known; and there shalt thou serve other gods, wood and stone.
37. And thou shalt become an astonishment, a proverb, and a byword, among all nations whither the Lord shall lead thee.
38. Thou shalt carry much seed out into the field, and shalt gather but little in; for the locust shall consume it.
39. Thou shalt plant vineyards, and dress them, but shalt neither drink of the wine, nor gather the grapes; for the worms shall eat them.
40. Thou shalt have olive trees throughout all thy coasts, but thou shalt not anoint thyself with the oil; for thine olive shall cast his fruit.
41. Thou shalt beget sons and daughters, but thou shalt not enjoy them; for they shall go into captivity.
42. All thy trees and fruit of thy land shall the locust consume.
43. The stranger that is within thee shall get up above thee very high; and thou shalt come down very low.
44. He shall lend to thee, and thou shalt not lend to him: he shall be the head, and thou shalt be the tail.
45. Moreover all these curses shall come upon thee, and shall pursue thee, and overtake thee, till thou be destroyed; because thou hearkenedst not unto the voice of the Lord thy God, to keep his commandments and his statutes which he commanded thee:
46. And they shall be upon thee for a sign and for a wonder, and upon thy seed for ever.
47. Because thou servedst not the Lord thy God with joyfulness, and with gladness of heart, for the abundance of all things;

48. Therefore shalt thou serve thine enemies which the Lord shall send against thee, in hunger, and in thirst, and in nakedness, and in want of all things: and he shall put a yoke of iron upon thy neck, until he have destroyed thee.
49. The Lord shall bring a nation against thee from far, from the end of the earth, as swift as the eagle flieth; a nation whose tongue thou shalt not understand;
50. A nation of fierce countenance, which shall not regard the person of the old, nor shew favour to the young:
51. And he shall eat the fruit of thy cattle, and the fruit of thy land, until thou be destroyed: which also shall not leave thee either corn, wine, or oil, or the increase of thy kine, or flocks of thy sheep, until he have destroyed thee.
52. And he shall besiege thee in all thy gates, until thy high and fenced walls come down, wherein thou trustedst, throughout all thy land: and he shall besiege thee in all thy gates throughout all thy land, which the Lord thy God hath given thee.
53. And thou shalt eat the fruit of thine own body, the flesh of thy sons and of thy daughters, which the Lord thy God hath given thee, in the siege, and in the straitness, wherewith thine enemies shall distress thee:
54. So that the man that is tender among you, and very delicate, his eye shall be evil toward his brother, and toward the wife of his bosom, and toward the remnant of his children which he shall leave:
55. So that he will not give to any of them of the flesh of his children whom he shall eat: because he hath nothing left him in the siege, and in the straitness, wherewith thine enemies shall distress thee in all thy gates.
56. The tender and delicate woman among you, which would not adventure to set the sole of her foot upon the ground for delicateness and tenderness, her eye shall be evil toward the husband of her bosom, and toward her son, and toward her daughter,

57. And toward her young one that cometh out from between her feet, and toward her children which she shall bear: for she shall eat them for want of all things secretly in the siege and straitness, wherewith thine enemy shall distress thee in thy gates.
58. If thou wilt not observe to do all the words of this law that are written in this book, that thou mayest fear this glorious and fearful name, The Lord Thy God;
59. Then the Lord will make thy plagues wonderful, and the plagues of thy seed, even great plagues, and of long continuance, and sore sicknesses, and of long continuance.
60. Moreover he will bring upon thee all the diseases of Egypt, which thou wast afraid of; and they shall cleave unto thee.
61. Also every sickness, and every plague, which is not written in the book of this law, them will the Lord bring upon thee, until thou be destroyed.
62. And ye shall be left few in number, whereas ye were as the stars of heaven for multitude; because thou wouldest not obey the voice of the Lord thy God.
63. And it shall come to pass, that as the Lord rejoiced over you to do you good, and to multiply you; so the Lord will rejoice over you to destroy you, and to bring you to nought; and ye shall be plucked from off the land whither thou goest to possess it.
64. And the Lord shall scatter thee among all people, from the one end of the earth even unto the other; and there thou shalt serve other gods, which neither thou nor thy fathers have known, even wood and stone.
65. And among these nations shalt thou find no ease, neither shall the sole of thy foot have rest: but the Lord shall give thee there a trembling heart, and failing of eyes, and sorrow of mind:
66. And thy life shall hang in doubt before thee; and thou shalt

fear day and night, and shalt have none assurance of thy life:

67. In the morning thou shalt say, Would God it were even! and at even thou shalt say, Would God it were morning! for the fear of thine heart wherewith thou shalt fear, and for the sight of thine eyes which thou shalt see.
68. And the Lord shall bring thee into Egypt again with ships, by the way whereof I spake unto thee, thou shalt see it no more again: and there ye shall be sold unto your enemies for bondmen and bondwomen, and no man shall buy you.

CHAPTER 109

Marriages, Out-of-Wedlock Births Are Bloodline Curses in America

Unfortunately, many boys, girls, women and men are guilty of having sexual intercourse resulting in pregnancies of the females. These scenarios are very prevalent in all races, creeds, religions and nationalities all over the world. We can't just point our fingers at specific groups of people. All are guilty of those sins. There are very few virgins who have abstained from having sexual intercourse prior to their marriage. The male gender is equally to blame along with the females.

Ezekiel 16 (KJV)

26. Thou hast also committed fornication with the Egyptians thy neighbours, great of flesh; and hast increased thy whoredoms, to provoke me to anger.

Acts 15 (KJV)

20. But that we write unto them, that they abstain from pollutions of idols, and from fornication, and from things strangled, and from blood.
29. That ye abstain from meats offered to idols, and from blood, and from things strangled, and from fornication: from which if ye keep yourselves, ye shall do well. Fare ye well.

Acts 21 (KJV)

25. As touching the Gentiles which believe, we have written and concluded that they observe no such thing, save only that they keep themselves from things offered to idols, and from blood, and from strangled, and from fornication.

Romans 1 (KJV)

17. For therein is the righteousness of God revealed from faith to faith: as it is written, The just shall live by faith.
18. For the wrath of God is revealed from heaven against all ungodliness and unrighteousness of men, who hold the truth in unrighteousness;
19. Because that which may be known of God is manifest in them; for God hath shewed it unto them.
20. For the invisible things of him from the creation of the world are clearly seen, being understood by the things that are made, even his eternal power and Godhead; so that they are without excuse:
21. Because that, when they knew God, they glorified him not as God, neither were thankful; but became vain in their imaginations, and their foolish heart was darkened.
22. Professing themselves to be wise, they became fools,
23. And changed the glory of the uncorruptible God into an image made like to corruptible man, and to birds, and fourfooted beasts, and creeping things.
24. Wherefore God also gave them up to uncleanness through the lusts of their own hearts, to dishonour their own bodies between themselves:
25. Who changed the truth of God into a lie, and worshipped and served the creature more than the Creator, who is blessed for ever. Amen.

26. For this cause God gave them up unto vile affections: for even their women did change the natural use into that which is against nature:
27. And likewise also the men, leaving the natural use of the woman, burned in their lust one toward another; men with men working that which is unseemly, and receiving in themselves that recompence of their error which was meet.
28. And even as they did not like to retain God in their knowledge, God gave them over to a reprobate mind, to do those things which are not convenient;
29. Being filled with all unrighteousness, fornication, wickedness, covetousness, maliciousness; full of envy, murder, debate, deceit, malignity; whisperers,
30. Backbiters, haters of God, despiteful, proud, boasters, inventors of evil things, disobedient to parents,
31. Without understanding, covenantbreakers, without natural affection, implacable, unmerciful:
32. Who knowing the judgment of God, that they which commit such things are worthy of death, not only do the same, but have pleasure in them that do them.

References by: Clarence Page

News & Notes, September 27, 2005 · Forty years ago, a government report on the state of the black family in America warned that almost one out of four black children were born to unmarried mothers. Recent figures suggest that now, almost 70 percent of black children are born out of wedlock.

The Breakdown of the Black Family
References by: Lana Hampton

One of the most tragic developments to emerge within the American black community is the steady erosion of the black family. With a high percentage of teen pregnancies and 70% of all black families being headed by a woman, the traditional black family, which has historically been a strength of the black community, is now in danger of extinction.

The U.S. has the highest rate of teenage pregnancies and births in the western industrialized world, costing us 7 billion dollars annually. Each year, almost 1 million teenage women--10% of all women aged 15-19 and 19% of those who have had sexual intercourse--become pregnant. One out of three Americans is born out-of-wedlock. The stats are 70% for blacks and 45% for Hispanics.

According to the Population Resource Center, out-of-wedlock teen births differ greatly by race. In 1995, 94 percent of black teens who gave birth were unmarried whereas 72 percent and 75 percent of births to white and Hispanic teens respectively were out-of-wedlock. The largest increases in out-of-wedlock births have been among white teens. Teens account for 31% of all out-of-wedlock births.

Teen mothers:

- are more likely to give birth to babies with a low birth weight
- are more likely to have children who perform poorly in school
- are less likely to have children who complete high school (only 1/3 of those receive a diploma) ~are much less likely to have obtained a college degree by the age of 30 (1.5% graduate from college) ~are much more likely to wind up on welfare (80% will look to the government to support their child(ren) and themselves).
- son's are more likely to wind up in prison
- daughter's are more likely to become teen mothers themselves
- are more likely to have children in special education (there's

a higher percentage of developmental disabilities in babies born to teen mothers).

How has this happened? Why in the black community, a community who historically has had socially conservative views? One obvious explanation is the decline in marriage rates. This is across the board, racially, but for blacks this decline is even more pronounced.

One widespread theory is that the government pays girls to get pregnant. Of course that's not their intent, but it is, in fact, what the government does. If a teen gets pregnant, she receives welfare. If not outright encouragement, it's definitely positive reinforcement.
Additionally, some teens lack education, regarding pregnancy, which should come from the family. Bu, we know we can't always rely on parents to do good parenting, but it's way past time for some parents to start. Boredom, too, is one reason given when teens are asked why they got pregnant.

Many poor black teens have low self-esteem, and therefore have little selfrespect. Many teens feel that they have few options in life. In poverty stricken, inner-city neighborhoods, there are few positive role models for children.

Rebellion has also been cited as a reason some teens become pregnant. What has also been vocalized, by teens, is the need for love - love, in this case, from the baby. Peer pressure also has a large impact on teen pregnancy. When positive social support is missing, teens have an assortment of negative influences to choose from.

So, what do we do about this dilemma? I recommend Abstinence Education programs. They have been proven to be effective. Washington policymakers should be aware of the consequences of early sexual activity, the undesirable contents of conventional "safe sex" education programs, and the findings of the professional literature concerning the effectiveness of genuine abstinence programs. More on Abstinence Education Programs.

As previously stated, the decline of people getting married has been named as one reason for a higher rate of out-of-wedlock births. By the age of 30, 81% of white women marry, 77% of Hispanic women and only 52% of black women.

One explanation for the decline in marriage among black women is the small pool of marriageable black men. Joblessness, incarceration and higher mortality are the principal reasons for the small pool. Another theory states that the legacy of slavery, where blacks were frequently separated from their families, has carried over to the present day. The problem with this theory is that marriage rates for blacks were high, like everyone else's until the 1960s, so how can they explain the long period of time when blacks did marry in large numbers?

One of the most cited and respected theories comes from an unlikely source Daniel Patrick Moynihan, the senator from New York, who is now deceased. Even though Moynihan was a Democrat, his legendary Moynihan Report, is often cited by conservatives when discussing urban policy. The report was based on studies done by black sociologist, Franklin Frazier. The Moynihan Report, subtitled, The Case for National Action, cited current social programs, such as welfare, as the reason for problems in the black community - problems such as out-of-wedlock births and lower marriage rates. The report predicted, with accuracy, that welfare would begin the destruction of the American black family.

In 1965 many, on the left, tried to discredit the report calling it "cold and scientific." They preferred a more feel-good type of discourse. This report had a strategy to keep black families in tact and yet many on the left rejected it.

In addition to Moynihan's input regarding the breakdown of the black family, George Gilder, a Fellow at Harvard, began inquiries into the causes of poverty. In his well known book, Invisible Man, Gilder states:

> The release of large numbers of young men from the bonds and disciplines of marriage and family, says Gilder, always leads to a threat to social stability. Men find structure and purpose and become responsible men through marriage and work. Without a stable family order, in which adult men civilize the young men, terror necessarily rules. No array of daycare centers, police powers, social welfare agencies, psychiatric or drug clinics, special schools and prisons, can have any significant effect. When men are deprived of any family role and robbed of male discipline, they will turn to the perennial male equalizers, that is, greater physical strength and aggression.

The chief cause of poverty, says Gilder, is the utter failure of socialization of young men through marriage. Yet nearly all the attention, subsidies, training opportunities and so-called therapies of the welfare state focus on helping women function without marriage. The welfare state attacks the problem of the absent husband by rendering him entirely superfluous. In the black community, we see the consequences of these malevolent social policies on a monumental scale. (Courtesy of Issues & Views)

Then there's the Radical Feminist approach which takes this view: Despite the reasonable and limited scope of the President's proposal, it should come as no surprise that radical feminists view it with great alarm. Denunciation of the very idea of promoting healthy marriage has been widespread and shrill in the conventional mode of radical feminists:

> NOW President Kim Gandy declared: "I think promoting marriage as a goal in and of itself is misguided." She added that

> "Finding a man--the [Bush] administration's approved ticket out of poverty--is terrible public policy. Marrying women off to get them out of poverty is not only backward, it is insulting to women." More on the Radical Feminist approach.

So, what do we do about the decimation of the traditional black family? Well, the Bush Administration has implemented sound policy aimed at strengthening the family. The Department of Health and Human Services, under the Bush administration, has developed a special initiative to support and strengthen the roles of fathers in families. This initiative is guided by the following principles:

- All fathers can be important contributors to the well-being of their children.
- Parents are partners in raising their children, even when they do not live in the same household.
- The roles fathers play in families are diverse and related to cultural and community norms.
- Men should receive the education and support necessary to prepare them for the responsibility of parenthood.
- Government can encourage and promote father involvement through its programs and through its own workforce policies.

The Department's activities account for those circumstances under which increased involvement by a father or a mother may not be in the best interest of the child. This is true for a small number of children, however. The Department strongly supports family preservation and reunification efforts when they do not risk the safety of the child.

As part of welfare reauthorization George Bush plans on following through with the Healthy Marriage Initiative. Recognizing the widespread benefits of marriage, both for individuals and for society, the federal welfare reform legislation that was enacted in

1996 set forth clear goals to increase the number of two-parent families and reduce out-of-wedlock childbearing.

According to..............,For decades, radical feminists depicted marriage as an oppressive institution that was injurious to women and children. In reality, facts show exactly the opposite: In general, marriage has profoundly beneficial effects on women, children, and men.

Foremost is the positive impact of marriage in alleviating poverty among mothers and children. On average, a mother who gives birth and raises a child outside of marriage is seven times more likely to live in poverty than is a mother who raises her children within a stable married family.Over 80 percent of long-term child poverty in the United States (where a child is poor for more than half of his or her life) occurs in never-married or broken households. Moreover, the economic benefits of marriage are not limited to the middle class; some 70 percent of nevermarried mothers would be able to escape poverty if they were married to the father of their children. More on the benefits of marriage.

The black family, historically, has been the foundation of the black community that and the church. We need to work on rebuilding our families. I don't believe it is too late to turn this situation around. It will, however, take an effort from those of us who support family to get this message out to those who need it most. Sound policy and sound practices work every time.

CHAPTER **110**

Marriage Is Biblically Honored Only Between a Male and a Female

There is a growing phenomenon of marriages or civil unions among same sex people. Many of these United States have changed there laws and regulations to legally allow same sex marriages and civil unions of these same sex couples without recognizing that those actions are an abomination to Almighty God. Immorality is at an all time high in America. These actions of immorality is a great curse upon these United States, her possessions and her territories as well. We can attribute these sins to global warming and climate change over this little world. Although, we can improve our environment by reducing air pollution and such, but this has changed our climate, nor is it causing global warming as been wrongly suggested by our leaders.

Male (Man) And Female (Woman) Marriage.

Heterosexuals. The union of two couples was originated by God with the first marriage of our father Adam and our mother Eve. This was a male and a female bonded together in what is called a marriage.

Genesis 2:21-24 (KJV), "21) And the Lord God caused a deep sleep to fall upon Adam, and he slept: and he took one of his ribs, and closed up the flesh instead thereof;

22. And the rib, which the Lord God had taken from man, made he a woman, and brought her unto the man.
23. And Adam said, This is now bone of my bones, and flesh of my flesh: she shall be called Woman, because she was taken out of Man.
24. Therefore shall a man leave his father and his mother, and shall cleave unto his wife: and they shall be one flesh." Christ went on to reiterate what His Father has previously said in the following verses of scripture:

Matthew 19:6 (NKJV), "So then, they are no longer two but one flesh. Therefore what God has joined together, let not man separate."

In addition to becoming one body, we Christians become one spirit as the Holy Ghost dwells in us.

1 Corinthians 6:17 & 19 (KJV), "But he that is joined unto the Lord is one spirit.

19. What? Know ye not that your body is the temple of the Holy Ghost which is in you, which ye have of God, and ye are not your own?"

Hebrews 13:4 (KJV), "Marriage is honorable in all, and the bed undefiled: but whoremongers and adulterers God will judge."

Homosexual or Gay Marriages.

Same sex marriages. So called marriage between two (2) females or two (2) males are not biblically ordained marriages. They are satanic catastrophes and are abominations to God.

Romans 1:26-27 (Living), "26) That is why God let go of them and let them do all these evil things, so that even their women turned against God's natural plan for them and indulged in sex with each other.

27. And the men, instead of having a normal sex relationship with women, burned with lust for each other, men doing shameful things with other men and, as a result, getting paid within their own souls with the penalty they so richly deserved."

This type of so called marriage shouldn't be condoned or honored as such. God didn't ordain that two (2) males, Adam and Sam should marry as one, neither did he ordain that two (2) women, Eve and Evelyn should marry as one in marriage. These are in fact demonic marriages of Satan.

CHRISTIAN AND WORLDLY MARRIAGES.

There are commonly two types of marriages which can be characterized as secular (worldly) and Christian marriages. Christian marriages are those institutions where both couples are in fact Christians. It is also imperative that the officiate or the person performing the rights of marriage be a Christian as well. All must be on one accord with one mind and one Spirit (Holy Spirit) when Christianity is involved.

Secular Marriages

A secular marriage falls into the all others category. These are couples who aren't confessed Christians. They can not claim the rights to God's blessings through our Savior Jesus Christ. Although they may have a Christian minister or a Christian officiate perform their rights of marriages, they will not be endowed with God's blessings on their marriages since they are not Christians, themselves.

Justice Of The Peace Marriages

On the other hand, when Christian couples go to have their rights of marriages performed by Justices of the Peace or some other officials who are not Christians, the rights of their marriage ceremonies are falling on deaf ears. God will not hear a sinner, but only when he/she is repenting and coming to salvation in Jesus Christ.

John 9:31 (KJV) "Now we know that God heareth not sinners: but if any man be a worshipper of God, and doeth his will, him he heareth."

1 John 4:6 (KJV) "We are of God: he that knoweth God heareth us; he that is not of God heareth not us. Hereby know we the spirit of truth, and the spirit of error."

If you are Christian couples whom you had a non Christian perform your rights of ceremony, you can rectify this by praying to God in the name of Jesus Christ by asking forgiveness for going to the world for His spiritual blessings. God will honor the intents of your heart even though ignorance played a deciding role in your decision. Then thank God through Jesus Christ for His forgiveness. Next, ask God to blessing your marriage and sever any evil ties between you, your marriage and the non Christian who performed the marriage ceremony. Thank Him for this blessing also.

If you feel comfortable in having your pastor perform another rights of marriage ceremony, you may, but it is not necessary. God has already performed it through His Holy Spirit (Who is here in earth with us) before you finished your prayer. We also have comfort in knowing that God, Almighty knows the intent of our hearts and He will bless us accordingly, but He will not have us ignorant in our wisdom, knowledge and understanding of His will for us in marriage.

.

Christian Marriages

The biblical marriage is an institution in its self. It is an entity by its self. A marriage of this sort is honored and respected by God, Almighty because He ordained it. A question might be asked, "Since

God Almighty Himself ordained marriage, does He recognize all marriages done under the guise of Christianity?" The answer is no He doesn't. Both couples of the marriage must be Christians. In essence, they must be saved. Although God tells us not to be unequally yoked together with unbelievers, He will still honor and respect that Christian who enters a marriage with an unbeliever.

2 Corinthians 6:14 (KJV), "Be ye not unequally yoked together with unbelievers: for what fellowship hath righteousness with unrighteousness? And what communion hath light with darkness?"

However, God doesn't recognize unbelievers in any sense of the word unless they are seeking salvation. Unfortunately, the unbeliever will enjoy the blessings bestowed upon their Christian mates, but not on their own faith or lack of faith which separates them from salvation in Almighty God's Son, Jesus.

Wisdom, Knowledge and Understanding.

Once we as Christians have obtained the wisdom, knowledge, and understanding in God's word, we can then conduct ourselves according to His word even when it comes to seeking a mate, dating, and marrying our mates whom God Himself has chosen for us before the foundation of the earth. He will not send to you a mate who is incompatible, unstable, not sincere, evil, etc. He or she will be the perfect mate for you. Your mate will not be chosen by the standards of the world's choices. When God chooses your mate, He will keep in mind the type of mate you desire and are looking for along with His choice for you. As a matter of fact, your perfect mate was already selected with the desires of your heart in mind, even before the foundation of the world.

Ephesians 1:4 (KJV), "According as He hath chosen us in Him before the foundation of the world, that we should be holy and without blame before Him in love:" In the Apocrypha Book of Tobit 6:18,

".....But do not be afraid, for she was set apart for you before the world existed," This was a very interesting story of a God fearing man named Tobiah who was seeking a wife with the help of an angel by the name of Rafael who guided, protected and aided him in the search for his wife. Unbeknownst to Tobiah, God had already selected his wife before the foundation of the world.

Note: The book of Tobit is found in "The Modern Reader's Bible" printed in 1910 and the Catholic's denominational bible, "The New American Bible". This book of Tobit is not found in Christian or Jewish bibles as a recognized book of the bible. In 1955 there were fragments of the Aramaic and Hebrew languages from lost dead sea scrolls (centuries old) found in cave IV at Qumran. The location of this cave is a mile or so West of the Northwestern corner of the dead sea. Some theologians differ on the authenticity or their lack in recognizing that these books were prophetically inspired by God, Almighty. You see, we Christians have blessings which no other humans on earth enjoy or can even imagine.

God Directs Our Paths

God directs our paths as we walk (pattern our lives) based on our faith in Jesus Christ through His Holy Spirit.

Romans 6:4 (KJV), "Therefore we are buried with Him by baptism into death: that like as Christ was raised up from the dead by the glory of the Father, even so we also should walk in newness of life."

Proverbs 3:6 (KJV), "In all thy ways acknowledge Him, and He shall direct thy paths." So, He will definitely direct you to your mate.

Ask For A Spirit-Filled Mate

The key is to ASK Him for your "SPIRIT FILLED HUSBAND OR

WIFE". He will certainly grant your request. Just make sure that you are in His will by obeying His every command.

UNSAVED POTENTIAL MATE?

Many people make the mistake of rationalizing with themselves by saying that they can make a person into what they desire them to be once they are married. If their potential mate is a drunk, they feel they can make them change and sober up. If they feel the person is a prostitute, they believe that with the right care and nurturing, change is almost certain. If you are a Christian and desire to marry a prostitute (harlot), here are admonishments or teachings you should be aware of and also here is what you are faced with since you belong to God.

Romans 12:1 (KJV), "I beseech you therefore, brethren, by the mercies of God, that ye present your bodies a living sacrifice, holy, acceptable unto God, which is your reasonable service."

1 Corinthians 6:15-18 (KJV), "15) Know ye not that your bodies are the members of Christ? Shall I then take the members of Christ, and make them the members of an harlot? God forbid.

16. What? Know ye not that he which is joined to an harlot is one body? For two, saith He, shall be one flesh.
17. But he that is joined unto the Lord is one spirit.
18. Flee fornication. Every sin that a man doeth is without the body; but he that committed fornication sinneth against his own body.
19. What? Know ye not that your body is the temple of the Holy Ghost which is in you, which ye have of God, and ye are not your own?
20. or ye are bought with a price: therefore glorify God in your body, and in your spirit, which is God's."

Unsaved Mates/Spouses

Christians must understand that if they find for themselves a persons who aren't Christians for their mates, they are essentially defying God, hindering their ministries, and blocking some their blessings as well. Satan and his demons could reek havoc with this type of marriage because they've just opened the door of their marriage with possibly opened invitations into their marriages, their families, their homes and all aspects of their lives. Of course strong Christians can block the fiery darts of Satan. Now, if you are already married to an unsaved spouse, this is what the Apostle Paul said by Holy inspiration:

1 Corinthians 7:12-16 (KJV), "12) But to the rest speak I, not the Lord: If any brother hath a wife that believeth not, and she be pleased to dwell with him, let him not put her away.

13. And the woman which hath an husband that believeth not, and if he be pleased to dwell with her, let her not leave him.
14. For the unbelieving husband is sanctified by the wife, and the unbelieving wife is sanctified by the husband: else were your children unclean; but now are they holy.
15. But if the unbelieving depart, let him depart. A brother or a sister is not under bondage in such cases: but God hath called us to peace.
16. For what knowest thou, O wife, whether thou shall save thy husband? Or how knowest thou, O man, whether thou shalt save thy wife?"

Obey God and seek a Christian mate to marry from the start. You have to start by praying to God to send you a Spirit filled mate, believe and then wait for Him to do so. If God has put a ministry on your heart, you must accept it and start working on it. He will not give a mate to you until you obey Him. Start obeying Him and you won't go wrong this way. You will then have a firm foundation from which to build your marriage relationship, your family and of course your Christian environment.

Love Your Unsaved Spouse

Apply the above paragraph to your situation. Now, what about if both of you were sinners and still out in the world when you got married, but now one of you is a born-again Christian? Beautiful! Your marriage is on its way to a Christian environment, albeit halfway. Pray for that unsaved mate daily. Stand in the gap for that mate on a daily basis. Don't offend your mate by highlighting that you are born-again with an all righteous attitude. Sometimes we Christians can be so heavenly minded that we are no earthly good.

Gently lead him/her to Christ by your unwavering love, respect, and your support (not evil) to them through your actions of Christian behaviors. Don't be quick to point out his/her faults as a sinner. Don't constantly nag him/her about going to church with you. On special occasions, let's say that your church or some organization is having a choir concert, you would approach your mate and say, "Honey, we are having a big choir coming in on Saturday night (whatever it is) for a concert, would you like to come?" Now you don't have to say "HONEY" as your lead-in. Say whatever is your pet name that you normally use to communicate to your mate.

Exercise Your Christian Walk

There are a few things you need to consider before marriage and even in the present marriage as well. Many people inadvertently bring tons of baggage into their marriages simply because they are unaware of them or that they are unaware they are doing such. let us consider the following as guidelines for Christians:

CEREMONY. It matters not that your ceremony is held in a church, chapel or some religious building. It can be in the convenience of your home, backyard or some other suitable environment. The main thing to consider is that it shouldn't be at a place recognizable as a sinners gathering place.

CHRISTIAN MINISTER. By all means ask your pastor or choose a member of the clergy within your church to perform your ceremony. If you have some special clergy in mind, choose him or her. A Christian marriage should be performed by a Christian clergy. By doing this you will be in store for double blessings from upon high. JUSTICE OF PEACE, JUDGE, MAYOR OR OTHER OFFICIALS.

Officials in the capacities of government are biblically not representatives of God. Although God ordained governments to exist, he didn't necessarily ordain the government officials who fill those positions to represent Him. Jesus said that where two (2) or three (3) are gathered in His name, there He will be in their midst also. Government officials belong to "CAESAR" which is the world. Who owns the world in a spiritual sense? Satan owns the world. This is not to say that we don't have Christians working as government officials, we do. Although we are in this world, but we are not of this world. Think about the fact that elected officials can't bestowed upon you any spiritual blessings by the mere fact of their positions or statue. They can give a lot on Caesar's side, but not on God's side.

HEAD OF HOUSEHOLD. God is the Head of Christ; and God ordained that our Savior Jesus Christ as the Head of Man; and He ordained man as the head of his wife which is his partner in his household.

1 Corinthians 11:3 (KJV), "But I would have you know, that the head of every man is Christ; and the head of the woman is the man; and the head of Christ is God. Ephesians 5:22-25 (KJV), "22) Wives, submit yourselves unto your husbands, as unto the Lord.

23. For the husband is the head of the wife, even as Christ is the Head of the church: and He is the Savior of the body.
24. Therefore as the church is subject unto Christ, so let the wives be to their own husbands in every thing.
25. Husbands, love you wives, even as Christ also loved the church and gave Himself for it:"

ABORTIONS. (See title and paragraphs on abortions). Actually birth begins before conception according to God, Almighty. Birth begins before the foundation of the world. God knows us before we entered our mothers womb, even before conception.

Ephesians 1:4 (KJV), "According as He hath chosen us in Him before the foundation of the world, that we should be holy and without blame before Him in love:"

Jeremiah 1:5 (KJV), "Before I formed thee in the belly I knew thee: and before thou camest forth out of the womb I sanctified thee,....."

When people rationalize that an embryo is not yet a human, they are only fooling themselves, because Satan knows what the bible says about our beings before the foundation of the world. Satan and his demons are here to kill, steal and destroy and certainly put a lie upon your heart about abortion. Abortion is murder where a life is taken.

John 10:10 (KJV), "The thief cometh not, but for to steal, and to kill, and to destroy: I am come that they might have life, and that they might have it more abundantly." ADULTERY AND INFIDELITY (world's name). Christians should not have sex with someone outside of their marriages because it is a sin of adultery for ones who are married. It is a sin of fornication for ones who are single. Adultery and fornication are both abominations to God, Almighty.

Exodus 20:14 (KJV), "Thou shalt not commit adultery."

This commandment by God was suitable back in the old biblical days and just as true today in the 20th century. However, back then when acts of adultery were committed, the adulterer and the adulteress were allowed to be put to death.

Leviticus 20:10 (KJV), "And the man that committeth adultery with another man's wife, even he that committeth adultery with his neighbor's wife, the adulterer and the adulteress shall surely be put to death."

This particular commandment was under the Dispensation of Law (Law of Moses). When Christ went to the cross, this commandment was disannulled. The participation in sex with partners other than the one you are married to is adultery and infidelity which are definitely sins.

- ABOMINATION TO GOD - Adultery is a definite abomination to God. Not only is your marriage vow broken, but you've sinned against God.

- OPENED DOORS TO SATAN - You've also opened the door for Satan and his demons to come into your marriage and your once Christian environment to reek all kinds of havoc with you and your family. Satan and his demons will have free reign with you and your family because you have opened doors to your once sealed marriage.

- MARRIAGE UNION BROKEN - Where you were once made into a union of one (1), you are now a merged union of at least three(3), including yourself, your mate, the other person(s) with Satan and his head demons also. These demons could represent murder, suicide, mental instability, multiple personalities, prostitution, drugs, etc., etc., etc.

- CHILD(REN) - BLOODLINE/STEP CHILD(REN) - Read the title on adopting children. There could possibly be things in your blood line which could be passed down to your children. You must consider your offspring before you decide to conceive and give birth to your child(ren). Question relatives about their knowledge of sins committed or occult practices.

* SPIRITUAL NOURISHMENT AND NURTURING - You must consider your child(ren)'s spiritual nourishment and nurturing. The bible tells us to bring up a child in a way in which we would want them to be and when they are grown, they will not depart from it.

* BLOODLINE SINS (GENERATIONAL SINS) - Read the title on adopting children. If there are any questionable sins in your blood line, you must ask God to forgive you for them, thank Him, then ask Him to sever all ties between you and those particular sins. After you've done this, then tell Satan God has forgiven you for that particular sin. Tell Satan and his head demons of that plagued sin curse to leave you and your family immediately because you are covered by Jesus Christ's blood.

If you or any member of your blood family has ever dealt with the occult, horoscopes, Ouija boards, fortune telling, psychic networks, palm readers, seances or anything of this nature, you must ask God to forgive you and sever all ties to them, thank Him, then tell Satan what you've just been forgiven of those sins and tell Satan and his head demons over each one of those sins to leave you immediately. When you include the head demons in your prayer, you are also including every demon under that head demon. So, you don't have to name each and every demon which could amount to essentially hundreds or even thousands.

* ADOPTED/ADOPTING CHILD(REN) - Read the title on adopting children. Normally you won't readily know the spiritual background of the child(ren) you intend to adopt as your own. However, you must consider the worse possible scenario before you adopt your

child(ren). This is where you must totally depend upon God's Holy Spirit, the Holy Ghost to help you in your prayer or petition to God, Almighty for your potential child(ren). You then must be the intercessor for the child(ren). You must ask God to forgive the child(ren) of any generational sins, sicknesses and diseases. Thank God for this blessing. After this, ask God to sever all ties of generation sin(s) of your child(ren) and thank Him for this blessing.

Now, tell Satan and his head demons over any generational sins, sicknesses, and diseases of your child(ren) to leave immediately because they have heard what you've ask God, Almighty and He has granted your request. Tell Satan also that your child(ren) are covered by the blood of Jesus Christ. As a Christian you have this authority over Satan, his head demons, and any other demons. You basically want to do the same thing that you would do above for the child(ren) you would birth or have already given to birth.

CHURCH AFFILIATION. You must affiliate with some Christian group such as a Church to be nurtured spiritually, fellowship, inspiration, self edification, prayer, praise and worship of God Almighty, Jesus Christ and the Holy Spirit. You will also need to find your place to serve within that Church as soon as possible and do it on a regular basis.

Hebrews 10:25 (KJV), "Not forsaking the assembling of ourselves together, as the manner of some is; but exhorting one another: and so much the more, as ye see the day approaching."

Families should worship together at the same church or place of worship. The husband should not be a member of one denomination where he worships and the wife a member of another denomination where she and possibly the children worship. Find a church affiliation in which the whole family will be comfortable with in worshiping God. Jesus tells us to forsake not the assembling of ourselves together. That is, we should not stay at home and just watch evangelists on the television or just listen to them on the radio. There is nothing wrong with this in itself, but how can we share with our fellow Christians about our walk with Christ or the heart aches we've experienced during the week. We can't exhort or encourage one with another without having some fellowship.

GOD CALLS PASTORS. You can identify a pastor who is really called by God to preach His word. One such sign is "SPEAKING IN TONGUES". If your particular pastor doesn't speak in tongues or prohibits the speaking of tongues in the congregation, then that pastor is neither called to preach, nor is that person called to pastor. He or she is still a babe in Christ without power.

Mark 16:17 (KJV) "And these signs shall follow them that believe; In my name shall they cast out devils; they shall speak with new tongues;"

Mark 16:20 (KJV) "And they went forth, and preached every where, the Lord working with them, and confirming the word with signs following. Amen."

Jeremiah 3:15 (KJV), "And I will give you pastors according to mine heart which shall feed you with knowledge and understanding."

Ephesians 4:11 (KJV), "And He gave some, apostles; and some, prophets; and some, evangelists; and some pastors and teachers;"

We can't adequately learn without a teacher, or a preacher. We can't show love to someone through a television set or radio. We can't hear a word from God through our own pastor if we don't attend church or fellowship with our own congregation. God talks to true pastors whom He has called and chosen to pastor and not to merely someone sitting in the pastor's position of a church. Some are called and selected by God and some aren't.

CHURCH CALLED PASTORS - NOT GOD'S. The ones who aren't called by God appear to be doing God's will by attempting weekly bible studies, but aren't really brushing the surface of God's word. That is, they have no depth of their teachings. Above all, they aren't capable of listening to God's Holy Spirit for instruction and direction for that particular congregation.

Jeremiah 23:2 (KJV), "Therefore thus saith the Lord God of Israel against the pastors that feed my people; Ye have scattered my flock, and driven them away, and have not visited them: behold, I will visit upon you the evil of your doings, saith the Lord." What God is saying here is that these so called pastors are running his church people away because they are not adequately preaching and/or teaching them the serious information they need to walk with Christ in their daily struggles with life, nor are they visiting these people whom they've run away. These so called pastors can hardly speak on the basics of Christian survival.

Many congregations call or hire for themselves pastors to lead them without the true function of the gift of discernment by whom God has called to lead them. Some congregations base their criteria on high credentials of secular education including graduate degrees instead of discerning whom God has called to pastor them.

-

CULT PASTORS AND MINISTERS.

John 9:31 (KJV), "Now we know that God heareth not sinners: but if any man be a worshipper of God, and doeth His will, him he heareth."

Many so called ministers of various occults including the "NEW AGE" movement, Jehovah Witnesses and many other occult represent themselves as pastors or ministers of their so called congregations or membership groups. These so called pastors and ministers don't represent the God we love and serve. They represent a lie which is Satan and all of his demons under him. They can only make a mockery of God's unadulterated word.

Proverbs 14:9 (KJV), "Fools make a mock at sin: but among the righteous there is favor."

To MOCK is to imitate falsely which is a form of MOCKERY. Additionally, it leads on to disappointment of the ones being lead. It doesn't matter if they use the Holy Bible.

Ezekiel 22:5 (KJV), "Those that be near, and those that be far from Thee, shall mock Thee, which art infamous and much vexed."

Our God doesn't even hear them, nor does He bless them for trying to proclaim His word through lies of Satan.

Psalms 1:6 (KJV), "For the Lord knoweth the way of the righteous: but the way of the ungodly shall perish."

Proverbs 1:10 (KJV), "My son, if sinners entice thee, consent thou not."

In other words don't allow these sinners to encourage you to try their ways of life in no shape, form or fashion. Furthermore, don't except any kind of literature, books or bibles from them. Above all, don't financially support them, even if it is just one thin dime. Jehovah's Witnesses are good for asking for at least a dime or two for their literature. Don't support them in any way, shape or form. One final note, don't invite these sinners in your house unless you are otherwise proclaiming God's word in an effort to bring them to salvation.

STUDY YOUR BIBLE. You are admonished to study your bible to gain wisdom, knowledge and understanding of God's holy word. You must pursue your education of the bible by attending not only

Sunday School, Vacation Bible School, Worship services and other such classes provided in seminars, conventions, revivals and other informational programs of study.

2 Timothy 2:15 (KJV), "Study to show thyself approved unto God, a workman that needeth not to be ashamed, rightly dividing the word of truth."

Take your own bible to church on a regular basis so as to know what that pastor or that speaker is teaching and trying to convey to you. Don't take their word for what they are saying. Read for yourself, take notes, highlight scriptures in your own bible with a colored marker for future references, study and meditate on God's Word for absorption in your memory as much as possible. Start by taking your child(ren) to Sunday School. Find a class not only for your child(ren), but for yourself as well. If a midweek bible study is offered, avail yourself to it also.

Psychic Hotlines. Don't allow someone to tell you to have an open mind and a telephone to call the psychic hotline. Please, don't ever call the psychic hotline. You shouldn't ever have an opened mind. Your mind should always be filled with God's Word for meditation and prayer or some other good things such as listening to the Holy Spirit's guidance and teachings.

Joshua 1:8 (KJV), "This book of the law shall not depart out of thy mouth; but thou shalt meditate therein day and night, that thou mayest observe to do according to all that is written therein: for then thou shalt make thy way prosperous, and then thou shalt have good success."

ASK GOD FOR DISCERNMENT. As you grow in God's Word from milk to meat so to speak, ask God for the ability to distinguish between people of good and evil. Milk represents a new Christian or Babe in Christ. A babe in Christ is just like a new born baby, innocent without the knowledge of God's Word to walk on its own. You will first have to start walking. That is you must be weaned from milk to meat. When you start eating meat, then you can digest God's Word with the knowledge, wisdom, and understanding to be able to stand alone fight skillfully using God's Word, the sword. Now you are ready to ask God for the Gift of discernment of good and evil spirits. Look what King Solomon ask for and what God said to him in return:

1 King 3:9 (KJV), "Give therefore thy servant an understanding heart to judge thy people, that I may discern between good and bad: for who is able to judge this thy so great people?"

1 King 3:11 (KJV), "And God said unto him, Because thou hast asked this thing, and hast not asked for thyself long life; neither hast asked riches for thyself, nor hast asked the life of thine enemies; but hast asked for thyself understanding to discern judgement;"

GENERATIONAL SINS - DISEASES & SICKNESSES. Read the title on adopting children. Sins within a blood line normally trickles down through generations are known as generational sins such as diabetes, heart disease and many other diseases, sicknesses and ailments. It is quite frightening to see each generation of a particular family being effected by such demonic oppressions. You must know that you have an avenue to fight these oppressions through prayer and intercessory prayer for yourself and for your present generation to God. You must ask God to forgive you for these generational sins and to sever all earthy ties between you and those particular generational sins and oppressions. Then you must remember to tell Satan and his head demons to leave you immediately in the name of Jesus because God Almighty has not only forgiven you for all generational sins that you have inherited, but He has broken all ties between you and to each and every named generational sin.

DIVORCE - It is not part of a Christian's marriage vows.

1 Corinthians 7:39 (KJV), "The wife is bound by the law as long as her husband liveth; but if her husband be dead, she is at liberty to be married to whom she will; only in the Lord.

Notice that says "ONLY IN THE LORD". That new husband or wife must also be in the Lord. Now the bible does give provisions for divorce for acts of fornication (adultery) in the marriage.

Matthew 19:9 (KJV), "And I say unto you, Whosoever shall put away his wife except it be for fornication, and shall marry another, committeth adultery: and whoso marrieth her which is put away doth commit adultery."

Even adultery and fornication can be forgiven. We can forgive our spouses for adultery or our friends we are dating while we are single for committing fornication seventy times seventy (7x70=490 times) on a daily basis.

Matthew 18:21-22 (KJV), "21) Then came Peter to Him, and said, how oft shall my brother sin against me, and I forgive him? Till seven times?

22. Jesus saith unto him, I say not unto thee, Until seven times, Until seventy times seven." Most of the time when we do forgive somebody of a wrong against us, we figure three (3) acts of forgiveness should be enough. What about forgiving the 490 times daily?. We need to reassess our power of forgiveness. Let's start now by forgiving one another more than the three times. Let's at least think about the 490 times per day.

MAIDEN NAME USE. Many married females choosing to use their maiden names is a growing phenomenon. Many women feel they must establish themselves somehow as independent professional woman by using their maiden names along with their married names, their husbands last name.

Some women have gone so far as to retain their maiden names as their last names. This has not only caused confusion, the husband's last name has been omitted. There was a certain woman who used her maiden name as her last name. During such functions, socials or fellowships where this woman's husband attended with her, people were addressing him by his wife's maiden name. This was quite confusing. This lady saw the problem, submitted the necessary paperwork to her personnel office for a last name change, informed the employee staff of her new last name and she used her husband's last name with honor.

Christian woman must be aware that God recognizes the man as the head of a marriage. She leaves her family in order to become one with her husband. That means she must become one with his last name as well. There shouldn't be any confusion on who's last name is being used. It should be obvious that a husband's name is the name being used and not the female's maiden name.

SEPARATION. It is biblically correct if a married couple separates for awhile when marital problem exist and both need a cooling off period. Although, it is better that they not separate from each other because evil could creep into the marriage and defile it.

1 Corinthians 7:10-11 (KJV), "10) And unto the married I command, yet not I, but the Lord, Let not the wife depart from her husband:

11. But and if she depart, let her remain unmarried, or be reconciled to her husband: and let not the husband put away his wife." However, if at all possible stay together to work out your differences. Many evils which we can't imagine can or possibly will creep into the marriages because of our being apart from our mates. Things you wouldn't normally do could become part of your marriage such as adultery, lusts, etc. Start by forgiving one another, make up, and quickly iron out your differences. Ask God

to forgive both of you and pray for strength, courage, patience, more love between you, more wisdom, more knowledge and more understanding. Above all, ask God to allow you to be led by His Holy Spirit on a daily basis.

My, (Curtis) Great Grandmother and her husband were separated for a time. Her husband's last name was "Hall". During the separation, she allegedly had an affair with another man whose last name was "Crutcher". A son was born out of this adulteress affair. Her baby from this affair was given the last name "Hall" and he was my grandfather. So, my father and his brothers carried the name of "Hall" instead of "Crutcher". Our bloodline is from the Crutcher ancestors.

WHORES AND DOGS (FEMALE AND MALE PROSTITUTES, respectively). For your soul's sake, don't marry a known female prostitute (whore) or a known male prostitute (dog) because they are both abominations to God. God doesn't even desire them to give money to the Church no matter how much it is because they and their money are abominations to Him.

Deuteronomy 23:18 (KJV), "Thou shalt not bring the hire of a WHORE, or the price of a DOG, into the house of the Lord thy God for any vow: for even both these are abomination unto the Lord thy God.

Dog. Hebrew definition. 3611 Keleb, Keh'-leb (by euphemism) a male prostitute:--dog, that is the word dog is the euphemism or substitute word for a male prostitute.

Don't allow people around you who appear to be beautiful, handsome, wealthy or who have celebrity status to be your desired mate or spouse. This could compromise or overcome your Christian judgement for someone whom God can't stand and whom He won't directly bless while they are still in their sinful livelihoods and their sinful state of minds. However, there are many Christians in those categories whose livelihoods aren't reflective of those sinful state of minds. Use your Christian discernment to select your mate or spouse.

CHAPTER 111

Marriages, Interracial - Discriminations, Prejudices and Racism Curses

There are some races of people who spew out their prejudices at races of people other than their own. God never made any superior races of people. Black people of the African races aren't superior, white people of the Caucasian races aren't superior, nor are other races of people superior. God doesn't like racism or prejudices among the human races. Moses married an Ethiopian woman whose father was a Priest of God, Almighty. Aaron and his wife didn't like the fact that Moses married this black woman. Aaron's wife, Miriam was punished severely by God with leprosy until she became white as snow. This leprosy made her skin totally white in color and she did not have any dark color pigment in her skin. However, Miriam was later healed of this disease after her husband, Aaron prayed to God for her healing. There is another account of this in the bible which happened to a man and which followed his future generations as well. This man was named Gehazi who lied to his master, the Prophet Elisha. Gehazi was cursed with and received the leprosy that Naaman was previously plagued with and was healed of it by the Prophet Elisha.

2 Ki 5:27 (KJV) "The leprosy therefore of Naaman shall cleave unto thee, and unto thy seed for ever. And he went out from his presence a leper as white as snow."

Certain features, color of the skin and colors of the hair leads to the description of the generational skin color hair curses of the Caucasian race of people. This also gives credence to the leprosy color of this particular race of people. However, this doesn't mean that our white sisters and brothers are unclean.

Lev 13:30-31 (KJV) Then the priest shall see the plague: and, behold, if it be in sight deeper than the skin; and there be in it a yellow thin hair; then the priest shall pronounce him unclean: it is a dry scall, even a leprosy upon the head or beard.

Yellow. Hebrew definition. 6669. tsahob, tsaw-obe'; from H6668; golden in color:--yellow.

31. And if the priest look on the plague of the scall, and, behold, it be not in sight deeper than the skin, and that there is no black hair in it; then the priest shall shut up him that hath the plague of the scall seven days:

Lev 13:36-37 (KJV) Then the priest shall look on him: and, behold, if the scall be spread in the skin, the priest shall not seek for yellow hair; he is unclean.

37. But if the scall be in his sight at a stay, and that there is black hair grown up therein; the scall is healed, he is clean: and the priest shall pronounce him clean.

This was a generational curse to the Caucasian (white) race of people. This also leads to another topic on the origins of certain races of people, specifically dealing with the black and white skin colors.

Num 12:1-11 (KJV) And Miriam and Aaron spake against Moses because of the Ethiopian woman whom he had married: for he had married an Ethiopian woman.

2. And they said, Hath the LORD indeed spoken only by Moses? hath he not spoken also by us? And the LORD heard it.
3. (Now the man Moses was very meek, above all the men which were upon the face of the earth.)
4. And the LORD spake suddenly unto Moses, and unto Aaron, and unto Miriam, Come out ye three unto the tabernacle of the congregation. And they three came out.
5. And the LORD came down in the pillar of the cloud, and stood in the door of the tabernacle, and called Aaron and Miriam: and they both came forth.
6. And he said, Hear now my words: If there be a prophet among you, I the LORD will make myself known unto him in a vision, and will speak unto him in a dream.
7. My servant Moses is not so, who is faithful in all mine house.
8. With him will I speak mouth to mouth, even apparently, and not in dark speeches; and the similitude of the LORD shall he behold: wherefore then were ye not afraid to speak against my servant Moses?
9. And the anger of the LORD was kindled against them; and he departed.
10. And the cloud departed from off the tabernacle; and, behold, Miriam became leprous, white as snow: and Aaron looked upon Miriam, and, behold, she was leprous.
11. And Aaron said unto Moses, Alas, my lord, I beseech thee, lay not the sin upon us, wherein we have done foolishly, and wherein we have sinned.

CHAPTER 112

Marriages of Catholic Church Leaders Are Prohibited Against

God's anointed biblical day prophets and preachers were married including the Prophet Isaiah. Isaiah's wife was a prophetess who birth him a son whom God, Almighty gave him his name.

Isa 8:3 (KJV) "And I went unto the prophetess; and she conceived, and bare a son. Then said the LORD to me, Call his name Mahershalalhashbaz."

One of the major offenders of prohibiting marriage is within the Catholic church. Usually Priests, Nuns and persons of other offices are prohibited from entering into an institution of marriage with someone. The holy bible tells us that we have choices between staying single or marrying. There are no stipulations on our serving God whether we are single or whether we are married.

1 Tim 4:1-3 (KJV) Now the Spirit speaketh expressly, that in the latter times some shall depart from the faith, giving heed to seducing spirits, and doctrines of devils;

2. Speaking lies in hypocrisy; having their conscience seared with a hot iron;
3. Forbidding to marry, and commanding to abstain from

> meats, which God hath created to be received with thanksgiving of them which believe and know the truth.

Heb 13:4 (KJV) "Marriage is honourable in all, and the bed undefiled: but whoremongers and adulterers God will judge."

1 Cor 7:9 (KJV) "But if they cannot contain, let them marry: for it is better to marry than to burn."

1 Cor 7:28 (KJV) "But and if thou marry, thou hast not sinned; and if a virgin marry, she hath not sinned. Nevertheless such shall have trouble in the flesh: but I spare you."

1 Cor 7:36 (KJV) "But if any man think that he behaveth himself uncomely toward his virgin, if she pass the flower of her age, and need so require, let him do what he will, he sinneth not: let them marry."

CHAPTER 113

Military Accidental Deaths Exceed War Deaths

Motorcycle, Vehicle Accidents Dominate Off-Duty Summer Fatalities By Donna Miles
American Forces Press Service

WASHINGTON, July 11, 2008 – Midway through the "101 Critical Days of Summer," 50 service members have died in off-duty accidents, half on motorcycles, defense officials reported.

The 101 Critical Days of Summer refers to the period between Memorial Day weekend and Labor Day that typically sees a spike in vehicle and recreational accidents. "It's the time when more people get outside and enjoy off-duty activities and more people are traveling," said John Seibert, the Defense Department's assistant for safety, health and fire. "But unfortunately, it's also a time when we see more accidents." Motor vehicles remain the No. 1 cause of off-duty military deaths, and despite broad safety awareness efforts militarywide, that trend shows no sign of diminishing this summer. Thirty-seven servicemembers have died in motor vehicles since May 23.

Defense Secretary Robert M. Gates noted in a safety message to the field sent just before Memorial Day that 77 servicemen and –women were killed in private motor accidents during last year's 101 Critical Days of Summer.

Officials say they're particularly concerned about the incidence of motorcycle deaths – 25 militarywide since Memorial Day weekend. Citing high fuel prices and cash accumulated during deployments that are driving up motorcycles' popularity within the force, officials say they fear these numbers will only go up.

Eighteen of the Army's 23 off-duty fatalities since Memorial Day have involved privately owned vehicles. Of those, 12 soldiers were killed riding motorcycles and one, an all-terrain vehicle, reported J.T. Coleman from the Army's Combat Readiness and Safety Center at Fort Rucker, Ala.

Similarly, 10 of the 12 sailors who died in off-duty accidents since May 23 were involved in vehicle accidents, according to April Phillips from the Naval Safety Center in Norfolk, Va. Eight of the Navy fatalities involved motorcycles.

The Marine Corps reported eight off-duty losses since the 101 critical days of summer campaign launched. Six of the eight Marines died in vehicle accidents, with three killed on motorcycles, said Marine Lt. Col. Mike Miller, who heads up the Corps' ground safety branch in Washington.

The Air Force, experiencing one of its safest summers in a decade, reported seven off-duty deaths since the Memorial Day weekend. Of those, one involved a four-wheeled vehicle and two involved motorcycles, said Jewell Hicks from the Air Force Safety Center at Kirtland Air Force Base, N.M.

That's a significant improvement from last year, when 19 airmen died during the 101 critical days. Fifteen of those deaths resulted from vehicle accidents, and seven of the airmen were riding motorcycles.

Air Force Chief of Safety Maj. Gen. Wendell Griffin blamed speeding, loss of control and improper techniques while rounding curves as the leading causes behind the motorcycle deaths. He noted in a videotaped message to the Air Force launching this year's 101 Critical Days of Summer campaign that failure to wear a helmet and mixing alcohol with riding contributed to some of these crashes.

But Miller cited the growing popularity of sport bikes as another factor driving up motorcycle accidents. These high-performance motorcycles travel at extremely high speeds and can be difficult to control.

"It truly is like trading in your Dodge minivan for a Ferrari," Miller said. "You don't so much ride one of these as hang on for dear life."

It's little surprise that young servicemembers, attracted by the adrenaline rush sports bikes promise and their relatively low cost, are lining up to buy them. And while disturbing, officials say, it's also not surprising that they're contributing to more military deaths.

For example, 19 of the 21 motorcycle fatalities so far this fiscal year occurred on sport bikes, Phillips reported. Nine of the Army's 12 off-duty motorcycle deaths since the Memorial Day weekend involved sports bikes, Coleman said.

Miller said that while he doesn't yet have statistics to back up his hunch, he's sure they're driving up Marine Corps fatalities, too. He noted that the Marine Corps lost 19 Marines to motorcycle deaths during fiscal 2007. With almost a full quarter of fiscal 2008 ahead, that number hit 18 on July 10.

Intent on bucking this trend, the military is taking action. In addition to the basic motorcycle safety course all military riders must take, the services now promote specialized training for those who ride high-performance motorcycles.

The Motorcycle Safety Foundation's Military Sport Bike Course is now mandatory for all sailors who ride sport bikes, Phillips said. The course also is being offered to soldiers at a growing number of Army bases.

Meanwhile, the 2nd Marine Expeditionary Force at Camp Lejeune, N.C., which is leading the Marine Corps' sport bike safety effort, is contracting with a professional motorcycle school and expanding the training to several Marine Corps sites, Miller said.

The Air Force's Air Mobility Command developed a sport bike safety class that's mandatory for all its airmen. It provides the training materials on request to all other Air Force installations, explained Frank Kelly at the Air Force Safety Center.

Meanwhile, as the 101 critical days of summer continue, military leaders are urging vigilance and a focus on safety.

Gates emphasized in his safety message to the field each servicemember's responsibility in promoting motor vehicle safety. "Know that the choices you make at sporting events, barbecues and other summer activities can impair your judgment and reaction times, all of which are necessary for safe driving," he said.

He reminded servicemembers that most vehicle accidents involve alcohol, fatigue or excessive speed, and most are preventable. "Don't put your life or the lives of others in danger by making poor decisions," he said. "Your safety and the safety of those around you is in your hands." Army Brig. Gen. William Forrester, commander of the Army Combat Readiness and Safety Center, cited the 2008 July 4 holiday as the first in decades with no fatal off-duty accidents within the Army. "To put this into perspective, this is the first recorded fatality-free Fourth of July holiday period the Army has experienced since the U.S. Army Combat Readiness/Safety Center began keeping records in 1974," he said. Forrester noted, however, that three reserve-component soldiers who were not in a duty status were killed in motorcycle accidents during the holiday weekend.

The Air Force and Navy also reported fatality-free July 4 weekends in terms of off-duty accidents.

The Marine Corps suffered two off-duty fatalities during the holiday weekend. A corporal died July 5 after his motorcycle hit a curb and threw him onto the street, officials said. A staff sergeant was killed July 6 when his motorcycle veered off the road, struck a curb, then ran into a tree.

Military Deaths For Twenty Years

Bet you didn't know the following! I surely did not..

These are some rather eye-opening facts: Since the start of the 11 year war on terror in Iraq and Afghanistan, the sacrifice has been enormous. In the time period from the invasion of Iraq in March 2003 through now, we have lost over 3000 military personnel to enemy action and accidents. As tragic as the loss of any member of the US Armed Forces is, consider the following statistics:

The annual fatalities of military members while actively serving in the armed forces from 1980 through 2006:

1980	2,392
1981	2,380
1984	1,999
1988	1,819
1989	1,636
1990	1,508
1991	1,787
1992	1,293
1993	1,213
1994	1,075
1995	2,465
1996	2,318

8 Clinton years @13,417 deaths

1997	817
1998	2,252
1999	1,984
2000	1,983
2001	890
2002	1,007
2003	1,410
2004	1,887
2005	919
2006	920

7 BUSH years @ 9,016 deaths

If you are confused when you look at these figures...so was I. Do these figures mean that the loss from the two latest conflicts in the Middle East are LESS than the loss of military personnel during Mr. Clinton's presidency when America wasn't even involved in a war? I was even more confused; when I read that in 1980, during the reign of President (Nobel Peace Prize) Jimmy Carter, there were 2,392 US Military fatalities!

These figures indicate that many of our Media & Politicians will pick and choose. They present only those 'facts' which support their agenda-driven reporting. Why do so many of them march in lock-step to twist the truth? Where do so many of them get their marching-orders for their agenda? Our Mainstream Print and TV media, and many politicians like to slant that these brave men and women, who are losing their lives in Iraq, are mostly minorities! Wrong AGAIN--- just one more media lie! The latest census of Americans shows the following distribution of American citizens, by Race:

European descent (White)	69.12%
Hispanic	12.5%
Black	12.3%
Asian	3.7%
Native American	1.0%
Other	2.6%

Now... here are the fatalities by Race; over the past three years in Iraqi Freedom:

European descent (white)	74.31%
Hispanic	10.74%
Black	9.67%
Asian	1.81%
Native American	1.09%
Other	33%

These statistics are published by Congressional Research Service, and they may be confirmed by anyone at: http://www.fas.org/sgp/crs/natsec/RL32492.pdf (Please look at this report site if you have the chance.)

CHAPTER **114**

Million Man March Honored Allah, Not Almighty God

During the million man march, led by Minister Louis Farrakhan, Leader of the Nation of Islam when many of the men were interviewed, some mentioned that we serve the same god. Meaning that the Moslems and the Christians serve the same god. We take tremendous offense to that because God, Almighty in heaven is the one that we serve. Allah is a demon god. There are no connections whatsoever between God, Almighty and the demon, Allah. You should not say anything to give honor to demon gods.

Exo 23:24 (KJV) "Thou shalt not bow down to their gods, nor serve them, nor do after their works: but thou shalt utterly overthrow them, and quite break down their images."

Exo 23:25 (KJV) "And ye shall serve the LORD your God, and he shall bless thy bread, and thy water; and I will take sickness away from the midst of thee."

1 Ki 9:6 (KJV) "But if ye shall at all turn from following me, ye or your children, and will not keep my commandments and my statutes which I have set before you, but go and serve other gods, and worship them:"

1 Ki 9:7 (KJV) "Then will I cut off Israel out of the land which I have

given them; and this house, which I have hallowed for my name, will I cast out of my sight; and Israel shall be a proverb and a byword among all people:"

Exo 20:3-5 (KJV) Thou shalt have no other gods before me.

4. Thou shalt not make unto thee any graven image, or any likeness of any thing that is in heaven above, or that is in the earth beneath, or that is in the water under the earth:
5. Thou shalt not bow down thyself to them, nor serve them: for I the LORD thy God am a jealous God, visiting the iniquity of the fathers upon the children unto the third and fourth generation of them that hate me;

There are a few leaders in the Muslim race of people claiming the Islamic religion who have brought curses into their families and their future generations to come including, but limited to:

Minister Louis Farrakhan - Illnesses And Cancer Curses

Louis Farrakhan Reveals Cancer-Related Illness
Reprint Information

Book on Katie Couric Makes Waves
White House: We're Not Subject to FOIA
FBI Seeks 2 Mysterious Men on Ferry
Publisher: Conservatives Do Read As Much As Liberals Romney Shrugs Off Mormon History Film

Nation of Islam leader Louis Farrakhan, 73, has suffered new health problems relating to earlier diagnosed prostate cancer and has canceled all engagements, he said in a letter published on the Web site of his church.

"I have been suffering from the after-effects of an extremely high dose of radiated seed implantation that indeed killed the cancer cells that had broken the prostate capsule, but over time, these seeds have done severe internal damage," he said in the letter dated Sept. 11 and published online at http://www.noi.org.

"I am more than fortunate. I am blessed by Allah to be alive," he added.

Farrakhan, who once called Judaism a "gutter religion" and later said his comments were simply misinterpreted street talk, was a driving force behind the 1995 million-man march on Washington.

During a recent trip to Cuba, he said in the letter, doctors discovered an anal ulcer "similar to the ulcer that I had in 1998-1999 that almost caused the loss of my life."

Mohammed Ali's Parkinson's Disease Curses

Muhammad Ali's Fight
World Famous Muhammad Ali Now Fights Parkinson's Disease
© Jennifer Gerics
Jun 9, 2007
Muhammad Ali, Google Images

Muhammad Ali, a former prize-winning boxer, is currently fighting Parkinson's disease. His earlier life involved boxing, religious conviction, and ever-ready verbal jabs.

Malcolm X Paid The Ultimate Price - A Curse Of Death

On February 21, 1965, Malcolm X was shot to death as he delivered a speech in Manhattan's Audobon Ballroom. The following March, three men -- Talmadge Hayer, Norman Butler, and Thomas Johnson -- were convicted of murdering the 39-year-old black leader. Though prosecutors suggested at trial that the slaying was plotted as "an object lesson for Malcolm's followers," no direct evidence linked the Nation of Islam -from which Malcolm had publicly broken -- to the killing, though that speculation still thrives.

As another anniversary of the murder passes, we have compiled an extensive collection of documents chronicling the death of Malcolm X. Included in this package are New York Police Department, FBI, prison, hospital, grand jury, and medical examiner records that have never previously been disclosed. From ballistics evidence and eyewitness accounts to a chilling autopsy photo and the bullet-riddled documents found in Malcolm's breast pocket, these documents offer a remarkable picture of a brutal crime.

CHAPTER 115

Musical Instruments Are Not Allowed in Some Churches

Some churches including the Protestant Church of Christ, doesn't believe in having musical instruments in their churches. When they sing their songs and hymns, they have no musical instruments to accompany them. Not only are they missing the point of praising and worshiping God, but they are missing out on wonderful blessings as well. God, Almighty loves hearing the skillful playing of musical instruments when we sing praises to Him.

Psa 150 (KJV) Praise ye the LORD. Praise God in his sanctuary: praise him in the firmament of his power.

2. Praise him for his mighty acts: praise him according to his excellent greatness.
3. Praise him with the sound of the trumpet: praise him with the psaltery and harp.
4. Praise him with the timbrel and dance: praise him with stringed instruments and organs.
5. Praise him upon the loud cymbals: praise him upon the high sounding cymbals.
6. Let every thing that hath breath praise the LORD. Praise ye the LORD.

Here is a record of one such miracle that was manifested where

God's Glory appeared in a cloud when it was visually seen. This Glory was so powerful and thick that the musicians and singers couldn't continue to stand to minister. These are blessings that most miss out on because they fall short praising and worshipping our Heavenly Father, God Almighty. When you prohibit musical instruments from being in your churches, then you have voided out glorious blessings from heaven. Certainly, if musical instruments and/or musicians aren't available, then lift up your voices to sing praises to our heavenly Father. You will be blessed as well.

2 Chr 5:12-14 (KJV) Also the Levites which were the singers, all of them of Asaph, of Heman, of Jeduthun, with their sons and their brethren, being arrayed in white linen, having cymbals and psalteries and harps, stood at the east end of the altar, and with them an hundred and twenty priests sounding with trumpets:)

13. It came even to pass, as the trumpeters and singers were as one, to make one sound to be heard in praising and thanking the LORD; and when they lifted up their voice with the trumpets and cymbals and instruments of music, and praised the LORD, saying, For he is good; for his mercy endureth for ever: that then the house was filled with a cloud, even the house of the LORD;
14. So that the priests could not stand to minister by reason of the cloud: for the glory of the LORD had filled the house of God.

2 Chr 6:1 (KJV) "Then said Solomon, The LORD hath said that he would dwell in the thick darkness."

CHAPTER 116

New Age Era Is a Spirit of Deception

There is a new phenomenon called the New Age Era which is sweeping the world. This New Age era has nothing to do with Christianity, except that it is an abomination to God, Almighty. New Age is another lie from hell with its author and founder as Satan. New Age has no place in Christianity, whatsoever.

2 Pet 2:1 (KJV) "But there were false prophets also among the people, even as there shall be false teachers among you, who privily shall bring in damnable heresies, even denying the Lord that bought them, and bring upon themselves swift destruction."

2 Pet 2:2 (KJV) "And many shall follow their pernicious ways; by reason of whom the way of truth shall be evil spoken of."

2 Pet 2:3 (KJV) "And through covetousness shall they with feigned words make merchandise of you: whose judgment now of a long time lingereth not, and their damnation slumbereth not."

CHAPTER **117**

Oil and Natural Gas Are in Abundance in America

We are slaves to the oil tycoons overseas when it comes to our consumption of oil and gasoline. Offshore oil drilling is at the forefront of our leaders' debates. They are really over looking our abundance of oil and natural gas minerals here in these United States of America. The states of Arkansas and Louisiana have rivers of these mineral resources. We just need to provide for the abundance of oil pumps, natural pumps, and provide for those expensive refineries.

King David petitioned Almighty God as to what he should do after his enemies had seized his people, his goods, his wives and children. Almighty God told him to ***Pursue, Overtake, and Recover All***. This is what America needs to do, pursue all of the land that can be explored for oil and natural gas, overtake those grounds while honoring all mineral rights owners for drilling, and recover all of the oil and natural gas resources that we can to eliminate our dependence on foreign oil resources.

1 Samuel 30:8 (KJV)

And David inquired at the Lord, saying, Shall I pursue after this troop? shall I overtake them? And he answered him, Pursue: for thou shalt surely overtake them, and without fail recover all.

There are rivers of oil and natural gas resources in many states under lands in America that are not being recognized by governors, state congressmen and women, state senators and other state officials. We are steady crying and complaining about our dependence on foreign oil, but nobody is sounding the alarm that we have an abundance in rivers of oil and natural gas resources under the surfaces of our farm lands in the these United states of America.

Since many of our citizens don't have the financial resources to build their own refineries, then government could provide the necessary funds to mineral rights holders in the form of government provided subsidies and grants for the same. One alternative is provide other transportation avenues in the form of underground tank storage, then use tankers to transport the oil and gas to nearby refineries.

There was an individual in the state of Indiana who has a ten (10) acre farm. He had a well drill at a 1200 foot depth. He pumps about three (3) barrels per day. The natural gas that he pumps, he uses for his home. He has plans to drill more wells on his ten (10) acre farm in the future.

Arkansas

Arkansas has rivers of oil and gas just waiting to be drilled and used. There are at least two (2) major oil and gas shales: the Penters Shale and the Fayettville Shale which stretches across about ten (10) counties which is about one-hundred (100) miles long and approximatelly fifty (50) miles wide.

Louisiana

Louisiana is next door to Arkansas which has a river of oil and natural gas resources as well. Here, nobody is sounding the alarm of another niche of oil and natural gas resources. Even if we didn't start drilling on our national parks and animal reserve lands, we have abundance in these resources on our many farm lands.

Louisiana - Haynesville Shale Field

1 of the Largest Domestic Natural Gas Finds & the Stock Behind It

Barnett Shale Flowback

Treat and recycle frac flowback water in Barnett Shale formation

Marcellus Shale Play Field - Natural Gas Field North America Information

Marcellus Shale States: New York, Pennsylvania, Ohio, West Virginia

Message Board Bookmark and Share Bookmark this page

What is the Marcellus Shale Area?

The Marcellus Shale Rock Formation Field, which extends through Pennsylvania, New York, Ohio, and West Virginia, is a part of the Devonian Black Shale Field. This geology shale was reported to hold more then 1.9 trillion cubic feet back in 2002. This did not cause much excitement because the amount that could actually be extracted was low.

A new survey issued by Terry Englander, a geoscience professor at Pennsylvania State University, and Gary Lash, a geology professor at the State University of New York at Fredonia, surprised everyone as these men think the Marcellus Natural Gas Shale Play could hold up to 500 trillion cubic feet of Natural Gas. 50 TFC would be a realistic amount that could be recovered. All of this is made possible by new drilling techniques called Horizontal Drilling.

The United States produces roughly 30 trillion cubic feet (30 TFC) of natural gas every year and this number is going down as the price of natural gas continues to rise. If research reports are correct and Marcellus Shale holds 50 TFC's of recoverable natural gas, this would put the Appalachian Basin Natural Gas Shale into a different league.

The Marcellus Shale Deposit would be dubbed a natural gas super giant and would be one of the biggest natural gas fields in the United States. The Haynesville Shale is a similar Natural Gas Shale.

How is Natural Gas extracted from Marcellus Shale? Horizontal well drillers can get natural gas from vertical fractures of the shale, through the shale pores in which natural gas is trapped, and through absorbed minerals and grains in the shale. The problem with Horizontal Drilling is the cost. A vertical drilled well in the Red Hot Marcellus Shale Zone costs around $810,000 while a horizontal drilled well will cost you roughly 3 Million Dollars. With new horizontal drilling techniques, you have a better chance of getting high natural gas volumes.

As Natural Gas hovers in the $12 range, these new horizontal drilling techniques are well worth it. As long as Natural Gas prices remain above $7, the Marcellus Shale will be very active. Don't forget to check out these other shale plays just as hot as Marcellus. Marcellus Shale - Horn River Shale - Bakken Oil Shale - Fayetteville Shale Brazil Oil Field - Barnett Shale - Haynesville Shale

If anyone would like to add to my research, email me at tweid04@ gmail.com

Pennsylvania Warns Gas Companies to respect Natural Treasures at Marcellus Shale:

Pennsylvania has an estimated 2.8 trillion cubic feet of proved natural gas reserves in the ground awaiting development, according to the Pennsylvania Oil and Gas Association. Developing the Marcellus Shale formation requires large amounts of fresh water to fracture the shale in order to extract the natural gas. Recent inspections by DEP and its partners have uncovered violations that threaten the state's water resources and its environment. Department of Environmental Protection Secretary Kathleen McGinty had this to say:

"Over the past few weeks, DEP inspectors have observed a number of violations at drilling sites operated by companies that were new to Pennsylvania," said McGinty. "In light of those discoveries, we acted quickly to stop this harmful activity and felt it was necessary to bring all current and potential operators together to meet directly with the agencies responsible for protecting our water and other natural resources." Full Article Here

Companies Involved in the Marcellus Shale - Marcellus Shale Stocks

- EOG Resources EOG CEO - We've talked about the Marcellus some in the past, and really our position there hasn't changed. We currently have about 230,000 net acres primarily in Pennsylvania and primarily in North Western Pennsylvania. We did sell our shallow production in the Appalachians, but we maintained our deep rights under those leases. So currently, as I said, we're at about 230,000 acres.
- Penn Virginia PVA CEO - There is not a lot to speak about concerning the Marcellus. In general, I can tell you that we have initiated a leasing effort up in Pennsylvania like lot of the other companies you have heard about. It's not only a grass roots effort, but we are approaching it from a little bit of a different twist, as we are making an attempt on gaining some JVs underneath some shallow operators, shallow production type operators. And then we're going to try to approach that

way. So, in any case, we still think that we can at some point in time get a substantial acre position and initiate testing in the Marcellus.

- Rex Energy REXX Rex Energy announced today that on June 10, 2008, the company completed the fracture stimulation of its second Marcellus Shale vertical test well in western Pennsylvania. To date, the well has flowed back approximately 75% of its frac fluids and the company is encouraged by initial production tests. The company's Marcellus Shale prospective acreage has grown to approximately 88,000 gross (57,000 net) acres.
- Southwest Energy SWN - 4/25/08 Confernce Call - In some new ventures activity in Pennsylvania we currently have approximately 100,000 net undeveloped acres where we believe the Marcellus Shale is prospective. We are currently analyzing core on our first vertical well here and drilling our second.
- Range Resources RRC and MarkWest MWE strike deal at Marcellus Shale
- XTO Energy XTO buys Marcellus Shale stake from Linn Energy LINE
- Chesapeake Energy CHK CHK has over 1 million Marcellus Shale Acers

In addition, we believe our 1.2 million net acres of Marcellus and 300,000 net acres in the Haynesville are worth at least an additional $10 billion combined. And since those plays are still in their infancy we believe their values are likely to increase substantially over time, as the play become more proven.

- Equitable Resources EQT
- Cabot Oil & Gas COG
- Talisman Energy TLM TLM has a 640,000 acre position at Marcellus Shale Field with Hallwood Announcement
- Southwestern Energy SWN

In some new ventures activity in Pennsylvania we currently have approximately 100,000 net undeveloped acres where we believe the Marcellus Shale is prospective. We are currently analyzing core on our first vertical well here and drilling our second.

- Atlas Energy Resources ATN

Atlas Energy currently controls approximately 516,000 Marcellus acres in Pennsylvania, New York and West Virginia, of which approximately 242,000 of these acres are located in the Company's core Marcellus Shale position in southwestern Pennsylvania

- Trans Energy TENG completes first Well in Marcellus Shale Natural Gas Field 6/12/08

Our farm lands are such that we could construct enough wells while leaving enough to be farmed for our much needed crops for food consumption. My brother who lives in Arkansas says that at least one individual has opened up a station to provide natural gas refilling for automobiles fitted for using natural gas consumption.

Here in the metropolitan Washington, D.C. area, there are metro buses and other vehicles using natural gas with natural gas re-filling stations available.

Why isn't somebody pushing natural gas consumption in our vehicles? Natural gas burns more cleaner than gasoline. Propane is another alternative to gasoline. Propane is non toxic which is cleaner. It is a liquid propane gas without pollution.

CHAPTER 118

Ordinations of Gays (All Homosexuals) Are Biblically Forbidden

Some churches including, but not limited to the denominations of the Episcopalians and the United Church of Christ (UCC) actively ordained and use gay/homosexuals as pastors and other clergy positions. It really doesn't matter to them whether or not a spiritual call is on their lives. UCC is mainly concerned with academic credentials of such persons including their achievements in at least a degree in the bachelors level or above. No ability of spiritual discernment is desired by them.

Romans 1 (KJV)

26. For this cause God gave them up unto vile affections: for even their women did change the natural use into that which is against nature:
27. And likewise also the men, leaving the natural use of the woman, burned in their lust one toward another; men with men working that which is unseemly, and receiving in themselves that recompence of their error which was meet.

First of all, Almighty God does not call someone to preach His gospel who is an abomination in their choices to Him. Neither can they spiritually communicate to Him through His Holy Spirit, nor can they exercise any spiritual gifts or be given any of the gifts of the Holy

Spirit which are the tools of Christians. God has a five-fold ministry that he calls his minister into. Gays have been known to work in some of those ministries, but without a calling from Almighty God.

Ephesians 4 (KJV)

11. And he gave some, apostles; and some, prophets; and some, evangelists; and some, pastors and teachers;
12. For the perfecting of the saints, for the work of the ministry, for the edifying of the body of Christ:

1 Corinthians 12 (KJV)

28. And God hath set some in the church, first apostles, secondarily prophets, thirdly teachers, after that miracles, then gifts of healings, helps, governments, diversities of tongues.

Here is an example of what Almighty God did to gays or homosexuals in sin city called Sodom and Gomorrah .

Genesis 18 (KJV)

20. And the Lord said, Because the cry of Sodom and Gomorrah is great, and because their sin is very grievous;
21. I will go down now, and see whether they have done altogether according to the cry of it, which is come unto me; and if not, I will know.

Here you will see that the gay men were so wicked in those days that they wanted to have sex even with Almighty God's angels who appeared to be human men at Lot's house. Lot knew these gentlemen were angels and servants of Almighty God, so he offered his daughters to the men, but they refused them. They wanted the men instead as they had not natural affections for the opposite sex.

Genesis 19 (KJV)

1. And there came two angels to Sodom at even; and Lot sat in the gate of Sodom: and Lot seeing them rose up to meet them; and he bowed himself with his face toward the ground;
2. And he said, Behold now, my lords, turn in, I pray you, into your servant's house, and tarry all night, and wash your feet, and ye shall rise up early, and go on your ways. And they said, Nay; but we will abide in the street all night.
3. And he pressed upon them greatly; and they turned in unto him and entered into his house; and he made them a feast, and did bake unleavened bread, and they did eat.
4. But before they lay down, the men of the city, even the men of Sodom, compassed the house round, both old and young, all the people from every quarter:
5. And they called unto Lot, and said unto him, Where are the men which came in to thee this night? bring them out unto us, that we may know them.
6. And Lot went out at the door unto them, and shut the door after him,
7. And said, I pray you, brethren, do not so wickedly.
8. Behold now, I have two daughters which have not known man; let me, I pray you, bring them out unto you, and do ye to them as is good in your eyes: only unto these men do nothing; for therefore came they under the shadow of my roof.
9. And they said, Stand back. And they said again, This one fellow came in to sojourn, and he will needs be a judge: now will we deal worse with thee, than with them. And they pressed sore upon the man, even Lot, and came near to break the door.
10. But the men put forth their hand, and pulled Lot into the house to them, and shut to the door.
11. And they smote the men that were at the door of the house

with blindness, both small and great: so that they wearied themselves to find the door.

After the angels delivered Lot and his family from the city as they had found favor and grace with Almighty God, who did the following:

Genesis 19 (KJV)

24. Then the Lord rained upon Sodom and upon Gomorrah brimstone and fire from the Lord out of heaven;
25. And he overthrew those cities, and all the plain, and all the inhabitants of the cities, and that which grew upon the ground.
26. But his wife looked back from behind him, and she became a pillar of salt.

CHAPTER **119**

Original Christians Took a Stand for Jesus Christ

Christians (Christ-Like Persons)

The word "Christian" isn't found in the old testament bibles (KJV), but is found only 2 times in the new testament bibles (KJV). The word "Christian" was brought to us in

Acts 26:28 (KJV), "Then Agrippa said unto Paul, Almost thou persuadest me to be a Christian."

The Apostle Paul was witnessing to King Herod Agrippa to become a Christian, but he refused. The other account of a Christian is found in

1 Peter 4:15 (KJV), "Yet if any man suffer as a Christian, let him not be ashamed; but let him glorify God on this behalf.

Christians are set aside or separated from the rudiments of the world to that of followers of Jesus Christ, our Savior under the principles and guidelines of the New Testament. Well, you probably wondering by now, what were the people whom were chosen by God to do His will called under the principles of the Old Testament?

Under the Old Testament principles and guidelines, people who chose to do God's will with the belief, faith and hope of Jesus Christ's coming were called NAZARITES. These Nazarites were also set aside for God. They were separated from the world to be Princes and Princes' of the Prince Most High, Jesus Christ. Although these people were called Nazarites, their High Priest/Prince had not arrived in human form on earth as yet.

The High Priest/Prince, the NAZARENE who is Jesus is the first Christian while the Nazarites then became followers of the Nazarene, the Christian. As you see, the Nazarites received a new name or new title if you will. This title became that of a Christian. The point that we should remember is that we are people set aside for God's will and purpose. We need to also remember that we didn't choose God, He chose us before the foundation of the world.

Ephesians 1:4 (KJV), "According as He hat chosen us in Him before the foundation of the world, that we should be holy and without blame before Him in love:".

Before Christ went to the cross for our sins, He prayed to God, the Father and petitioned Him that all Christians should join Him in Heaven.

John 17:24 (KJV), "Father, I will that they also, whom thou hast given me, be with me where I am; that they may behold my glory, which thou hast given me: for thou lovedst me before the foundation of the world.

Jesus made an astounding promise to us before He left for heaven. He told us about His Father's mansions. He then went on to tell us that we couldn't follow Him back then, but we could later after His ascension to heaven.

John 14:2-3 (KJV),

2. "In my Father's house are many mansions: if it were not so, I would have told you. I go to prepare a place for you.
3. And if I go and prepare a place for you, I will come again, and receive you unto myself; that where I am, there ye may be also."

CHAPTER **120**

Owe No Man Nothing (i.e., Zip or Zero)

Our society is such that we credit at our disposal from buying automobiles, homes and many other items. Credit cards are very prevalent as well. Many people have gotten themselves in trouble with their using credit. Some have over extended themselves by using credit.

It seems that the majority people of our society have not learned to save for their desired purchases. Many have the attitudes that they desire to have that particular item, now and not wait by saving up for it.

The dire consequences are that they are now slaves to that credit monster and made it a part of their lives.

The bible admonishes us not become borrowers, but to become lenders.

Romans 13 (KJV)

8. Owe no man any thing, but to love one another: for he that loveth another hath fulfilled the law.

CHAPTER 121

Pray for the Peace of Israel and Jerusalem

Almighty God has admonished all Christians to pray for the peace of Jerusalem and Israel (All Jewish/Hebrew Nations). In doing such will reap us many blessings from God. If we fail to do such, then we will reap His wrath of curses, instead. So, it is very imperative that these United States of America hold stead fast to support Israel at all costs for our blessings to be performed.

Psalms 122 (KJV)

1. I Was glad when they said unto me, Let us go into the house of the Lord.
2. Our feet shall stand within thy gates, O Jerusalem.
3. Jerusalem is builded as a city that is compact together:
4. Whither the tribes go up, the tribes of the Lord, unto the testimony of Israel, to give thanks unto the name of the Lord.
5. For there are set thrones of judgment, the thrones of the house of David.
6. Pray for the peace of Jerusalem: they shall prosper that love thee.
7. Peace be within thy walls, and prosperity within thy palaces.
8. For my brethren and companions' sakes, I will now say, Peace be within thee.

9. Because of the house of the Lord our God I will seek thy good.

In the name of Almighty God in Heaven, and
In the name of Almighty Jesus Christ in Heaven, and
In the name of Almighty Holy Spirit, Who is on earth with us.
Praise You, Almighty God, and Praise You, Almighty Jesus Christ, and Praise You, Almighty Holy Spirit! Amen.

CHAPTER 122

Pray for Those Who Are in Authority

We are reminded to pray for our leaders and particularly those in authority over us. We are especially reminded to pray continually without ceasing. There are sayings that if Christians aren't praying, then God's Angels don't have anything to do. When we pray, God, Almighty dispatches his Angels on our behalf. Don't allow your angel to unemployed because you fail to pray to God, continually. Don't forget to pray for your supervisors, your Pastors, Judges at all levels of the Judiciary Systems, your congressmen and congresswomen, your senators, your city mayors and their staff, the state governors, the president and vice president of the United States of American and any other persons in authority.

1 Timothy 2 (KJV)

1. I exhort therefore, that, first of all, supplications, prayers, intercessions, and giving of thanks, be made for all men;
2. For kings, and for all that are in authority; that we may lead a quiet and peaceable life in all godliness and honesty.
3. For this is good and acceptable in the sight of God our Saviour;
4. Who will have all men to be saved, and to come unto the knowledge of the truth.

In the name of Almighty God in Heaven, and
In the name of Almighty Jesus Christ in Heaven, and
In the name of Almighty Holy Spirit, Who is on earth with us.
Praise You, Almighty God, and Praise You,
Almighty Jesus Christ, and
Praise You, Almighty Holy Spirit! Amen.

CHAPTER 123

Pray to Seek Almighty God's Face for More Blessings and Favors

Have you often times wondered why your prayers go un-answered? Maybe it is because you have not done the following to gain favor from Almighty God:

1. Humble yourself as a little child.
2. Turn from your wicked ways. Strive to do good in all of your ways.
3. Ask Almighty God for forgiveness after you have forgiven and reconciled your differences with someone else with whom you have a problem with., then you must pray to seek or see Almighty God's face by living an unrighteous life style on a daily basis, thereby turning from all of your wicked ways.

2 Chronicles 7 (KJV)

14. If my people, which are called by my name, shall humble themselves, and pray, and seek my face, and turn from their wicked ways; then will I hear from heaven, and will forgive their sin, and will heal their land.

In the name of Almighty God in Heaven, and
In the name of Almighty Jesus Christ in Heaven, and
In the name of Almighty Holy Spirit, Who is on earth with us.
Praise You, Almighty God, and Praise You, Almighty Jesus Christ, and Praise You, Almighty Holy Spirit!
Amen.

CHAPTER 124

Prayer Against Your Adversaries and Enemies

Heavenly Father, in the name of Your Precious Son, Jesus Christ and Your Precious Holy Spirit, I offer this prayer and supplication in Psalms 109:

Psalms 109 (KJV)

1. Hold not thy peace, O God of my praise;
2. For the mouth of the wicked and the mouth of the deceitful are opened against me: they have spoken against me with a lying tongue.
3. They compassed me about also with words of hatred; and fought against me without a cause.
4. For my love they are my adversaries: but I give myself unto prayer.
5. And they have rewarded me evil for good, and hatred for my love.
6. Set thou a wicked man over him: and let Satan stand at his right hand.
7. When he shall be judged, let him be condemned: and let his prayer become sin.
8. Let his days be few; and let another take his office.
9. Let his children be fatherless, and his wife a widow.
10. Let his children be continually vagabonds, and beg: let

them seek their bread also out of their desolate places.

11. Let the extortioner catch all that he hath; and let the strangers spoil his labour.
12. Let there be none to extend mercy unto him: neither let there be any to favour his fatherless children.
13. Let his posterity be cut off; and in the generation following let their name be blotted out.
14. Let the iniquity of his fathers be remembered with the Lord; and let not the sin of his mother be blotted out.
15. Let them be before the Lord continually, that he may cut off the memory of them from the earth.
16. Because that he remembered not to shew mercy, but persecuted the poor and needy man, that he might even slay the broken in heart.
17. As he loved cursing, so let it come unto him: as he delighted not in blessing, so let it be far from him.
18. As he clothed himself with cursing like as with his garment, so let it come into his bowels like water, and like oil into his bones.
19. Let it be unto him as the garment which covereth him, and for a girdle wherewith he is girded continually.
20. Let this be the reward of mine adversaries from the Lord, and of them that speak evil against my soul.
21. But do thou for me, O God the Lord, for thy name's sake: because thy mercy is good, deliver thou me.
22. For I am poor and needy, and my heart is wounded within me.
23. I am gone like the shadow when it declineth: I am tossed up and down as the locust.
24. My knees are weak through fasting; and my flesh faileth of fatness.
25. I became also a reproach unto them: when they looked upon me they shaked their heads.
26. Help me, O Lord my God: O save me according to thy mercy:

27. That they may know that this is thy hand; that thou, Lord, hast done it.
28. Let them curse, but bless thou: when they arise, let them be ashamed; but let thy servant rejoice.
29. Let mine adversaries be clothed with shame, and let them cover themselves with their own confusion, as with a mantle.
30. I will greatly praise the Lord with my mouth; yea, I will praise him among the multitude.
31. For he shall stand at the right hand of the poor, to save him from those that condemn his soul.

In the name of Almighty God in Heaven, and
In the name of Almighty Jesus Christ in Heaven, and
In the name of Almighty Holy Spirit, Who is on earth with us.
Praise You, Almighty God, and Praise You, Almighty Jesus Christ, and Praise You, Almighty Holy Spirit! Amen.

CHAPTER **125**

Prayer to Deliver You from Evil Actions and Violence

Heavenly Father, in the name of your Son, Jesus Christ and Your Precious Holy Spirit, please accept my prayer in Psalms 140 as follows:

Psalms 140 (KJV)

1. Deliver me, O Lord, from the evil man: preserve me from the violent man;
2. Which imagine mischiefs in their heart; continually are they gathered together for war.
3. They have sharpened their tongues like a serpent; adders' poison is under their lips. Selah.
4. Keep me, O Lord, from the hands of the wicked; preserve me from the violent man; who have purposed to overthrow my goings.
5. The proud have hid a snare for me, and cords; they have spread a net by the wayside; they have set gins for me. Selah.
6. I said unto the Lord, Thou art my God: hear the voice of my supplications, O Lord.
7. O God the Lord, the strength of my salvation, thou hast covered my head in the day of battle.
8. Grant not, O Lord, the desires of the wicked: further not his wicked device; lest they exalt themselves. Selah.

9. As for the head of those that compass me about, let the mischief of their own lips cover them.
10. Let burning coals fall upon them: let them be cast into the fire; into deep pits, that they rise not up again.
11. Let not an evil speaker be established in the earth: evil shall hunt the violent man to overthrow him.
12. I know that the Lord will maintain the cause of the afflicted, and the right of the poor.
13. Surely the righteous shall give thanks unto thy name: the upright shall dwell in thy presence.

In the name of Almighty God in Heaven, and
In the name of Almighty Jesus Christ in Heaven, and In the name of Almighty Holy Spirit on earth with us!
Praise You, Almighty God, and Praise You, Almighty Jesus Christ, and Praise You, Almighty Holy Spirit! Amen.

CHAPTER **126**

Prayer to Deliver You from Generational Curses and Other Curses

Heavenly Father,

in the name of Your Son, Jesus Christ and Your Precious Holy Spirit,

I break myself, my wife, my children, my grandchildren, and my great grandchildren from all generational curses, all Agent Orange (Viet Nam) curses, all Buddhist Monk's (Viet Nam) curses, all Satanic curses, and all Unknown curses including, but not limited to diabetes, high blood pressure, heart diseases, heart attacks, kidney diseases, strokes, blindness in the eyes, eye diseases, cancers, and arthritis to the ***third and fourth generations***,

Going back to:
My parents,
My grandparents, and to
My great grandparents,
To the third and fourth generations.

I loose myself, my wife, my children, my grandchildren, and my great grandchildren from all generational curses, all agent Orange (Viet Nam) curses, all Buddhist Monk's (Viet Nam) curses, all Satanic curses, and all Unknown curses including, but not limited to diabetes, high blood pressure, heart diseases, heart attacks, kidney diseases, strokes, blindness in the eyes, eye diseases, cancers, and arthritis to the third and fourth generations,

Going back to:
My parents,
My grandparents, and to
My great grandparents,
To the ***third and fourth generations***.

I cut and sever all bonds, all cords, all snares, all snares of death, all ties and all traps to myself, my wife, my children, my grandchildren and to my great grandchildren to the third and fourth generations from all links to all generational curses, all Agent Orange (Viet Nam) curses, all Buddhist Monk's (Viet Nam) curses, all Satanic curses, and all Unknown curses including, but not limited to diabetes, high blood pressure, heart diseases, heart attacks, kidney diseases, strokes, blindness in the eyes, eye diseases, cancers, and arthritis to the ***third and fourth generations***,

Going back to:
My parents,
My grandparents, and to
My great grandparents,
To the ***third and fourth generations***.

I rebuke all generational curses, all Agent Orange (Viet Nam) curses, all Buddhist Monk's (Viet Nam) curses, all Satanic curses, and all Unknown curses including, but not limited to diabetes, high blood pressure, heart diseases, heart attacks, kidney diseases, strokes, blindness in the eyes, eye diseases, cancers, and arthritis for myself, my wife, my children, my grandchildren and my great grandchildren to the ***third and fourth generations***.

Going back to:
My parents,
My grandparents, and to
My great grandparents,
to the ***third and fourth generations***.

I command that all generational curses, all Agent Orange (Viet Nam) curses, all Buddhist Monk's (Viet Nam) curses, all Satanic curses, and all Unknown curses including, but not limited to diabetes, high blood pressure, heart diseases, heart attacks, kidney diseases, strokes, blindness in the eyes, eye diseases, cancers, and arthritis ***come out now and leave immediately*** and ***never return forever*** for myself, my wife, my children, my grandchildren and my great grandchildren to the ***third and fourth generations***,

Going back to:
My parents,
My grandparents, and to
My great grandparents,
To the ***third and fourth generations***.

I bind my body, my wife's body, my children's bodies, my grandchildren's bodies, my great grandchildren's bodies to the third and fourth generations to outstanding healthy bodies and vessels without diseases and sickness.

I bind myself, my wife, my children, my grandchildren, and my great grandchildren to the Spirit of the Living ***God, God's Holy Spirit to the third and fourth generations***.

I bind myself, my wife, my children, my grandchildren, and my great grandchildren to God, Almighty's hedge of protection to the ***third and fourth generations***.

In the name of Almighty God in Heaven, and
In the name of Almighty Jesus Christ in Heaven, and
In the name of Almighty Holy Spirit, Who is on earth with us.
Praise You, Almighty God, and Praise You, Almighty Jesus Christ, and Praise You, Almighty Holy Spirit! Amen.

CHAPTER **127**

Prayer to Reverse Enemy Attacks Against You

Although I don't condone violence, you must protect yourself in a life or death situation. In this case you have to get yourself a leverage, (i.e., a baseball bat, skillet, a club, a pipe, a brick, etc.) and knock the evil hell out of the attacker to protect yourself. However, on the other hand try to safely escape the attacker if you are physically being attacked. Otherwise, here are some ideas to follow:

Love your attacker(s)/enemy(ies) as you will heap coals of fire on his/her head.

Do not avenge yourself or take vengeance upon your attacker/ enemy as God, Almighty said to leave the way open for His wrath as vengeance is His and He will repay.

Romans 12 (KJV)

19. Dearly beloved, ***avenge not ourselves***, but rather give place unto wrath: for it is written, ***Vengeance is mine***; I will repay, saith the Lord.
20. Therefore if thine enemy hunger, feed him; if he thirst, give him drink: for in so doing thou shalt ***heap coals of fire on his head***.
21. Be not overcome of evil, but overcome evil with good.

Pray the prayer listed below from Psalms 140. Pray this prayer on a daily basis until you see positive results.

> Father in heaven, please accept my prayer from Psalms 140,
> In the name of my personal Savior, Jesus Christ and
> In the name of Your Precious Holy Sprit, this my prayer:

Psalms 140 (KJV)

1. Deliver me, O Lord, from the evil man: preserve me from the violent man;
2. Which imagine mischiefs in their heart; continually are they gathered together for war.
3. They have sharpened their tongues like a serpent; adders' poison is under their lips. Selah.
4. Keep me, O Lord, from the hands of the wicked; preserve me from the violent man; who have purposed to overthrow my goings.
5. The proud have hid a snare for me, and cords; they have spread a net by the wayside; they have set gins for me. Selah.
6. I said unto the Lord, Thou art my God: hear the voice of my supplications, O Lord.
7. O God the Lord, the strength of my salvation, thou hast covered my head in the day of battle.
8. Grant not, O Lord, the desires of the wicked: further not his wicked device; lest they exalt themselves. Selah.
9. As for the head of those that compass me about, let the mischief of their own lips cover them.
10. Let burning coals fall upon them: let them be cast into the fire; into deep pits, that they rise not up again.
11. Let not an evil speaker be established in the earth: evil shall hunt the violent man to overthrow him.
12. I know that the Lord will maintain the cause of the afflicted, and the right of the poor.

13. Surely the righteous shall give thanks unto thy name: the upright shall dwell in thy presence.

In the name of Almighty God in Heaven, and
In the name of Almighty Jesus Christ in Heaven, and
In the name of Almighty Holy Spirit, Who is on earth with us.
Praise You, Almighty God, and Praise You, Almighty Jesus Christ, and Praise You, Almighty Holy Spirit! Amen.

CHAPTER 128

Prisons Are Over Crowded Due to Inequalities in Broken Systems

Many of the prisons in the Unites States of America are dangerously over crowded, mainly due to directed and blatant discrimination with vast over tones of racism. Most judges sitting on the court benches routinely grant excessive sentences to black Americans and other minorities over white Americans. Most of the time white Americans given slaps on their wrists for hard drug possessions while on the other hand, black Americans are given harsher sentences for possessions of crack cocaine or marijuana. Some of the judges aren't fit to serve as judges on dog fight events.

Prison systems are predominately corrupt at the least. There are blatant favoritism by prision guards. They allow gang leaders within the prisons to do as they will while their palms are being greased with monetary kick-backs as some inmates can afford to pay off the gurards.

The parole systems are corrupt, bias and legally conduct prejudices and racism against many inmates. Here's something that I found out about the Correctional Facility at Chillicothe, Ohio. The Adult Parole Board had continuously denied parolee candidates their opportunities for parole. One gentleman was on a work program where he learned a trade of automobile body repair and painting. He repaired and painted the prison's vehicle bodies. He received numerous certificate awards of appreciation for his outstanding works of achievements. He also attended the General Education Development (GED) program, even though he had previously graduated from high school. He came up for parole many times during his 20 year at Chillicothe, but was refused each and every time.

Here is the kicker part of this scenario. It was learned that the reason why the Adult Parole Board kept extending the inmates time in prison was to insure the security of the prison's employee job status. It was learned that if they paroled the inmates, which was about 17 inmates eligible for parole, it would jeopardized the prison's employee jobs. This is certainly unacceptable in the least. It is discrimination and legalized slavery (institutionalized).

When one rebel against God, Almighty, sickness, including directed prejudices and racism towards humanity; diseases and death could be part of your punishment.

Sickness and Disease Was Miriam's (Aaron's sister) Punishment For Prejudice and Racism.

Numbers 12 (KJV)

1. And Miriam and Aaron spake against Moses because of the Ethiopian woman whom he had married: for he had married an Ethiopian woman.
2. And they said, Hath the Lord indeed spoken only by Moses? hath he not spoken also by us? And the Lord heard it.
3. (Now the man Moses was very meek, above all the men which were upon the face of the earth.)
4. And the Lord spake suddenly unto Moses, and unto Aaron, and unto Miriam, Come out ye three unto the tabernacle of the congregation. And they three came out.
5. And the Lord came down in the pillar of the cloud, and stood in the door of the tabernacle, and called Aaron and Miriam: and they both came forth.

6. And he said, Hear now my words: If there be a prophet among you, I the Lord will make myself known unto him in a vision, and will speak unto him in a dream.
7. My servant Moses is not so, who is faithful in all mine house.
8. With him will I speak mouth to mouth, even apparently, and not in dark speeches; and the similitude of the Lord shall he behold: wherefore then were ye not afraid to speak against my servant Moses?
9. And the anger of the Lord was kindled against them; and he departed.
10. And the cloud departed from off the tabernacle; and, behold, Miriam became leprous, white as snow: and Aaron looked upon Miriam, and, behold, she was leprous.
11. And Aaron said unto Moses, Alas, my lord, I beseech thee, lay not the sin upon us, wherein we have done foolishly, and wherein we have sinned.
12. Let her not be as one dead, of whom the flesh is half consumed when he cometh out of his mother's womb.
13. And Moses cried unto the Lord, saying, Heal her now, O God, I beseech thee.
14. And the Lord said unto Moses, If her father had but spit in her face, should she not be ashamed seven days? let her be shut out from the camp seven days, and after that let her be received in again.
15. And Miriam was shut out from the camp seven days: and the people journeyed not till Miriam was brought in again.
16. And afterward the people removed from Hazeroth, and pitched in the wilderness of Paran.

Death Was Aaron's Punishment For Rebellion.

Numbers 20 (KJV)

24. Aaron shall be gathered unto his people: for he shall not enter into the land which I have given unto the children of

Israel, because ye rebelled against my word at the water of Meribah.

25. Take Aaron and Eleazar his son, and bring them up unto mount Hor:
26. And strip Aaron of his garments, and put them upon Eleazar his son: and Aaron shall be gathered unto his people, and shall die there.
27. And Moses did as the Lord commanded: and they went up into mount Hor in the sight of all the congregation.
28. And Moses stripped Aaron of his garments, and put them upon Eleazar his son; and Aaron died there in the top of the mount: and Moses and Eleazar came down from the mount.
29. And when all the congregation saw that Aaron was dead, they mourned for Aaron thirty days, even all the house of Israel.

CHAPTER **129**

Psychics and Fortune Tellers Are Satan's Representatives

Psychics And Fortune Tellers (Familiar spirits). The actual word "Psychic(s)" and "Fortune Tellers" are not found in the King James version of the bible, but are described as "familiar spirit(s) which relates to the field of satanic deceptions. This deception attempts to copy the Spiritual Gifts of Christian Prophecy and other Spiritual Gifts as well. They are essentially counterfeits to Almighty God's powers and Gifts.

Leviticus 19:31 (KJV), "Regard not them that have familiar spirits, neither seek after wizards, to be defile by them: I am the Lord your God."

Leviticus 20:6 (KJV), "And the soul that turned after such as have familiar spirits, and after wizards, to go a whoring after them, I will even set my face against that soul, and will cut him off from among his people."

One example is that of King Saul. Among other things, King Saul lost his life for consulting familiar spirits and he did not inquire or consult God, Almighty.

1 Chronicles 10:13-14 (KJV), "13) So Saul died for his transgression which he comitted against the LORD, even against the word of the

LORD, which he kept not, and also for asking counsel of one that had a familiar spirit, to inquire of it;

14. And inquired not of the LORD: therefore HE slew him, and turned the kingdom unto David the son of Jesse."

Psychic telephone networks and Psychic television programs are booming businesses all over the world, especially in the United States of America. People by the millions are hooked on so called benefits of being associated with psychics, Satan's representatives. These psychics lie about looking into one's future, one's wealth or future wealth, love, about communications with one's loved ones whom have past away, the so called appearance of one's love ones in seance sessions, counterfeit healings and much more. These are all counterfeits to God's blessings He has in store for His Saints, but not for those of the world.

OPEN MIND AND A TELEPHONE. The celebrities who are hosting these television shows will tell you that all you need is an open mind and a telephone to contact a psychic and start receiving joy, success and any other lies they want to tell you. What they are really telling you is that your mind must be opened to Satan and his demons so they can perform their counterfeits on you. They will actually be performing tricks on you by trying to imitate God's blessings.

- OPEN MIND. You must not open your mind to no one other than God, Almighty which includes His son Jesus Christ, and His Holy Spirit because they are one. You must meditate on God's Holy Word, the bible and do His commandments to the best of your abilities.
Joshua 1:8 (KJV), "This book of the law shall not depart out of thy mouth; but thou shall MEDITATE therein DAY and NIGHT, that thou mayest observe to do according to all that is written therein: for then thou shalt make thy way PROSPEROUS, and then thou shall have good SUCCESS."

1 Timothy 4:15 (KJV) "Meditate upon these things; give thyself wholly to them; that they profiting may appear to all"

Meditate. Hebrew definition. G3191. meletao, mel-et-ah'-o; from a presumed der. of G3199; to take care of, i.e.(by impl.) revolve in the mind:--imagine, (pre-) meditate.

You see, you can't have an opened mind if you continually meditate on the Lord, our God. When you totally mediate on the Lord, you will have great success and you will become prosperous in Him.
- TELEPHONE. There is normally a fee assessed with calling the Psychic 800, 900 or other numbered hotlines. Some fees start at around $3.99 per minute which is charged to your telephone number just to be lied to and/or have counterfeits performed on you. Our telephone line for communications is God's Holy Spirit. When we pray, the Holy Spirit intercedes for us and carries our prayers to Jesus Christ, our Savior. Jesus then intercedes our prayers to God, our Father whom in turns gives the commands back to the Holy Spirit for our success and our prosperity.

Mark 11:24 (KJV), "Therefore I say unto you, What things ye desire, when ye pray, believe that ye receive them, and ye shall have them."

Romans 8:26 & 34 (KJV) "26) Likewise the Spirit also helpeth our infirmities: for we know not what we should pray for as we ought: but the Spirit itself maketh intercession for us with groanings which cannot be uttered.

34. Who is he that condemneth? It is Christ that died, yea rather, that is risen, who is even at the right hand of God, who also maketh intercession for us."

You see, we don't have to pay for our communications or go through various long distant telephone carriers like AT&T, SPRINT, MCI, or other carriers. We don't even have to own a telephone and a telephone line. Our long distance carrier is none other than God's Holy Spirit who is available whenever we desire and wherever we are day or night. Incidently, we will never get a busy signal, nor will we get static on the line. We don't have to worry about some contractors or someone else cutting or damaging our communication line. The world doesn't have access to our communication source or path. We have access to a great monopoly of the best communications source in the universe.

Let's explore the following scriptures:

Deuteronomy 18:10-12 (KJV), "10) There shall not be found among you any one that maketh his son or his daughter to pass through the fire, or that useth divination, or an observer of times, or an enchanter, or a witch,

11. Or a charmer, or a consulter with familiar spirits, or a wizard, or a necromancer.
12. For all that do these things are an abomination unto the Lord: and because of these abominations the Lord thy God doth drive them out from before thee."

PASS THROUGH FIRE. Anyone who makes their son or daughter pass through fire is an abomination to God. You may have heard or actually been part of a party or gathering of people where certain games were played. These games included certain people with bare feet walking over red hot coals of fire without feeling the flames or the hot coals. Additionally, these people weren't even harmed. This is unnatural and certainly influenced by Satan and his demons. Those demons are protecting the person by actually standing or laying between the hot coals and the person whose walking over them. This is a lie and a counterfeit to God's divine protection.

DIVINATION (WITCHCRAFT AND SOOTHSAYER). H7081. qecem,

keh'-sem; from H7080. divination, divine sentence, witchcraft. H7080. qacam, kaw-sam; a prim. root; prop. to distribute, i.e. determine by LOT or MAGICAL SCROLL; by impl. to divine (-r, -ation), prudent, soothsayer, use divination.

Here are some of the tools used in divination:

DIVINING (DOWSING) RODS used to search the ground for sources of water and minerals are quite popular. Webster's Dictionary gives the following definition: "dowse (douz) vi. dowsed, dows'ing to search for a source of water or minerals by walking about with a divining rod (dowsing rod) -dows'|er n." Normally forked branches of trees are used with two (2) branches forked in a "V-shape" used for handles at one end with a single branch used for pointing at the other end. The person searching doing the search would hold the handles while slowly walking over an area of the ground. Once the extended pointed part of the branch starts to move by going down and up then the person (with the demon' help) has found the source for where the water or minerals are. There are also mechanical (electrical) devices available which treasure hunters use to find precious metals. These are dowsing devices where one rod is placed at a point and another rod is placed at a specified distance from the first one and both are connected by wires to the dowsing device. The device sends out signals within a preset radius for the desire source of minerals where the scanning process is then monitored on the device by listening for beeping sounds and/or viewing the device's's metered gauges. So, as you can see, this is high tech divination. Same thing, but different methods of high technical methods of divinations are also abomination to God, Almighty.

POWER GAMES OF DEMONIC INFLUENCE. There are various games on the market which includes, but not limited to 'DUNGEONS and DRAGONS" and the "OUIJA BOARD". One word of caution is that if you have concerns or doubts about you or your children, your loved ones or any other Christian participating or playing with such games, don't. Don't even go in the presence of such games being played. Such games allow the participant(s) to interact with Satan and/or his demons. This is an abomination to God, Almighty.

HEAVY METAL/HARD ROCK/GANGSTER RAP MUSIC. These types of music for entertainment are demonically influenced music. Christians shouldn't avail themselves to listening to these types of music. There is also what is called I believe "BACKWARD MASK" music. This is when records were played, you couldn't understand what was being said or sung. When the record was played by reversing the direction of the record, then you could understand the lyrics which were either praising Satan or blaspheming God and/or the heavenly host.

LOT(S) Vines Expository Dictionary: " Kleros denotes (a) an object used in casting or drawing lots, which consist of bits, or small tablets, of wood or stone (the probable derivation is from klao, to break); these were sometimes inscribed with the name of persons, and were put into a receptacle or a garment (a lap, Prov. 16:33), from which they were cast, after being shaken together; he whose lot first fell out was the one chosen." Modern day lots are used with decks of cards, crystal balls, pieces of paper thrown in a hat or basket and/ or various other methods or objects for drawing chances. Included are games of LUCK or CHANCE based on payment of money or something of value. Games of luck or chance for money or monetary gain include playing cards. shooting pool, shooting craps (dice), playing poker, playing slot machines, bingo, and purchasing raffle tickets just to name a few.

Let's explore luck (chance) and God's blessings.

LUCK (CHANCE). Receipients of the world who receive any type of improvements in their lives, success, money or anything of value in their lives is characterize to them as luck. Often times you'll hear

many people profess that they were lucky in one thing or another. Satan deals in luck, but not God. The world also gives credit to the forces of nature. Who is that force of nature? Satan, of course!
GOD'S BLESSINGS. Matthew 5:45 (KJV), "That ye may be the children of your Father which is in heaven: for He maketh His sun to rise on the evil and on the good, and sendeth rain on the just and on the unjust."

Although God blesses His own people whom are called by His name, worldly people receive His blessings as well. Blessings are given as a direct result of Christian prayers and their walk with Jesus Christ. As you can see, God provides rain and sunshine to his righteous people while the unrighteous or worldly people receive these blessings as well. Even in this, the world still gives credit to luck or in some cases, nature.

WITCHCRAFT (SORCERY) H3784. kashaph, kaw-shaf; a prim. root; prop. to whisper a spell, i.e. to inchant or practise magic;--sorcerer, (use) witch(-craft).

HOROSCOPE. MAGIC(IAN). Hebrew definition."H2748. chartom, khar-tome'; from the same H2747; a horoscopist (as drawing magical lines or cirles):--magician." The practice of using horoscopes and/or astrological signs falls into this category. Christians shouldn't get involved in the reading and/or following so called daily horoscopes found in newspapers, magazines and even booklets dedicated to horoscopes for each day and month of the year. If someone wants to know what your sign is, then tell them "Jesus Christ, my personal Saviour." Included are so called readings or palm readings to determine ones future or for some unknown knowledge of the person.

OBSERVER OF TIMES (HOROSCOPIST). Leviticus 19:26 (KJV), "Ye shall not eat any thing with the blood: neither shall ye use enchantments, nor OBSERVE TIMES."

Webster's Dictiounary definition: "Horoscope (hor'e skop') n. observer of the hour of birth, watcher, by metathesis, 1 the position of the planets and stars with relation to one another at a given time, esp. at the time of a person's birth, regarded in astrology as determining one's destiny 2 a chart of the zodiac signs and the positions of the twelve planets, etc. 3 a forecast based on such a chart, usually a set of twelve predictions for the twelve signs of the zodiac -- hor'o-scop'ic (-skap'ik) adj. -ho-ros-co-py (ho-res'ke pe) n."

God doesn't need or does He use charts, signs or wonders to predict our destiny as the sees through their eyes. All He has to do is speak the word and its done. As a mater fact He directs us and guides our paths automatically. We don't have to read the daily papers or some other literature to determine our destiny for a particular day or night. Actually, Satan doesn't even know our destiny in advance. What Satan and his demons do is to make their predictions for certain worldly persons who are into that sort of thing. Our support and our destiny is based upon our serving the true and living God whose Son is Jesus.

SORCERER (WITCHCRAFT) as explained by Vines Expository Dictionary as "1. Magos (a) one of a Median caste, a magician: (b) a wizard, sorcerer, a pretender to magic powers, a professor of the arts of witchcraft. 2. Pharmakos, an adjective signifying 'devoted to magical arts,' is used as noun, a sorcerer, especially one who uses drugs, potions, spells, enchantments. In sorcery, the use of drugs, whether simple or potent, was generally accompanied by incantations and appeals to occult powers, with the provision of various charms, amulets, etc., professedly designed to keep the applicant or patient from the attention and power of demons, but actually to impress the applicant with the mysterious resources and powers of sorcerer." Here you have learned that demons are the actual powers behind the sorcerer and all other displays of magical powers of sinful inflences.

ENCHANTER. " H5172. nachash, nawkhash' a prim. root; prop. to hiss, i.e. whisper (magic) spell;"

People who are not under the power of the Holy Ghost, that is saved, they can be subjects of spells being cast upon them. However, Christians through their own ignorance and lack of knowledge can also have spells cast upon them as well.

Webster's definition: "Spell (spel) a saying, tale, charm, akin to Goth spill, tale, 1 a word, formula, or form of words thought to have some magic power; incantation 2 seemingly magical power or irresistible influence; charm; fascination 3 a trance -- cast a spell on 1 to put into, or as into, a trance 2 to win the complete affection of"

CONSULTER. Hebrew definition. "H7592. sha'al, shaw-al', shaw-ale'; a prim. root; to inquire; by impl. to request; by extens. to demand:--ask (counsel, on), beg. borrow, lay to charge, consult, demand, desre,"

Psychics hire themselves out as consultants to the worldly populus. Celebrities and government are regular customers of psychics for consultations for not only in their personal lives, but for guidance in making decisions in government matters as well. We as Christians have the Spirit of the Living God, His Holy Spirit for counsel and to lead and to guide us in our daily lives. We don't have to go to another person to reap these benefits. However, we can touch and agree with another Christian for some special blessing we desire and are seeking God, Almighty for.

Matthew 18:19-20 (KJV), "19) Again I say unto you, That if two of you shall agree on earth as touching any thing that they shall ask, it shall be done for them of my Father which is in heaven.

20. For where two or three are gathered together in my name, there am I in the midst of them."

WIZARD. Hebrew definition. H3049. yidde'oniy, yid-deh-o-nee'; from H3045; prop. a knowing one; spec. a conjurer; (by impl.) a GHOST:--WIZARD. Webster's dictionary. "Wiz-zard (wiz'ard) n. 2 a magician; conjurer; socerer 3" Present day wizards are characterzied and defined in Webster's dictionary as follows:

WITCH (wich) n. sorcerer, to use magic, to separate (hence set aside for religious worship) 1 a) a woman supposedly having supernatural power by a compact with the devil or evil spirits; sorceress b) [Obs.] a man with such power (cf. WARLOCK).

Witches have been known to transform themselves into ghosts where they can what they call, "astro project" themselves through walls or from one place to another quite fast. They can then transform themselves back to their physical bodies once they arrive at their desired destination.

WARLOCK (wor'lak') n. compact, 1 a person who practices black magic; sorcere or wizard: the male equivalent of a witch (sense 1) 2 a conjurer or magician.

Warlocks have also been known to transform themselves into ghosts where they can what they call, "astro project" themselves through walls or from one place to another quite fast. They can then transform themselves back to their physical bodies once they arrive at their desired destination.

NECROMANCER (SEANCE PERFORMER). H1875. darash, daw-rash'; by impl. to seek or ask; spec. to WORSHIP:--ask, necromancer, question, require, search, seek for, out.
Webster's Dictionary definition on necromancy 1 the practice of claiming to foretell the future by alleged communication with the dead 2 black magic; sorcery.

SATANIC WORSHIPING. The worship of Satan by witches and

followers of satan in what is known as a "COVEN", a place for satanic worship, the counterfeit of Christian Churches.

Webster's dictionary: coven (kuv'an) a gathering or meeting, esp. of witches. Satanism (sat'n iz'em) worship of Satan; esp., the principles and rites of a cult which travesties Christian ceremonies--Sa'tan ist n.

SEANCE (sa'ans). Webster's Dictionary definition: a meeting or session; now specif., a meeting at which a MEDIUM seeks or professes to communicate with the spirits of the dead. MEDIUM. 7 a person through whom communications are supposedly sent to the living from spirits of the dead.

COUNTERFEIT RESURRECTION. Seances are counterfeits to the actual resurrection of the dead. Only God, Almighty's power can raise the dead, but not Satan or his demons. Satan and his demons know exactly what our loved ones looked like at the time of their deaths and/or their funerals. These demonic spirits are great imposters. They can appear to you as your loved ones and even speak to you. My beloved precious ones, these are demons talking to you and these are demons making their appearance to you. Do not participate in or go near a seance in session, neither take part in such. Your curiosity will put your soul in danger.

DEATH IS UNTIL JUDGEMENT FOR LOST SOULS. When humans die their bodies are gone until judgement time. However, Christians' bodies will be resurrected upon the return of our Lord and Savior, Jesus Christ.

Revelation 20:12-13 (KJV), 12) And I saw the dead, small and great, stand before God; and the books were opened: and another book was opened, which is the book of life: and the dead were judged out of those things which were written in the books according to their works.

13. And the sea gave up the dead which were in it; and death and hell delivered up the dead which were in them: and they were judged every man according to their works."

They will not reappear to us again on this earth.

RESURRECTION OF THE DEAD IN CHRIST. When Christ returns for the Church (Christians) the dead in Christ shall awaken from the dead to return to heaven with Him.

1 Thesalonians 4:16-17 (KJV), "16) For the Lord Himself shall descend from heaven with a shout, with the voice of the archangel, and with the trump of God: and the dead in Christ shall rise first:

17. Then we which are alive and remain shall be caught up together with them in the clouds, to meet the Lord in the air: and so shall we ever be with the Lord."

PSYCHIATRY can be defined as a relm of the psychic phenomenon. Psychiatrist normally use hypnosis in determining the ills and ailings of their patients. They can't help their own minds and souls, so how can they heal somebody elses. They need help themselves.

ACUPUNCTURE is a false sense of healing with needles of some sort. This type of so called healing opens one up for demon possession and should be avoided.

HYPNOSIS is a form of a trance where one allows his or her mind to be controlled by satanic forces. This is where a person has lost control of his or her mind, body and soul. Christians, you should never allow yourselves to be put in a hypnotic trance, ever.

MARTIAL ARTS seems to be a harmless form of an exercise, mind control, and self defense, with MIND OVER MATTER. Mind over matter is the key. You must be able to exercise it in order to get your strength and power over your opponent. Your strength and power actually comes from demonic forces. This includes all types of martial arts. None are safe for Christians.

TRANSCENDENTAL MEDITATION is another form of a mind over matter in that one tries to meditate above ones own mind and out of the universe so to speak. Christian should meditate only on God's word, the Bible.

PALM READINGS by the palm of the hand by palm readers is another lie which involves the demonic entities also. Your so called predicted future will be carried out by none other than the assigned demons to fool you that these things which came to past or is coming to past are your blessings from God, Almighty. Christians, stay away from PSYCHICS and/or PALM READERS.

CHAPTER **130**

Racism, Discriminations and Prejudices in Churches

Unfortunately, hatred wears three common hats called racism, discrimination, and prejudice. They can be found around the world and are taught and carried over from one generation to another. These evil spirits are prevalent from the child rearing stages of our lives to our present everyday lives of our secular environments. Racism is not only a facet of life across different races or nationalities of people, but often time within a particular race and nationality.

Just because people are labeled as Christians doesn't mean that prejudices and racism are non existent in their lives and their churches. We have experienced prejudices in our church. There are certain cliques or groups of people who are given favoritism when some sort of selection processes avail themselves to certain people who are in the roles of authority.

Prov 26:26 (KJV) "Whose hatred is covered by deceit, his wickedness shall be showed before the whole congregation."

Prov 26:27 (KJV) "Whoso diggeth a pit shall fall therein: and he that rolleth a stone, it will return upon him."

Ezek 35:11 (KJV) "Therefore, as I live, saith the Lord GOD, I will even do according to thine anger, and according to thine envy which thou hast used out of thy hatred against them; and I will make myself known among them, when I have judged thee.

We have experienced year after year when election of new officers were in order for the coming year. This particular pastor would influence the selection process by his favorable recommendations for some and his disapproval for others. The selection process has nothing to do with ones spiritual growth in this particular church, but who may make decision in favor of this particular pastor's desires. Insecurity plays a big role in his life including the problem of his self esteem and his outlook on life in Christendom. This pastor seems to be insecure in everything he does in the church. When God puts a pastor in a church, he or she has nothing to be insecure about. One thing is for certain, you can't do God's will when you are depending on self, your soul power. You must depend on God's Holy Spirit and Him only. Many pastors and preachers seek power, money and yes, sex.

Zec 4:6 (KJV) "Then he answered and spake unto me, saying, This is the word of the LORD unto Zerubbabel, saying, Not by might, nor by power, but by my spirit, saith the LORD of hosts."

When we are still in self, then we are motivated by self and not by God's Holy Spirit. Unfortunately, self is the powerful works of the flesh. This is when we use the power of our soul instead of letting the Holy Spirit use His power. We must first be in tune with the Holy Spirit before we can be used by Him. God tells us in His word what the works of the flesh are, then He tells us what the fruits of the Spirit are as well.

Gal 5:19-24 (KJV) Now the works of the flesh are manifest, which are these; Adultery, fornication, uncleanness, lasciviousness,

20. Idolatry, witchcraft, hatred, variance, emulations, wrath, strife, seditions, heresies,

21. Envyings, murders, drunkenness, revellings, and such like: of the which I tell you before, as I have also told you in time past, that they which do such things shall not inherit the kingdom of God.
22. But the fruit of the Spirit is love, joy, peace, longsuffering, gentleness, goodness, faith,
23. Meekness, temperance: against such there is no law.
24. And they that are Christ's have crucified the flesh with the effections and lusts.

CHAPTER **131**

Rape (Forced or Not Mutually Consensual Sex) Is Strictly Forbidden

Unfortunately, church folks and ministers have allowed themselves to be caught up in rape cases. Some have forced themselves not only on those of the opposite sex, but those of the same sex (abomination to God) as well without their consent. Some ministers have gone so far as to tell their victims to keep it a secret by not telling anyone concerning their episodes with them. Some of the victims have suffered mentally. They are devastated in that their bodies were immorally violated. This is a mark that some victims will carry with them for the rest of their lives. In biblical days, there were very harsh punishments for raping somebody as illustrated below in the following scriptures.

Deu 22:23-30 (KJV) If a damsel that is a virgin be betrothed unto an husband, and a man find her in the city, and lie with her;

24. Then ye shall bring them both out unto the gate of that city, and ye shall stone them with stones that they die; the damsel, because she cried not, being in the city; and the man, because he hath humbled his neighbour's wife: so thou shalt put away evil from among you.
25. But if a man find a betrothed damsel in the field, and the man force her, and lie with her: then the man only that lay with her shall die:

26. But unto the damsel thou shalt do nothing; there is in the damsel no sin worthy of death: for as when a man riseth against his neighbour, and slayeth him, even so is this matter:
27. For he found her in the field, and the betrothed damsel cried, and there was none to save her.
28. If a man find a damsel that is a virgin, which is not betrothed, and lay hold on her, and lie with her, and they be found;
29. Then the man that lay with her shall give unto the damsel's father fifty shekels of silver, and she shall be his wife; because he hath humbled her, he may not put her away all his days.
30. A man shall not take his father's wife, nor discover his father's skirt.

CHAPTER 132

Rebuke Not, Nor Disrespect an Elderly Man or Woman

God tells us to honor and respect senior citizens or our elders whether they are our parents, grandparents or not. We are suppose to respect older people as if they were our parents. Many youngsters misconstrue the fact that they are bound to the authority of senior human beings whether they are children, teenagers, or over 21 years of age. They still are commanded to obey and honor their elders/senior citizens.

1 Timothy 5 (KJV)

1. Rebuke not an elder, but intreat him as a father; and the younger men as brethren;
2. The elder women as mothers; the younger as sisters, with all purity.
3. Honour widows that are widows indeed.

I heard an Apostle, who is also a Pastor having a conversation with one of his preachers (Elder) who had elderly people in his congregation. He told the preacher that in doing his job that he could disregard that person was a senior citizen because he was over that senior citizen or words to that effect. This is not the kind of teachings that I would like to hear concerning elderly people.

CHAPTER **133**

Sabbath Day Commandments Are for Jews (Hebrews), (i.e., the Twelve Tribes of Israel)

Christians Are Not Under Old Testament Law

Colossians 2 (KJV)

16. Let no man therefore judge you in meat, or in drink, or in respect of an holyday, or of the new moon, or of the ***sabbath days***:

Colossians 2:16 (Simple English) "So, don't let anyone condemn you for what you eat or drink, or a religious festival, or the new moon holiday, or ***Sabbaths***."

Churches such as the 7th Day Adventist Churches celebrate and worship with their services being held on Saturdays, which they call their Sabbath Day of celebration or their worship day. Actually, there is nothing wrong with celebrating or worshiping Almighty God, the Father, Almighty God, the Son, and Almighty God, the Holy Spirit on Saturdays. However, we as Christians are admonished to serve them on every day of the week, not just on Saturday or Sundays. Most Christians choose Sunday in which they come together and worship the Holy Trinity. However, the 7th Day Adventist Churches believe that they are required to worship on Saturday in their attempts to fulfill their purported requirements of keeping the Sabbath Day Holy.

That commandment was strictly for the Jewish/Hebrew nation of people religion. That commandment is still prevalent today for all Jewish religious practicing Jews or Orthodox Jews.

Jews/Hebrews Are Still Under The Law

Leviticus 19 (KJV)

1. And the Lord spake unto Moses, saying,
2. Speak unto all the congregation of the children of Israel, and say unto them, Ye shall be holy: for I the Lord your God am holy.

3. Ye shall fear every man his mother, and his father, and keep my ***sabbaths***: I am the Lord your God.

Exodus 20 (KJV)

8. Remember the sabbath day, to keep it holy.

Jews are still bound by the dispensation of Law in the bible. Remember, they are still looking for their King to come forth. They denied Jesus, their original King, who brought in the dispensation of Grace to us. Christians are under the dispensation of Grace and are no longer under the dispensation of Law where the Jews are still bound by the Dispensation of the Law. Therefore, they still have to keep the Sabbath Day, Holy.

CHAPTER 134

Sacrifices to Devils or Satan (i.e., Other Gods) Are Strictly Forbidden

Our heavenly Father is a jealous and righteous God who also created everything within and without our universe. We can certainly kindle His anger by honoring other little gods even though they may be physical objects and/or designs, they have demons attached to them.

Deu 32:17-25 (KJV) They sacrificed unto devils, not to God; to gods whom they knew not, to new gods that came newly up, whom your fathers feared not.

18. Of the Rock that begat thee thou art unmindful, and hast forgotten God that formed thee.
19. And when the LORD saw it, he abhorred them, because of the provoking of his sons, and of his daughters.
20. And he said, I will hide my face from them, I will see what their end shall be: for they are a very froward generation, children in whom is no faith.
21. They have moved me to jealousy with that which is not God; they have provoked me to anger with their vanities: and I will move them to jealousy with those which are not a people; I will provoke them to anger with a foolish nation.
22. For a fire is kindled in mine anger, and shall burn unto the lowest hell, and shall consume the earth with her increase,

and set on fire the foundations of the mountains.

23. I will heap mischiefs upon them; I will spend mine arrows upon them.
24. They shall be burnt with hunger, and devoured with burning heat, and with bitter destruction: I will also send the teeth of beasts upon them, with the poison of serpents of the dust.
25. The sword without, and terror within, shall destroy both the young man and the virgin, the suckling also with the man of gray hairs.

CHAPTER **135**

Saints or Sainthood Automatically Includes All Christians

Saints Are Automatically Appointed By God's Grace And Mercy.

Almighty God in heaven tells us through His holy word in Romans that we are already Saints because we are holy and living sacrifices unto Him. Catholics go through the rituals of canonizing or appointing some of their late members which proves nothing because if their selected ones lived their lives acceptable to God, they are already appointed as Saints.

Romans 12:1 (KJV), "I beseech you therefore, brethren, by the mercies of God, that ye present your bodies a living sacrifice, holy, acceptable unto God, which is your reasonable service."

So, as you can see, we are obligated to keep our bodies pure, blameless, consecrated and holy as saints. In some denominations, some people are **selected, canonize or appointed saints** by man on earth which doesn't even amount to a hill of beans. God doesn't recognize man's appointments of saints because it is His Son, Jesus' authority and power to so and not man's.

The following scriptures give credence to people set aside as holy and as saints versus the wicked.

Psalms 37:28 KJV), "For the Lord, loveth judgement, and forsaketh not his saints; they are preserved for ever: but the seed of the wicked shall be cut off."

If man was allowed to select and make certain people saints, then most of the world including Christians would be essentially lost and damned along with the wicked. Notice the next scripture with the word "COVENANT" in it.

Psalms 50:5 (KJV), "Gather my saints together unto me; those that have made **COVENANT** with me by sacrifice."

The covenant mentioned in Psalms 50:5 is an agreement between God and His saints as well as a promise from Him to His saints. First, God made us a promise of salvation through His Son, Jesus as being the LIGHT of the Gentiles and the Church (the Christians). He talks about this in Isaiah.

Isaiah 42:6 (KJV), "I the LORD have called thee in righteousness, and will hold thine hand, and will keep thee, and give thee for a COVENANT of the people, for a LIGHT of the gentiles; "

Whether we accept the fact or belief or not that we are naturally born in sin, we have involuntarily made a covenant with death and an agreement with hell. God sent His Son, Jesus to die for our sins which put an awakening effect on death and a hot furnace effect on hell.

Isaiah 28:18 (KJV), "And your covenant with death shall be disannulled, and your agreement with hell shall not stand; when the overflowing scourge shall pass through, then ye shall be trodden down by it."

Essentially, we've been given a release on life of our souls from eternal death to life everlasting and our eternal home will not be in hell, but heaven. Finally, this verse also emphasizes that when Christ was sacrificed for us, He took victory over Satan and hell (overflowing scourge). Satan and his demons are doing and will do everything in their power to destroy (trodden down) Christians.

Biblically speaking when we become born-again Christians, we become saints at that moment because we are **SAVED** from God's wrath:

Mark 16:16 (KJV), "He that believeth and is baptized shall be saved; but he that believeth not shall be damned."

Within various church denominations, predetermined ceremonies on how we should be baptized once we believe is done in a variety of ways including the sprinkling of water on a new convert's or baby's head (baby dedications). The Greek translation refers to "fully wet." Baptism through submersion represents the burial and resurrection of Christ.

Sprinkling/Pouring Water Baptisms. Sprinkling and the pouring of water on candidates for baptism don't represent Christ's death, nor do they represent His resurrection in the sense of the bible representations, either literally or figuratively. We must be fully submersed in water as is the will of Almighty God.

Submersion In Water Baptisms. When John baptized our Lord and Savior, Jesus Christ, He was fully submersed in water. When His body went under water, it represented His death. When He rose out of the water, it represented His resurrection.

Mat 3:13 (KJV) "Then cometh Jesus from Galilee to Jordan unto John, to be baptized of him."

Mat 3:14 (KJV) "But John forbad him, saying, I have need to be baptized of thee, and comest thou to me?"

Mat 3:15 (KJV) "And Jesus answering said unto him, Suffer it to be so now: for thus it becometh us to fulfil all righteousness. Then he suffered him."

Mat 3:16 (KJV) "And Jesus, when he was baptized, went up straightway out of the water: and, lo, the heavens were opened unto him, and he saw the Spirit of God descending like a dove, and lighting upon him:"

Mat 3:17 (KJV) "And lo a voice from heaven, saying, This is my beloved Son, in whom I am well pleased."

Paul talked about baptism in I Corinthians where he mentioned the word "WASHED" as being fully wet. So, how can one wash by sprinkling or just by pouring water on someone? Common sense would lend you the wisdom that if you wanted to thoroughly wash your clothes, you would want them fully submerge in water to get the full effect of cleanliness.

1 Cor 6:11 (KJV) "And such were some of you: but ye are washed, but ye are sanctified, but ye are justified in the name of the Lord Jesus, and by the Spirit of our God."

Washed. Greek definition. 628. apolouo, ap-ol-oo'-o; from G575 and G3068; to **wash fully**, i.e. (fig.) have remitted (reflex.):--wash (away).

God gives us an example of how we should partake in water baptism in the following scriptures:

SAVED (BORN-AGAIN). We are saved from God, Almighty's eternal wrath forever. We don't have to worry about the Great White Throne Judgment where Satan, his demons and all lost people will spend eternity.

Romans 6:4 (KJV), "Therefore we are buried with Him by baptism into death: that like as Christ was raised up from the dead by the glory of the Father even so we also should walk in newness of life."

Romans 6:5 (KJV), "For if we have been planted together in the likeness of His death, we shall also in the likeness of His resurrection:"

SANCTIFIED as being holy and set aside from the world:

1 Corinthians 6:11 (KJV), "And such were some of you: but ye are washed, but ye are sanctified, but ye are justified in the name of the Lord Jesus, and by the Spirit of our Lord."

JUSTIFIED, that is we are made righteous through the shedding of Jesus Christ's blood on the cross for our sins. You see, No man or woman can appoint us as saints by no means except God, the Father, God the Son, and God the Holy Spirit. As Christians we must be in control of our total self which is our body, our soul and our spirit. The way we can be in control of ourselves is through our spirit (the Holy Spirit) within us. Although the Holy Spirit doesn't force us to do anything, He will if we are submissive enough to allow Him to nudge us and convict our hearts if we attempt to do something wrong. He is essentially our watchdog and our guide because we are set aside from the people of the world (unbelievers).

Acts 13:39 (KJV) "And by him all that believe are justified from all things, from which ye could not be justified by the law of Moses."

Rom 3:24 (KJV) "Being justified freely by his grace through the redemption that is in Christ Jesus:" Rom 3:25 (KJV) "Whom God hath set forth to be a propitiation through faith in his blood, to declare his righteousness for the remission of sins that are past, through the forbearance of God;"

Rom 3:26 (KJV) "To declare, I say, at this time his righteousness: that he might be just, and the justifier of him which believeth in Jesus."

Rom 3:28 (KJV) "Therefore we conclude that a man is justified by faith without the deeds of the law."

Rom 5:1 (KJV) "Therefore being justified by faith, we have peace with God through our Lord Jesus Christ:" Rom 5:9 (KJV) "Much more then, being now justified by his blood, we shall be saved from wrath through him." Rom 8:33 (KJV) "Who shall lay any thing to the charge of God's elect? It is God that justifieth."

1 Cor 6:11 (KJV) "And such were some of you: but ye are **washed**, but ye are sanctified, but ye are justified in the name of the Lord Jesus, and by the Spirit of our God."

Washed. Greek definition. 628. apolouo, ap-ol-oo'-o; from G575 and G3068; to wash fully, i.e. (fig.) have remitted (reflex.):--wash (away).

ROYAL INHERITANCE . Although we are in the world, we are not of this world. We are from the stock of a kingdom of a ROYAL inheritance, a priestly fraternity bestowed on us from our King, Jesus.

1 Peter 2:9, (KJV), "But ye are a chosen generation, a royal priesthood, an holy nation, a peculiar people; that ye should show forth the praises of Him Who called you out of darkness into His marvellous light."

CHAPTER **136**

Salvation Is the Key to Your Everlasting Life after Your Physical Death

ARE YOU REALLY SAVED OR BORN-AGAIN?

We must have sincere desires in our hearts to change from our sinful lives that we lead to that of salvation through Jesus Christ, God's only Son. We must believe in God the Father, God the Son and God the Holy Spirit. God is a third (3) partition God Head, i.e., God the Father, Jesus the Son and the Holy Spirit. These are all one. When we are physically born, we are born in sin. We have a body and soul which comprises only two (2) heads in one. The only way we can have a relationship with the God head, we must be born-again which is also called being saved and also heirs to salvation. Once we are born-again (saved), we are filled with God's Holy Spirit. Now we are three (3) partition persons or 3 heads in one. We have a body, a soul, and the Holy Spirit. We have a link to God in heaven through Jesus Christ by way of Gods Holy Spirit.

Before we become heirs to salvation we must repent of our sins to Jesus Christ, the Son of God Almighty in heaven.

Acts 2:38 (KJV) "Then Peter said unto them, Repent, and be baptized every one of you in the name of Jesus Christ for the remission of sins, and ye shall receive the gift of the Holy Ghost."

Rom 10:9 (KJV) "That if thou shalt confess with thy mouth the Lord Jesus, and shalt believe in thine heart that God hath raised him from the dead, thou shalt be saved."

Rom 10:10 (KJV) "For with the heart man believeth unto righteousness; and with the mouth confession is made unto salvation." Your prayer to be saved should be something similar to this while you raise your hands towards heaven:

> "Jesus Christ in heaven,
> I am a sinner,
> I believe inYou,
> I believe that You died for my sins,
> I believe God, Almighty raised You from the dead, I believe in God, Almighty, Your Father in heaven, I believe in God, Almighty's Holy Spirit,
> Please forgive me of all of my sins,
> Please cleanse me throughout, and
> Please come into my heart Lord, Jesus.
> Thank You, Master!.
> Amen."

Acts 2:38 (KJV), "Then Peter said unto them, Repent, and be baptized every one of you in the name of Jesus Christ for the remission of sins, and ye shall receive the gift of the Holy Ghost."

What are you saved from? This is the ultimate question. The word "SAVED" on the secular side of the house is used synonymous with material possessions such as saved money, family heirlooms and/or other saved possessions. Saving money usually involves some sort of an account at a savings institution such as a bank. This bank account provides a means for checks and balances. However, the word saved on the spiritual side of the house takes on a completely different meaning. "Saved" means you are an heir to salvation. You have an account in heaven called the book of life with your name in it.

Revelation 3:5 (KJV), "He that overcometh, the same shall be clothed in white raiment; and I will not blot out his name out of the book of life, but I will confess his name before my Father, and before his angels."

This is heaven's means and ways for checks and balances of your spiritual savings account. Before your name was written in the book of life, you had to repent and be baptized. This baptism should have been by water baptism through submersion.

During the days of Noah, only eight souls were saved by water.

1 Peter 3:20-21 (KJV), (20) "Which sometimes were disobedient, when once the longsuffering of God waited in the days of Noah, while the ark was a preparing, wherein few, that is, eight souls were saved by water.

21. "The like figure whereunto even baptism doth also now save us **(not the putting away of the filth of the flesh, but the answer of a good conscience toward God,)** by the resurrection of Jesus Christ:".

Likewise, we must partake in water baptism through submersion. We are buried with Christ by baptism into death and raised in the likeness of His resurrection.

Romans 6:4-5 (KJV), (4) "Therefore we are buried with Him by baptism into death: that like as Christ was raised up from the dead by the glory of the Father, even so we also should walk in newness of life."

5. "For if we have been planted together in the likeness of His death, we shall be also in the likeness of His resurrection:".

We are saved from hell's furnace of fire forever.

Matthew 13:49,50 (KJV), (49) "So shall it be at the end of the world: the angels shall come forth, and sever the wicked from among the just,"

50. "And shall cast them into the furnace of fire: there shall be wailing and gnashing of teeth." This is the eternal wrath of God, Almighty for the sins we've committed and/or that we will subsequently commit.

Christians are identified as heirs to SALVATION.

1 Thessalonians 5:9 (KJV), "For God hath not appointed us to wrath, but to obtain salvation by our Lord Jesus Christ,".

Salvation doesn't mean that you are saved from worldly problems and/or bad situations. As a matter of fact, things may just get worse. Once you take a firm stand for Christ, all hell will break loose. We do mean that literally. You'll loose some worldly friends, you will be attacked from all directions by hell's forces. Satan, and all of his head demons and filthy imps will attack everything that you possibly own or gain: you, your relatives, your friends, and/or anybody whom you are remotely connected to including any property(ies) and possessions you may own or acquire.

Salvation is the first level of anointing that God blesses us with. This level of anointing renders us what is called "BABES IN CHRIST". As babes in Christ, we can only digest the milk of His word.

Hebrews 5:12 (KJV), "For when for the time ye ought to be teachers, ye have need that one teach you again which be the first principles of the oracles of God; and are become such as have need of milk, and not of strong meat.".

Hebrews 5:13 (KJV), "For every one that useth milk is un-skillful in the word of righteousness: for he is a babe.".

Therefore, as babes in Christ, we need to read and study God's word regularly.

2 Timothy 2:15 (KJV), "Study to show thyself approved unto God, a workman that needeth not to be ashamed, rightly dividing the word of truth.".

As we read and study God's word, we'll become more skillful in using it. There are many passages of scriptures in God's word a babe in Christ won't be able to comprehend or understand. Although babes in Christ have this new born-again life, they still have their secular knowledge and experiences they can comfortably refer to rather than being led by the Holy Spirit while trying to understand God's word. This is a learned process in being guided by the Spirit of the Living God. Getting rid of old habits will be a gradual process. Some old habits will vanish immediately, but others can take awhile. It all depends on the person and that person's faith. Everybody's faith is not the same. Some people's faith is weak and some others are strong. Pray and ask God for a stronger faith on a daily basis.

Being filled with the Holy Spirit. Getting our prayer language is the second level of anointing that God bestows on us. This level of anointing is where we we can pray to God, Almighty in the Spirit. It is a language similar to the Holy Ghost's gift of "Speaking In Tongues". The difference is that your prayer is only between you, God, Jesus, and the Holy Spirit. The Holy Spirit's gift of speaking in tongues can be interpreted by another Christian who possess the gift of interpretation tongues or someone who understand the language that you are speaking. This is where you could be speaking in any language in the world. This is a sign that your are a Christian.

Power is the third anointing that God bestows on us. This level of anointing will come after much prayer and praise after your requests to Him. Additionally, one has to be weaned from the milk of God's word to the meat of His word. Being filled with the Holy Spirit gives you the opportunity to have access to one or more of the nine gifts of the Spirit. In your bible read the following scriptures in 1 Corinthians 12:1-12. If you desire God to bestowed one or more of the gifts of the Spirit upon you, begin to earnestly and sincerely pray to Him. Praise Him while lifting up holy hands to heaven and thanking Him for that gift.

When you pray, you should always thank God for something that you ask of Him before you end your prayer even though you may not physically see it. Whatever you do, please don't beg Him for that gift. Start by giving God the sacrifice of praises regularly and you'll start seeing a big difference in your life as you grow closer to Him. Normally, when one is baptized in the Holy Spirit, the gift of speaking in tongues will be evident.

1 Cor 14:22 (KJV) "Wherefore tongues are for a sign, not to them that believe, but to them that believe not: but prophesying serveth not for them that believe not, but for them which believe."

This is where God bestows upon you a heavenly language where you can pray to Him in the Spirit as well as in the language of men. If you are not praying to God in tongues, then you should not speak in tongues among other people without an interpreter because the Church won't understand what you're saying. However, if you are alone in your secret prayer closet, then speak in tongues (heavenly language) to God as much as you so desire. As a matter of fact, it delights God when you pray or speak to Him in the Spirit (tongues - heavenly language). You can also have the anointing to speak a foreign language in the tongues of men. If someone understands what you are saying, then they can interpret it for you.

This only comes with much prayer and fasting. Fasting can take on the form of the sacrifice of praises to God, Jesus, and the Holy Spirit every day and throughout the day. Developing a very close an intimate relationship with the Holy Spirit is another form of fasting. You still are required to direct your prayers to God, the Father through Jesus Christ, the Son. However, you can talk to God's Holy Spirit, ask Him questions, seek His advice and assistance.

Acts 1:8 (KJV) "But ye shall receive power, after that the Holy Ghost is come upon you: and ye shall be witnesses unto me both in Jerusalem, and in all Judaea, and in Samaria, and unto the uttermost part of the earth."

Receiving this anointing could take many years of trials and tribulations before you see the Holy Spirit's power being manifested in your life and your ministry. God tells us in Peter what we should do because Satan and his demons will definitely be on our heels, both day and night.

1 Pet 5:8 (KJV) "Be sober, be vigilant; because your adversary the devil, as a roaring lion, walketh about, seeking whom he may devour:"

1 Pet 5:9 (KJV) "Whom resist stedfast in the faith, knowing that the same afflictions are accomplished in your brethren that are in the world."

1 Pet 5:10 (KJV) "But the God of all grace, who hath called us unto his eternal glory by Christ Jesus, after that ye have suffered a while, make you perfect, stablish, strengthen, settle you."

1 Pet 5:11 (KJV) "To him be glory and dominion for ever and ever. Amen."

You have to completely die to self will, your soul power which is probably the most difficult part of the fast. You will be tried and tried and tried........... God has to make us sure that we are certain that we won't abuse or misuse His power. With power, miracles can be manifested, personal dealings will be manifested, healing of sickness and diseases of other people through you (the vessel) can be manifested, angels can physically appear to you, and God's shield of protection will be around you where Satan and his demons will have no access to you. We must always remember to give God the credit for blessings manifested through our anointing. We don't have power to do anything. We are only vessels for God to work through. So, we shouldn't put our chests out and say, "I did this or I did that", say rather, "The Holy Spirit did this or the Holy Spirit did that". The Holy Spirit carries out God's command of all blessings, miracles and healing.

Before Job was afflicted by Satan, he had a hedge around him which was God's shield of protection. God removed the shield or hedge from Job so that Satan could test him with afflictions. This is what we previously mentioned about being tried, and tried. However these trials didn't change Job's love, dedication, nor his walk with God, Almighty. We must be able to withstand our trails as well. Job passed the test. God healed him and blessed him even more so than He did at first.

SOULS NEVER DIE

Jehovah Witnesses (Occult), Not A Church Portrays Great Ignorance And Deceit.

Christians must understand that our souls never die. All souls belong to God, Almighty who made us. Even when we die in Christ, our souls live on. Contrary to popular beliefs of various cults who represent themselves as churches including the CULT, Jehovah Witnesses. Jehovah Witnesses will point out to Christians that their bibles claim in black and white that their souls dies. The particular scripture in which they famously like to use is:

Ezekiel 18:4 (KJV), "Behold, all souls are mine, as the soul of the father, so also the souls of the son is mine: THE SOUL THAT SINNETH, IT SHALL DIE."

As we explore the Hebrew translation of the word "soul" and the Greek translation of the word "soul", you'll see why although spelled the same, they are distinctively defined with different meanings.

HEBREW WORD "SOUL". Let's explore the Hebrew translation for the word "soul".

Soul. Hebrew definition. H5315. nephesh, neh'-fesh; (from H5314; naphash, naw-fash'; a prim. root: to breathe) prop. a breathing creature, i.e. animal or (abstr.) vitality; used very widely in a lit., accommodated or fig. sense (bodily or mental):--any, appetite, beast, body, breath, creature (person).

There are many other definitions that can be included, but the breathing creature in which we are referring to is a person's body and the breath it needs in order to live. In the above scripture both the body and breath are referred to as the soul. Let's take a look at the phrase "The soul that sinneth, it shall die". Now, wouldn't you agree that the breath in itself can't sin? With breath in our bodies, we can sin. So then, when we have done a portion of sinning, we are prone to die, wouldn't you agree again? Here is another scenario about the livelihood of breath for us to consider. If one person sinned and if the Jehovah's claim was true, then all of us including every living creature would be dead because breath would be dead. So, as you see, the definition of this particular soul refers to the physical body and not our breath. However, the breath can leave an individual body, but still reside in other living bodies. In essence the soul (breath) never dies.

One case in point is when the Prophet Elijah was summoned to the bedside of a child with whom his breath left him resulting in his death. As you can recall above in Ezekiel 18:4 where God said that all souls were His. Elijah knew this and prayed to God and ask Him to let that child's soul (breath) come into him again. The child's soul did come into him again and he did live again.

1 King 17:21-22 (KJV), "21) And he stretched himself upon the child three times, an cried unto the Lord, and said, O Lord my God, I pray Thee, let this child's soul come into him again.

22. And the Lord heard the voice of Elijah; and the soul of the child came into him again, and he revived."

There was no death on that child's soul (breath) whatsoever. It had merely returned to the owner, God Almighty.

GREEK WORD "SOUL". Matthew 10:28 (KJV), "And fear not them which kill the body, but are not able to kill the soul: but rather fear Him which is able to destroy both soul and body in hell."

Let's explore the Greek translation for the word "soul" in this particular scripture.

Soul. Greek definition. G5590. psuche, psoo-khay; from G5594, i.e. (by impl.) spirit, thus distinguished on the one hand from G4151, which is the rational and IMMORTAL SOUL.

Let's see what definition Webster's dictionary have the word "Immortal". Immortal (im mort'l) adj. 1. Not mortal; deathless; living or lasting forever.

Here you'll find that the soul is a spirit which man, neither can kill, nor can he destroy it. The soul doesn't die as the Jehovah's Witnesses occult would have you believe.

So as you can readily see, death comes to the soul (body), but not the soul (spirit). You can also see how Satan uses his deceptive meanings for words spelled exactly alike, but with two completely different meanings. We can now conclude that the spiritual soul lives forever and never dies.

CHAPTER 137

Satan Must Receive Permission from Almighty God before Attacking Christians

The bible tells us to pray continuously, that is on a daily basis. Satan is on his job on a daily basis making accusations on Christians to Almighty God on a daily basis. So, we need to be sure that we are prayed up on a daily basis. Praying several or more times a day won't hurt, not one bit. Keep seeking Almighty God's face on a daily basis.

Revelation 12:10 (KJV), "...... for the accuser of our brethren is cast down, which accused them before our God day and night.".

There is a cliche, "IF SATAN IS NOT BOTHERING YOU, THEN YOU AREN'T BOTHERING HIM". Simply put, if you aren't doing anything to further God's kingdom, nor are you actively seeking to bring souls to Christ, then Satan won't bother you until he decides to destroy you, kill you, or steal your joy and happiness.

Job 2:1 (KJV) "Again there was a day when the sons of God came to present themselves before the LORD, and Satan came also among them to present himself before the LORD."

Job 2:2 (KJV) "And the LORD said unto Satan, From whence comest thou? And Satan answered the LORD, and said, From going to and fro in the earth, and from walking up and down in it."

John 10:10 (KJV), "The thief cometh not, but for to steal, and to kill, and to destroy: I am come that they might have life, and that they might have it more abundantly.".

Rev 12:10 (KJV) "And I heard a loud voice saying in heaven, Now is come salvation, and strength, and the kingdom of our God, and the power of his Christ: for the accuser of our brethren is cast down, which accused them before our God day and night." As a matter of fact, Satan may bestow upon you many counterfeit blessings, worldly pleasures and possessions while you weren't doing anything for God because you were still lost in sin and a child of Satan.

CHAPTER 138

Satanic Territorial Rights Violations Reap You More Curses

There are certain places where Satan and his demons take as their territories. They will reek havoc with humans if they come into those territories. Christians must not be ignorant of such territories, especially places of satanic worship, celebrations, and satanic sacrifices.

Touching Satan's Ground

- Visiting the Dome of The Rock in Jerusalem
- Visiting Satanic Covens (meeting place for Satanist)
- Touching Santa Claus figurines, statues and/or accessories
- Visiting persons dressed in Santa Claus clothing
- Satanic sacrificial grounds and properties
- Visiting King Tut's Display during it's tours
- Obelisk (residence of Ra, Sun God - demon) - A 4-sided pillar
- Visiting the Washington Monument (Obelisk), Washington D.C.
- Visiting the Obelisk at St. Peter's Bascilica, Rome
- Visiting the Obelisk at Central Park, New York City
- Visiting Fortune Tellers properties
- Visiting spiritualist properties
- Visiting tarot card readers properties

- Visiting palm readers properties
- Visiting drug houses or properties
- Visiting homosexual houses or properties
- Visiting Jehovah Witness' properties
- Visiting Islamic properties
- Visiting Moslem properties
- Visiting Masonic, Shriner, or Eastern Star properties
- Visiting Buddhist Temples and/or properties
- Visiting Hindu properties
- Visiting Mormon Temples and/or properties
- Visiting houses or properties of prostitution
- Visiting properties of pornography
- Visiting properties where abortions are performed (murder institutions) including some hospitals
- Visiting mental institutions and/or hospitals of the mentally insane
- Visiting psychiatric wards of hospitals
- Visiting death chambers, facilities, rooms, etc. for capital punishment (government sanctioned murders):
- Electric chair facility for murdering
- Gas chambers for murdering
- Lethal injection rooms or chambers for murdering
- Places for firing squads for murdering
- Facilities for hanging persons for murdering
- Visiting Places for persons to consume poisons for murdering
- Visiting places of euthanasia (killing or causing the death of so called hopelessly sick and/or injured persons)
- Visiting witch doctor properties
- Visiting properties where Native Indians perform their rituals
- Visiting any and all properties dedicated to other gods

We can bring curses in our lives by touching Satan's ground. When you touch objects and things that are dedicated to Satan, you are in fact in violation of his territorial rights. Buddhist statues, geisha girl (oriental prostitutes) dolls/ oriental fans with geisha girl art design/ possibly chop sticks from foreign countries, and many such objects dedicated to the gods of the oriental religions. These things or objects are Satan's ground and must not be touched by Christians. Jerusalem and other historical holy cities are visited by many people including Christians. Many Christians have visited and are presently visiting Jerusalem and other historically biblical cities. Unfortunately, Christians have visited places of worship of other religions and some of these places are in fact cursed. One of the places of worship is the DOME OF THE ROCK, the Temple Mount. Many of us Christians have desired to visit the Dome of The Rock which is a Moslem Mosque (Temple) where Moslems worship. This particular mosque is built right over the original TEMPLE MOUNT of the jews. So, Christians consider the Temple Mount of significant biblical historical value. However, the Moslem Mosque is a temple of Satan and many Christians don't know this.

My wife visited that particular temple, the Moslem Mosque. One of the things that you have to do is take your shoes off because the Moslems consider that temple a sacred temple. If you don't take off your shoes, then you don't get to enter the Moslem Mosque. So, you have to take off your shoes in honor of the demon, ALLAH. Wait a minute! This is similar to what God had Moses to do when he was approaching a certain ground as he came before the Lord.

Exo 3:5 (KJV) "And he said, Draw not nigh hither: put off thy shoes from off thy feet, for the place whereon thou standest is holy ground."

Acts 7:33 (KJV) "Then said the Lord to him, Put off thy shoes from thy feet: for the place where thou standest is holy ground."
There is nothing holy about the demon Allah or his ground. Allah is not the god that we serve.

1 Ki 9:7 (KJV) "Then will I cut off Israel out of the land which I have

given them; and this house, which I have hallowed for my name, will I cast out of my sight; and Israel shall be a proverb and a byword among all people:"

Exo 20:3-5 (KJV) Thou shalt have no other gods before me.

4. Thou shalt not make unto thee any graven image, or any likeness of any thing that is in heaven above, or that is in the earth beneath, or that is in the water under the earth:
5. Thou shalt not bow down thyself to them, nor serve them: for I the LORD thy God am a jealous God, visiting the iniquity of the fathers upon the children unto the third and fourth generation of them that hate me;

CHAPTER 139

Schools Prohibit Their Students from Praying by Federal and Local Governments

Churches have allowed our children to be plagued with curses in allowing prayer to be taken out of our school systems all over the entire United States of America by the federal government. They allowed one woman to win a lawsuit in a court of law by taking prayer out of schools by the name of the late Madalyn Murray O'Hare, who was a proclaimed atheist (hater of God, Almighty). Christians however, allowed Satan and his demons to have the right to exist in our school systems, but we denied God the right to enter and exist in our school systems.

With all of the killings in our schools across the United States of America, people are questioning one to the other as to where God was when these killings were happening. Well, let's remember that God was no longer welcomed in our school system by the federal government. So, He wasn't there to assist them or their children. The founding fathers of America were great advocates of prayer in the schools and daily prayers in them were normal. As a matter of fact, Congress still has some sort of prayer in their chambers before a session with a local minister leading them on some occasions. Remember also that Satan and his demons have free reign in all of the public school systems and they have certainly reeked havoc in them. Our moral standards are at an all time low as we are constantly plagued with the lawful denial or legal disallowal of our children's rights to having prayer in our schools.

Psa 5:3 (KJV) "My voice shalt thou hear in the morning, O LORD; in the morning will I direct my prayer unto thee, and will look up."

Psa 6:9 (KJV) "The LORD hath heard my supplication; the LORD will receive my prayer."

Psa 42:8 (KJV) "Yet the LORD will command his lovingkindness in the daytime, and in the night his song shall be with me, and my prayer unto the God of my life."

Psa 54:2 (KJV) "Hear my prayer, O God; give ear to the words of my mouth." Psa 65:2 (KJV) "O thou that hearest prayer, unto thee shall all flesh come."

Psa 66:20 (KJV) "Blessed be God, which hath not turned away my prayer, nor his mercy from me." Psa 69:13 (KJV) "But as for me, my prayer is unto thee, O LORD, in an acceptable time: O God, in the multitude of thy mercy hear me, in the truth of thy salvation."

Psa 88:13 (KJV) "But unto thee have I cried, O LORD; and in the morning shall my prayer prevent thee."

Prov 15:8 (KJV) "The sacrifice of the wicked is an abomination to the LORD: but the prayer of the upright is his delight."

Prov 15:29 (KJV) "The LORD is far from the wicked: but he heareth the prayer of the righteous." Prov 28:9 (KJV) "He that turneth away his ear from hearing the law, even his prayer shall be abomination."

Isa 26:16 (KJV) "LORD, in trouble have they visited thee, they poured out a prayer when thy chastening was upon them."

In the name of Almighty God in Heaven, and
In the name of Almighty Jesus Christ in Heaven, and
In the name of Almighty Holy Spirit, Who is on earth with us.
Praise You, Almighty God, and Praise You, Almighty Jesus Christ, and Praise You, Almighty Holy Spirit! Amen.

CHAPTER 140

Secular (i.e., Worldly) vs. Christian Types of Celebrations

Secular celebrations are commonly misconstrued with the Christian traditions of worshiping God, Almighty, His Son, Jesus and His Holy Spirit.

Not only are secular type parties and fellowships prevalent, but the commercialization of products and services by retailers depend on this niche for marketing and profits.

Marketing strategies are developed around certain holidays or holy days such as the 4th of July, Easter, Thanksgiving, Christmas and New Years. We as Americans celebrate the 4th of July to commemorate the freedom which we so richly enjoy. Easter is a day set aside for family reunions, picnics, bar-b-ques, and/or family gatherings. Retailers such as store owners enjoys selling easter candy, bunny rabits whether they are alive or just stuffed animals, chicken eggs for boiling and coloring, clothing (Easter frocks) and easter baskets. Thanksgiving provides the retailers a market for selling turkeys, hams and many other food products for this special day. Thanksgiving day is a great day festivity where families get together for dinner to celebrate in their own way the birth of American. Christmas is probably the greatess holiday for targeting consumers for marketing and selling. The Christmas season can either break or make retailers in the quest to sell an abundance of goods and services. The Christmas season is the biggest profit period of the year. The next largest season for celebrations is New Years day. Parties are prevalent everywhere. Party foods, liquors: soft drinks and alcoholic drinks, goods and services are very marketable for New Years celebrations.

We as Christians should be really aware or cognizant of whether we are to celebrate as the secular world does or whether we should worship God instead. The bible admonishes us not to celebrate as the secular world does. Many times we are found doing what the world does just because they represent the majority and it seems like the thing to do. Just because the majority says it is right, it is not necessarily the truth. Let's see what God tells us to do in the verse referenced by two different translations of the Bible. Although they reflect different definitions, they are actually saying the same thing with the abilities to enhance our understanding.

Colossians 2:16 (Revised Standard) "Therefore let no one pass judgement on you in questions of food and drink or with regard to a festival of a new moon or a sabbath." Colossians 2:16 (Simple English) "So, don't let anyone condemn you for what you eat or drink, or a religious festival, or the new moon holiday, or Sabbaths." JULY 4TH is a family oriented holiday combined with family vacations. Families usually come together for family reunions, class reunions and/or various other reunions. This is a grand opportunity for Christians to attend such functions to witness for Jesus Christ. This is in fact a form of worshiping for all Christians who participates in such events or functions. Let your light so shine that men, women, boys and girls will see Jesus in you. This is a pagan holiday and certainly not a Christian one.

EASTER is a day set aside to recognize the death and resurrection of our Lord and Savior Jesus Christ. We don't recognize Easter as a day of celebration, but a special day to praise, worship and recognition our Lord, Jesus. The world anticipates and celebrates the days immediately preceding Easter as high volume sales days before this day arrives for profits. Easter is really a pagan holiday. Easter is not a holy day in itself. Christians have taken or set aside this day as a day for special worship of God, Almighty for His Son's death on the cross for our sins.

HALLOWEEN (October 31st) is a special satanic day of worship with various costume parties and gatherings. Children are allowed to participate by dressing up in their costumes as they travel door-to-door for tricks or treats. This seems harmless for children to do, but they are really honoring Satan and his demons by participating in such. Many parents are ignorant of this fact and allow their children to do such. Christians no doubt have their own versions in participating in various functions held at churches. Even having functions at church with costumes aren't good ideas. It is still a form of worshiping Satan and his demons. Christians shouldn't wear costumes even at a church sponsored function, neither on Halloween day, nor night. Christians shouldn't do anything which gives credence to the celebration of halloween.

THANKSGIVING is day set aside as a holiday of giving thanks and dinners by the American people to commemorate the Pilgrim's celebration of the good harvest of 1621. Christians should be giving thanks on a daily basis including Thanksgiving day.

CHRISTMAS DAY is a pagan holiday which the merchants and retailers love. During mid August, some merchants and retailers start their marketing strategies for selling their wares targeted at Christmas shoppers for so called Christmas gifts, dinners, parties and such. Christians often use and should use this pagan holiday for family gatherings and a special day for worshipping God for the birth of His Son, Jesus while they commemorate His birth. Santa Claus has no place in the Christian life. He is a satanic diversion from Jesus Christ, our hero. It is a representation of the pagan holiday, Christmas. Participating in the gift buying craze is representive of the pagan holiday as well. Many people go in debt just to buy someone a gift because it was in their tradition to do so. This is satanic bondage and shouldn't be. Christians should sever all ties between the pagan holiday rituals of the pagan holiday called Christmas. Although Christmas sounds like a religious holy day, it really isn't. Some will say that Christmas is a combination of "Christ" and "Mas(s)" is a deception. Christianity has nothing to do with the formation of Christmas day.

NEW YEARS DAY is another pagan holiday which brings many celebrations of parties, events, and/or vain promises for doing better during the cominig year. Traditional ethnic dishes are normally cooked and served for superstitous reasons. Here again, Christians should be aware of the reasons for this pagan holiday and abstain from participating in such parties and/or celebrations.

CHAPTER **141**

Sex with Animals Is Strictly Forbidden

Unfortunately, humans do have sex with animals. There was such a case where a woman was having sex with her dog when a male friend came into her apartment as he had a key to get in. When he came into the apartment it excited the dog. When the dog tried to withdraw, he couldn't do it normally. He tore the insides of the woman because his penis was swollen inside of her as what happens when dogs have sex. Unfortunately, the woman died after that episode. So, sex for humans is only permitted between a male and a female.

Some boys and men have been known to have sex with some of the animals on farms, such as hogs, sheep and/or other animals as well.

Leviticus 18 (KJV)

23. Neither shalt thou lie with any beast to defile thyself therewith: neither shall any woman stand before a beast to lie down thereto: it is confusion.

CHAPTER 142

Skinny People with Celiac Disease

Often times, we have seen skinny people who can eat up a storm of food and not gain a pound. On the other hand we see obese or over weight people who eat just a little bit of food, but constantly gain weight. Food and drinks are not always the culprit in a person's body. Sometimes, it is a medical condition which spurs either weight loss or weight gain. So, we need to be very careful and accuse someone of over eating or not eating enough because of their physical appearances of looking too skinny or looking too fat. One such medical condition for some skinny people is the "Celiac" diseases.

Celiac Disease

Celiac disease is a digestive disease that damages the small intestine and interferes with absorption of nutrients from food. People who have celiac disease cannot tolerate a protein called gluten, found in wheat, rye, and barley. Gluten is found mainly in foods but may also be found in products we use every day, such as stamp and envelope adhesive, medicines, and vitamins.

CHAPTER **143**

Snakes (Coach Whips) Were Not Fables (i.e., Old Wives Tales)

We are admonished not to be taken by fairy tales, old wives tales and just plain old lies. However, there is a so-called fable concerning what old people talked about concerning what is known as "Coach Whip Snakes". Stories have been told about these snakes by different old folks from several Southern states. These people have told several stories of their experiences seeing these snakes. Well, "Ripley's Believe It Or Not" publishers don't really believe that such a snake existed. Here is one such so-called fable that I believe was actual in that the snake did exist at one time. Creditable Christian people have shared their experiences about seeing these mysterious snakes.

1 Timothy 1 (KJV)

4. Neither give heed to fables and endless genealogies, which minister questions, rather than godly edifying which is in faith: so do.

Strong's Dictionary Definition:

|3366| nor
|4337| to pay attention
|3454| to tales

While growing up on the farms in Arkansas, I, Curtis, heard many old people talk about the Coach Whip Snake. Some years ago somebody decided to contact Ripley's Believe It Not organization in an attempt to add that story to their archives for publishing in their books as well. Ripley's denied that such a snake existed. I have actually talked to a sweet old lady who has now gone from this life to heaven. Just recently, I have heard of another account of the snake from a source in North Carolina.

A sweet old lady, Ms. Cora Shepard, who was a tenet in a house which we owned in Arkansas told us that when she was younger, she was standing in a field on a farm in Arkansas when she saw a dust cloud. As she stood watching, she noticed that two (2) coach whip snakes battling it out by whipping each other with their tails. The snakes finally stopped battling, entwined themselves into a wheel and started rolling towards her. Fortunately, she was able to out run them out of the field without being harmed by them.

Just recently, our Christmas guest, Johnathan Gaither of Baltimore, Maryland told us of an old man who was farming by plowing with his tractor in a field in North Carolina. When the farmer stopped his tractor, this snake started beating the side of the tractor tire with its tail. It seemed to him that tail was stiff like a club. Fortunately, the farmer didn't leave the safety of his tractor or else he could have been beaten to death by that snake. The farmer summarized that maybe he had disturbed the snakes nest in the field. I told Johnatan that the snake sounded like the coach whip snake that I had heard so much about over the years.

CHAPTER **144**

Snakes (Serpents) Previously Had Legs as Substantiated in Biblical Scriptures

There is another account and substantial proof that creation is real over the lie, "evolution'. Before Adam and Eve fell from Grace to sin, they talked to a serpent who not only could communicate with them in their language, but who had legs and could walk as other animals would. After the serpent allowed himself to be used by Satan who in turn fooled Eve into taking a bite of the forbidden fruit from its tree, God punished the serpent by taking away its language to further communicate with humans, by taking away its legs, and allowing it to crawl on its belly for the rest of its life.

This proof came as a discovery in 1997 when a fossil was found of a prehistoric snake with hind legs. This substantiates what the Bible says about the serpent before the fall of man and woman from the Grace of Almighty God.

Genesis 3 (KJV)

1. Now the serpent was more subtil than any beast of the field which the Lord God had made. And he said unto the woman, Yea, hath God said, Ye shall not eat of every tree of the garden?
2. And the woman said unto the serpent, We may eat of the fruit of the trees of the garden:

3. But of the fruit of the tree which is in the midst of the garden, God hath said, Ye shall not eat of it, neither shall ye touch it, lest ye die.
4. And the serpent said unto the woman, Ye shall not surely die:
5. For God doth know that in the day ye eat thereof, then your eyes shall be opened, and ye shall be as gods, knowing good and evil.
6. And when the woman saw that the tree was good for food, and that it was pleasant to the eyes, and a tree to be desired to make one wise, she took of the fruit thereof, and did eat, and gave also unto her husband with her; and he did eat.
7. And the eyes of them both were opened, and they knew that they were naked; and they sewed fig leaves together, and made themselves aprons.
8. And they heard the voice of the Lord God walking in the garden in the cool of the day: and Adam and his wife hid themselves from the presence of the Lord God amongst the trees of the garden.
9. And the Lord God called unto Adam, and said unto him, Where art thou?
10. And he said, I heard thy voice in the garden, and I was afraid, because I was naked; and I hid myself.
11. And he said, Who told thee that thou wast naked? Hast thou eaten of the tree, whereof I commanded thee that thou shouldest not eat?
12. And the man said, The woman whom thou gavest to be with me, she gave me of the tree, and I did eat.
13. And the Lord God said unto the woman, What is this that thou hast done? And the woman said, The serpent beguiled me, and I did eat.
14. And the Lord God said unto the serpent, Because thou hast done this, thou art cursed above all cattle, and above every beast of the field; upon thy belly shalt thou go, and dust shalt thou eat all the days of thy life:

15. And I will put enmity between thee and the woman, and between thy seed and her seed; it shall bruise thy head, and thou shalt bruise his heel.
16. Unto the woman he said, I will greatly multiply thy sorrow and thy conception; in sorrow thou shalt bring forth children; and thy desire shall be to thy husband, and he shall rule over thee.
17. And unto Adam he said, Because thou hast hearkened unto the voice of thy wife, and hast eaten of the tree, of which I commanded thee, saying, Thou shalt not eat of it: cursed is the ground for thy sake; in sorrow shalt thou eat of it all the days of thy life;
18. Thorns also and thistles shall it bring forth to thee; and thou shalt eat the herb of the field;
19. In the sweat of thy face shalt thou eat bread, till thou return unto the ground; for out of it wast thou taken: for dust thou art, and unto dust shalt thou return.
20. And Adam called his wife's name Eve; because she was the mother of all living.
21. Unto Adam also and to his wife did the Lord God make coats of skins, and clothed them.
22. And the Lord God said, Behold, the man is become as one of us, to know good and evil: and now, lest he put forth his hand, and take also of the tree of life, and eat, and live for ever:
23. Therefore the Lord God sent him forth from the garden of Eden, to till the ground from whence he was taken.
24. So he drove out the man; and he placed at the east of the garden of Eden Cherubims, and a flaming sword which turned every way, to keep the way of the tree of life.

LAS (SMU) — Researchers from Southern DalMeth Newodist University have described an intriguing species of fossil snake with legs that was found in a limestone quarry north of Jerusalem.

Newspaper published in the March 17 issue of the journal Science, SMU paleontologist Louis Jacobs In a journal and several international co-authors say the fossil snake is important because it provides new information on the evolution of snakes.

The fossil snake, which lived 95 million years ago, is named Haasiophis terrasanctus after a Hebrew University professor named George Haas who obtained it from quarry workers more than 20 years ago. The well-preserved fossil sat largely unstudied in storage until Mike Polcyn, an SMU graduate student in paleontology, brought back pictures of it and other undescribed specimens that he took while on a business trip to Israel in 1996.

"We immediately decided we needed to go back and organize a joint project to research and publish on this unique location and the animals preserved there," Polcyn said.

Haasiophis is a little over a meter long and has hind legs about 2 cm long that extend all the way to the toe bones. Its head and lower jaws are intact.

"It is extremely rare to find a fossil snake head preserved because they usually get spread and scattered," Jacobs said.

Louis Jacobs searching for fossils

Haasiophis is the second limbed snake to come from the limestone quarry near the villages of 'Ein Yabrud, north of Jerusalem. George Haas published a description of the first limbed snake, Pachyrachis problematicus, in 1979, but at the time he placed it not as a snake but as a marine lizard known as a dolichosaur. Some scientists believe Pachyrachis represents the most primitive snake known and provides evidence of a link between mosasaurs – giant swimming lizards of the Cretaceous Period – and true snakes.

In the past 20 years, however, researchers have developed more quantitative methods of evaluating relationships between species based on unique anatomical details. The analysis of the head and jaws of Haasiophis presented in the Science article places it closer to more advanced terrestrial snakes such as boas and pythons and suggests that neither Pachyrachis nor Haasiophis has anything to do with snake origins.

"As a result of this analysis, it seems less likely that snakes evolved from mosasaurs," Jacobs said.

Scientists believe snakes evolved from a group of lizards prior to 100 million years ago. During the evolutionary process, their headbones changed, they developed long bodies with specialized vertebra and muscles, and they lost their legs.

Jacobs said analysis of Haasiophis indicates that snake feeding apparatus, body form and locomotor pattern all evolved before the hind legs were lost.

"The fact Haasiophis had legs means that either snakes lost their legs more than once or they re-evolved them," Jacobs said. He speculates that the tiny legs on Haasiophis were somehow used in reproduction and stimulation, much like the spurs on anacondas are used today. They are too small in relation to the reptile's whole body to have helped it move.

Analysis of Haasiophis also adds to the debate over whether snakes originated on land or in the sea. Haasiophis lived in the sea, and Jacobs believes it may represent the first invasion of the sea by snakes.

A large view of the entire snake fossil

During the Cretaceous Period, the area that includes the Middle East

was a shallow sea with patches of reef and limestone deposition, much like the modern-day Bahamian reef. At one point about 95 million years ago, the sea level fell, making a quiet area on this limestone shelf. Animals washed into the area and fell to the bottom. With no scavengers to eat the bodies, they eventually fossilized within the limestone. Paleontologists also have found fossils of sharks, turtles, primitive mosasaurs and plants in the 'Ein Yabrud quarry.
Rocks in the Dallas/Fort Worth area are similar in age to those at 'Ein Yabrud, suggesting that limbed snakes such as Haasiophis could once have lived in Texas.

"It's not beyond possibility," Jacobs said.

Lou Jacobs with a dinosaur skeleton at the Dallas Museum of Natural History

Jacobs is a professor of Geological Sciences in SMU's Dedman College and president of SMU's Institute for the Study of Earth and Man. Most recently he has served as director ad interim of the Dallas Museum of Natural History. He has conducted extensive field research in Pakistan, Mexico, Kenya, Cameroon, Malawi and Yemen, as well as in Texas and other parts of the United States. He is the author of Lone Star Dinosaurs (1995), Cretaceous Airport (1993) and Quest for the African Dinosaur: Ancient Roots of the Modern World (1993), as well as numerous scientific papers.
Co-authors with Jacobs and Polcyn on the March 17 Science paper include Eitan Tchernov of Hebrew University, Olivier Rieppel of the Field Museum in Chicago and Hussam Zaher of the Universidade de Sao Paulo in Brazil. Tchernov and Rieppel were both students of George Haas.

CHAPTER **145**

Souls (Spirits) Never Die

Christians must understand that our souls never die. All souls belong to God, Almighty who made us. Even when we die in Christ, our souls live on. Contrary to popular beliefs of various cults who represent themselves as churches including the CULT, Jehovahs Witnesses. Jehovahs Witnesses will point out to Christians that their bibles claim in black and white that their souls dies. The particular scripture in which they famously like to use is:

Ezekiel 18:4 (KJV), "Behold, all souls are mine, as the soul of the father, so also the souls of the son is mine: THE SOUL THAT SINNETH, IT SHALL DIE."

As we explore the Hebrew translation of the word "soul" and the Greek translation of the word "soul", you'll see why although spelled the same, they are disticntively define with different meanings.

HEBREW WORD "SOUL". Let's explore the Hebrew translation for the word "soul". H5315. nephesh, neh'-fesh; (from H5314; naphash, naw-fash'; a prim. root: to breathe) prop. a breathing creature, i.e. animal or (abstr.) vitality; used very widely in a lit., accommodated or fig. sense (bodily or mental):--any, appetite, beast, body, breath, creature (person). There are many other definitions that can be included, but the breathing creature in which we are referring to is a person's body and the breath it needs in order to live. In the above scripture both the body and breath are referred to as the soul. Let's take a look at the phrase "The soul that sinneth, it shall die". Now, wouldn't you agree that the breath in itself can't sin? With breath in our bodies, we can sin. So then when we have done a portion of sinning, we are prone to die, wouldn't you agree again? Here is another scenario about the livelihood of breath for us to consider. If one person sinned and if the Jehovah's claim was true, then all of us including every living creature would be dead because breath would be dead. So, as you see, the definition of this particular soul refers to the physical body and not our breath. However, the breath can leave an individual body, but still reside in other living bodies. In escence the soul (breath) never dies.

One point in case is when the Prophet Elijah was summoned to the bedside of a child with whom his breath left him resulting in his death. As you can recall above in Ezekiel 18:4 where God said that all souls were His. Elijah knew this and prayed to God and ask Him to let that child's soul (breath) come into him again. The child's soul did come into him again and he did live again. 1 King 17:21-22 (KJV), "21) And he stretched himself upon the child three times, an cried unto the Lord, and said, O Lord my God, I pray Thee, let this child's soul come into him again. 22) And the Lord heard the voice of Elijah; and the soul of the child came into him again, and he revived." "There was no death on that child's soul (breath) whatsoever. It had merely returned to the owner, God Almighty.

GREEK WORD "SOUL". Matthew 10:28 (KJV), "And fear not them which kill the body, but are not able to kill the soul: but rather fear Him which is able to destroy both soul and body in hell." Let's explore the Greek translation for the word "soul" in this particular scripture. G5590. psuche, psoo-khay; from G5594, i.e. (by impl.) spirit, thus distinguished on the one hand from G4151, which is the rational and IMMORTAL SOUL. Let's see what definition Webster's dictionary have the word "Immortal". Immortal (im mort'l) adj. 1.

Not mortal; deathless; living or lasting forever. Here you'll find that the soul is a spirit which man can't kill or can't destroy. It doesn't die as the Jehovah's Witnesses would have you believe.

So as you can readily see, death comes to the soul (body), but not the soul (spirit). You can also see how Satan uses his deceptive meanings for words spelled exactly alike, but with two completely different meanings. We can now conclude that the spiritual soul lives forever and never dies.

Souls/Spirits Return Back To Almighty God In Heaven

King David, in his petition and request for Almighty God's protection from his enemies, he committed his Spirit/Soul back to the Heavenly Father. Our, Savior and Master, Jesus Christ while He was yet on the cross before his final crucifixion, he sent his Spirit and Soul back to our Creator, Almighty God in Heaven.

Psalms 31 (KJV)

5. Into thine hand I commit my spirit: thou hast redeemed me, O Lord God of truth

Luke 23 (KJV)

46. And when Jesus had cried with a loud voice, he said, Father, into thy hands I commend my spirit: and having said thus, he gave up the ghost.

As we explore the Hebrew translation of the word "soul" and the Greek translation of the word "soul", you'll see why although spelled the same, they are distinctively defined with different meanings.

HEBREW WORD "SOUL". Let's explore the Hebrew translation for the word "soul".

Soul. Hebrew definition. H5315. nephesh, neh'-fesh; (from H5314; naphash, naw-fash'; a prim. root: to breathe) prop. a breathing creature, i.e. animal or (abstr.) vitality; used very widely in a lit., accommodated or fig. sense (bodily or mental):--any, appetite, beast, body, breath, creature (person).

There are many other definitions that can be included, but the breathing creature in which we are referring to is a person's body and the breath it needs in order to live. In the above scripture both the body and breath are referred to as the soul. Let's take a look at the phrase "The soul that sinneth, it shall die". Now, wouldn't you agree that the breath in itself can't sin? With breath in our bodies, we can sin. So then, when we have done a portion of sinning, we are prone to die, wouldn't you agree again? Here is another scenario about the livelihood of breath for us to consider. If one person sinned and if the Jehovah's claim was true, then all of us including every living creature would be dead because breath would be dead. So, as you see, the definition of this particular soul refers to the physical body and not our breath. However, the breath can leave an individual body, but still reside in other living bodies. In essence the soul (breath) never dies.

One case in point is when the Prophet Elijah was summoned to the bedside of a child with whom his breath left him resulting in his death. As you can recall above in

Ezekiel 18:4 where God said that all souls were His. Elijah knew this and prayed to God and ask Him to let that child's soul (breath) come into him again. The child's soul did come into him again and he did live again.

1 King 17:21-22 (KJV), "21) And he stretched himself upon the child three times, an cried unto the Lord, and said, O Lord my God, I pray Thee, let this child's soul come into him again.

22. And the Lord heard the voice of Elijah; and the soul of the child came into him again, and he revived."

There was no death on that child's soul (breath) whatsoever. It had merely returned to the owner, God Almighty.

GREEK WORD "SOUL". Matthew 10:28 (KJV), "And fear not them which kill the body, but are not able to kill the soul: but rather fear Him which is able to destroy both soul and body in hell."
Let's explore the Greek translation for the word "soul" in this particular scripture.

Soul. Greek definition. G5590. psuche, psoo-khay; from G5594, i.e. (by impl.) spirit, thus distinguished on the one hand from G4151, which is the rational and IMMORTAL SOUL.

Let's see what definition Webster's dictionary have the word "Immortal". Immortal (im mort'l) adj. 1. Not mortal; deathless; living or lasting forever.

Here you'll find that the soul is a spirit which man, neither can kill, nor can he destroy it. The soul doesn't die as the Jehovah's Witnesses occult would have you believe.

So as you can readily see, death comes to the soul (body), but not the soul (spirit). You can also see how Satan uses his deceptive meanings for words spelled exactly alike, but with two completely different meanings. We can now conclude that the spiritual soul lives forever and never dies.

Moses And Elias After Their Long Deaths Talked To Jesus

Matthew 17 (KJV)

1. And after six days Jesus taketh Peter, James, and John

his brother, and bringeth them up into an high mountain apart,

2. And was transfigured before them: and his face did shine as the sun, and his raiment was white as the light.
3. And, behold, there appeared unto them Moses and Elias talking with him.

Many People Rose From Their Graves After Jesus' Resurrection

Matthew 27 (KJV)

50. Jesus, when he had cried again with a loud voice, yielded up the ghost.
51. And, behold, the veil of the temple was rent in twain from the top to the bottom; and the earth did quake, and the rocks rent;
52. And the graves were opened; and many bodies of the saints which slept arose,
53 And came out of the graves after his resurrection, and went into the holy city, and appeared unto many.

A Poor Man Goes To Heaven And A Rich Man Goes To Hell

Luke 16 (KJV)

19. There was a certain rich man, which was clothed in purple and fine linen, and fared sumptuously every day:
20. And there was a certain beggar named Lazarus, which was laid at his gate, full of sores,
21. And desiring to be fed with the crumbs which fell from the rich man's table: moreover the dogs came and licked his sores.
22. And it came to pass, that the beggar died, and was carried by the angels into Abraham's bosom: the rich man also died, and was buried;

23. And in hell he lift up his eyes, being in torments, and seeth Abraham afar off, and Lazarus in his bosom.
24. And he cried and said, Father Abraham, have mercy on me, and send Lazarus, that he may dip the tip of his finger in water, and cool my tongue; for I am tormented in this flame.
25. But Abraham said, Son, remember that thou in thy lifetime receivedst thy good things, and likewise Lazarus evil things: but now he is comforted, and thou art tormented.
26. And beside all this, between us and you there is a great gulf fixed: so that they which would pass from hence to you cannot; neither can they pass to us, that would come from thence.
27. Then he said, I pray thee therefore, father, that thou wouldest send him to my father's house:
28. For I have five brethren; that he may testify unto them, lest they also come into this place of torment.
29. Abraham saith unto him, They have Moses and the prophets; let them hear them.
30. And he said, Nay, father Abraham: but if one went unto them from the dead, they will repent.
31. And he said unto him, If they hear not Moses and the prophets, neither will they be persuaded, though one rose from the dead.

When Jesus Christ was on the cross being crucified to death, He looked up towards Heaven and gave up his Spirit to His Father, Almighty God.

Luke 23 (KJV)

46. And when Jesus had cried with a loud voice, he said, Father, into thy hands I commend my spirit: and having said thus, he gave up the ghost.

Another such case was when Stephen was being stoned to death, he looked up towards heaven and saw Jesus Christ on the right side of Almighty God and he requested that Jesus receive his spirit as well.

Acts 7 (KJV)

59. And they stoned Stephen, calling upon God, and saying, Lord Jesus, receive my spirit.
60. And he kneeled down, and cried with a loud voice, Lord, lay not this sin to their charge. And when he had said this, he fell asleep.

CHAPTER **146**

Spankings or Whippings of Your Own Children Are Biblically Correct

Churches should be ashamed of themselves for allowing outsiders such as the law officials and governments to dictate to their members on how to raise their children. Older generations including our parents and grandparents punished us with switches they cut from trees, razor straps, belts, paddles, rulers, ironing cords or whatever was available to produce the process of whipping. Spankings were the softer side of whippings which was usually done with the hands on one's buttocks or more bluntly, one's butt. These types of punishments really got our attention to say the least. We learned a great deal of respect for not only our parents, but any grownups, elderly persons, and senior people around the ages of our grandparents. Nowadays, if you whip your children and your neighbor learn of it and calls the police, you could be arrested and hauled off to jail for child abuse. Now, there are some people out there who really do abuse children and they should be arrested and locked up and charged for abusing children. There is a difference between correcting your child and abusing your child. Christians should have the knowledge, wisdom and understanding to know the difference. We are admonished by God, Almighty to chastise our children by using the tools of corrections such as belts, paddles or our hands. These seem to get the children's attention when just talking to them doesn't work at times.

Prov 10:13 (KJV) "In the lips of him that hath understanding wisdom is found: but a rod is for the back of him that is void of understanding."

Prov 13:24 (KJV) "He that spareth his rod hateth his son: but he that loveth him chasteneth him betimes."

Prov 14:3 (KJV) "In the mouth of the foolish is a rod of pride: but the lips of the wise shall preserve them."

Prov 22:15 (KJV) "Foolishness is bound in the heart of a child; but the rod of correction shall drive it far from him." Prov 23:13 (KJV) "Withhold not correction from the child: for if thou beatest him with the rod, he shall not die."

Prov 23:14 (KJV) "Thou shalt beat him with the rod, and shalt deliver his soul from hell." Prov 26:3 (KJV) "A whip for the horse, a bridle for the ass, and a rod for the fool's back."

Prov 29:15 (KJV) "The rod and reproof give wisdom: but a child left to himself bringeth his mother to shame."

CHAPTER 147

Stem Cell (Embryonic) Research - Killing and Murdering Babies

One of Almighty God's Ten (10) Commandments tells that we should not kill. Many researchers believe that if the female's embryo is not yet a human. They had better think again because He knew us before the foundation of this world. Simply speaking, he knew us before an embryonic egg and sperm came together to fertilize and form it.

Exodus 20 (KJV)

13. Thou shalt not kill.

God said that he knew us before the foundation of the world. So, why do ignorant an unlearned, and self-serving people proclaim that embryos aren't humans? As soon as a woman conceives, she has a human being in her womb.

Luke 2 (KJV)

21. And when eight days were accomplished for the circumcising of the child, his name was called Jesus, which was so named of the angel before he was conceived in the womb.

Ephesians 1 (KJV)

4. According as he hath chosen us in him before the foundation of the world, that we should be holy and without blame before him in love:

1 Peter 1 (KJV)

20. Who verily was foreordained before the foundation of the world, but was manifest in these last times for you,

John 17 (KJV)

24. Father, I will that they also, whom thou hast given me, be with me where I am; that they may behold my glory, which thou hast given me: for thou lovedst me before the foundation of the world.

Many people are in favor of stem cell research from murdered babies; some with their own selfish reasons in mind. Mrs. Nancy Reagan, the late former President Ronald Reagan's widow. Many of the members of the House of Delegates, both Congressmen and Congresswomen, and some members of the United States Senate as well.

Not only are the citizens of the United States of American in a serious state of moral deficiency, but the lawmakers, and the judicial system as well. We as U.S. citizens are in a very sad state of affairs. The United States of America is in danger of losing God, Almighty's protective hedge around her. The 911 terrorist and Hurricane Katrina that hit the gulf states including New Orleans, Louisiana, Biloxi, Mississippi and states were just a so-called mother nature fluke. These disasters were wake-up calls to set our spiritual lives in order because God is certainly watching us and taking notes.

Just recently, there was an outbreak of the "Swine Flu" which not only infiltrated these United States of America, her territories, and her possessions, but it has infiltrated other Continents around the world as well. Our actions of sin is the main culprit of such epidemics of swine flu and many other epidemics which humanity experiences.

CHAPTER 148

Suicides (Any) Are Quick Flights to Hell's Fire and Brimstone

Suicide bombers have been white washed in their minds to believe that they are martyrs for their cause or someone else's. They also believe that they will go to heaven for a better life, also. This is far from the truth. Any type of suicide is murder or killing.

Suicide bombers accomplish two things: They kill themselves and if they are successful, they murder or kill others.

Suicidal individuals believe they can end whatever problems they are dealing with a further belief that they ended it all. This is far from the truth. Their problems have only begun. They have prepared their earthly life for an instant life in hell's fire forever, which is throughout eternity. They will also be judged by God, Almighty for all of their sins and of course for murdering themselves as well.

Suicides assisted by others are as individual suicides as well. The ones who assists someone to commit suicide is just as guilty as they are. They now have blood on their hands as well as murder. Any body who assists someone in suicide are guilty including doctors, nurses, attendants, etc.

Matthew 5 (KJV)

21. Ye have heard that it was said by them of old time, Thou shalt not kill; and whosoever shall kill shall be in danger of the judgment:

Psalms 10 (KJV)

1. Why standest thou afar off, O Lord? why hidest thou thyself in times of trouble?
2. The wicked in his pride doth persecute the poor: let them be taken in the devices that they have imagined.
3. For the wicked boasteth of his heart's desire, and blesseth the covetous, whom the Lord abhorreth.
4. The wicked, through the pride of his countenance, will not seek after God: God is not in all his thoughts.
5. His ways are always grievous; thy judgments are far above out of his sight: as for all his enemies, he puffeth at them.
6. He hath said in his heart, I shall not be moved: for I shall never be in adversity.
7. His mouth is full of cursing and deceit and Fraud: under his tongue is mischief and vanity.
8. He sitteth in the lurking places of the villages: in the secret places doth he murder the innocent: his eyes are privily set against the poor.

Psalms 94 (KJV)

1. O Lord God, to whom vengeance belongeth; O God, to whom vengeance belongeth, shew thyself.
2. Lift up thyself, thou judge of the earth: render a reward to the proud.
3. Lord, how long shall the wicked, how long shall the wicked triumph?

4. How long shall they utter and speak hard things? and all the workers of iniquity boast themselves?
5. They break in pieces thy people, O Lord, and afflict thine heritage.
6. They slay the widow and the stranger, and murder the fatherless.

Hosea 6 (KJV)

9. And as troops of robbers wait for a man, so the company of priests murder in the way by consent: for they commit lewdness.

Matthew 19 (KJV)

17. And he said unto him, Why callest thou me good? there is none good but one, that is, God: but if thou wilt enter into life, keep the commandments.
18. He saith unto him, Which? Jesus said, Thou shalt do no murder, Thou shalt not commit adultery, Thou shalt not steal, Thou shalt not bear false witness,
19. Honour thy father and thy mother: and, Thou shalt love thy neighbour as thyself.

Romans 1 (KJV)

29. Being filled with all unrighteousness, fornication, wickedness, covetousness, maliciousness; full of envy, murder, debate, deceit, malignity; whisperers,
30. Backbiters, haters of God, despiteful, proud, boasters, inventors of evil things, disobedient to parents,
31. Without understanding, covenant breakers, without natural affection, implacable, unmerciful:
32. Who knowing the judgment of God, that they which commit such things are worthy of death, not only do the same, but have pleasure in them that do them.

CHAPTER **149**

Swine Flu Viruses Epidemic in America and Around the World

The swine flu virus epidemic is another resulting case of what our sins can bring upon us. Almighty God is not please with us and so He allows plagues like the swine flu to infiltrate our lives. This swine flu has not only caused many of our fellow humans sickness, but also death as well. As long as we are not continuously seeking Almighty God's face, then these and many more plagues will infiltrate our lives and wreak havoc on our societies.

Health Chiefs Warn Against 'Sneaky' Flu Virus
2 days ago

GENEVA (AFP) — Global health chiefs warned against the "sneaky" swine flu virus but said a vaccine could be ready as early as June as Russia reported its first confirmed case of the disease.

"This is a subtle, sneaky virus, it does not announce its presence or arrival in a new country with sudden explosion of patients seeking medical care or requiring hospitalisation," said Margaret Chan, head of the World Health Organisation (WHO).

She warned that "countries especially in the developing world, where populations are most vulnerable, should prepare to see more than the present small number of severe cases."

WHO The spread in impoverished nations was one of the signals that the WHO was keeping an eye on before it declares a pandemic, instead of simply relying on geographical spread under its influenza rulebook.

But in some good news amid rising cases around the world, the WHO said the first vaccine against the A(H1N1) virus could be ready by the end of next month.

"We're hopeful that by the end of June, by the beginning July, this will be the time that commercial companies will be in a position of being able to make a vaccine," said WHO's interim Assistant Director General Keiji Fukuda.

The WHO's latest figures put the overall number of infections worldwide at more than 11,100, including 86 deaths.

But Fukuda added the daily count of the rising number of cases around the world was becoming irrelevant.

"The numbers themselves have become a little bit more irrelevant," interim assistant director general Keiji Fukuda told journalists. "They will increasingly not reflect what's going on.

"Countries such as the United States are moving away from large-scale testing of cases," he said.

Fukuda added though that experts were still mulling whether to give the go-ahead for production as this may reduce or halt the manufacture of vaccines for seasonal flu.

A study released Friday said the various A(H1N1) swine flu strains spreading across the globe react to antibodies in the same way, boosting the chances of a common vaccine for all of them.

The study, published in Science, says the virus has probably been circulating unnoticed in pig populations for some time, and it calls for more careful monitoring of swine populations. It confirms that the new pathogen originated with pigs, and is a mix of a previously known virus that already contained avian, swine and human genetic segments with two other genes from Eurasian swine viruses never before detected outside Asia.

Understanding the origins of the novel A(H1N1) virus could help scientists prevent the pathogen from emerging in a new -- and potentially more virulent -- form, the researchers said.

"These findings are critically important for our global public health," said Nancy Cox, chief of the Influenza Division of the US National Center for Immunization and Respiratory Diseases in Atlanta, Georgia and a co-author of the study.

Moscow Friday recorded its first case of the virus, as 11 Spanish soldiers were also diagnosed with the disease.

A Russian national on a flight from the United States was diagnosed with the A(H1N1) virus, the country's public health chief Gennady Onishchenko said.

"He feels normal and is receiving adequate medical care," Interfax quoted Onishchenko as saying. "He does not have a temperature. His condition is stable."

In Spain, 11 soldiers at a military school were diagnosed with swine flu, although their symptoms are mild, while in Rome two high schools were closed after four students back from the United States fell ill.

The United States said meanwhile it will invest one billion dollars to develop key components for a swine flu vaccine and conduct clinical studies into its efficacy.

US Health Secretary Kathleen Sebelius said the money will come from already existing funds and will be used to place orders with companies licensed to produce flu vaccine for antigens -the ingredient in a vaccine that causes the body to develop antibodies -- and adjuvants, which boost the body's immune response.

- Australia Confirms Melbourne Schoolboy as 14th Swine Flu Victim Bloomberg - 1 hour ago
- Melbourne teen diagnosed with swine flu
- Melbourne Herald Sun - 2 hours ago
- Ninth Victorian swine flu case confirmed
- The Age - 3 hours ago
- Suspected A/H1N1 flu cases in Brazil fall to 13
- Xinhua - 3 hours ago

Almighty God has warned us that if we obey His commandments, many blessings are in store for us. On the other hand if we will not obey His commandments and follow after other gods, there are curses in store for us.

Deuteronomy 11 (KJV)

1. Therefore thou shalt love the Lord thy God, and keep his charge, and his statutes, and his judgments, and his commandments, alway.
2. And know ye this day: for I speak not with your children which have not known, and which have not seen the chastisement of the Lord your God, his greatness, his mighty hand, and his stretched out arm,
3. And his miracles, and his acts, which he did in the midst of Egypt unto Pharaoh the king of Egypt, and unto all his land;
4. And what he did unto the army of Egypt, unto their horses, and to their chariots; how he made the water of the red sea to overflow them as they pursued after you, and how the Lord hath destroyed them unto this day;

5. And what he did unto you in the wilderness, until ye came into this place;
6. And what he did unto Dathan and Abiram, the sons of Eliab, the son of Reuben: how the earth opened her mouth, and swallowed them up, and their households, and their tents, and all the substance that was in their possession, in the midst of all Israel:
7. But your eyes have seen all the great acts of the Lord which he did.
8. Therefore shall ye keep all the commandments which I command you this day, that ye may be strong, and go in and possess the land, whither ye go to possess it;
9. And that ye may prolong your days in the land, which the Lord sware unto your fathers to give unto them and to their seed, a land that floweth with milk and honey.
10. For the land, whither thou goest in to possess it, is not as the land of Egypt, from whence ye came out, where thou sowedst thy seed, and wateredst it with thy foot, as a garden of herbs:
11. But the land, whither ye go to possess it, is a land of hills and valleys, and drinketh water of the rain of heaven:
12. A land which the Lord thy God careth for: the eyes of the Lord thy God are always upon it, from the beginning of the year even unto the end of the year.
13. And it shall come to pass, if ye shall hearken diligently unto my commandments which I command you this day, to love the Lord your God, and to serve him with all your heart and with all your soul,
14. That I will give you the rain of your land in his due season, the first rain and the latter rain, that thou mayest gather in thy corn, and thy wine, and thine oil.
15. And I will send grass in thy fields for thy cattle, that thou mayest eat and be full.
16. Take heed to yourselves, that your heart be not deceived, and ye turn aside, and serve other gods, and worship them;

17. And then the Lord's wrath be kindled against you, and he shut up the heaven, that there be no rain, and that the land yield not her fruit; and lest ye perish quickly from off the good land which the Lord giveth you.
18. Therefore shall ye lay up these my words in your heart and in your soul, and bind them for a sign upon your hand, that they may be as frontlets between your eyes.
19. And ye shall teach them your children, speaking of them when thou sittest in thine house, and when thou walkest by the way, when thou liest down, and when thou risest up.
20. And thou shalt write them upon the door posts of thine house, and upon thy gates:
21. That your days may be multiplied, and the days of your children, in the land which the Lord sware unto your fathers to give them, as the days of heaven upon the earth.
22. For if ye shall diligently keep all these commandments which I command you, to do them, to love the Lord your God, to walk in all his ways, and to cleave unto him;
23. Then will the Lord drive out all these nations from before you, and ye shall possess greater nations and mightier than yourselves.
24. Every place whereon the soles of your feet shall tread shall be yours: from the wilderness and Lebanon, from the river, the river Euphrates, even unto the uttermost sea shall your coast be.
25. There shall no man be able to stand before you: for the Lord your God shall lay the fear of you and the dread of you upon all the land that ye shall tread upon, as he hath said unto you.
26. Behold, I set before you this day a blessing and a curse;
27. A blessing, if ye obey the commandments of the Lord your God, which I command you this day:
28. And a curse, if ye will not obey the commandments of the Lord your God, but turn aside out of the way which I command you this day, to go after other Gods, which ye have not known.

CHAPTER **150**

Tattoos in the Skin of the Body Hold Deadly Little Secrets

The Holy Bible cautions us against such things as tattoos, carvings, and piercing of our skins. Science and the medical field have proven that doing such puts one at risk for many diseases and sicknesses which are in some cases very deadly, indeed.

Leviticus 19 (KJV)

> 28. Ye shall not make any cuttings in your flesh for the dead, nor print any marks upon you: I am the Lord.

Terry Watkins
Dial-the-Truth Ministries

TATTOO'S DEADLY LITTLE SECRET

That harmless little "innocent" tattoo may have a little secret hiding inside.

A very deadly little secret. . .

Underneath that harmless tattoo is a very serious risk of acquiring a deadly blood-borne disease such as AIDS, Hepatitis B, Hepatitis C, tetanus, syphilis, tuberculosis and other blood-born diseases.

An alarming research study recently published by Dr. Bob Haley and Dr. Paul Fischer at the University of Texas Southwestern Medical School in Dallas uncovered that the "innocent" commercial tattoo may be the number one distributor of hepatitis C. The study was published in the journal Medicine (Haley RW, Fischer RP, Commercial tattooing as a potentially source of hepatitis C infection, Medicine, March 2000;80:134-151). Dr. Haley, a preventative medicine specialist and a former Center for Disease Control (CDC) infection control official, is exceptionally knowledgeable to prepare the study.

Dr. Haley concludes, "We found that commercially acquired tattoos accounted for more than twice as many hepatitis C infections as injection-drug use. This means it may have been the largest single contributor to the nationwide epidemic of this form of hepatitis."

Incredible. According to Dr. Haley's research you are twice as likely to be infected with hepatitis C from getting a tattoo from a tattoo shop than shooting up dope! With over 20 million Americans wearing a tattoo – and growing by leaps and bounds – we are likely staring down the barrel of a mammoth deadly epidemic.

The study also found that people who get tattooed in a commercial tattoo parlor were nine times more likely to get hepatitis C! That's nine times more likely to be infected by a deadly, fatal disease. And Dr. Haley is not referring to "backyard-prison-tattoos" but a tattoo from a "sanitized" commercial tattoo shop.

Did you know the deadly disease hepatitis C kills over 10,000 people a year? And sky-rocketing. . . Currently 4 million Americans are chronically infected with hepatitis C and rising. . . And according to Dr. Haley, it's number one channel -- the deadly tattoo. . . Courtesy of your friendly commercial tattoo parlor.

There is the documentated case of a 22-year-old grocery store employee who simply received his $45 tattoo. And four weeks later

– needed a liver transplant! (Mryna L. Armstrong and Lynne Kelly, Tattooing, Body Piercing, and Branding Are on the Rise, The Journal of School Nursing, Feb. 2001, Vol 17 No. 1, p.15)

When you consider hepatitis B can be transmitted with as little as 0.00004 ml of blood, and can live on blood contaminated surfaces, such as needles, tattoo machines, tables, etc. for over two months, the risk of hepatitis is very real indeed.

IMPORTANT: It's strongly advised for people who have tattoos to get a Hepatitis check. And soon. . . Hepatitis can lie unnoticed for many years while doing serious damage. The sooner hepatitis is detected the better the chances for survival. If you have a tattoo – get checked.

WebMD warns of the "Russian Roulette" tattoo procedure -- as each stick of the tattoo needle opens you up to contracting a deadly disease:

"Hepatitis C is spread by infected blood and infected needles, which is the virus' connection with tattooing. Tattoos involve lots of needles making lots of sticks in the skin. Each stick carries potential for contamination -- and not just with hepatitis, but also HIV, . . ."

Still want a tattoo?

Ask actress Pamela Anderson about the harmless tattoo. Pamela contracted the deadly hepatitis C from a simple, small finger "TOMMY" tattoo.

The fact of tattoos spreading deadly diseases is nothing new. It's been known and documented for years.

According to the Hepatitis Control Report, Spring 2001, "Outside the United States, several studies have connected the practice [tattoos] to hepatitis B and C virus transmission. . ."

"Tattooing poses health risks because the process exposes blood and body fluids. Because of this a person who gets tattooed risks getting a disease or infection that is carried through blood. These blood-borne diseases include hepatitis B and C, tetanus, and HIV." (Bonnie B. Graves, Tattooing and body piercing, p. 40)

"By the middle of the nineteenth century, it was becoming more and more apparent that the practice was not without its medical hazards. For instance, in 1853 the first case was reported of syphilis, transmitted not in the old fashioned way, but via the tattooist's needle." (Ronald Scutt, Art, Sex and Symbol, 1974, p. 133)

"In the late 1950's, a New York City boy contracted blood poisoning from being tattooed with an unsterilized needle."

(Laura Reybold, Everything you need to know about the dangers of tattooing and body piercing, p. 17)

In 1961 an outbreak of hepatitis B in New York City was linked to the tattoo. And the "ultra-liberal" New York City outlawed the deadly tattoo from 1961 until 1997!

Did you know the American Red Cross prohibits donors from donating blood for 12 months one complete year -- after getting tattooed? Their Blood Donation Eligibility Guidelines under "Tattoo" reads, "Wait 12 months after a tattoo. This requirement is related to concerns about hepatitis."

Get this. . . According to research published in the Journal of School Health, 70 percent of 642 adolescents surveyed in a study reported hemorrhaging while being tattooed. (Donald Staffo , The Tuscaloosa Times, January 10, 2001)

Despite the attempt of many tattoo websites to nullify the possibility of contracting HIV / AIDS from a tattoo, the Center for Disease Control (CDC) gives a different answer:

"Can I get HIV from getting a tattoo or through body piercing?

A risk of HIV transmission does exist if instruments contaminated with blood are either not sterilized or disinfected or are used inappropriately between clients. CDC recommends that instruments that are intended to penetrate the skin be used once, then disposed of or thoroughly cleaned and sterilized." (www.cdc.gov/hiv/pubs/faq/faq27.htm)

Why are tattoos so vulnerable to deadly diseases?

Simple. Because the tattooist is puncturing thousands of tiny potential disease bearing wounds with very little, if any, serious state or federal health regulations. And not only that, many of the customers receiving a tattoo are drug-users, criminals, rock artists, deviants and homosexuals who just happen to be the major carriers of the deadly blood-borne diseases such as AIDS and hepatitis.

And there exists no or very little federal or state laws enforcing any serious sterilization regulations. It is basically up to the tattoo shop owner to sterilize or not sterilize his tattooing tools and procedures.

"Where tattooing is legal, however there is little or no government regulation of tattoo artists. . . Since there is little regulation of tattoo artists, however, it is important to recognize that, as in any field, there may be unscrupulous or incompetent practitioners. Tattooing opens your body to potential infection, disease, and scarring."

(Laura Reybold, Everything you need to know about the dangers of tattooing and body piercing, p. 18)

On their web site, the world-renown, Mayo Clinic sounds a warning about the dangers of the commercial tattoo shop and lack of serious health regulations:

"Keep in mind that tattoo parlors and piercing venues are not held to the same sterility standards as doctors' offices and hospitals. Few states have hygienic regulations to ensure safe tattooing practices in commercial tattoo parlors, and even fewer monitor and enforce standards." (Body piercing and tattoos: More than skin deep, Mayo Clinic, www.mayoclinic.com)

WebMD also acknowledges the lack of sterile regulations missing in most tattoo shops:

"By and large, tattoo artists and shops are not required -- by state or local governments -- to follow the same sterile operating practices as other operations that use needles, like hospitals and doctor's offices."

Dennis Dwyer, executive director of the tattoo's industry voluntary-self-monitoring organization Alliance for Professional Tattoo Artists (APT) readily admits the problem, "Many people are trying their best to provide safe tattooing. But this industry has a lot of nonconformists," (Pamela Anderson Says She Has Hepatitis C, WebMD Medical News, March 21, 2002, content.health.msn.com/content/article/1678.50634)

Tattoo industry expert Professor Myrna Alexander of Texas Tech University, who has researched the tattoo industry for 10 years, warns, "There are some very reputable tattoo artists out there. They work hard, and their studios are as clean as medical clinics. They do a good job because they believe what they are doing is art. The problem is, there are many who don't." (Pamela Anderson Says She Has Hepatitis C, WebMD Medical News, March 21, 2002, content.health.msn.com/content/article/1678.50634)

Most tattoo shops do not and will not advise you to the real potential for serious health dangers. Despite the vast amount of research available (just search the Internet) many tattooist still refuse to acknowledge the very serious health dangers the tattoo invites. OTHER LITTLE DANGERS

Besides the possibility of killing you with fatal diseases such as AIDS and hepatitis, the "harmless" tattoo provides an arm-load of other ailments.

Tattoos can cause chronic skin disorders such as sarcoid, keloid scarring, allergic dermatitis, photosensitivity reactions, psoriasis, and benign or malignant tumors. (www.saintmarys.edu/~health/dyk0010.html) Many people experience infection and allergic reaction to the tattoo ink.

Also, the pigments in tattoo ink contain small metal fibers such as iron oxide. These metal fibers can cause intense burning pain during an MRI procedure. Some medical institutions refuse to perform MRIs on people with tattoos. The MRI is an important medical procedure and this risk should not be taken lightly. (www.ezpermanentmakeup.com/IronOxideLetters.htm) And every prick is an invitation for blood-bourne diseases such as hepatitis and AIDS.

Think before you get that tattoo. . .

A tattooing machine can puncture the skin 3,000 times a minute. And every one of those thousands of punctures creates a hole 1/64 to 1/16th of an inch into the dermis that literally invites infection and disease. Every single puncture of the tattoo needle opens up the real possibility of AIDS, Hepatitis B, Hepatitis C, tetanus, tuberculosis and about any other blood-borne disease. With the average tattoo taking about 60 minutes that equals 180,000 tiny "Russian Roulette" puncture wounds providing a potential path to a very deadly infectious disease.

Beware!

Your tattoo could have inserted more than harmless ink in your exposed flesh.

Psalm 38:5-8 (KJV)

5. My wounds stink and are corrupt because of my foolishness.
6. I am troubled; I am bowed down greatly; I go mourning all the day long.
7. For my loins are filled with a loathsome disease: and there is no soundness in my flesh.
8. I am feeble and sore broken: I have roared by reason of the disquietness of my heart.

CHAPTER **151**

Taxation Without Representation - Washington DC's Citzens Are Curses Against Them

The almost 600,000 citizens which comprises around 57% of black citizens living in our nations capital, Washington, D.C. citizens are merely cursed and living in a high tech system of slavery instituted by their nation's majority white masters, the U.S. Congress and the U.S. Senate with whom I will call Mr. Charlie and Miss Charlotte, respectively. The majority of the members of the Supreme Court stand idly by with their subtle support and without lifting a finger to help correct this evil.

These citizens are taxed as other citizens in the 49 other states of America. They have a Congresswoman, The Honorable Eleanor Holmes Norton, representing them without the benefit or right of casting her vote for her citizens which she represent in Washington, District of Columbia, our nation's Capitol. Honorable Holmes-Norton is doing an outstanding job with one of her hands tied behind her back as she puts her best foot forward for her citizens.

Mr. Charlie and Miss Charlotte are holding up over ½ million votes that these citizens could possibly cast for their selected Congress seat with voting rights, their selected Senate seat, and most certainly, their selected persons for president of these United States. These votes could turn the good-old-boy tides around for a change to more of a majority vote instead of the fixed voter collegiate state processes where the white majority stand to benefit as those states have a white majority voter base.

This high tech slavery has prevented these black citizens from having a vote in the U.S. Congress, even though they have a Congressional Representative in place. They are taxed without representation. That is because they can not cast their vote to help select a president of their choice. They have been denied the benefits of statehood in the District of Columbia.

Mr. Charlie and Miss Charlotte have instrumentally and legally perpetrated their discriminations, their prejudices, and their blatant racism at the highest levels of the federal governments without remorse, without sympathy, without love, without repercussions from our Supreme Deity, Almighty God. Bottom line, these evil curses will not go unpunished.

Almighty God hates racial discriminations, racial prejudices, racism perpetrated by any member of His human creation. As an example of his hatred for these evil curses, he took vengeance of one of his Prophetess by the name of Miriam, the sister of the Priest named Aaron who was the Spokesman for Moses. Moses married a black woman who was an Ethiopian woman. In their racist rage, they angered Almighty God. He told them to go out of the Tabernacle. He them directed his wrath upon Miriam.

Numbers 12 (KJV)

1. And Miriam and Aaron spake against Moses because of the Ethiopian woman whom he had married: for he had married an Ethiopian woman.
2. And they said, Hath the Lord indeed spoken only by Moses? hath he not spoken also by us? And the Lord heard it.
3. (Now the man Moses was very meek, above all the men which were upon the face of the earth.)
4. And the Lord spake suddenly unto Moses, and unto Aaron, and unto Miriam, Come out ye three unto the tabernacle of the congregation. And they three came out.

5. And the Lord came down in the pillar of the cloud, and stood in the door of the tabernacle, and called Aaron and Miriam: and they both came forth.
6. And he said, Hear now my words: If there be a prophet among you, I the Lord will make myself known unto him in a vision, and will speak unto him in a dream.
7. My servant Moses is not so, who is faithful in all mine house.
8. With him will I speak mouth to mouth, even apparently, and not in dark speeches; and the similitude of the Lord shall he behold: wherefore then were ye not afraid to speak against my servant Moses?
9. And the anger of the Lord was kindled against them; and he departed.
10. And the cloud departed from off the tabernacle; and, behold, Miriam became leprous, white as snow: and Aaron looked upon Miriam, and, behold, she was leprous.
11. And Aaron said unto Moses, Alas, my lord, I beseech thee, lay not the sin upon us, wherein we have done foolishly, and wherein we have sinned.
12. Let her not be as one dead, of whom the flesh is half consumed when he cometh out of his mother's womb.
13. And Moses cried unto the Lord, saying, Heal her now, O God, I beseech thee.
14. And the Lord said unto Moses, If her father had but spit in her face, should she not be ashamed seven days? let her be shut out from the camp seven days, and after that let her be received in again.
15. And Miriam was shut out from the camp seven days: and the people journeyed not till Miriam was brought in again.
16. And afterward the people removed from Hazeroth, and pitched in the wilderness of Paran.

CHAPTER 152

Terrorist 911 Attack and Hurrican Katrina Disasters

The terrorist 911 attack on the twin towers at New York and failed attempts on the United States National Capitol Building and theWhite House building in Washington, D.C. and the Hurricane Katrina disasters in the Gulf Coasts which devastated New Orleans, Louisiana and Biloxi, Mississippi are really wake-up calls to American and warnings that she is on the wrong path towards rampart increasing of sins and immorality at a rapid pace. Below are some of the things that have open the doors of America to disasters which include, but not limited to the following sins and rebellious actions against Almighty God's Word:

1. Abortions - Murdering babies legally as well as illegally.
2. Stem Cell Research - Murdering babies for research.
3. Fornication - Sexual intercourse of unmarred couples.
4. Adultery/Infidelity - Sexual intercourse of married people outside of their marriage.
5. Incest - Sexual intercourse with close relatives.
6. Homosexuality (i.e., gay couples) - Sexual intercourse or sexual acts with same sex mates.
7. Rape - forced sex on an un-consenting person.
8. Pedofile actions - sexually molesting children.
9. Prejudices and racism against fellow humans.
10. Serving idol gods over Almighty God.

11. Outlawed the freedom to pray in our schools and in some public buildings.
12. Immigration Reform - Racism and discrimination (institutionalized).
13. Collegiate Voting System - Prejudicial, discrimination, and racism directed at the vast majority. Those types of votes are targeted at the lilly white population for desired results.
14. Washington, D.C. denied statehood (racial overtones) as well as voter rights and representations. The District is under Jim Crow rule and slavery at the least. The majority black citizens still have to bow and shuffle to Mr. Charlie.
15. Wicca, witchcraft, and worshiping Satan.
16. Seeking the services and advisements of fortune tellers, psychics or soothsayers.
17. Children disobedient and disrespecting their parents, their grandparents, and other grownups.
18. Killers/murderers of human beings.
19. Robbers and thieves - forcefully seizing goods from others and taking things of others at will.
20. Worshiping in occult religions over Christianity.
21. Seances - attending meeting with a Medium officiating the attempts to call up dead people for their clients to talk to them. Actually, demons can manifest to look like the dead person and also mimic their voices. No one reach dead people through such methods.
22. Churches denying priest the opportunities marry, especially in the Catholic churches under their Pope in Rome, Italy. There is no such commandment by Almighty God.
23. Alcoholism - habitual and excessive consumption of alcoholic beverages.
24. Drug addictions - habitual and excessive consumption of drugs.
25. Drug dealing - the selling or the directing of selling drugs illegally.

26. Gluttony - the excessive or habitual over eating of food and or drinks.
27. Shop Lifting - stealing goods, money, or things without paying for them.
28. Lotto or Lottery - official gambling by purchasing lottery tickets of chance.
29. Casinos - legalized gambling with various games of chance.
30. Gangs - organized violent groups with evil means of persuasion in mind.
31. Mobs - highly organized criminals forces to illegally obtain money, property, things with a bottom line of organized crime.

Now here is an example of a punishment of death to a Priest by the name of Aaron who worked with the Prophet Moses. Aaron had rebelled against Almighty God's Word, so God punished him with death. Death is also given to America as well.

Numbers 20 (KJV)

24. Aaron shall be gathered unto his people: for he shall not enter into the land which I have given unto the children of Israel, ***because ye rebelled against my word at the water of Meribah***.
25. Take Aaron and Eleazar his son, and bring them up unto mount Hor:
26. And strip Aaron of his garments, and put them upon Eleazar his son: and Aaron shall be gathered unto his people, and shall die there.
27. And Moses did as the Lord commanded: and they went up into mount Hor in the sight of all the congregation.
28 And Moses stripped Aaron of his garments, and put them upon Eleazar his son; and ***Aaron died*** there in the top of the mount: and Moses and Eleazar came down from the mount.
29. And when all the congregation saw that Aaron was dead,

they mourned for Aaron thirty days, even all the house of Israel.

30. Almighty God warns us what will happen if we obey His commandments and what will happen to us if we don't obey and follow His commandments. There are very serious consequences when we disobey His commandments and follow after idol gods.

Deuteronomy 28 (KJV)

1. And it shall come to pass, if thou shalt hearken diligently unto the voice of the Lord thy God, to observe and to do all his commandments which I command thee this day, that the Lord thy God will set thee on high above all nations of the earth:
2. And all these blessings shall come on thee, and overtake thee, if thou shalt hearken unto the voice of the Lord thy God.
3. Blessed shalt thou be in the city, and blessed shalt thou be in the field.
4. Blessed shall be the fruit of thy body, and the fruit of thy ground, and the fruit of thy cattle, the increase of thy kine, and the flocks of thy sheep.
5. Blessed shall be thy basket and thy store.
6. Blessed shalt thou be when thou comest in, and blessed shalt thou be when thou goest out.
7. The Lord shall cause thine enemies that rise up against thee to be smitten before thy face: they shall come out against thee one way, and flee before thee seven ways.
8. The Lord shall command the blessing upon thee in thy storehouses, and in all that thou settest thine hand unto; and he shall bless thee in the land which the Lord thy God giveth thee.
9. The Lord shall establish thee an holy people unto himself, as he hath sworn unto thee, if thou shalt keep

the commandments of the Lord thy God, and walk in his ways.

10. And all people of the earth shall see that thou art called by the name of Lord; and they shall be afraid of thee.
11. And the Lord shall make thee plenteous in goods, in the fruit of thy body, and in the fruit of thy cattle, and in the fruit of thy ground, in the land which the Lord sware unto thy fathers to give thee.
12. The Lord shall open unto thee his good treasure, the heaven to give the rain unto thy land in his season, and to bless all the work of thine hand: and thou shalt lend unto many nations, and thou shalt not borrow.
13. And the Lord shall make thee the head, and not the tail; and thou shalt be above only, and thou shalt not be beneath; if that thou hearken unto the commandments of the Lord thy God, which I command thee this day, to observe and to do them:
14. And thou shalt not go aside from any of the words which I command thee this day, to the right hand, or to the left, to go after other gods to serve them.
15. But it shall come to pass, if thou wilt not hearken unto the voice of the Lord thy God, to observe to do all his commandments and his statutes which I command thee this day; that all these curses shall come upon thee, and overtake thee:
16. Cursed shalt thou be in the city, and cursed shalt thou be in the field.
17. Cursed shall be thy basket and thy store.
18. Cursed shall be the fruit of thy body, and the fruit of thy land, the increase of thy kine, and the flocks of thy sheep.
19. Cursed shalt thou be when thou comest in, and cursed shalt thou be when thou goest out.
20. The Lord shall send upon thee cursing, vexation, and rebuke, in all that thou settest thine hand unto for to do, until thou be destroyed, and until thou perish quickly;

because of the wickedness of thy doings, whereby thou hast forsaken me.

21. The Lord shall make the pestilence cleave unto thee, until he have consumed thee from off the land, whither thou goest to possess it.
22. The Lord shall smite thee with a consumption, and with a fever, and with an inflammation, and with an extreme burning, and with the sword, and with blasting, and with mildew; and they shall pursue thee until thou perish.
23. And thy heaven that is over thy head shall be brass, and the earth that is under thee shall be iron.
24. The Lord shall make the rain of thy land powder and dust: from heaven shall it come down upon thee, until thou be destroyed.
25. The Lord shall cause thee to be smitten before thine enemies: thou shalt go out one way against them, and flee seven ways before them: and shalt be removed into all the kingdoms of the earth.
26. And thy carcase shall be meat unto all fowls of the air, and unto the beasts of the earth, and no man shall fray them away.
27. The Lord will smite thee with the botch of Egypt, and with the emerods, and with the scab, and with the itch, whereof thou canst not be healed.
28. The Lord shall smite thee with madness, and blindness, and astonishment of heart:
29. And thou shalt grope at noonday, as the blind gropeth in darkness, and thou shalt not prosper in thy ways: and thou shalt be only oppressed and spoiled evermore, and no man shall save thee.
30. Thou shalt betroth a wife, and another man shall lie with her: thou shalt build an house, and thou shalt not dwell therein: thou shalt plant a vineyard, and shalt not gather the grapes thereof.
31. Thine ox shall be slain before thine eyes, and thou shalt

not eat thereof: thine ass shall be violently taken away from before thy face, and shall not be restored to thee: thy sheep shall be given unto thine enemies, and thou shalt have none to rescue them.

32. Thy sons and thy daughters shall be given unto another people, and thine eyes shall look, and fail with longing for them all the day long; and there shall be no might in thine hand.
33. The fruit of thy land, and all thy labours, shall a nation which thou knowest not eat up; and thou shalt be only oppressed and crushed alway:
34. So that thou shalt be mad for the sight of thine eyes which thou shalt see.
35. The Lord shall smite thee in the knees, and in the legs, with a sore botch that cannot be healed, from the sole of thy foot unto the top of thy head.
36. The Lord shall bring thee, and thy king which thou shalt set over thee, unto a nation which neither thou nor thy fathers have known; and there shalt thou serve other gods, wood and stone.
37. And thou shalt become an astonishment, a proverb, and a byword, among all nations whither the Lord shall lead thee.
38. Thou shalt carry much seed out into the field, and shalt gather but little in; for the locust shall consume it.
39. Thou shalt plant vineyards, and dress them, but shalt neither drink of the wine, nor gather the grapes; for the worms shall eat them.
40. Thou shalt have olive trees throughout all thy coasts, but thou shalt not anoint thyself with the oil; for thine olive shall cast his fruit.
41. Thou shalt beget sons and daughters, but thou shalt not enjoy them; for they shall go into captivity.
42. All thy trees and fruit of thy land shall the locust consume.
43. The stranger that is within thee shall get up above thee very

high; and thou shalt come down very low.

44. He shall lend to thee, and thou shalt not lend to him: he shall be the head, and thou shalt be the tail.

45. Moreover all these curses shall come upon thee, and shall pursue thee, and overtake thee, till thou be destroyed; because thou hearkenedst not unto the voice of the Lord thy God, to keep his commandments and his statutes which he commanded thee:

46. And they shall be upon thee for a sign and for a wonder, and upon thy seed for ever.

47. Because thou servedst not the Lord thy God with joyfulness, and with gladness of heart, for the abundance of all things;

48. Therefore shalt thou serve thine enemies which the Lord shall send against thee, in hunger, and in thirst, and in nakedness, and in want of all things: and he shall put a yoke of iron upon thy neck, until he have destroyed thee.

49. The Lord shall bring a nation against thee from far, from the end of the earth, as swift as the eagle flieth; a nation whose tongue thou shalt not understand;

50. A nation of fierce countenance, which shall not regard the person of the old, nor shew favour to the young:

51. And he shall eat the fruit of thy cattle, and the fruit of thy land, until thou be destroyed: which also shall not leave thee either corn, wine, or oil, or the increase of thy kine, or flocks of thy sheep, until he have destroyed thee.

52. And he shall besiege thee in all thy gates, until thy high and fenced walls come down, wherein thou trustedst, throughout all thy land: and he shall besiege thee in all thy gates throughout all thy land, which the Lord thy God hath given thee.

53. And thou shalt eat the fruit of thine own body, the flesh of thy sons and of thy daughters, which the Lord thy God hath given thee, in the siege, and in the straitness, wherewith thine enemies shall distress thee:

54. So that the man that is tender among you, and very delicate,

his eye shall be evil toward his brother, and toward the wife of his bosom, and toward the remnant of his children which he shall leave:

55. So that he will not give to any of them of the flesh of his children whom he shall eat: because he hath nothing left him in the siege, and in the straitness, wherewith thine enemies shall distress thee in all thy gates.
56. The tender and delicate woman among you, which would not adventure to set the sole of her foot upon the ground for delicateness and tenderness, her eye shall be evil toward the husband of her bosom, and toward her son, and toward her daughter,
57. And toward her young one that cometh out from between her feet, and toward her children which she shall bear: for she shall eat them for want of all things secretly in the siege and straitness, wherewith thine enemy shall distress thee in thy gates.
58. If thou wilt not observe to do all the words of this law that are written in this book, that thou mayest fear this glorious and fearful name, The Lord Thy God;
59. Then the Lord will make thy plagues wonderful, and the plagues of thy seed, even great plagues, and of long continuance, and sore sicknesses, and of long continuance.
60. Moreover he will bring upon thee all the diseases of Egypt, which thou wast afraid of; and they shall cleave unto thee.
61. Also every sickness, and every plague, which is not written in the book of this law, them will the Lord bring upon thee, until thou be destroyed.
62. And ye shall be left few in number, whereas ye were as the stars of heaven for multitude; because thou wouldest not obey the voice of the Lord thy God.
63. And it shall come to pass, that as the Lord rejoiced over you to do you good, and to multiply you; so the Lord will rejoice

over you to destroy you, and to bring you to nought; and ye shall be plucked from off the land whither thou goest to possess it.

64. And the Lord shall scatter thee among all people, from the one end of the earth even unto the other; and there thou shalt serve other gods, which neither thou nor thy fathers have known, even wood and stone.
65. And among these nations shalt thou find no ease, neither shall the sole of thy foot have rest: but the Lord shall give thee there a trembling heart, and failing of eyes, and sorrow of mind:
66. And thy life shall hang in doubt before thee; and thou shalt fear day and night, and shalt have none assurance of thy life:
67. In the morning thou shalt say, Would God it were even! and at even thou shalt say, Would God it were morning! for the fear of thine heart wherewith thou shalt fear, and for the sight of thine eyes which thou shalt see.
68. And the Lord shall bring thee into Egypt again with ships, by the way whereof I spake unto thee, thou shalt see it no more again: and there ye shall be sold unto your enemies for bondmen and bondwomen, and no man shall buy you.

The one thing that I am grateful for is the United States of America's steadfastness and support of Israel and the Jewish nations. God said that He would bless those who bless Israel. I believe that this is the one thread that is keeping the U.S. afloat so far. She sure as hell is not doing anything else right.

Genesis 12 (KJV)

1. Now the Lord had said unto Abram, Get thee out of thy country, and from thy kindred, and from thy father's house, unto a land that I will shew thee:
2. And I will make of thee a great nation, and I will bless thee,

and make thy name great; and thou shalt be a blessing:

3. ***And I will bless them that bless thee, and curse him that curseth thee: and in thee shall all families of the earth be blessed.***

CHAPTER 153

Tithing (10% of Salary Donations) Is Not Commanded in the New Testament Bibles

Tithing, donating 10% of ones salary and/income to churches is a commandment given under old testament law. When Jesus went to the cross, He disannulled not only the priesthood, but also the command to tithe. However, Orthodox Jews/Hebrews, meaning people who are born as jews/hebrews and practice that religion are still under the Dispensation of Law. They are still bound by the commandments under the old testament law, including tithing.

I, (Curtis) and my family were members of Heritage Fellowship United Church of Christ, Reston, Virginia during the late 1990s. The United Church of Christ Headquarters graciously moved our presiding pastor who wasn't actually performing as a pastor should have performing. The pastorship was then vacant. We had to search for another pastor. Meanwhile, we were also searching for an interim pastor who was a seventy-five year old was a Methodist minister.

The minister's name was Dr. Bishop (Dr. B.). Dr. B. Would always emphasize the point that tithing was very high on his agenda in the church. He would give tithes several times over without thinking about it. We have seen him do just that. When there was a need for additional funds in the church he would give probably more than any of the members. He really believed in Malachi 3:3-11. Dr. Bishop and his lovely wife owned two (2) Cadillac automobiles, a fine home, and a comfortable retirement pension. One night after picking up one of the Cadillacs, he turned in the path of an oncoming truck. Dr. Bishop was killed instantly. My point is that the promises made in Malachi 3:8-11 did not save his life after all of the donations that he made to the church. It's great to give to your local church, even 20% or more of your earnings is even greater, your donations to any church or religious organization is only part of your walk with Jesus Christ. The key is to obey and follow all of Almighty God's commandments. Before you ask Almighty God to bless you or anybody else, bless Almighty God, first by saying, "Praise, Almighty God" or "Hallelujah", then say "Almighty God, please bless me" or "Almighty God, please bless America" or such words to that effect.

We have attempted to give you the old testament commands under the Dispensation of Law and also of the commandments under our present age, the Dispensation of Grace below.

New Testament Priest, Jesus Christ

When Jesus Christ, our Lord, was born, He became our Priest forever after the order of King and Priest Melchisedec. We are no longer bound by old testament laws, including the need to be tithers.

Hebrews 7 (KJV)

15. And it is yet far more evident: for that after the similitude of Melchisedec there ariseth another priest,
16. Who is made, not after the law of a carnal commandment, but after the power of an endless life.
17. For he testifieth, Thou art a priest for ever after the order of Melchisedec.

New Testament Command To Give (Dispensation of Grace)

Luke 6 (KJV)

38. Give, and it shall be given unto you; good measure, pressed down, and shaken together, and running over, shall men give into your bosom. For with the same measure that ye mete withal it shall be measured to you again.

Old Testament Command To Give

Many church pastors sometimes over emphasize to their congregations the importance of bringing a tenth (10th of gross salaries) in to support the church and its ministries. This is a great starting point to share in their giving. However, to stress that this is a mandate for Christians, is not correct. The pastors will beat their congregations over their heads with the book of Malichi.

Malachi 3 (KJV)

8. Will a man rob God? Yet ye have robbed me. But ye say, Wherein have we robbed thee? In tithes and offerings.
9. Ye are cursed with a curse: for ye have robbed me, even this whole nation.
10. Bring ye all the tithes into the storehouse, that there may be meat in mine house, and prove me now herewith, saith the Lord of hosts, if I will not open you the windows of heaven, and pour you out a blessing, that there shall not be room enough to receive it.
11. And I will rebuke the devourer for your sakes, and he shall not destroy the fruits of your ground; neither shall your vine cast her fruit before the time in the field, saith the Lord of hosts.

Hebrews 7 (KJV)

1. For this Melchisedec, king of Salem, priest of the most high God, who met Abraham returning from the slaughter of the kings, and blessed him;
2. To whom also Abraham gave a tenth part of all; first being by interpretation King of righteousness, and after that also King of Salem, which is, King of peace;
3. Without father, without mother, without descent, having neither beginning of days, nor end of life; but made like unto the Son of God; abideth a priest continually.
4. Now consider how great this man was, unto whom even the patriarch Abraham gave the tenth of the spoils.
5. And verily they that are of the sons of Levi, who receive the office of the priesthood, have a commandment to take tithes of the people according to the law, that is, of their brethren, though they come out of the loins of Abraham:
6. But he whose descent is not counted from them received tithes of Abraham, and blessed him that had the promises.
7. And without all contradiction the less is blessed of the better.
8. And here men that die receive tithes; but there he receiveth them, of whom it is witnessed that he liveth.
9. And as I may so say, Levi also, who receiveth tithes, payed tithes in Abraham.
10. For he was yet in the loins of his father, when Melchisedec met him.
11. If therefore perfection were by the Levitical priesthood, (for under it the people received the law,) what further need was there that another priest should rise after the order of Melchisedec, and not be called after the order of Aaron?
12. For the priesthood being changed, there is made of necessity a change also of the law.
13. For he of whom these things are spoken pertaineth to

another tribe, of which no man gave attendance at the altar.

14. For it is evident that our Lord sprang out of Juda; of which tribe Moses spake nothing concerning priesthood.
15. And it is yet far more evident: for that after the similitude of Melchisedec there ariseth another priest,
16. Who is made, not after the law of a carnal commandment, but after the power of an endless life.
17. For he testifieth, Thou art a priest for ever after the order of Melchisedec.

Disannulment Of Earthly Priests And Tithing (Dispensation of Law)

Jesus Christ took the place of earthly priests. He is our Priest throughout eternity. Since we were commanded to give our tithes to the priests, not only were the priest's positions disannulled, but also the requirements to tithe. The commandment to tithe was under the Dispensation of Law. Christians aren't under the Dispensation of Law, but under the Dispensation of Grace. Thus, we must abide by the commandments under the Dispensation of Grace.

18. For there is verily a disannulling of the commandment going before for the weakness and unprofitableness thereof.
19. For the law made nothing perfect, but the bringing in of a better hope did; by the which we draw nigh unto God.
20. And inasmuch as not without an oath he was made priest:
21. (For those priests were made without an oath; but this with an oath by him that said unto him, The Lord sware and will not repent, Thou art a priest for ever after the order of Melchisedec:)
22. By so much was Jesus made a surety of a better testament.
23. And they truly were many priests, because they were not suffered to continue by reason of death:

24. But this man, because he continueth ever, hath an unchangeable priesthood.
25. Wherefore he is able also to save them to the uttermost that come unto God by him, seeing he ever liveth to make intercession for them.
26. For such an high priest became us, who is holy, harmless, undefiled, separate from sinners, and made higher than the heavens;
27. Who needeth not daily, as those high priests, to offer up sacrifice, first for his own sins, and then for the people's: for this he did once, when he offered up himself.
28. For the law maketh men high priests which have infirmity; but the word of the oath, which was since the law, maketh the Son, who is consecrated for evermore.

CHAPTER **154**

Viet Nam Veterans Syndromes - Post-War Suicides

The results of war, humanity-to-humanity is devastating to the body, soul and spirit of humanity. When, I, Curtis was stationed at 2d Armored Division, Fort Hood, Texas, they had a motto, "Hell On Wheels". Well, war is not only hell on wheels, but hell in the air, hell on the ground, and hell to the atmosphere as a whole. Anytime that our human elements are linked to any spirits of war, it sets up hell on humanity.

When leaders of any continent on earth declares war and sends its citizens into that war, they could or not have the blessings of Almighty God in Heaven on their side. If Almighty God is on their side, then so be it, but if He is not, then that leader has blood on his or her hand. A petition for repentance and forgiveness is then in order for that leader.

The most important key element of humanity and our troops sent into war is the power and strength of spirituality with that link to Divine power to heaven. I feel that 99.99 percent of Chaplains are not equipped, nor anointed to impart or disseminate any anointing of the Spirit to our troops. Many Chaplains are well educated, of high ranks in their branch of service, but not spiritually anointed as ones called and anointed by Almighty God. Ministry is not a vocation as such, but a calling.

Preachers Must Be Called By Almighty God

Romans 10 (KJV)

13. For whosoever shall call upon the name of the Lord shall be saved.
14. How then shall they call on him in whom they have not believed? and how shall they believe in him of whom they have not heard? and how shall they hear without a preacher?
15. And how shall they preach, except they be sent? as it is written, How beautiful are the feet of them that preach the gospel of peace, and bring glad tidings of good things!
16. But they have not all obeyed the gospel. For Esaias saith, Lord, who hath believed our report?

Ephesians 4 (KJV)

11. And he gave some, apostles; and some, prophets; and some, evangelists; and some, pastors and teachers;
12. For the perfecting of the saints, for the work of the ministry, for the edifying of the body of Christ:

Warnings Against Leaders Of Nations Who Obey Not Almighty God!

Exodus 5 (KJV)

1. And afterward Moses and Aaron went in, and told Pharaoh, Thus saith the Lord God of Israel, Let my people go, that they may hold a feast unto me in the wilderness.
2. And Pharaoh said, Who is the Lord, that I should obey his voice to let Israel go? I know not the Lord, neither will I let Israel go.
3. And they said, The God of the Hebrews hath met with us:

let us go, we pray thee, three days' journey into the desert, and sacrifice unto the Lord our God; lest he fall upon us with pestilence, or with the sword.

Almighty God's Wrath Against Humanity

Exodus 9 (KJV)

15. For now I will stretch out my hand, that I may smite thee and thy people with pestilence; and thou shalt be cut off from the earth.
16. And in very deed for this cause have I raised thee up, for to shew in thee my power; and that my name may be declared throughout all the earth.

Agent Orange Defoliate Chemical Curses

Agent Orange was the name given to chemical used to kill the leaves on trees and shrubs and bushes used as barriers and hiding places for the Viet Cong, the U.S. Soldiers enemies, whom they were fighting. Agent Orange helped the soldiers on the one hand, but has deemed to highly dangerous on the other hand to the soldier's physical health. Those chemicals were sprayed with air planes piloted by members of the United States Air Force.

Over the years since the Viet Nam conflict, many veterans who have served in Viet Nam during certain periods of time have all contracted various diseases, sicknesses and cancers as results of coming in contact with those Agent Orange chemicals. Many veterans have already lost their lives because of this highly toxic chemical.

Our Orkin Pest Control representative shared with us his experiences when he served in Viet Nam. I believe he said that he served in Viet Nam around the year of 1968. He was serving with a 25-member team when he was wounded in his head with shrapnel from a grenade. He was medically evacuated back to a hospital, possibly Walter Reed Army Medical Hospital, Washington, D.C. before the Air Force started spraying Agent Orange. However, his comrades of 24-members were still there when the spraying started. All of them contracted diseases, sicknesses, and cancers from the effects of the Agent Orange chemicals. He went on to say that unfortunately, all of those members are now dead.

I, Curtis, am also a victim of Agent Orange. I contracted diabetes, diabetic neuropathy in the legs and feet, kidney disease, eye diseases, eye blindness, high blood pressure and diseases as well.

Buddhist Monk's Curses

I learned that when soldiers arrived at Ton Se Nut Air Base, Viet Nam, Buddhist Monks would stand at the end of the run way and chant curses upon the soldiers coming in to Viet Nam. This is a curse coupled with the Agent Orange curse that has drastically effected our veterans who have served their country in the Republic of Viet Nam, a conflict that the United States of America did not win. Many lives have been lost not only in battle over there, but in peace time after the soldiers returned home with a another battle of diseases, sicknesses, and cancers which destroyed their physical health in their bodies.

Over 100,000 US Vietnam
Vet Suicides To Date!
http://rense.com/general77/hdtage.htm

VIETNAM STATISTICS

This list tells it all. These statistics could change many hearts.

We, the U.S. have lost over 158,000 American lives to the Vietnam war and that count is still rising.

Approx 58,000 in Vietnam. 100,000 or more to suicide and most of those occurred after the men came home.

This accurate accounting gives us persepective on the cost of current and future wars.

from Fallen Leaves, Broken Lives By Edward Tick
Utne magazine

CHAPTER 155

White Supremacy People Are Headed Straight to Hell's Fire and Brimstone

The media reports that there are up to 200,000 White Supremacy people in a number of hate groups around the United States of America. Most people are quite aware of the hate group called the Klu Klux Klan, but not aware of the many other hate groups that these White Supremacy people are involved in to perpetrate their hatred and ignorance.

CHAPTER **156**

Whore-mongers, (i.e., Gays, Homosexuals, Prostitutes, Transsexuals & Adulterers)

Psalms 11 (KJV)

6. Upon the wicked he shall rain snares, fire and brimstone, and an horrible tempest: this shall be the portion of their cup.

Sexual Perverts Destroyed By Almighty God

Luke 17 (Kjv)

29. But the same day that Lot went out of Sodom it rained fire and brimstone from heaven, and destroyed them all.

Leviticus 19 (KJV)

29. Do not prostitute thy daughter, to cause her to be a whore; lest the land fall to whoredom, and the land become full of wickedness.

Unfortunately there are people in the church who feel they have to have sex with whomever. It doesn't matter to them if the person(s) are single or married. It makes no difference to them one way or the other. They must have sex with somebody. They are in fact defiling their bodies tremendously. The stakes are very high here. These persons are abomination to God, Almighty. They really don't have eternal life in these situations.

1 Cor 6:9 (KJV) "Know ye not that the unrighteous shall not inherit the kingdom of God? Be not deceived: neither fornicators, nor idolaters, nor adulterers, nor effeminate, nor abusers of themselves with mankind,"

1 Tim 1:10 (KJV) "For whoremongers, for them that defile themselves with mankind, for menstealers, for liars, for perjured persons, and if there be any other thing that is contrary to sound doctrine;"

Heb 13:4 (KJV) "Marriage is honourable in all, and the bed undefiled: but whoremongers and adulterers God will judge."

Rev 21:8 (KJV) "But the fearful, and unbelieving, and the abominable, and murderers, and whoremongers, and sorcerers, and idolaters, and all liars, shall have their part in the lake which burneth with fire and brimstone: which is the second death."

Rev 22:15 (KJV) "For without are dogs, and sorcerers, and whoremongers, and murderers, and idolaters, and whosoever loveth and maketh a lie."

James 4:4 (KJV) "Ye adulterers and adulteresses, know ye not that the friendship of the world is enmity with God? whosoever therefore will be a friend of the world is the enemy of God."

Exodus 7 (KJV)

11. Then Pharaoh also called the wise men and the sorcerers: now the magicians of Egypt, they also did in like manner with their ***enchantments***.
12. For they cast down every man his rod, and they became serpents: but Aaron's rod swallowed up their rods.

Exodus 7 (KJV)

22. And the magicians of Egypt did so with their enchantments: and Pharaoh's heart was hardened, neither did he hearken unto them; as the Lord had said.
23. And Pharaoh turned and went into his house, neither did he set his heart to this also.
24. And all the Egyptians digged round about the river for water to drink; for they could not drink of the water of the river.
25. And seven days were fulfilled, after that the Lord had smitten the river.

Num 21:6 (KJV) "And the LORD sent fiery serpents among the people, and they bit the people; and much people of Israel died."

23,000 People Perished In The Cities Of Sodom And Gomorrah

1 Cor 10:8 (KJV) " Neither let us commit fornication, as some of them committed, and fell in one day three and twenty thousand."

1 Cor 10:9 (KJV) "Neither let us tempt Christ, as some of them also tempted, and were destroyed of serpents."

CHAPTER 157

Wine (Only) Represents Jesus Christ's Cleansing Blood

Many people, including pastors, ministers, and lay members of many churches confuse wine with grape juice. Some of these churches use grape juice as a wine. I, (Curtis) have witness the use of cool-aid as a form of communion wine along with Ritz crackers as a kosher bread (without ingredients of baking powder, yeast, salt, milk, baking soda or such).

Jesus Christ's blood has cleansing powers without human sicknesses or diseases. His blood is not polluted with any humanities frailties. It is pure and powerful which has cleansed our bloodlines through salvation. So, he chose to use wine instead of grape juice to symbolically represent his blood. Why would He use an alcoholic beverage to represent his cleansing blood power. Let's take a look at the wine and grape juice beverages for their cleansing properties.

Grape Juice

Grape juice is made from the juices of fresh grapes. They are full of impurities, have a lot of vitamins, taste good, but does not have cleansing properties to speak of. It is referred to as the fruit of the vine.

Wine or New Wine (Fermented)

1 Corinthians 11

26. For as often as ye eat this bread, and drink this cup, ye do shew the Lord's death till he come.

Joel 1 (KJV)

5. Awake, ye drunkards, and weep; and howl, all ye drinkers of wine, because of the new wine; for it is cut off from your mouth.

Hosea 4 (KJV)

11. Whoredom and wine and new wine take away the heart.

Matthew 9 (KJV)

17. Neither do men put new wine into old bottles: else the bottles break, and the wine runneth out, and the bottles perish: but they put new wine into new bottles, and both are preserved.

Grape juice in its regular form doesn't have the power, nor the strength to burst open a bottle or container as does new wine or fermented grape juice.

Wine is also made from fresh grapes as well. It was previously in the form of grape juice. However, wine is allowed to set and work itself (ferment) for approximately forty (40) days or more until it is fermented with an alcoholic content. Alcohol is a cleansing composition which is used as a sterilization substance in cleasing purposes. Medical professionals use alcohol to clean areas for injections of needles in someone's body. Alcohol is used in industrial environments, personal environments, home environments and many other uses. So, as you can see the alcohol content in wine represents purity as Christ's blood is pure. Wine is also referred to as the fruit of the vine.

When Jesus Christ attended that famous wedding with His mother, Mary, he turned that pot of water into wine, but not into grape juice, punch or kool-aid.

When my wife and I were ministers at First Mount Zion Baptist Church, Dumfries, Virginia, we were associated with many young ministers who would in our ministers' meetings always challenged the Elderly Pastor concerning the use of wine during Communion Services at the church. Most were ignorant and untrained. Although the Pastor was that knowledgeable, either, he did get the use of wine use in communion services right.

We have attended some churches who serve both wine and grape juice during their communion services. The would arrange on the center rows of the communion serving tray about two rows with glasses of wine and the remainder of the glasses on the outer rows with grape juice. This enabled the congregation to have choices on which one of the beverages that they wanted to consume. Some people had problems on consuming wine in church due to their ignorance and unbelief.

CHAPTER 158

Wives Tales and Fables Are Forbidden

Our Bible tells not to sit around listening to old wives tales and fables, specifically nasty jokes and such. We should fill our minds and hearts with the Word of God continually on a daily basis. There is an old saying in the computer world: Garbage In, Garbage out (GIGO). So, whatever you put in you is what will eventually come out. When you hear people attempt to express themselves, they constantly use curse words. Some people cannot adequately express themselves without having to use curse words. They programmed their minds with a vocabulary of curse words, so when they speak that is all they have by way of their expressions. Put something good in your mind. Put God's word in your mind. Put spiritual songs in your mind. Continually put prayers in your mind, don't leave it void, because Satan will fill it with his garbage.

1 Timothy 4 (KJV)

7. But refuse profane and old wives' fables, and exercise thyself rather unto godliness.

For a start, put praises in your heart towards Almighty God on a continuous basis. Just make it a habit in praising Him. You can also send up praises to our Savior and Master Jesus Christ as well as to the Spirit of the living God, the Holy Spirit as well. Here is what Almighty God said in the 150th Psalms:

Psalms 150 (KJV)

1. Praise ye the Lord. Praise God in his sanctuary: praise him in the firmament of his power.
2. Praise him for his mighty acts: praise him according to his excellent greatness.
3. Praise him with the sound of the trumpet: praise him with the psaltery and harp.
4. Praise him with the timbrel and dance: praise him with stringed instruments and organs.
5. Praise him upon the loud cymbals: praise him upon the high sounding cymbals.
6. Let every thing that hath breath praise the Lord. Praise ye the Lord.

CHAPTER **159**

Wives and Husbands Must Submit to Each Other

One of the key issues in a marriage is ultimately that of respect towards each other. Although the husband is the head of the wife in the marriage while Jesus Christ is the Head of the Church, he must give honor and respect to his wife. Also, the wife must give respect and honor to her husband as well. They must be mutually in agreement on things concerning their family and their way of living. This doesn't mean that the husband should rule with force or without respecting his wife's input on their subject matters at hand. There will be times when the wife may not have anything to input to a subject matter, then the husband has the final authority in such cases.

The husband must realize that no matter what decisions are made in the family, the husband is held accountable to Almighty God. Meaning, if the family is going off the right path of righteousness, then the husband will be held accountable, possibly because the husband failed to teach his family the ways of Almighty God.

1. Wives, submit to your own husbands.
2. Husbands, honor and respect your wives.
3. Be of One (1) Mind (i.e., On One Accord), so your prayers won't go unanswered.

1 Peter 3

1. Likewise, ye wives, be in subjection to your own husbands; that, if any obey not the word, they also may without the word be won by the conversation of the wives;
2. While they behold your chaste conversation coupled with fear.
3. Whose adorning let it not be that outward adorning of plaiting the hair, and of wearing of gold, or of putting on of apparel;
4. But let it be the hidden man of the heart, in that which is not corruptible, even the ornament of a meek and quiet spirit, which is in the sight of God of great price.
5. For after this manner in the old time the holy women also, who trusted in God, adorned themselves, being in subjection unto their own husbands:
6. Even as Sara obeyed Abraham, calling him lord: whose daughters ye are, as long as ye do well, and are not afraid with any amazement.
7. Likewise, ye husbands, dwell with them according to knowledge, giving honour unto the wife, as unto the weaker vessel, and as being heirs together of the grace of life; that your prayers be not hindered.
8. ***Finally, be ye all of one mind, having compassion one of another, love as brethren, be pitiful, be courteous:***

About the Authors

Dr. Curtis G. Hall's ancestry and genealogy spans from and includes: Native American Indian (Cherokee and Choctaw Tribes), and Black African Jew. Curtis is a U.S. Army Retiree and a Viet Nam Veteran who served twenty years and five days on active military duty. He served among various other tours: a tour at the Pentagon, Washington, D.C., two tours in Southeast Asia: one tour in the Northern region of South Korea and one tour in the Republic of Da Nang, Vietnam. He then served two tours in Europe: Fischbach and Pirmasens, Germany (same tour) and Verona, Italy. Curtis is also a civil service retiree where he retired as a Computer Scientist. Curtis holds a Doctor of Philosophy degree with a distinction in Computer Science and a Doctor of Divinity degree with a distinction in Theology, both from Trinity College and University. Curtis is also a graduate from the International Bible Institute and Seminary, Orlando, Florida. Curtis is also a Past Pastor and Assistant Pastor. He holds Ordination Credentials from the International Seminary, Plymouth, Florida.

Dr. Carolyn Hall's ancestry and genealogy spans from and includes: Native American Indian (Cherokee Tribe), and Black African Jew. Carolyn holds a Doctor of Philosophy degree with a distinction in Computer Science and a Doctor of Philosophy Degree with a distinction in Theology from Trinity College and University. She is also a graduate of the International Bible Institute and Seminary, Orlando, Florida and Central Jersey Bible Institute, New Jersey. She holds Ordination Credentials from the International Seminary, Plymouth, Florida. Carolyn served twelve years in the U.S. Air Force where she served at various bases: a tour at McQuire Air Force Base, New Jersey, Thule, Greenland and The Pentagon, Washington, D.C. She presently is still serving her country as an Information Technology Specialist with the Department of Defense with 36 years and counting.

Curtis and Carolyn have a combined total of over 70 years in the gospel ministry. Both are called by God, Almighty to proclaim His holy word by preaching, speaking and teaching. They are inspired to speak, teach and preach the gospel through any means necessary including the media as they are lead by the inspiration of the Holy Spirit as He gives them utterance. Both, Curtis and Carolyn love to explore the bible in doing their research for increased knowledge of God's word. They also love to use their expository skills with ease in disseminating God's word as they are lead to do so with inspirations from God, Almighty's Holy Spirit. Curtis is a preacher who has served as a pastor, assistant pastor, management trustee, bible teacher, Sunday school teacher and has held various other positions in the church. Carolyn is a preacher, choir soloist, bible teacher and Sunday school teacher among other duties within the church..

Curtis and Carolyn are the proud parents of two daughters, Cheryl (from Curtis's previous marriage) and Vanessa and one son, Patrick. Cheryl, the oldest daughter is the mother of two daughters and 2 sons, while her brother, Patrick (from Curtis's previous marriage) is the father of two sons and a daughter. Vanessa, the youngest daughter is a graduate of Northern Virginia Community College, Alexandria, VA. She holds an Associate of Applied Arts Degree in Music, and Associate of Applied Science Degree in Network Engineering. She is also a graduate of Strayer University. She holds a Bachelor's Degree in Computer Network Engineering. A word of knowledge was not only revealed to us by the Holy Spirit, but He also revealed to others also that Vanessa has a calling from God, Almighty on her life. We believe God's calling on her life includes, but not limited to the ministry of leading others at her young age, music, preaching and teaching ministries.

www.ingramcontent.com/pod-product-compliance
Lightning Source LLC
Chambersburg PA
CBHW060424100426
42812CB00030B/3297/J
9780970178602